Fourth Edition

THE CRIMINAL EVENT

An Introduction to Criminology in Canada

VINCENT F. SACCO
Queen's University

LESLIE W. KENNEDY
Rutgers University

THOMSON

NELSON

Australia   Canada   Mexico   Singapore   Spain   United Kingdom   United States

THOMSON

NELSON

The Criminal Event: An Introduction to Criminology in Canada, Fourth Edition

by Vincent F. Sacco and Leslie W. Kennedy

Associate Vice President, Editorial Director:
Evelyn Veitch

Editor-in-Chief, Higher Education:
Anne Williams

Executive Editor:
Ann Millar

Senior Marketing Manager:
Lenore Taylor

Senior Developmental Editor:
Rebecca Rea

Permissions Coordinator:
Melody Tolson

Senior Content Production Manager:
Julie van Veen

Production Service:
ICC Macmillan Inc.

Copy Editor:
James R. Coggins

Proofreader:
Dianne Fowlie

Indexer:
Bernice Eisen

Production Coordinator:
Ferial Suleman

Design Director:
Ken Phipps

Interior Design Modifications:
Artplus

Cover Design:
Johanna Liburd

Cover Image:
Jeff Spielman/Getty Images

Compositor:
ICC Macmillan Inc.

Printer:
Edwards Brothers

Library and Archives Canada Cataloguing in Publication Data

Sacco, Vincent F., 1948–
The criminal event: an introduction to criminology in Canada / Vincent F. Sacco, Leslie W. Kennedy.—4th ed.

Includes bibliographical references and indexes.
ISBN-13: 978-0-17-610279-1
ISBN-10: 0-17-610279-5

1. Criminology—Textbooks.
2. Crime—Canada—Textbooks.
I. Kennedy, Leslie W., 1951–
II. Title.

HV6025.S23 2007   364
C2006-903405-2

Table of Contents

PART THREE   DOMAINS OF CRIME   233

CHAPTER EIGHT   CRIME AND THE FAMILY AND HOUSEHOLD   234

Preface

When we wrote the first edition of *The Criminal Event* in the early 1990s, Canadian criminologists were attempting to explain the drop in crime, to make sense of claims about highly dangerous young delinquents ("super predators"), and to document the successes (and failures) of community policing. At the time, there was much more interest in understanding the motivations of offenders and the experiences of victims than in comprehending the broader contexts in which crime occurs.

In the last decade and a half, some things have remained the same, and many others have changed. Police are still involved in community crime prevention, and crime rates have stayed low. Situational crime prevention has become much more popular and has been responsible, at least in part, for crime rate reductions. The claims about super predators have been debunked.

Concerns about safety continue unabated, as do debates about the effectiveness of various police strategies. However, in the time since our first writing, we have also witnessed a new concern about public security that has captivated the public, changed policing, and made Canadians' concerns about safety much more globally based. With the new concern about the threat of terrorism, the police are now more likely to be engaged in counter-terrorism programs that put local crime into a new light. Canada, like much of the rest of the world, has been touched by the immediate threat of terrorist attack. The need to plan for emergencies, to detect and thwart attacks, and to lead recovery have added new responsibilities to police agencies.

During this period, the criminology discipline has seen a more widespread acceptance of the approach offered in our book—an approach which seeks to examine the settings and the transactional character of crime and not just why criminals act in the way that they do. Integrated approaches which attempt to account for the location, time, and situational context of crime have become more commonplace. Increasingly criminologists acknowledge that an event perspective allows us to look at all relevant aspects of the crime experience. This approach also facilitates efforts at prevention, deterrence, and harm reduction.

As we have tried to do in previous editions, this revision discusses the dominant theories of crime, the most important empirical approaches to its study, and the many research findings that inform our understanding of crime. We have updated how these approaches relate to contemporary challenges for police, public agencies, and the public itself in the search for safety and security.

As well, we have made some additional efforts to enhance the readability of the book. To this end, we begin each chapter with learning objectives and end each with suggestions for further reading. The literature on criminology is vast, and it is important that students read beyond any textbook introduction.

Our overall approach emphasizes an understanding of criminology as a body of knowledge and not a buffet selection of large numbers of equally viable views and conclusions. Unlike some of our colleagues, we do not believe that "nothing is knowable" or that empirical truths reside only in the minds of the observers. As the late Richard Wright advised textbook writers to do, we have tried to close the gap between the image of our discipline as it appears in this introduction to the field and the image which appears in the more significant professional journals.

One again we are grateful to everyone who has helped us at each stage of this process. As always, it was a pleasure working with several solidly professional and good-humoured individuals at Thomson Nelson. Joanna Cotton deserves special thanks for initiating work on this edition. Rebecca Rea at each step provided invaluable assistance and oversaw the project's completion. In particular, her careful assessment of the feedback from users of the book got us on the right track very early in the process. Naman Mahisauria, Melody Tolson, and Julie van Veen performed invaluable roles during the production process. The several reviewers who took time to give us their views of what did and did not work in earlier editions importantly influenced the way in which the revisions were undertaken.

Vincent Sacco would like to thank his friends and colleagues at Queen's University and elsewhere who offered advice and assistance. Conversations with Steve Baron, Rob Beamish, Nadine Blumer, Larry Comeau, Ron Gillis, Roberta Hamilton, Fiona Kay, Carl Keane, Reza Nakhaie, Elia Zureik, and Bob Silverman often influenced how he thought about the pedagogical tasks involved in revising a textbook. Michael Monaghan provided helpful guidance at several points. Michelle Ellis, Lynn O'Malley, Emily Theriault, Wendy Schuler, and Joan Westenhaefer helped with the manuscript in a large number of very practical ways. As always, he is very appreciative of the opportunity to teach (and learn from) the best students in the country. Of course, he is most thankful to his family. Katherin ("my daughter the social worker") has always shown him that any issue is debatable. Dan, his favourite film critic, introduced him to punk music in the earliest stages of this project, and as the project ends, he is a devout fan (Long Live B-R!). Tiia continues to be his most important friend, supporter, and reality checker. He loves you all.

Les Kennedy would like to thank Vince Sacco for shouldering most of the responsibility for this edition. Vince coordinated the effort with our friends at Thomson Nelson and managed a great deal of the change in content. Les appreciates his efforts and continued friendship. This book has had great staying power, and a big part of this is the great relationship that the authors have developed over the years. Les would also like to thank his staff, colleagues, students, and friends at Rutgers University, particularly Norm Samuels and Steve Diner for the ongoing support they have shown over the years. His greatest thanks go to Ilona, for her endless optimism, encouragement, and love, and Alexis and Andrea, for their inspiration, courage, and sense of adventure. A special appreciation goes to his late mother, who continues to inspire him with her love of learning and her sense of morality, and his father, who has taken on old age with a smile and a twinkle in his eye.

We would also like to thank the numerous readers retained by Thomson Nelson to review the *The Criminal Event* and give suggestions for the fourth edition, including:

Joseph H. Michalski, University of Western Ontario
Janet Hoffman, Lambton College of Applied Arts and Technology
Carla Hotel, Douglas College
Larry R. Comeau, Sheridan Institute of Technology and Advanced Learning

Part 1

Foundations

What Is Criminology?
Defining and Constructing the Problem of Crime

LEARNING OBJECTIVES:

- introduce criminology as a discipline
- consider the images of crime and criminal justice which confront us daily in the mass media and other forms of popular culture
- identify and discuss some myths about crime
- discuss the meaning and importance of the legal conceptualization of crime
- distinguish between consensus and conflict models of law creation
- consider alternative conceptualizations of crime, namely the view of crime as norm-violation and as social control
- identify the conceptual limitation of "offender-centred" conceptualizations of crime

INTRODUCTION

Every day we are confronted with many different accounts of crime events in our neighbourhoods and cities, and in other neighbourhoods and cities across the country. These crimes include stabbings in back alleys; beatings of wives carried out by estranged husbands; schoolyard thefts; major commercial frauds in which lending agencies have fleeced clients of their savings; and Internet scams which promised rewards to eager investors. We must find ways to make sense of these crime events, which on the surface appear quite different from one another.

In this book, it is our central contention that there are consistent ways for us to approach these and other crimes, ways that allow us to make sense of them and to place them in a broader context. We may not always be able to understand why people do certain things, but at the very least we can search for explanations of crime by examining such factors as circumstances and offender and victim characteristics. What factors led up to the act? Who else was involved? Where did the event take place? What did the police do? We also want to know what was done after the event occurred to deal with its consequences. What punishment was handed down to ensure that similar events do not happen again? The examples presented above at first seem to be unique social events; in fact, they share many characteristics that enable us to classify them the same way—that is, as criminal events.

In presenting an overview of explanations of crime, we will introduce the major theories of criminology as well as the research methods and data that are used to test hypotheses and to identify trends in crime. We will also present findings from the considerable research literature, with particular emphasis on crime that occurs at home, during leisure, and at work. Because explanations of crime heavily influence views on how society should respond to it, it is important to understand what the current public policy responses are and how they can be changed to deal more effectively with crime.

The discipline of criminology has gained in stature and credibility over the years. It has also developed strong traditions, many of which are complementary and some of which are at odds with one another, as will be seen. We begin, therefore, with a look at criminology as a discipline as it is practised in Canada and other countries. After this, we will review some of the more important factors that influence the study of crime.

WHAT IS CRIMINOLOGY?

The Modern Study of Criminology

Modern criminology draws on a number of different disciplines. In Canada and elsewhere, criminology is less a distinct discipline and more a field of study that is influenced by the insights and perspectives of both natural and social sciences (Gartner, 2000). Criminologists attempt to understand not only the motivations of the offender but also the circumstances leading up to the act and its consequences for the victim(s), for others in the community, and for society at large. Criminologists are also asked to suggest how society should respond to crime (Should policing strategies be changed? Should crime prevention programs be developed?). Finally, criminologists monitor how changes in the laws and their interpretation affect how people behave in society and, in turn, how agents of social control respond to this behaviour.

Because criminology is an interdisciplinary field, people with quite different types of training are involved in the study of crime. Criminologists can be trained as historians, psychologists, political scientists, economists, or legal scholars. Increasingly, criminology is taught in criminal justice programs which are staffed by faculty from these many different disciplines. It is still true, however, that when it is taught outside criminology and criminal justice departments, criminology is treated as a subdiscipline of sociology. Sociology has been the most important home of criminological training in North America because sociologists tend to be more involved than other researchers in the study of social problems. Also, most of the major figures in criminological history have been sociologists by training; this fact is then reflected in the courses that are offered. In contrast (Sampson, 2000), European criminologists are more often found in law schools, which gives criminological research a more legal orientation on that continent.

Canadians have been doing research in criminology for a long time. The interests of Canadian researchers cover the entire range of topics in criminology. Recent examples include youth crime (Doob and Cesaroni, 2004), cyber-crime (McMullen and Perrier, 2003), violence against women (Johnson and Hotten, 2003), policing (Van Brunschot, 2003), and money laundering (Schneider, 2004). In this book, we draw on both Canadian and international research. Criminology as a field of study has been growing most strongly in the United States, spurred by federal funding in the 1970s and 1980s in response to social disorder in American cities. More recently, the U.S. government has generously funded studies of drug-related and organized crime. Even more recently, the events of September 11, 2001 have focused criminological attention on the problems of terrorism and security. Even so, U.S. federal funding for criminological research is low relative to the amounts committed to other areas, such as medical and biophysical research. This is the case even though criminological research is often expensive. This is particularly true with respect to large-scale victimization surveys and longitudinal studies of offenders.

Not surprisingly, many critics ask what effects state funding has on the ways in which the discipline of criminology is practised (Savelsberg et al., 2002). This is a reasonable concern to raise. When government agencies make money available for particular kinds of research projects or particular kinds of college or university programs, they play an important agenda-setting role. To a considerable degree,

WHAT IS IT?

Criminology

Taking an interdisciplinary approach, criminologists attempt to understand (a) the factors that prompt or fail to inhibit criminal motivation, (b) the circumstances leading up to the act, and (c) the consequences of the act for the victim(s), for others in the community, and for society at large. Criminologists are also asked to suggest how society should respond to crime. Finally, criminologists monitor how changes in the laws and their interpretations affect how people behave in society and, in turn, how agents of social control respond to these behaviours.

5

Chapter 1: What Is Criminology?
Defining and Constructing
the Problem of Crime

the need to finance large research projects could lead criminologists to focus their attention on some problems rather than others (Walters, 2003). The effects of this process could be subtle and long-term but no less real. As critical students of criminology, we want to think about how both government funding and the political beliefs of the criminologists themselves (Walsh and Ellis, 1999) might influence the work that criminologists do and the ways in which they do it.

There is a great deal of interest in the study of crime in countries outside North America. For example, many countries have conducted large-scale victimization surveys. In Britain, the British Crime Survey (Nicholas et al., 2005) has been used heavily to develop policing policy, community crime prevention programs, and offender programs. Again, we will draw on the findings of such work in this book.

Our presentation will be heavily influenced by recent thinking in criminology—thinking that strongly emphasizes the routine nature of crime and maintains that individual lifestyles bring offenders and victims together in time and space to create crime opportunities. The crime that results creates consequences for all parties concerned, including consequences resulting from police intervention or the actions of third parties.

A logical place to begin the study of criminology, however, is with an examination of the images of crime which constitute so much of our popular culture, unlike many other fields of study (nuclear physics, for instance), most people approach the field of criminology with at least a vague sense that they understand the subject matter. To a considerable degree, this understanding is fed by television, movies, urban legends, and other forms of folk knowledge. Often, the images that come to us via popular media get in the way of our efforts to make systematic sense of crimes and those who are involved in them. For this reason, it is a good idea to subject these images to some critical scrutiny.

THE PUBLIC'S INTEREST IN CRIMINAL EVENTS

Crime News

The Interest in Crime News

While there are differences across media types and across communities with respect to the amount of coverage that crime receives (Liska and Baccaglini, 1990), generally speaking crime is widely reported by all popular news media (Sacco, 1995). Why is this? The simple answer is that audiences are interested in such stories: crime news "sells" (Gordon and Heath, 1981). Some readers/viewers perceive crime news as an important source of "facts"; others are caught up in the dramatic and sometimes lurid nature of crime news.

Katz (1987) contends that the public's fascination with crime news has little to do with a search for the truth about crime or with the dramatic qualities of crime reporting. Rather, he maintains, crime news allows audience members to work out their own positions on moral questions of a general yet also personal nature. For example, many crime stories deal with the competence or insensitivity of offenders. As Katz (1987: 50) expresses it, we read accounts of "ingenious, vicious, and audacious crimes of deception that trick the close scrutiny of diligent customs inspectors, of the most bloody murders, of big heists in broad daylight." Stories such as these demonstrate to the audience the nature and limits of human competence and human sensitivity. They interest the audience because the dilemmas of assessing personal competence and of maintaining one's own moral sensibility are routinely encountered in daily life. For Katz (1987: 72), reading crime news is a "ritual moral exercise [and as such] appears to serve a purpose similar to the morning shower, routine physical exercise, and shaving."

The Content of Crime News

Studies on the content of crime news have yielded interesting findings (Howitt, 1998). *First*, there seems to be little relationship between the amount of *crime news* and the amount of *crime* (as measured, for instance, in official statistics). In other words, objectively measured trends in crime do not correspond closely with trends in the amount of crime news (Garofalo, 1981a; Katz, 1987). *Second*, the amount of attention the media give to crime depends on the type of offence. Violent, relatively rare crimes such as homicide are emphasized, whereas property crimes, white-collar offences, and other nonviolent, frequently occurring crimes are underreported (Chermak, 1998; Randall, Lee-Sammons, and Hagner, 1988). *Third*, crime news exaggerates the proportion of offences that result in arrest (Sacco and Fair, 1988; Skogan and Maxfield, 1981); that is, the media portray the police as far more effective than they really are (Eschholz et al., 2004). *Fourth*, the media focus their attention on the early stages of criminal justice processing (detection and arrest); the later stages of legal processing are largely ignored (Hans, 1990).

Also, media coverage is notable not only for what it includes but also for what it excludes. Crime reporting is often criticized for ignoring the relationship between crime and broad social conditions. Humphries (1981) suggests that news reports associate criminal violence with youth, maleness, and minority membership and ignore how labour markets and related

7

Chapter 1: What Is Criminology?
Defining and Constructing
the Problem of Crime

institutions have historically shaped employment opportunities and the size and composition of the pool of people vulnerable to arrest. This tendency to portray crime as perpetrated mainly by pathological individuals precludes alternative explanations. For instance, a report about a single mother accused or convicted of child abuse may describe her as "disturbed" and ignore the following questions: "Was the mother receiving welfare or was she unemployed? Was the child attending a day-care program or receiving any other social services? Had the mother been a victim of child abuse?" (Gorelick, 1989: 423).

The biased nature of crime reporting is obvious in Voumvakis and Ericson's 1984 study of newspaper accounts of attacks against women in Toronto. The accounts covered in this study offered explanations for the violent "crime wave" but did so by emphasizing (a) how the victims' actions placed them at risk, (b) the need for a more coercive—and presumably more effective—response from the criminal justice system, and (c) the pathology of offenders. Voumvakis and Ericson maintained that these terms of reference, although not necessarily unreasonable, were restrictive in that they ruled out alternative interpretations, especially ones that would have linked crimes against women to more general patterns of gender inequality. Reporting that emphasizes the need for more police, for more punishment, and for more vigilance by women does not allow for a discussion of broader programs of social reform. More recently, and more generally, Stone (1993) examined how the Toronto media treat the topic of violence against women; she found that efforts to frame the problem of female victimization in the terms of reference of various feminist perspectives were generally absent from such reports.

The Sources of Crime News

Studies of news production practices emphasize how judgments of "newsworthiness" come to be applied to categories of events (Chibnall, 1977; Fishman, 1978). These judgments reflect how journalists perceive their society, the work they are engaged in, and the audiences they serve. For several reasons, criminal events—especially violent ones—conform closely to the professional values of journalists (Ericson, Baranek, and Chan, 1987).

First, such incidents have spatial and temporal characteristics that lend themselves easily to news production routines. Murders, thefts, and sexual assaults are discrete events. They are also "short term"—that is, they happen between one newspaper edition and the next, or one newscast and the next. *Second,* reports of criminal events are easily understood by audiences and so require little in the way of background information. Also, because there is an almost limitless supply of crime news, the number of crime-related stories can be expanded or reduced depending on the needs of media decision makers and on the amount of space or time that must be filled on any given day (Warr, 1991). *Third*, many crimes lend themselves to a dramatic narrative form that features the exploits of clearly defined "good guys" and "bad guys" (Ericson, 1991).

News organizations rely heavily on a continuous flow of crime news. As a result, they have developed well-defined relationships with those they perceive as reliable and credible suppliers of that news (Gordon and Heath, 1981). The police are the main source of crime news: the "police wire," the press release, the news conference, and the beat reporter provide the link between the world of crime and the news media (Ericson, Baranek, and Chan, 1987). Because the police can supply a steady stream of stories that are "entertaining, dramatic, amusing and titillating" (Ericson, 1991: 207), journalists implicitly adopt a police perspective on the problem of crime (Fishman, 1981).

The relationship between police and journalists is mutually beneficial (Katz, 1987). Journalists are allowed regular access to a valued news commodity; also, they gain credibility, authority, and objectivity when they refer to the police as the official spokespeople on crime. At the same time, the police are able to present themselves as experts on crime and as "owners" of the problem of crime.

All of this helps explain why interpersonal violent crimes such as homicide and robbery receive greater coverage than crimes by or against businesses (Ericson, 1991). The established sources—journalist relationships that exist with respect to "common" crimes—generally do not exist in the case of business crimes. Furthermore, stories about business crime are often judged as less newsworthy because they tend to be more complex, less dramatic, and more difficult to personalize (Randall, Lee-Sammons, and Hagner, 1988).

Crime Drama

Crime drama has always been important to television. From *Dragnet, The Untouchables,* and *Racket Squad* to *Law and Order* and *CSI,* every decade has witnessed countless lawyers, police detectives, and private investigators engaged in the prime-time pursuit of law and order. Crime drama conforms closely to television's stylistic and commercial requirements (Beckett and Sasson, 2000; Sumser, 1996). These programs rely heavily on suspense and violent action, and provide a format in which both can be maximized (Sparks, 1992). As crimes are investigated, and as wrongdoers are pursued and brought to justice, opportunities abound for car chases, fistfights, and gunplay.

9

Chapter 1: What Is Criminology?
Defining and Constructing
the Problem of Crime

The essentially escapist nature of television crime drama is well recognized. No one really expects crime dramas to provide a realistic portrait of crime and criminals. The images have more to do with the needs of the medium than with a desire to accurately map reality (Beckett and Sasson, 2000). Still, it is worth noting that crime in television drama, like crime in the news, tends to be disproportionately violent (Lichter et al., 1994). Also, television criminals are generally older than their real-life counterparts—closer to the age of the audience. Real-life offenders are often poor; on television they are more likely to be affluent. In crime dramas, any association between crime and minority group membership tends to be downplayed in order to avoid alienating a significant segment of the viewing audience (which would clearly not be in the best interests of a commercial medium). In sum, television criminals are typically "white materialists, motivated by greed and lasciviousness" (Newman, 1990: 263).

The distinction between television news and television drama is less clear than it once was (Fishman and Cavender, 1998; Tunnell, 1998; Welch, 2000). Programs such as *America's Most Wanted* and *Cops,* and the many shows that make use of amateur video to tell crime stories, combine traditional news documentary techniques with the familiar narrative style of dramatic television. These program formats (sometimes labelled "infotainment" or "reality television") have proliferated because they are popular with audiences and relatively inexpensive to produce (Kooistra and Mahoney, 1999). Crime, like other social problems, continues to be a source of both entertainment and income in the mass media (Gusfield, 1989).

Some General Characteristics of Crime Media

Despite all of the differences between types of media and types of content within media, it is possible to discuss a small number of broad generalizations with respect to the ways in which crime is discussed (Sacco, 2005).

Atypicality

One such characteristic is the tendency for news and entertainment media to focus on the rare and the unusual. Of course, this is part of what we mean by the term "news." Although homicides are the crimes which occur least frequently, they are the kinds of crime that one is most likely to encounter in newscasts and dramatic offerings (Paulsen, 2003). Gang rampages, (McCorkle and Miethe, 2002) and acts of terrorism (real or imagined) (Jenkins, 2003) are more likely to attract the attention of media than are the much more routine and mundane actions of property offenders.

It is common for Canadians to think that this tendency to give in to the sensationalist and the bizarre in crime coverage is a fault of American media from which Canadians are relatively immune. However, there is research to suggest that Canadian and American newscasts are more similar than they are different in this respect (Dower, 2004). Such similarities may have more to do with the nature of commercial media and the need to gather large undifferentiated audiences than with national identities.

Simplicity

One defining feature of most forms of popular culture is the tendency to simplify complex realities for the purposes of mass production. News stories tend to be brief, to the point, and, in the case of television, very heavy on visual presentation. Complicated media investigations about corporate wrongdoing end up being presented as stories about individual victims and malevolent corporate actors. Often emotion is emphasized at the expense of rational discourse. Stories that do not require an extensive background on the part of the audience are preferable to those which do.

Organized crime provides a particularly interesting case in point (Bernstein, 2002). As we will see in later chapters, the phenomenon we call organized crime can be understood as a kind of social activity which is bound up with the complexities of particular kinds of cultural and economic realities. Too often, however, media treatments of organized crime focus on crude ethnic stereotypes and simple-minded ideals about criminal conspiracies. British criminologist Michael Woodiwiss (2001) argues that the there has been a kind of "dumbing" of the discourse around organized crime which prevents a comprehensive and reasoned understanding of the issue.

Personification

Crime news tends to be people news. In the most extreme form, our celebrity-obsessed culture seems to be most interested in celebrity crimes. There has been no shortage of such cases in recent years. The murder trials of actors OJ Simpson and Robert Blake, the charges of shoplifting directed against actress Winona Ryder and politician Svend Robinson, and the countless charges of sexual misconduct and substance abuse leveled against professional athletes have all occupied far more media time than the circumstances of the crimes themselves would have suggested they merited.

Even when crimes don't involve celebrities, it is, for instance, the mind of the serial killer or the pain of the victim which fascinates us. Television

11

Chapter 1: What Is Criminology?
Defining and Constructing
the Problem of Crime

programs such as *America's Most Wanted* (Cavender, 1998) assign the participants in crimes clear-cut and unambiguous roles as villains, victims, and
heroes. The use of music, personal detail, and point-of-view photography
encourages the viewer to take the role of the victim.

One need only think of the way in which most North American media
responded to the events of September 11, 2001 to realize the extent to which
this tendency to personification is deeply ingrained in popular cultural presentations. Despite the geopolitical complexities which, it might be argued,
gave rise to the incidents of that day, the media quickly turned them into a
story about the personal conflict between President George W. Bush and
Osama Bin Laden. In a way that seemed to borrow heavily from the narrative
form of the movie western, the conflict was reduced to the President telling
media audiences that as far as he was concerned, Bin Laden was "wanted dead
or alive" just as posters in the old west had described desperados of an earlier
period.

Status Quo Orientation

Although some observers claim that the media are too liberal, many social
critics suggest just the opposite. In other words, they maintain that the broad
tendency of media is to reinforce existing social conditions and reaffirm
existing power relationships.

With respect to crime specifically, we can see several kinds of evidence
which are consistent with this conclusion. Crime news, for instance, seems to
disproportionately focus on the crimes of the poor and the powerless rather
than on the crimes of the powerful. The average newscast is usually much
more concerned with garden variety offences such as murder, sexual assault,
and robbery than with crimes by governments or by corporations. Even when
attention is focused on corporate crimes, the tendency is to treat the offence as
the work of irresponsible corporate managers or rogue corporations rather
than to question the nature of the broader economic arrangements which
make such crimes possible. To some degree at least, the inherently conservative
nature of so much crime reporting in the media reflects the influences which
crime sources are able to exert directly or indirectly over content (Hall et al.,
1978). As well, especially with respect to commercial media, the desire of the
large conglomerates which own television and radio stations and newspapers
is to attract and hold both advertisers and audiences (Bagidikian, 2004).
Messages which threaten the economic advantages of either might not be all
that welcome.

Talking about Crime

People do more than read crime news and watch crime shows on television; they also talk about crime (Sasson, 1995). Unfortunately, social scientists seem less interested in the two-way conversations people have with each other than in the (largely) one-way conversations that the mass media have with their audiences. A major study of reactions to crime in three major American cities found that people cited their friends and neighbours, rather than the mass media, as their principal sources of information about local crime conditions (Skogan and Maxfield, 1981). That being said, talk about crime often focuses on events that have received heavy media play. Media coverage of serial killings, child abductions, and crimes committed by or against celebrities is likely to generate considerable public discussion. Much talk also centres on crime in the local environment. Residents of high-crime neighbourhoods tend to talk more about crime (Skogan and Maxfield, 1981); they are also more likely to be personally acquainted with crime victims and thus to have more stories to tell about crime and its consequences.

In their study on fear of crime among the elderly, Kennedy and Silverman (1985) reported the surprising finding that respondents who expressed high levels of fear also had higher levels of contact with family members. The continuous cautions that the elderly (especially those living on their own) received from their families actually may have exacerbated their fears.

Crime in Rumour and Legend

Sometimes talk about crime seems to bear only a tenuous relationship to reality. In 1956, news spread throughout Taipei that a number of children had been slashed with what seemed to be razor blades (Jacobs, 1965). In another famous episode in 1944, many residents of Mattoon, Illinois, were said to be the victims of a "phantom anesthetist" who entered their homes and sprayed them with a paralyzing gas (Johnson, 1945). In 1969, the story spread through the city of Orléans, France, that Jewish dress shop owners were kidnapping young women and selling them into the "white slave trade" (Morin, 1971). More recently, stories have arisen in many North American communities about the threat posed to children by Halloween sadists, who poison or otherwise contaminate the "treats" they dispense to unsuspecting children (Best, 1990).

There was no evidence to corroborate any of these stories. Their fanciful quality suggests a close kinship with the sociological concept of "rumour" (Rosnow, 1988; Rosnow and Fine, 1976; Locher, 2002). Like all rumours, they represented forms of improvised news in that they expressed anxieties and

Improvised news
Similar to rumour; expresses anxieties and uncertainties about some aspect of social life.

13

Chapter 1: What Is Criminology?
Defining and Constructing
the Problem of Crime

uncertainties about some aspect of social life (Shibutani, 1966). For example, Best (1990) contends that the spread of stories about Halloween sadists during the 1970s was a response to three forms of social strain that characterized the period. The *first* was increasing public concern over the vulnerability of children to child abuse and other victimizing experiences. The *second* was the general increase in the fear of crime and in the threats posed to personal safety by anonymous strangers. The *third* was an increasing mistrust of people outside one's group. Best (1990: 143) characterized the Halloween sadist as a symbolic expression of these three anxieties: "The sadist, like other dangers, attacks children—society's most vulnerable members; the sadist, like the stereotypical criminal, is an anonymous, unprovoked assailant; and the sadist, like other strangers, should be met with suspicion rather than trust."

Folklorists use the term **urban legend** to characterize many of the crime stories that travel along interpersonal channels of communication (Brunvand, 1981, 1984, 1986, 1989). Brunvand (1984: ix) describes these legends as "highly captivating and plausible, but mainly fictional oral narratives that are widely told as true stories." Urban legends are widely circulated; typically they deal with attempted abductions in shopping malls or amusement parks, psychopaths who terrorize babysitters, criminally insane killers who stalk couples on lover's lanes, and the theft of organs from still living victims (Donovan, 2004; Radford, 2003). While these stories vary in their details from place to place and over time, their moral substance has remarkable durability.

Urban legend
Captivating and plausible fictional oral narratives that are widely regarded as true stories.

Wachs (1988) contends that crime folklore has considerable entertainment value, in that the stories, whether told or heard, provide opportunities for dramatic and often humorous release. She further characterizes these stories as "cautionary tales" that advise listeners of the dangers of urban life and the need for constant vigilance.

Some urban legends are more newsworthy than others. Stories about bicycle thieves generally have less currency than stories about killers on the loose. While talk about corporate and white-collar criminals seems to be rare, it does exist (Kapferer, 1989). In recent years, for instance, stories have circulated that some major businesses are under the control of satanic cults (Brunvand, 1984) or are willfully contaminating food products (Kapferer, 1989). In some inner-city African-American communities, rumours circulate which suggest that certain tobacco companies and fast-food outlets are run by genocidal, racist organizations (Pipes, 1997; Turner, 1993).

Sometimes stories have very real consequences even after they have been exposed as hoaxes. In March of 2005, a media scare erupted when a diner at a

---

BOX 1.1

The Fiend under the Car

Many of the urban legends people transmit through their conversations (and increasingly via the Internet) concern the actions of violent strangers. One such story, which began to circulate widely in the mid-1990s, focused on "teenage punks" or "gangsters" who, it was said, hid beneath cars parked in supposedly safe places such as suburban shopping malls. According to the most popular forms of the story, the offender struck when the passenger was standing next to the car, opening the door. At that point, he slashed the victim's ankles with a knife. When the victim bent over in pain or shock, she was robbed or raped by the offender. Several aspects of this story should be noted:

- The victim was typically female, and the offender was typically male.
- Robbery was commonly regarded as the motive for the crime, but sometimes it was claimed that the attack was part of a gang initiation.
- The colour of the offender was only rarely specified. When it was specified, the offender was said to be black.
- While such crimes have been attributed to many different places, no verifiable incidents have been discovered.

The popularity of this story may reflect its value as a cautionary tale about the dangers that lurk even in those places in the urban (and suburban) environment where people expect to feel safe. The tale also has parallels with stories that many adults heard as children about murderous fiends or mythical monsters hiding under their beds.

Source: www.snopes.com

San Jose, California, Wendy's restaurant said that she had found a finger in a bowl of chili. Restaurant officials indicated that there was no way in which the finger could have gotten into the chili, especially without a severed finger having been reported somewhere during the production process. Subsequently, the woman who made the report was charged with fraud, and it was discovered that she had a history of attempting to make false claims against corporations. However, the initial report and the extensive media attention it was granted cost the chain about $2.5 million in lost revenue. Concerns have been raised not only about the serious consequences of such hoaxes but also about the media's role in sounding the alarm and perpetuating public doubts about a product.

Crime myths
Distorted and misleading pieces of information that nevertheless are accepted as fact.

Crime Myths

Much of what we see on television or hear during late-night storytelling sessions can be described as **crime myths** (Kappeler and Potter, 2004)—that is,

15

Chapter 1: What Is Criminology?
Defining and Constructing
the Problem of Crime

distorted and misleading information that is nevertheless accepted as fact. For instance, many people believe these crime myths:

- The elderly are more likely to be victimized than any other group in society.
- Most crime is violent.
- Serial killers account for a substantial number of murders each year.
- Rates of victimization have risen dramatically in recent years.
- The risk of wife assault increases substantially on Super Bowl Sunday.

Yet, according to the best social scientific evidence, none of these statements is true.

According to Kappeler and Potter (2004), crime myths serve several important social functions. *First*, they help us organize our views about crime and the criminal justice system by providing a ready-made framework that clearly identifies criminals, victims, and crime fighters. *Second*, these myths support and maintain established views about crime. *Third*, they help us fill the gaps in our knowledge that social science has not yet filled, or cannot fill. *Fourth*, they provide an emotional outlet for our responses to crime and help establish channels for transforming emotions into action.

Because crime myths are so pervasive and so durable, they sometimes damage our objectivity. Marcus Felson (2002) contends that ten myths—that is, fallacies derived from popular culture—obscure our understanding of the empirical realities of crime:

The dramatic fallacy The media's emphasis on strange and violent crimes that are shrouded in mystery leads us to believe that such incidents are typical. Felson points out that most crime is not very dramatic at all. Property crime is far more common than violent crime. Furthermore, most of the violent crime that does occur is "minor" (that is, it involves minor injuries or no injuries). Homicide, in contrast, is statistically rare.

The cops and courts fallacy There is a tendency in the media to exaggerate the justice system's role in producing and preventing crime. Felson suggests that the frequency and distribution of crime have more to do with the social organization of everyday life than with the practices of the police or the courts.

The not-me fallacy The crudely drawn portraits of offenders in many television shows and films lead us to believe that offenders are fundamentally different from the rest of us. However, many people who do not think of themselves as criminals have certainly committed criminal acts. Also, our own tendency to obey the law may have less to do with our innate goodness than with the absence of temptation to offend.

The innocent youth fallacy We tend to think of youth as a time of innocence, and the media support the view that offenders are likely to be middle-aged. However, all of the available research indicates that for most common types of crime, adolescence and young adulthood are high-risk ages for both offending and being victimized.

The ingenuity fallacy The media often encourage us to think that the typical offender is a criminal genius (as, for example, in the films about the fictional serial killer Hannibal Lecter). Felson points out that in fact most crime requires little planning or intelligence. The most common types of crime are quickly and easily committed, and the offenders who commit them are unskilled.

The organized-crime fallacy Organized and white-collar crime exist. However, Felson reminds us that most crime is not organized. Moreover, crime organizations that do exist tend to be loose and informal rather than rigid. Presentations in films of well-structured hierarchical criminal syndicates are highly exaggerated versions of the reality.

The juvenile gang fallacy Juvenile gangs figure prominently in media treatments of crime. However, gangs are less well structured and less "corporate" than the media often lead us to believe.

The welfare-state fallacy Felson argues that while those who hate the welfare state blame it for crime, those who like the welfare state claim that crime problems result from the fact that the welfare state is insufficiently developed. In contrast, Felson contends that crime in industrial nations really has little to do with the extensiveness of the welfare state. Felson is quick to point out that he is not opposed to fighting poverty or inequality; but it is important, he adds, to detach crime from any kind of knee-jerk reaction to other social problems.

The agenda fallacy People with a political or social agenda often link that agenda to conclusions about the causes or prevention of crime. Anti-daycare advocates may claim that children in daycare are more likely to grow up to be offenders. Pro-gun advocates may claim that firearm ownership is a powerful crime deterrent. Too often, claims such as this are made in the absence of empirical evidence. It is important to disentangle our understanding of crime from the political agendas of those who speak to us through the media.

The whatever-you-think fallacy A final "fallacy" to which Felson directs our attention relates to the view of some criminologists that what is and is not a crime varies so much from one society to the next that it becomes impossible to say what crime—and therefore what criminology—is. Felson's view is that while the definition of crime varies between cultures, it does so more narrowly than is sometimes assumed.

17

Chapter 1: What Is Criminology?
Defining and Constructing
the Problem of Crime

BOX 1.2

The Mythology of Random Violence

A central concern of many contemporary crime myths is the theme of random violence. Urban legends, media portrayals, and political rhetoric about "new" categories of crime such as "home invasion," "car jacking," and "serial murder" reinforce the public's view that random violence—in many different forms—has become a significant social problem. But what exactly is random violence? And how accurate are the claims made about it in popular culture? An informative answer to questions such as these is provided by sociologist Joel Best in *Random Violence: How We Talk about New Crimes and New Victims* (1999).

According to Best, the concern about random violence reflects three assumptions: that such violence is patternless, that it is pointless, and that it is on the rise. Best contends that all three assumptions are highly questionable.

- Patternless   If by the term random we mean without pattern, then clearly violence is not random. Based on the social scientific evidence, it is completely incorrect to assume that all members of this society face an equal risk of becoming crime victims. The research in fact tells us that risks vary dramatically by age, by gender, by social class, and by a range of lifestyle indicators. Based on the horror stories we read in the mass media, we might think that we are all equally likely to be murdered. Actually, the evidence shows that young, socially disadvantaged males are far more likely to be killed than other Canadians.

- Pointless   The violent crimes we read about in the newspaper often seem senseless. Why would one youth beat up another youth over a pair of gym shoes? And why would a child "out of the blue" attack his classmates with a gun? But whether an act is pointless is very much a matter of perspective. Very often, violent offenders believe that they had valid reasons for doing what they did. They often say they were "angry" or "tired of being pushed around." Of course, we may not see these as valid reasons, and we may claim that their acts were pointless. But this circular reasoning implies that the acts were pointless by definition. The participants may have seen their actions as very sensible.

- On the rise   A big part of the concern about random violence is that it is becoming more common. Indeed, many people believe that crime rates are climbing even though the statistical evidence reveals strong trends in the opposite direction. Moreover, claims about whether violence is getting worse or getting better assume that some point of historical reference exists against which comparisons can be made. For example, rates of many kinds of crime are higher now than they were in the 1950s but lower now than they were a few years ago. In short, glib overall statements about how random violence may be spiralling out of control are surely exaggerated.

In the chapters that follow, the gap separating cultural myth from empirical reality will become more and more apparent. It is useful to begin where Felson's discussion of fallacies ends—with a consideration of what crime is.

CONCEPTUALIZING CRIME

Criminology, like all of the social (and other) sciences, is built on three foundations: theory, research, and conceptualization. *Theories* attempt to explain the relationships between categories of phenomena. *Research* refers to the studies that criminologists conduct in the "real world" to test their theories or to generate new ones. The nature of criminological theory and research is a central issue in later chapters of this book. *Concepts* are general terms that are used for classifying objects, persons, relationships, or events. In other words, concepts are the linguistic categories that we use to classify those aspects of social or physical reality that interest us. A central concept in the field of criminology is, of course, crime. In day-to-day conversation, we use this term in a very casual manner; in the context of this book, it is important for us to look more closely and more precisely at it. What do criminologists mean by it? What acts and behaviours does crime include? What does it exclude?

This is an extremely important matter because how we conceptualize crime dictates the questions we ask about it. We want to try to figure out what is the best way to think about crime for analytical purposes. What is crime like? What features do crimes share in common that are of interest to us as criminologists? It is important to point out that it does not really make sense to say that concepts are right or wrong. Instead, we can think of them as being more or less useful to us for particular purposes.

Below, we focus on three conceptualizations: crime as *legal construct*, crime as *normative violation*, and crime as *social control*. While these differ from one another in some important ways, it will become apparent that they share an important characteristic in common—they all define crime in offender-centred terms.

Crime
A behaviour that breaks the criminal law and is liable to public prosecution and punishment.

Crime as Lawbreaking

The dominant way of thinking about crime is in legal terms. In other words, we define crime relative to law. Thus, crime is conceptualized as a behaviour that breaks the law and is liable to public prosecution and punishment. Thus, the law may be understood as a form of social control that evaluates the moral nature of the behaviour in question. When we describe an act as criminal, we imply that the act is disvalued. It is a form of wrongdoing that "good people" should avoid at the risk of punishment. One of the major

WHAT IS IT?

Crime

In legal terms, crime is defined as behaviour that breaks the law and is liable to public prosecution and punishment. A criminal intention (*mens rea*) without the action (*actus reus*) is not a crime.

19

Chapter 1: What Is Criminology?
Defining and Constructing
the Problem of Crime

functions of the law is to deter people from engaging in the behaviour that it prohibits. The law comprises a set of written rules that are supported by state authority and accompanied by a standardized schedule of penalties.

Brantingham, Mu, and Verma (1995) note that although Canada has over 40,000 different federal and provincial statutes and municipal bylaws, only those which are defined by federal law are technically crimes. The principal piece of Canadian criminal law is the Criminal Code, a federal piece of legislation that includes most but not all of the categories of offending we normally think of as crimes.

Context

The fact that someone behaves in a way that *seems* to be inconsistent with the requirements of the law does not mean that he or she has committed a crime. To be criminal in a legal sense, an act must be intentional (Boyd, 2000). The mere physical act—known legally as the *actus reus*—is not enough. There must also be a willful quality to the act—what the law refers to as *mens rea*. Moreover, to be criminal, an act must be committed in the absence of a legally recognized defence or justification (Boyd, 2000). For example, while the law defines assaultive behaviour as a crime, a particular assaultive act may not be criminal if it was accidental (rather than intentional) or was committed in self-defence (and is therefore legally justifiable).

Actus reus
The mere physical criminal act.

Mens rea
The willful quality of a criminal act.

Individual Accountability

All criminal law derives from a model of behaviour that is based on individual psychology. Individuals must employ judgment in controlling their acts so that accidents do not occur. Since intent is part of the definition of crime, prosecutors must establish such purpose in the perpetrator. They sometimes try to do this by constructing the motive; however, establishing a motive does not establish guilt. A criminal intention (*mens rea*) without the action (*actus reus*) is not a crime. Intent and action together are required to obtain a criminal conviction.

Courts can also define the criteria used in judging guilt. In some situations, individuals commit acts that they do not have the power to prevent. These cases are covered by a judgment of competence, which may be restricted because of age, duress, self-defence, or insanity.

Age With respect to age, the criminal behaviours of youths are regulated by the **Youth Criminal Justice Act**, which was passed by Parliament in 2002 and became effective in 2003. According to the YCJA, a youth, or young person, is someone who is twelve years or older but less than eighteen years old. Thus, the law recognizes that though young people must be held responsible for their

YCJA
The *Youth Criminal Justice Act* was passed by the Parliament of Canada in 2002, and became effective in 2003. The Act details the principles, rules, and procedures regarding youthful offenders.

Duress defence
Some unlawful constraint or influence used to force an individual to commit an act that he or she otherwise would not have committed.

Self-defence
Actions taken to protect oneself or one's property, involving reasonable force, in the face of a threat.

actions, age is a relevant factor in determining how responsibility is to be assigned.

Duress   Individuals operating under duress can claim that they did not intend to commit a crime and therefore are not guilty. For this defence to succeed, the accused must prove that some unlawful constraint or influence was used to force him or her to commit an act that he or she otherwise would not have committed (Rush, 1994). Duress is often difficult to prove. The degree of force used must be commensurate with the degree of harm the individual perceived was being directed his or her way. Duress is never a defence against murder.

Self-Defence   Self-defence involves actions taken to protect oneself or one's property, involving reasonable force, in the face of a threat. These cases are not always straightforward, and our view of self-defence is evolving. Originally, the doctrine of self-defence held that the danger must be immediate and severe in order for criminal actions to be justified. More recently, in delineating situations in which self-defence claims may be made, the law has begun to recognize issues such as the power differential between the victim and the offender, and/or the presence of a long-term pattern of abuse and the fear that might be associated with it. An example of this is the "battered woman syndrome." A battered woman who has killed her abuser may claim self-defence if she had reasonable cause to think that her life was in danger (regardless of whether she had actually been physically abused in the immediate incident). The Supreme Court of Canada has accepted the argument of self-defence in these cases.

Insanity   It is up to the defence to prove a state of insanity; the prosecution is not required to prove sanity. In effect, this restricts the extent to which an individual can claim that a limited capacity to form intent resulted from mental breakdown.

Legal and Social Controls

The legal system plays an important role in managing criminal events. Legal definitions of crime may appear to be immutable—that is, determined by clear-cut rules of evidence in establishing guilt or innocence—but in reality, they are not. Legal responses are often heavily influenced by circumstances, public tolerance, and judicial discretion. The police and the courts apply the law not only to prevent crime and punish criminals but also to reduce social conflict. Any study of crime needs to account for behaviour that is disorderly or dangerous but not yet unlawful. Alternative or informal legal responses set

21

Chapter 1: What Is Criminology?
Defining and Constructing
the Problem of Crime

the outside limits of criminality by redefining the criminal justice system's responses to misbehaviour.

The law is only one form of social control (Black, 1976). Social life is also regulated by informal expectations about how people should and should not behave. Whether we call these expectations etiquette, professionalism, or simply good taste, people evaluate the morality of each other's behaviour and respond accordingly in a variety of ways. Gossip, ridicule, and ostracism are all forms of social control, and involve fewer formal social processes than do legal forms. When actions are classified as crimes, much more is implied than a mere condemnation of the behaviour. When we call an act a crime, we are implying that the problem will be processed in a particular way and that specific state agencies will assume responsibility for solving it. In other words, to label a particular deed a crime is to assign "ownership" of the problem at hand to the police, the courts, and other criminal justice agencies.

If a problem is defined as one that involves an uninformed public acting on the basis of incomplete or incorrect information, experts in education might be expected to provide a solution. If a problem is defined as one that results from some medical condition, mental or physical health professionals will dominate efforts to solve it. When behaviour is deemed criminal, the issue will likely be surrendered to law enforcement and crime prevention specialists. Clearly, these alternative approaches have dramatically different consequences. As Gusfield (1989) notes, it makes a real difference whether we see social problems as involving people who are troubled or people who are troublesome.

Those who conceptualize crime in legal terms find it useful to distinguish between crime *mala in se* and crime *mala prohibita*. This distinction alerts us to the fact that not all crimes resonate to the same degree with popular morality. Crimes *mala in se* are crimes that are seen as wrong in and of themselves. They are acts that most people would see as wrong even if they were not against the law, and that have been widely condemned both historically and cross-culturally. Murder, robbery, and other predatory crimes are examples of crimes *mala in se.* In contrast, some types of behaviours are not as widely or as consistently condemned. Crimes *mala prohibita* are acts that are wrong not in and of themselves but by prohibition. Alcohol consumption and certain sexual activities, for instance, are viewed as criminal only in some societies and only at some points in history. This *mala in se/mala prohibita* distinction forces us to recognize that laws might differ with respect to the moral force they can exert. Because this point is an important one, it is advisable to consider the broader issue of the relationship between law and morality.

Mala in se
Crimes that are perceived historically and cross-culturally as wrong.

Mala prohibita
Crimes that are condemned through prohibition.

BOX 1.3

The Insanity Defence in Canada

In 1992, the section of the Criminal Code relating to a defence of insanity was amended. The changes were intended to reflect modern psychiatric terminology and to clarify how and when the defence should be applied. The new terminology referred to a "defence of mental disorder" rather than insanity. Unlike in the case of other kinds of defences, when the insanity defence is successful, it does not result in a verdict of "not guilty" but in a verdict of "not criminally responsible on account of mental disorder." The person in question usually will be institutionalized rather than go free.

For a variety of understandable reasons, the insanity defence is often the focus of considerable controversy.

For instance, in 1999 a Winnipeg man named Robert Chaulk was charged with the New Year's Eve slaying of two of his neighbours. Chaulk had been the central figure in an earlier Supreme Court ruling that widened the definition of criminal insanity to include those who are unable to recognize the moral depravity of their crimes.

In June 1987, Chaulk and a co-accused were convicted of first-degree murder in the stabbing and beating death of an 83-year-old Winnipeg man named George Haywood. During their trial, defence psychiatrists had argued that the pair suffered from a rare condition called "folie à deux." The term implies that the offenders had experienced a joint psychotic episode. However, the jurors found the two guilty, and they were sentenced to life with no chance of parole for 25 years.

However, in 1990 the Supreme Court of Canada ordered a new trial after re-examining the Criminal Code "moral-wrong test." The Court found that an individual can claim insanity not only if he or she fails to understand that a criminal act is legally wrong but also if he or she cannot comprehend the degree to which the act is morally wrong. In a retrial, the jurors found the two defendants not guilty by reason of insanity.

Chaulk received two life sentences for the New Year's Eve 1999 killings, but the case did much to focus attention on the legal meaning of insanity. Many critics of the justice system question how great a role psychiatric testimony should play in legal proceedings.

On November 23, 2001, a 74-year-old resident of Belleville, Ontario named Robert Lloyd stabbed his wife to death in their home. Lloyd attempted to plead insanity but was not successful. However, in 2003, his charge was reduced from second-degree murder to manslaughter. According to media reports, Lloyd showed no signs of mental illness before or immediately after the crime despite a family history of mental disorder. In the months following the murder, he did start to express concerns that members of the Masonic Lodge were after him, and he told at least one doctor that the crime was a mercy killing. Several psychiatrists had examined the accused. In reference to the case, Justice Richard Byers said that the crime was not about the theories proposed by the various doctors who examined Lloyd but about the murder itself. This, however, is a distinction that is not easily made either in courtrooms or in the court of public opinion.

Sources: Black, W. "Getting away with Murder." *Belleville Pioneer* (online edition). October 25, 2003. http://www.thepioneer.com/oct25_editorial.htm

Roberts, D. "Insanity Rulings Blasted after Killings in Winnipeg." *Globe and Mail.* January 5, 1999: A1, A7.

Roberts, D. "Man Gets Two Life Sentences in Killings." *Globe and Mail.* December 4, 1999: A2. Used by permission.

23

Chapter 1: What Is Criminology?
Defining and Constructing
the Problem of Crime

Crime, Politics, and the Law

Where do criminal laws come from in the first place? Two answers to this question have been advanced (Grattet, Jenness, and Curry, 1998; Kueneman, 2000). The first is that laws arise from a social consensus about morality and about the need to respond to particular types of events in particular ways. The second is that reactions to crime have more to do with power, conflict, and inequality than with social consensus.

At a very broad level, these approaches differ with respect to how they perceive the role of social interests (Bockman, 1991). According to consensus theorists, society's members have many interests in common, and their reactions to crime serve these collective interests. Laws are written and enforced to meet the needs of the majority. Deviation from these laws is generally accepted as reason for punishment. Conflict theorists, for their part, contend that in a complex society, different social groups may pursue different interests, and how well they succeed at this depends on how powerful they are. In this sense, reactions to crime reflect particular class, cultural, or other social interests rather than broader collective interests.

The Consensus View

In the study of law, the concept of social consensus is meant to alert us to the apparently broad-based agreement in society regarding what kinds of acts are serious crimes warranting direct and immediate intervention, and what kinds are not. **Consensus theory** is associated with a number of important scholars, most notably the famous French sociologist Emile Durkheim (1897), who wrote in the nineteenth century about the relationship between law and morality.

For Durkheim, the role that law plays depends on the kind of social solidarity which is characteristic of a particular society. In this respect, Durkheim distinguished between "mechanical" and "organic" solidarity, the former being more characteristic of less complex, more traditional societies and the latter being more characteristic of contemporary urban societies. In mechanical societies, social solidarity rests upon what people have in common. It is their shared beliefs and values which connect them to each other. In such societies, the role of law is to reflect this "collective conscience." Thus, in mechanical societies, law emerges out of and

Consensus theory
Theory proposing that laws and punishment are enforced in order to maintain the collective interests shared by members of society.

WHAT DOES IT MEAN?

Consensus versus Conflict

Social consensus is meant to alert us to the apparent broad-based agreement in society regarding what kinds of acts are serious crimes and deserving of direct and immediate intervention, and what types are not. Conflict approaches contend that responses to crime must be seen as part of a larger struggle between groups attempting to use the law, or legal control, in the pursuit of their own interests.

reflects the common morality, and when offenders are punished, this act expresses what the members of the society share in common.

In contrast, organic societies are characterized by a complex division of labour in which people play different but complementary roles. The basis of social solidarity is not what people share with each other so much as it is how people need each other. In such societies, the role of law is not to punish and repress but to integrate and mediate the parts of society in the context of this complex division of labour. The role of law, therefore, is to provide restitution rather than express common moralities. Of course, no society is completely mechanical or completely organic, and solidarity typically rests on some combination of these social forces.

These are powerful ideas which have importantly influenced the ways in which other scholars have thought about the role of law in contemporary society (Parsons, 1951; Pound, 1943). Thus, it can be suggested that even in a complex, highly differentiated society such as our own, people who differ from one another in terms of gender, age, ethnicity, and social class are likely to agree on certain basic moral standards.

Punishment is directed toward a commonly agreed-on set of behaviours that offend social mores. We punish murderers more severely than we punish other criminals because of the general social consensus that murder is among the most serious infractions a person can commit. By passing laws, we "criminalize" behaviours that are widely understood as threatening to our shared values. We attach the most severe penalties to those crimes which offend most deeply our sense of collective morality.

Consistent with this view, a large body of public opinion research indicates that, by and large, our legal responses to crime reflect widespread social sentiments (Goff and Nason-Clark, 1989; Johnson and Sigler, 2000).

The consensus position has attracted much criticism. Opponents of this view have argued that it oversimplifies the complex relationships among groups pursuing different interests with varying levels of resources. In measuring consensus in public opinion surveys, we confront the question of where the consensus came from in the first place. It is one thing to argue that consensus spontaneously emerges from the collective will of the population. It is quite another to suggest that consensus results from the fact that some individuals have a vested interest in reacting to criminal events in a particular way and are able to convince the rest of the population that their world view is the right one. In either case, we might find that public opinion data reveal widespread agreement on the relative seriousness of different crimes.

Conflict, Power, and the Law

In contrast to the consensus view, conflict theory asserts that even where a consensus exists regarding what constitutes a serious crime and what does not, we must take into consideration the source of the consensus. Moreover, it is incorrect to maintain that this consensus is a spontaneous product of group life. As one critic of the consensus position has noted:

> Laws do not simply appear miraculously on our law books and do not reflect "society's" values. Instead, the acts and people we call "criminal" and our concern with crime at any given time reflect the activity of groups in this society seeking legal support for economic, ideological and status interest (Sheley, 1991: 39).

From this standpoint, definitions of crime must be seen as part of a larger struggle among groups attempting to use the law, or legal control, in the pursuit of their own interests.

Conflict theory
Theory that argues that in a complex society, social groups may pursue different interests, and the achievement of success depends on how powerful they are. Responses to crime are interpreted as part of a larger struggle among groups that attempt to use law, or legal control, in pursuit of their own interests.

BOX 1.4

Don't Some Laws Reflect Consensus?

The view that laws emerge out of and reflect special interests seems to be contradicted by the common sense observation that at least some laws seem to reflect the interests of everyone in society. For example, laws against murder, robbery, and sexual assault would seem to be in the interest of everyone, not just those who have the most power.

However, the late British sociologist Steven Box (1981) argued that it is not really correct to say that the law prohibits murder, sexual assault, and robbery. Rather, it prohibits certain types of these behaviours, and at the same time does not prohibit behaviours committed by more powerful people that are equally or even more destructive.

With respect to murder, for instance, Box wrote:

> The criminal code defines only some types of killing as murder; it excludes, for example, deaths which result from negligence such as employers' failure to maintain safe working conditions in factories or mines . . . or deaths which result from government agencies' giving environmental health risks a low priority . . . or death resulting from drug manufacturers' failure to conduct adequate research on new chemical compounds before conducting aggressive marketing campaigns. [Therefore] criminal laws against murder, rape, robbery and assault do protect us all, but they do not protect the less powerful from being killed, sexually exploited, deprived of their property, or physically or psychologically damaged through the greed, apathy, negligence and the accountability of the relatively more powerful (48–9).

Identifying Competing Social Groups

There is little agreement among scholars as to what constitutes competing groups. Marxian scholars locate attempts to control the mechanisms for reacting to crime in the conflicts between social classes (Chambliss, 1986; Reiman, 2003). For these theorists, class conflict is a central feature of capitalist societies. The powerful economic classes, which own property and industries, seek to expand and consolidate their control of the less powerful classes, which must sell their labour to the capitalist classes in order to survive. The legal machinery provides one important means by which they can do so (Schissel, 1992).

Marxian scholars also encourage us to recognize that industries that pollute the environment and victimize consumers are generally treated less harshly than street criminals who, say, rob convenience stores (Michalowski and Bohlander, 1976). This is because the criminalization and aggressive prosecution of these actions by industries would not be consistent with capitalist interests. Marxians argue that the average person might well agree that the cold-blooded killer of a convenience store night clerk should be treated more harshly than the CEO of a corporation that sells defective—and potentially dangerous or even lethal—products, but this does not demonstrate evidence of a spontaneous consensus about what types of crimes are more serious. It merely demonstrates how powerful interests are able to manipulate the consciousness of the members of a capitalist society.

Other proponents of the conflict position favour a model of group relations that is more diffuse than the one embraced by the Marxians. For them, laws and other aspects of the legal machinery reflect interests other than class (Bernard, 1981; Gusfield, 1963; Turk, 1976). Conflicts arise between cultural, lifestyle, and ethnic groups, and the factors propelling groups to use the legal machinery in the service of their interests are often diverse. When social groups are involved in conflicts, they do not always fight on a level playing field. Groups vary in their access to the resources that allow them to influence social outcomes. The machinery of legal control can be thought of as one of these resources. Groups may wish to see laws passed in order to have their values officially recognized by society; or they may wish to use the law to control a group that they believe threatens their values or social position.

Consensus *and* Conflict

It is probably too simple to think that a choice has to be made between the consensus and conflict models since both ideas have something of value to offer.

What kinds of compromise are possible? One kind of compromise might be that conflicts and consensus are useful explanations of different types of

27

Chapter 1: What Is Criminology?
Defining and Constructing
the Problem of Crime

crimes. Perhaps crimes such as murder are acts which violate the widely shared sentiments which the law embodies. Other crimes might reflect the ability of some in society to impose their moral definitions on others. The history of Canadian drug laws provides an example of the latter process (Cook, 1969; Comack, 1986). Most scholars agree that Canada's earliest drug laws, which took effect in the first decade of the twentieth century, emerged out of racial and class conflict—especially in Western Canada. Because such laws, in the first instance, were directed again Chinese opium merchants, it has been argued that the real role of these laws was to contain Asian immigration and trade and thus exert class control (Fischer et al., 2003). The laws against marijuana which followed in 1923 were no doubt influenced by the racist propaganda of writers such as Emily Murphy and by American propagandists who argued that marijuana could turn users into an army of psychotic killers (Fischer et al., 2003).

A second example of law as a conflict process concerns the so-called "safe street laws" which swept the country in the last years of the twentieth and the first years of the twenty-first centuries (Carnochan, 2005; Gatez, 2004). In many cities, these laws were ostensibly directed towards "squeegiers" who were said to harass and threaten "honest" and "decent" citizens who were trying to go about their business. In reality, the laws were directed against the poorest and most marginal segments of urban society. The real effect of such legislation was to make it a crime to be homeless. These laws emerged out of a conflict between the dispossessed and marginalized and various anti-poverty coalitions on the one side and policing organizations, politicians, headline writers, and downtown business interests on the other.

In this case, the distinction between homicide laws and drug laws (or anti-panhandling laws) might be seen as the distinction made earlier between crimes mala in se and crimes mala prohibita. In the former case, we understand crimes as acts that violate a widely shared consensus enshrined in law. In the latter, we think about crime as the product of an ability of those with more power to criminalize those with less power.

Another kind of compromise might suggest that consensus and conflict describe law creation at different stages of the process. Thus, while laws might be born in conflict, they often end in consensus. One reason for this is that laws affect moral judgments. In other words, because we live in a society that treats X as a crime, we come to believe over time that X is indeed wrong. So, with the example above, we end up thinking that killing a convenience store clerk is indeed more serious than a corporation selling defective products because we live in a society which seems to take the former so much more seriously than the latter.

Feminist

A theoretical orientation that critically assesses power relationships in society particularly as those relationships relate to gender inequality.

Feminist Approaches

In the feminist view, felicity and harmony are regarded as the highest values, and much emphasis is placed on the themes of caring, sharing, nurturing, and loving. According to Harris (1991):

> This contrasts sharply [with] the orientation that values power and control above all else. Where the central goal is power, power conceived as "power over" or control, people and things are not viewed as ends in themselves but as instruments for the furtherance of power. Hierarchical institutions and structures are established both to clarify power rankings and to maintain them. The resulting stratifications create levels of superiority and inferiority, which carry differential status, legitimacy, and access to resources and other benefits. Such divisions and exclusions engender resentment and revolt in various forms, which then are used to justify greater control (88).

A major part of the feminist effort, Harris suggests, involves attempts to identify and confront characteristics and values that are not conducive to the full realization of human potential. Feminists also reject negative values that are used to justify stereotyping and that work to support the groups in power (Daly and Maher, 1998). The feminist view proposes that the emphasis on control (which is epitomized in incarceration) be replaced by an emphasis on strategies that address the serious disharmony in society. The potential for crime and violence can be reduced by undermining social inequalities and enhancing social interaction (Boritch, 1997; van Wormer and Bartollos, 2000). More recent views of gender and crime emphasize the importance of cultural values imbedded in patriarchal views of social relations, which have been used to justify greater aggression in men and more submissive roles for women. As women have become more increasingly involved in crime, there is a larger issue about economic equality leading to equal opportunity for crime, a view that has not gone unchallenged in the research literature. In particular, the critiques have been directed at how we use stereotypical views of social relationships to explain the influence of gender on crime, ignoring the underlying social, economic, and political forces that influence these relationships.

Battered Women and Crime

The feminist reinterpretation of social control is consistent with general trends in the legal landscape, where more and more claimants are not only representing certain groups as victims but also negotiating to have offenders considered in a

29

Chapter 1: What Is Criminology?
Defining and Constructing
the Problem of Crime

different light. This is particularly evident with respect to the cases of women who kill their husbands after suffering long-term physical abuse. What has confounded the courts in dealing with these cases is that often there is no evidence of self-defence at the time of the murder and, in many instances, the crime actually seems to have been premeditated. Advocates contend that women charged with such crimes should not be judged solely on the evidence gathered on the scene. Rather, adjudication of the act should include consideration of the pattern of abuse that preceded it.

As stated earlier, the courts have come to accept **battered woman syndrome** as a defence. This syndrome is characterized by a sense of helplessness: as a result of ongoing violence, women come to believe that they can neither leave the abusive relationship nor act effectively to reduce the physical abuse; thus, violence is their only recourse. Striking back when the abuser is asleep or otherwise vulnerable makes the act seem premeditated.

Battered woman syndrome
The sense of helplessness felt by women who come to believe that they can neither leave an abusive relationship nor effectively act to reduce the violence.

Until quite recently, women who killed their abusive partners in such circumstances were routinely convicted of manslaughter or murder and were often sentenced to long prison terms. But in the late 1970s and early 1980s, the courts began to allow expert witness testimony regarding battered woman syndrome and how it was possible for the experience of long-term abuse to have imparted a sense of imminent personal danger (generally required in a self-defence plea) in a woman who killed an abusive partner (Gillespie, 1989). In many other nations, battered woman syndrome is still not recognized as a special justification for homicide. However, in North America, expert witness testimony is allowed in such cases, and this testimony influences court verdicts.

The Focus on Offenders

Legal conceptualizations of crime, whether they are rooted in consensus visions or in conflict ones, are much more concerned with criminal behaviour than they are with actual criminal events (Gould, 1989). In other words, when it comes to deciding what a crime is or whether a crime has occurred, the law focuses on what offenders *do* rather than on other event elements. From a legal standpoint, crime is largely synonymous with the actions of the offender. By implication, when criminologists resort to legal conceptualizations, they are encouraging us to think about crime as merely something that offenders do. This is a rather narrow vision of crime. If crimes are equivalent

WHAT DOES IT MEAN?
Battered Woman Syndrome
This syndrome is characterized by a sense of helplessness. Women come to believe that they cannot leave an abusive relationship and that they cannot act effectively to reduce the violence.

to offenders' actions, the only interesting questions appear to be those relating to those actions. This discourages us from asking other questions—relating, for instance, to the roles of victims and bystanders—that may be equally important.

Other Conceptualizations

Conduct Norms

Many social scientists have argued that legal conceptualizations of crime are too limited, and have suggested alternative ways of thinking about crime. One early critic, the sociologist Thorsten Sellin (1938), maintained that the use of legal definitions to delimit the subject matter of criminology violated a fundamental criterion of scientific inquiry. According to Sellin, the scientist must be free to use his or her own terms in attempting to understand any phenomenon, including crime. Legal definitions surrender the boundaries of the field of criminology to politicians and legislators. Moreover, Sellin maintained, because laws reflect diverse administrative needs, the acts that the law defines as criminal often have very little in common. Smoking marijuana, homicide, "disturbing the peace," and sexual assault differ from one another in a variety of ways. If the criminologist wants to understand what causes crime, Sellin argued, the effort will be stymied by the heterogeneous nature of the subject matter.

Sellin's solution was to reconceptualize crime in ways that made more sense, sociologically speaking. According to him, instead of thinking about the subject matter of criminology as "acts that violate the law," it was more helpful to conceptualize the field as the study of violations of norms of conduct. Norms of conduct are widely shared cultural rules about which people feel strongly. For Sellin, acts that violated these rules shared an important characteristic: they defied broadly held expectations of what constituted appropriate conduct. Thus, in the present era, homicide and sexual assault violate conduct norms (so defined), but smoking marijuana and disturbing the peace do not. While this conceptualization may be less comprehensive than the legal definition, Sellin believed that it was more useful since it only included acts that had important behavioural similarities.

Predatory and Moralistic Violence

A very different way of conceptualizing crime has been advanced by sociologist Donald Black. In a 1983 paper, Black argued that much of what the justice system regards as crime is understood as something quite the opposite by those whom it labels as offenders. Seen in this way, assaults, vandalism, and even murder can be understood as quests for justice (Agnew, 1990; Katz, 1987; Lee, 2000). This position recognizes that those who are judged to be offenders

Norms
Rules that govern social activities and define social roles, role relations, and standards of appropriate conduct.

31

Chapter 1: What Is Criminology?
Defining and Constructing
the Problem of Crime

often feel victimized by those against whom they offend. Studies of homicide have shown that the eventual victim is often the first party to have brandished a weapon or threatened deadly force (Luckenbill, 1977; Wolfgang, 1958). Similarly in many cases of assault, offenders may feel that they are merely responding to verbal or physical transgressions on the part of others (Felson, Baccaglini, and Ribner, 1985; Luckenbill, 1984). A wife who shoots her husband after years or decades of abuse may question a justice system that categorizes her as the offender and the husband as the victim. Such examples, Black maintains, encourage us to recognize that social control is behind many different kinds of crime and that there is real social scientific value to be derived from thinking about crime as a form of social control.

Social control
The regulatory institutions of society—especially the law enforcement and judicial systems—and how they operate, encompassing rule enforcement at all levels.

It is important, Black argued, to distinguish such "moralistic crime" from predatory crime. Predatory crime (or violence) involves the exploitation or the appropriation of the property or the person of another. Many sexual assaults, robberies, and break and enters would be examples of predatory crimes. In most of these incidents, the offender exploits or plunders the victim and there is no prior relationship between them (Jensen, 2002).

Black argued that the failure to make the distinction between predatory and moralistic crime leads to confusion for the criminologist. This is because so many homicides and assaults are moralistic rather than predatory. This means that, as forms of behaviour, they have very little in common with predatory crimes such as shoplifting or sexual assault. Indeed, as a form of behaviour, moralistic crimes have more in common with law than they do with predatory crimes. Because they are efforts to seek justice, they involve one person defining another's behaviour as wrong and treating it accordingly. Of course, to say that the man who kills his wife after he finds out she has had an affair has committed a "moralistic crime" is not to say that we agree with the action. It is only, Black says, to identify its key behavioural characteristics so as to clarify the task of criminological analysis.

Conceptual Limitations

On the subject of defining crime, Robert Bursik and Harold Grasmick have written:

> Unlike some other substantive areas examined within the social sciences, one of the most problematic issues in the area of criminology actually involves defining the behavior that we study. While this may seem to be a curious state of affairs to an outside observer, some very tricky conceptual and theoretical problems arise in this seemingly simple task (1993: 19).

The alternative conceptualizations offered by Sellin, Black, and others remind us that the central subject matter of criminology can be defined in a number of different ways. As stated, conceptualizations are not right or wrong; they are merely more or less useful. Obviously, thinking about crime as a violation of law, a violation of conduct norms, and a form of social control are three different ways of defining the subject matter. That being said, all three conceptualizations share an important feature: they are offender-centred. In other words, they conceptualize crime as the act of the offender. As we will see in later chapters, there is another and potentially more useful view: that crime is primarily an event.

SUMMARY

Criminology is a broad-based perspective in that it is concerned with all aspects of crime and social control. Moreover, it is an interdisciplinary field, which means that psychologists, historians, geneticists, legal scholars, and the practitioners of many other disciplines contribute to our criminological understanding.

Most of us approach the study of crime with many preconceptions, which we develop mainly through the images we confront in popular culture. Films, television, newspapers, and informal storytelling sessions often focus on tales of crime and violence. These images originate in the media's need to entertain mass audiences, and often bear little relationship to what criminologists learn from more careful studies of the phenomenon of crime. In later chapters, we will regularly question the understandings of crime that popular culture underwrites.

In this chapter, we also discussed the conceptualization of crime—that is, what the term is intended to mean when used in the context of criminological discussion. Most commonly, crime is understood as an act that violates the law. Law itself can be understood as emerging out of processes of social consensus and/or social conflict.

However, other conceptualizations of crime are possible—for example, it can be seen as a violation of conduct norms, or a form of social control. That being said, the overarching trend in contemporary criminology is to conceptualize crime in offender-centred terms. In other words, however we define crime, we implicitly define it as something an offender *does*—as an act an offender commits. In the remainder of this book, we adopt an alternative position. Instead of treating crime as an *act* that an offender commits, we treat it as an *event* in which others are involved aside from the offender. In the next chapter, we consider the character and the implications of crime-as-event.

33

Chapter 1: What Is Criminology?
Defining and Constructing
the Problem of Crime

QUESTIONS FOR REVIEW AND DISCUSSION

1. What is the difference between an action in which there is no intent to harm and an action in which an individual has this intent?
2. How well do you think consensus arguments explain the laws against pornography?
3. Should people who have psychological problems always be excused for their crimes? If not, why not?
4. In what ways do your family and friends talk about crime? How does this influence your sense of how much crime there is? How does their discussion of crime compare with what you read or hear through the media?
5. Is news reporting of crime accurate? Discuss the factors that may create distortions relating to the extent and incidence of crime.

RECOMMENDED READINGS

Boyd, N. 2002. *Canadian Law: An Introduction.* 3rd ed. Toronto: Nelson Thomson.

Kappeler, V.E., and G.W. Potter. 2004. *The Mythology of Crime and Criminal Justice* 4th ed. Long Grove, IL: Waveland Press.

Krajicik, D.J. 1998. *Scooped: How Media Miss Real Story While Chasing Sex, Sleaze and Celebrity.* New York: Columbia University Press.

Walters, R. 2003. *Deviant Knowledge: Criminology, Politics and Policy.* Cullompton: Willan Publishing.

INFOTRAC® COLLEGE EDITION

Explore InfoTrac® College Edition, your online university library, which includes hundreds of popular and scholarly journals in which you can find articles related to the topics in this chapter. Visit InfoTrac® through your web browser (**www.infotrac-college.com**) or through this book's website (**www.criminalevent-4e.nelson.com**).

WHAT'S ON THE WEB?

For chapter links and quizzes, check out the accompanying website at **www.criminalevent-4e.nelson.com**.

Chapter 2 The Criminal Event

LEARNING OBJECTIVES:

- introduce the concept of the criminal event
- show how an event-centred definition of crime expands analytical possibilities beyond those associated with an offender-centred definition
- discuss the major elements of the criminal event, including the offender, the victim, the bystanders, the police, and the social setting
- show that crime is not randomly distributed in time, space, or the social structure
- introduce the concept of the "social domain"
- describe a model of the criminal event which includes precursors, transactions, and aftermath

Criminal event
Comprises its precursors, including the locational and situational factors that bring people together in time and space; the event itself, including how the interactions among participants define the outcomes of their actions; and the aftermath of the event, including the reporting to the police, their response, the harm done, the redress required, and the long-term consequences of the event in terms of public reactions and the changing of laws.

In this chapter, we introduce the concept of the **criminal event** and explain how crime takes place through the convergence of motivated offenders with victims and various third parties. We also discuss the three stages of criminal events: precursors, transactions, and aftermath. **Precursors** relate to the way the law defines acceptable behaviour in society and to the ways people in the community define morality. Precursors also include the various factors that bring offenders and victims together. **Transactions** are the exchanges that take place during the event, as well as its situational context. Key considerations here include the offender's behaviour, the role of the victim, and the effects that third parties—including the police—have on the event. The **aftermath** refers to the consequences of the crime, including the harm to the victim, the punishment of the offender, and public reactions to the crime.

INTRODUCTION

In this chapter, we provide an organizational framework for our integrated approach to the analysis of crime and crime control. This framework emphasizes the study of crime as **criminal events** (Brantingham, Brantingham, and

Taylor, 1993; Gould, 1989; Meier, Kennedy, and Sacco, 2001). Throughout most of the history of criminology, researchers have tried to understand crime largely in terms of the actions of criminal offenders (Meier et al., 2001; Miethe and Meier, 1994). The simple implication of this approach is that a crime represents little more than the expression of the will of a person who is motivated to behave criminally. If this view is valid, the task of the criminologist is to try to explain why some people behave criminally, while the task of the police and other criminal justice agencies is to prevent offenders from behaving criminally or to capture and reform them after they have done so.

Although we cannot hope to understand crime in society without reference to the lawbreaker, it is also true—as noted earlier—that there is much more to crime than the offender. In many cases, crimes also involve victims who resist their victimization and in so doing affect the course of action (Kleck and Sayles, 1990; Weaver et al., 2004). Furthermore, crimes often involve bystanders and witnesses, whose presence can deter an offender or whose apparent tacit approval of the offender's actions can facilitate the commission of the crime. Bystanders or victims may also summon the police, whose appearance at the scene may affect the response of offenders.

The criminal event cannot be separated from the physical and social setting in which it occurs (Miethe and Regoeczi, 2004; Miethe and Meier, 1994; Sherley, 2005). Many forms of crime are intricately linked to the routine activities in which both victims and offenders engage, and to the usual places in which these activities occur (Sherman, Gartin, and Buerger, 1989). More generally, criminal events involve the public, whose response to perceived increases in crime levels results in pressure on police to pursue more aggressively some categories of offenders. On an even broader scale, crimes involve the actions of lawmakers and the social groups to whom they are responsive. The concept of the criminal event encourages us to conceptualize crime in terms that encompass but also extend beyond the study of offenders. In other words, rather than being *individual* events, crimes are *social* events (Haen Marshall, 2004; Meier, Kennedy, and Sacco, 2001).

CRIMES AS SOCIAL EVENTS

To characterize crimes as "events" is to recognize them as incidents that occur at particular times and in particular places. Like any other type of social event—a dinner party, a corporate board meeting, a car accident—criminal events are more likely to happen in specific circumstances and to involve

BOX 2.1

The Diverse Character of Criminal Events

Case One

On December 26, 2005, a Boxing Day shopping excursion became a setting for violence as a 15-year-old woman was killed and six other people were injured when gunmen sprayed a crowd of bystanders at one of the busiest intersections in Toronto. The young woman, the 52nd gun homicide of the year in Toronto, was apparently caught in the crossfire between two well-armed groups attempting to settle some outstanding grievance through the use of force.

Case Two

On May 11, 2004, an elderly Windsor resident received a telephone call from a male person who purported to be an employee of her bank. The caller identified himself as "Mr. Fox" and told her that the bank suspected that one of its employees had fraudulently removed $4,800 from her VISA account. Mr. Fox requested her help in catching the employee in the act, and she agreed. He subsequently instructed her to go to her bank and attempt to withdraw another $4,800 from her VISA account. If she was successful, he would meet her outside and then return the money to her VISA account. Mr. Fox cautioned the victim not to tell anyone of their conversation, as the bank did not yet know which bank employees could be trusted. The victim subsequently went to her bank and took $4,800 out of her VISA account. She exited the bank and was met by "Mr. Fox." He took the money from her and told her to go right home and wait for his call. The victim returned to her home. She eventually got suspicious and called her bank, at which time she learned that she had been scammed. (Windsor Police Department Scam Alert, http://www.police.windsor.on.ca/Senior%20Moment/scam_alert.htm)

Case Three

Sometime late one night, Vilem Luft stabbed his wife, Bohumila, to death in their Kitchener home. He next took a rifle and shot his daughter and their three sons. Then he shot himself (Wood, 2000: 35).

Case Four

Fans of Martha Stewart had always thought of her as an expert on all matters domestic and a gracious hostess. In 2002, however, another image of her emerged from press reports. It was alleged that she had taken advantage of insider information, which had allowed her to sell stock shares at a high price before the value of the stock fell dramatically. In 2004, she was found guilty of four counts of obstruction of justice and lying to investigators about a curiously timed stock sale.

specific types of people. This conceptualization of crime runs counter to the common tendency to think about criminal events as merely the by-product of chance. People speak of the crime victim as having been "unlucky." They maintain that crimes occur because some people are "in the wrong place at the wrong time." If such events are accidents, however, they are *systematic* accidents (Felson, 1987). Like many other surprises in life, criminal events are made more or less likely by the choices people make about how and where they spend their time, energy, and money.

The term *event* also suggests an *episodic* quality. Criminal events, like all forms of social events, have a beginning and an end. This is not to deny that the participants in the event may have had a prior association or—in the case of a homicide, for instance—that some form of conflict may have predated the event (Miethe and Regoeczi, 2004; Luckenbill, 1977). It *is* to suggest, however, that the criminal event has its own dimensions, which are both related to and distinct from what went on before it. In a similar way, we can speak of the aftermath of criminal events, in which other social processes are set in motion. Much of the daily business of the criminal justice system is part of the aftermath of criminal events. Offenders are accused and tried, court dispositions are carried out, and victims must learn to cope with the pain of victimization (Miller et al., 1996). Also, members of the public who learn about criminal events through mass media reports or conversations with neighbours may become more concerned about their personal safety or about the crime problem and its effect on society (Sacco, 2005).

The *social* character of criminal events derives from the fact that they involve interactions between people. If the event has several offenders, these offenders interact with one another as well as with victims and bystanders (if any) (Warr, 2002; Weerman, 2003). In turn, the police interact with these participants and others. Even an act of vandalism involving a lone youthful offender and an unoccupied school building has social dimensions. A sticker on the door advising that the property is patrolled by security guards may encourage the offender to weigh the risks associated with the offence. Conversely, a run-down building with broken windows may be read by the offender as an announcement that no one cares about the appearance of the property (Kelling and Coles, 1996). In either case, the offender reads the signs, interprets them—using past experience as a guide—and then acts accordingly. The vandalism itself may be intended as a message to other youths or to unpopular teachers.

In this way, the behaviour of each participant in the criminal event intersects with and influences the behaviour of other participants. This interaction does much to determine the course of the event, the stages through which it proceeds and the extent to which it will be judged as serious. In order to fully appreciate the complexity of criminal events, we must understand their

BOX 2.2

Stranger Violence In Winnipeg

Using police data, Elizabeth Comack, Vanessa Chopyk, and Linda Wood (2000) were able to examine violence in the context of various kinds of social relationships. The data were collected over a five-year period (1991–1995). Despite the widespread concern about violence at the hands of strangers, the authors found that of the 1002 cases of violence in their sample, only 16 percent involved individuals not known to each other. One-third of the events did conform to the public stereotype of street crime in that they occurred in public places or secluded areas. Yet about half of the incidents involving individuals not known to each other occurred at or near bars, stores, or gas stations. In many cases, the complainants were security guards or bouncers. Moreover, despite the perception that violent offenders are often people of colour, the authors reported that 50 percent of the males charged with violence against strangers were Caucasian. In addition, the researchers found that:

- violence involving strangers was about as likely to happen during the day as in the evening or late at night
- while Aboriginal people are more likely to be over-represented in crime statistics, their crimes more typically involve members of their own communities, especially their intimate partners and other family members
- stranger violence has a relatively low rate of injury, owing in part to the fact that many of these crimes are robberies in which the offenders seek to obtain property rather than to inflict harm on people.

behavioural and situational elements (Birkbeck and LaFree, 1993; Haen Marshall, 2004). A consideration of the principal participants in these events provides a useful starting point.

OFFENDERS

Offender Characteristics

Criminological research indicates that particular social characteristics are associated with a higher likelihood of offender involvement in criminal events. For most offences, offenders tend to be young, disadvantaged males. The relationship between age and offender status has been well documented (Felson, 2002; Gottfredson and Hirschi, 1990; Courtwright, 1998). Involvement in offending is highest among those in late adolescence and early adulthood (see Figure 2.1). Property crime offending peaks at a somewhat earlier age than does violent offending (Flowers, 1989). Property crime arrests peak at age 16, and then drop by half by age 20; violent offending reaches a peak at around age 18

Figure 2.1

Persons Accused of Property Crimes and Violent Crimes by Age, Canada, 2003

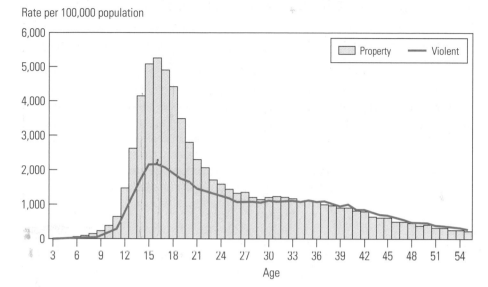

Rate per 100,000 population

(U.S. Department of Justice, 1988). Crimes such as embezzlement, fraud, and gambling do not conform to this general trend: they are characterized by higher levels of involvement somewhat later in the life cycle (Steffensmeier and Allan, 1995).

This pattern is evident at all stages of the criminal justice system from arrest to incarceration. Thus, police data from the year 2003 show that people aged 15 to 24 represented only 14 percent of the total population but accounted for 45 percent of those accused of property crimes and 32 percent of persons accused of violent crimes (Bunge et al., 2005). For the year 2003/2004, court data indicated that younger adults were also over-represented in court when compared to the age distribution of the adult population (Thomas, 2004). People aged 18 to 24 comprised 12 percent of the adult population, but accounted for 31 percent of all cases in adult criminal court. Similarly, persons 25 to 34 years of age accounted for 28 percent of adult court cases but only 18 percent of the adult population.

The association between youthfulness and crime has led many criminologists to argue that over time, crime trends will vary as the proportion of the population in the highest risk age group changes (Ouimet, 2002; Sprott and Cesaroni, 2002). Criminologist Peter Carrington (2001) used existing population data to forecast the ways in which crime rates might be expected to change into the middle of the 21st century. Assuming other factors are held constant, Flowers argued that declines in crime levels could be expected as the population of Canada continues to age. Not surprisingly, his analysis suggests that the kinds of crimes committed by teenagers (such as robbery) would show the sharpest decline, while the kinds of crimes most often committed by older adults (such as impaired driving) would be less affected by the shifts in the average age of the population.

Offender status is also strongly related to gender (Boritch, 1997; Bunge et al., 2005; Graham and Wells, 2003; Kruttschnitt, 2002). Data collected at all stages of the criminal justice system in this country and elsewhere support the general conclusion that men more than women engage in offending behaviour. Statistics compiled from 122 policing agencies (which cover 61 percent of all recorded crime in Canada) draw a typical portrait of who is more likely to be accused by the police of committing a crime (Wallace, 2004). For all broad categories of crime, men tend to dominate the data. For instance, men were the accused in 84 percent of the violent crimes and 78 percent of the crimes against property. For all crimes reported to the police, males comprised 81 percent of the accused. The differences between men and women are usually strongest in the case of crimes of violence. In 2003, men were the accused in 90 percent of the homicides, 98 percent of the sexual assaults, and 91 percent of the robberies.

A similar kind of pattern is evident in data that come from the courts. In the 2003/2004 reference year, 83 percent of those cases which came to an adult court involved a male (Thomas, 2004). Although males accounted for the majority of cases, the gender balance varied by type of crime. For Crimes against the Person and Criminal Code Traffic offences, 85 percent of cases involved males; however, males were involved in 77 percent of Crimes against Property. Females accounted for significant percentages of the accused in only a relatively small number of offences; these included: prostitution (43 percent), fraud (29 percent), and theft (28 percent). A similar situation obtains in the case of youth court. In the reference year 2003/2004, males accounted for 79 percent of the youth court cases, and they were represented at higher rates than females in all of the age groups which appeared before the court (Thomas, 2005).

In a similar way, the majority of offenders admitted to sentenced custody were male. In the reference year 2002/03, women represented only 10 percent of provincial/territorial admissions and 5 percent of federal admissions (Johnson, 2004).

While the rate at which women are arrested has increased somewhat over the past 30 years, the offending rates of males continue to be higher than those of females in virtually every category of crime. Also noteworthy is that most of the increase in women's offences during this period related to property crime; the violent crime offence rates for females have remained fairly steady (Boritch, 1997: 30). Although, as we pointed out in Chapter 1, some recent evidence indicates that the gender gap in offending has been closing (Chen and Gilles, 2004), much of the rhetoric about the "new female criminal" appears to overstate the case (Boritch, 1997: 37; Hartnagel, 2000). For most types of criminal events, offending is still very much a male activity.

For many "common" varieties of crime, such as assault, burglary, robbery, and homicide, offending is associated with social and economic disadvantage (Miethe and McCorkle, 1998). This finding emerges most clearly when the most serious forms of crime are examined (Harris, 1991). While the evidence is far from consistent, there is much research to suggest that rates of crime are linked to social indicators such as the level of inflation, rate of unemployment, and level of inequality (Bunge et al., 2005; Daly et al., 2001). At the level of the individual, the data suggest that offenders tend to be unemployed, temporarily employed, or employed in part-time, unskilled, or semi-skilled jobs (Baron, 2004; Flowers, 1989).

Offending is also associated with minority group membership (Roberts and Melchers, 2003). This association has been extensively documented with respect to African-Americans in the United States and Aboriginal people in Canada (Sampson, 1985; Silverman and Nielsen, 1992; Wood and Griffiths, 2000). The over-representation of Aboriginal people at all stages of criminal justice system processing has been noted by several researchers (Roberts and Doob, 1997; Roberts and Melchers, 2003). While Aboriginal people make up about 3 percent of the population, they comprise a much larger proportion of admissions to custody in all jurisdictions. In the year 2002/03, Aboriginal people accounted for 21 percent of the admissions to provincial/territorial sentenced custody, 18 percent of federal custody admissions, 14 percent of probation intakes, and 17 percent of conditional sentence admissions (Johnson, 2004). Of course, these rates reflect the very high levels of social and economic precariousness which is closely associated with minority status (La Prairie, 2002; Blackstock et al., 2004).

In contrast, corporate crimes do not suggest a pattern linking criminal offending and minority status. Instead, with respect to crimes of this type, offenders tend to be "predominantly well-educated people with good jobs" (Snider, 1992: 320).

TABLE 2.1

Profile of Incarcerated Offender Populations in Canada, 2004

Overall Population

	Male		Female	
	Number of Offenders 12,034	%	Number of Offenders 379	%

Profile

Age Group				
Less than 18	5	0.4	—	—
18–19	125	1	6	2
20–29	3,354	28	125	33
30–39	3,889	32	138	36
40–49	2,950	25	73	19
50+	1,711	14	37	10

Aboriginal Inmates

	2,193	%	108	%
Age Group				
Less than 18	2	.09	—	—
18–19	36	2	2	2
20–29	795	36	54	50
30–39	748	34	34	31
40–49	432	20	15	14
50+	180	8	3	3

Source: Solicitor General of Canada. *Basic Facts about the Correctional Service of Canada.* 2005 Edition. Ottawa: Public Works and Government Services Canada.

An emphasis on the social and demographic characteristics of individual offenders should not deflect attention from the fact that offending very often has collective dimensions. For example, most youthful delinquent acts are committed in groups rather than by individuals (Tanner, 2001; Venkatesh, 1997; Warr, 2002). Criminal events involving corporate offending or organized crime may involve several complex levels of organization (Gordon, 2000; Pearce and Snider, 1995). Offender organization strongly affects the course of criminal events.

TABLE 2.2

Adults (18+) Charged, by Gender (Selected Offences, %), 2003

Offence Type	Male	Female
Homicide	90	10
Attempted murder	85	15
Assaults	82	18
Sexual assaults	98	2
Other sexual offences	97	3
Abduction	42	58
Robbery	91	9
Violent crime—total	**84**	**16**
Break and enter	93	7
Motor vehicle theft	91	9
Fraud	71	29
Theft over $5,000	82	18
Theft under $5,000	70	30
Property crime—total	**78**	**22**
Mischief	87	13
Arson	83	17
Prostitution	51	49
Offensive weapons	82	18
Criminal code—total	**81**	**19**
Impaired driving	87	13
Cannabis offences	88	12
Cocaine offences	82	18
Other drug offences	84	16

Source: M. Wallace. "Crime Statistics in Canada 2003." Statistics Canada, *Juristat*, Catalogue No. 85-002, 24(6): 25. Used by permission of Statistics Canada.

Offender Perceptions

When asked to explain their actions, offenders typically offer two types of accounts: excuses and justifications (Scott and Lyman, 1968). When offering an excuse, an individual admits that a given act was wrong but denies responsibility for it. When offering a justification, on the other hand, an individual accepts responsibility for the act but denies its immorality. These two types of accounts produce distinct interpretations of offenders, their victims, and their offences.

Excuse
Denial of responsibility for an acknowledged wrongful act.

Justification
Accepting responsibility for the act while denying the immorality of the act.

BOX 2.3

Risk Factors, Gender, and Delinquency

Researchers interested in the study of offending behaviour have sought to determine the factors that place individuals at higher risk of criminal activity. For example, Linda Simourd and Donald Andrews (2000) attempted to identify risk factors with respect to juvenile misbehaviour. In particular, they were interested in whether the factors that seem to put youth at risk of delinquency differ across gender. In other words, is a factor such as associating with antisocial peers indicative of an equally high risk of delinquent involvement for both males and females? The authors used a technique called meta-analysis to review the results of a large number of studies done over 30 years. The major findings of their analysis included the following:

- The general risk factors that were important for female youths were also important for male youths. In addition, no particular risk factor was important for a particular gender.
- In descending order, the most important risk factors for male and female youths were antisocial attitudes and peers, temperament or misconduct problems, educational difficulties, poor parent–child relations, and minor personality variables (in regard to areas such as empathy and moral reasoning).
- In contrast, lower social class, family structure or parental problems, and personal distress were not strongly related to delinquency.
- When various sample and study characteristics were taken into account, the general pattern of results was unchanged.

A study of convicted rapists found that though offenders generally admitted their offences, they denied that they were to blame for what had happened (Scully and Marolla, 1984). By offering excuses relating to the use of drugs or alcohol or persistent "emotional problems," they attempted to deflect blame from themselves. In a similar way, police who used excessive force against suspects explained away their actions as a natural outcome of the strong emotions that arise in police work (Hunt, 1985). White-collar offenders have tended to argue that they committed their crimes out of ignorance or an inattention to detail and, furthermore, that their actions must be considered in the context of an otherwise law-abiding life. Even contract killers may offer rationalizations for the murders they are paid to commit. According to Levi (1981), organized-crime hit men often claim that if they hadn't shot someone (that is, fulfilled their "contract"), someone would have shot them.

HOW DO THEY DIFFER?

Excuses versus Justifications

An excuse admits that a given act is wrong but denies responsibility for the act. A justification, on the other hand, accepts responsibility for the act but denies its immorality.

Offenders may even claim that their crime had positive effects. For example, white-collar criminals may argue that their actions saved a failing business and thereby preserved jobs. They may also favourably compare their offences with those of "real" criminals such as robbers and rapists (Benson, 1985). People who are guilty of workplace theft or income tax evasion often defend their actions by arguing that "everyone does it" and "the only real crime is getting caught."

Offenders' accounts may also make reference to the culpability of victims (Presser, 2003). A rapist may contend that the victim seduced him or that she said no but really meant yes (Scully and Marolla, 1984). These justifications do not deny the accusation, but they do deny the moral and legal interpretations that others attach to the behaviour. In cases of police violence, some types of people are defined by the police as legitimate targets of physical force because they are known "cop haters" or troublemakers (Hunt, 1985).

Offenders' accounts often reflect pervasive cultural beliefs (Presser, 2003). For instance, a rapist's excuses and justifications will borrow from more general sexist beliefs in the blameworthiness of sexual assault victims. Also, the cultural environment and the historical period partly determine the degree to which an offender's account is plausible. In the late twentieth century, people tend to reject demonic possession as an excuse for crime, yet such accounts would have been accepted in an earlier period. For another example, the "culture" of large bureaucracies currently allows white-collar offenders to deny personal responsibility for their actions (Benson, 1985), yet public sentiment is beginning to hold these individuals accountable (Snider, 1992).

Offender accounts also alert us to the fact that we apply the label of "offender" with only relative certainty. Most of us are unequivocal in our judgment of the man who hides in the bushes and sexually assaults a woman who happens by. Until recently, however, we have been reluctant to apply the label "rapist" to a man who has behaved violently toward a woman he knows well. Many people believe that a husband who assaults his wife has somehow committed a less serious act than has a stranger who assaults another stranger (Bograd, 1988).

Our judgments about the suitability of an offender label may be further complicated by the social context in which the offending occurs. A homicide that results from a heated argument between drunken patrons of a bar may not seem as clear-cut as one that occurs in a more sedate environment. When we draw attention to the relationship between offender labels and offender characteristics, to the victim–offender relationship, or to the social setting, we are suggesting that the study of the offender is inseparable from the study of other dimensions of the criminal event.

It is worth noting that not only offenders but also their family members offer excuses and justifications for criminal conduct. Hazel May (1999) conducted in-depth interviews with people related to offenders who had been convicted of murder. Offenders' relatives, she found, like offenders themselves, have a need to understand murder as something other than "the purposeful act of an 'evil' person" (May, 1999: 503).

VICTIMS

"Victimless" Crimes

For many types of criminal events, it is useful to recognize a victim role. Victims include people whose purses are stolen, whose homes are broken into, or who are murdered in the course of the event. For other event categories, such as drug use and gambling offences, victims cannot be said to exist in any direct and immediate way, although many would argue that it is incorrect to consider such offences victimless crimes (Schur, 1965; Meier and Geis, 1997).

The issue of whether the law should be applied to victimless crimes revolves around the idea of harm. While there is widespread support for legalizing various forms of vice, great concern persists as to the potential negative effects of doing so. The prevailing view is that vice is not victimless and needs to be regulated through criminal law.

Those who propose removing the legal sanctions associated with victimless crimes argue that policing these acts represents an over-reach of the law and that consenting adults should have the freedom to partake in certain activities. Furthermore, criminalization tends to affect only the disadvantaged and others who cannot pursue these activities in private (Wagner, 1997). Advocates of legalization also argue that many of the problems associated with victimless crimes would be eliminated if these behaviours were permitted in regulated (but legal) environments. From their perspective, it is not the behaviour itself but rather the fact that it has been driven underground that gives rise to the surrounding criminal subcultures.

Surveys of direct victims of crime demonstrate that involvement in criminal events as a victim, like involvement as an offender, is not a random matter. In fact, many of the social characteristics associated with offending are also associated with victimization. For one thing, like offenders, victims of crime tend to be young. According to a 2004 national study of victimization risk, the

Victimless crimes
Criminal events in which a victim does not exist in any direct and immediate way. Examples: gambling or abusing drugs by personal choice.

Canadian General Social Survey (GSS), the highest rates of both violent and property crimes were experienced by people aged 15 to 24. The overall rate of violent crime for young people was about 18 times the rate for those over 65 (see Table 2.3). This overall finding regarding age difference in victimization risk is consistent with the findings of similar surveys done in the United States and elsewhere (Kennedy and Sacco, 1998; Nicholas et al., 2005). Despite much talk about a crime wave against the elderly, people over 65 are the least likely to be victims of crime (Fattah and Sacco, 1989). According to many surveys, the rates of victimization for those 65 or older are lower than the rates for any other age group (Sacco and Nakhaie, 2001).

Surveys of crime victims also show that gender differences vary by type of crime. For instance, the 2004 GSS revealed that while males experienced a robbery rate of 13 per 1,000, women experienced a substantially lower rate—8 per 1,000. Regarding assault, males had a rate of 91 per 1,000, females 59 per 1,000. With respect to sexual assault, the rate for men was 7 per 1,000, for women 35 per 1,000 (Gannon and Mihorean, 2005). Note that several researchers question whether surveys such as the GSS accurately portray the levels of women's victimization—an issue we will return to in the next chapter.

The link between social disadvantage and victimization is less clear-cut, as it varies by the type of event (Cohen, Kluegel, and Land, 1981; Miethe and McCorkle, 1998). When it comes to serious crimes of violence, studies generally support the conclusion that poor people and ethnic minorities are more likely to become victims (Mirrlees-Black et al., 1998, Zawitz et al., 1993). In Canada, Aboriginal people comprised about 19 percent of those accused of homicide and about 15 percent of homicide victims in 2003 (Kong and Beattie, 2005). Our ability to describe relationships involving crime and ethnicity is impaired by the fact that data on the relationship between ethnicity and crime are not routinely collected in Canada except in cases of homicide. While many argue that high quality data regarding race/ethnicity are required for rational policy development and for the construction of comprehensive social scientific explanations, not everyone agrees (Kong and Beattie, 2005). The contentious question of whether such data should be collected at all is one to which we will return in the next chapter.

With respect to some forms of household theft, and personal theft that does not involve contact between the offender and the victim, the risks of victimization are greater for higher-income groups (Laub, 1990; Sacco and Johnson, 1990). Table 2.4 shows the data from the national survey of crime victims undertaken by Statistics Canada in 2004; it reveals that in general,

Canadian General Social Survey (GSS)
A large Canadian national survey that periodically has as a focus criminal victimization, crime prevention behaviour, and perceptions of crime.

TABLE 2.3

Violent Victimization Rates per 1,000 Population by Victim Characteristics, Age 15+, Canada, 2004

Characteristic	Rates
Total Rate	106
Sex	
Female	102
Male	111
Age	
15 to 24	226
25 to 34	157
35 to 44	115
45 to 54	62
55 to 64	45
65 and over	12*
Marital Status	
Married	52
Common Law	131
Single	203
Widow or Widower	—
Separated or Divorced	159
Main Activity	
Working at a job	114
Looking for work	207*
Student	183
Household work	78
Retired	18*
Other	167*
Evening Activities (Number per Month)	
Less than 10	44
10 to 19	77
20 to 29	104
30 and more	174
Household Income	
0 to 14,999	156
15,000 to 29,999	104
30,000 to 39,999	105
40,000 to 59,999	94
60,000 and over	106
Location of Home	
Urban	112
Rural	84

__ estimate is too unreliable to publish; *use with caution

Source: M.Gannon and K. Mihorean. 2005. "Criminal Victimization in Canada 2004." Statistics Canada, *Juristat*, No. 85-002-XPE, 25(7): 23. Used by permission.

TABLE 2.4

Household Victimization Rates per 1,000 Households by Household Income, Canada, 2004

Income Level	Total Household Crime	Break and Enter	Motor Vehicle Theft	Theft Household Property	Vandalism
0–14,999	160	41	21	59	39
15,000–29,999	223	36	42	84	60
30,000–39,999	257	50	39	93	74
40,000–59,999	267	41	49	93	84
60,000+	300	42	56	104	98

Source: M.Gannon and K. Mihorean. 2005. "Criminal Victimization in Canada 2004." Statistics Canada, *Juristat*, No. 85-002-XPE, 25(7): 26. Used by permission.

the risks of various forms of household victimization increase with household income.

Victim Perceptions

Like offenders, victims may be reluctant to define events in which they are involved as crimes. In some situations, a crime—even while it is underway—may involve ambiguous or unfamiliar elements that are not readily understood as criminal victimization. A study of mugging victims reported that many of those who were victimized did not immediately define the event as a predatory crime; some even thought the mugger was a neighbour in search of assistance or someone playing a joke (Lejeune and Alex, 1973).

Willingness to label an event a crime generally depends on the degree of coherence between the victim's definition of a "typical crime" and the characteristics of the event in question (Greenberg, Ruback, and Westcott, 1984). However, some crimes are inherently more ambiguous than others. With many forms of sexual victimization, the event may be very difficult for the victim to label. One study found that women who were sexually assaulted did not define the act as rape unless sexual intercourse was involved (Scheppele and Bart, 1983). Crime definitions are generally less ambiguous when the event's illegality is obvious (Agnew, 1985b).

The issue of family violence provides an especially vivid illustration of the importance of victim definition processes (Mihorean, 2005). It has been well documented that women are reluctant to label as criminal or abusive the violence that occurs in an intimate relationship (Johnson, 1996). As with sexual assault, Western culture until recently strongly tended to blame women for their victimization in domestic relationships. Women who remain in abusive relationships may be labelled "sick" or "masochistic," or accused of "bringing it on themselves." If they attempt to flee the abuse or confront the abuser, they often find that few supports are available (Johnson and Bunge, 2000). Moreover, these actions may increase rather than reduce the risk of future victimization. As parents, in-laws, and neighbours choose sides, many blame the victim for breaking up the family; they may even suggest that if she really loves her children, she should "make the best of it." All of this discourages the woman from viewing herself as a victim. Acknowledging that one's mate is an abuser is the first and hardest step in re-evaluating and changing one's life circumstances and may well bring on violent retaliation by the abusive partner. A denial of the violent character of the victimization and the victimizer may result in the abused partner tolerating conditions that an outsider would think intolerable (Ferraro and Johnson, 1983).

BYSTANDERS AND WITNESSES

Criminal events often involve others aside from offenders and victims. In many events, bystanders are more than passive spectators (Cooney, 1998). By their mere presence they may deter an offender from committing a crime, or prevent an incident from escalating (Decker, 1995). Conversely, they may facilitate the offender's actions. For example, a young male who is insulted by someone in the presence of his peers may be inclined to respond aggressively.

Bystanders may also call the police or offer to act as witnesses. What bystanders do, if anything, depends on several factors. For example, their actions may be influenced by their view of or relationship to the victim and/or offender (Steffensmeier and Steffensmeier, 1977), by their assessment of the personal costs associated with intervention, and by their confidence in their ability to intervene (Shotland and Goodstein, 1984).

Bystanders are also affected by what they perceive to be transpiring between victim and offender. According to Shotland and Straw (1976), bystanders are less likely to intervene in a violent assault perpetrated by a man against a woman if they perceive them to be married rather than strangers. Davis (1991) suggests that when people witness adults physically abusing

Bystanders
Criminal event participants whose presence may affect the course of action even though they are not centrally involved in the event as offenders or victims.

children in public, their reluctance to intervene in a "private matter" outweighs their concern for the child's welfare.

From the perspective of bystanders, criminal events are often ambiguous. We do not expect to witness a crime, and we may be so engrossed in our own activities that an event may be well under way before it comes to our attention (Hartman et al., 1972). By the time we make sense of the event and think of a response, it may be too late. The presence of several bystanders tends to reduce the likelihood that any one bystander will assist a victim, especially if the bystanders are strangers to one another and do not share a common cultural frame of reference (Shotland, 1976). One bystander among many is required to accept only part of the responsibility for not acting; he or she may rationalize that somebody else would take action if something were seriously wrong.

THE POLICE AND CRIME

When an event comes to their attention, the police may invoke a wide array of discretionary powers (e.g., collecting evidence, investigating the claims of the victims, and arresting the offender or offenders). In short, the police have the power to "certify" an event as a crime by assessing the match between the event as they understand it and their working knowledge of what the law disallows.

How do the police become involved in situations that they might designate as crimes? It is worth emphasizing here the distinction between proactive and reactive policing. Black (1970) notes that with **proactive policing**, the police become involved when their own investigative or patrol activities bring to their attention events that may be designated as crimes. Only about 10 percent of the time do the police become involved as a result of proactive policing. In contrast, with **reactive policing**, the police become involved in criminal events when asked to do so by a member of the public. So it is important to understand the circumstances in which citizens request police intervention.

Proactive policing
Police involvement in incidents as a result of their own investigative or patrol activities, which bring to their attention events that may be designated as crimes.

Reactive policing
Police involvement in criminal events at the request of a member of the public.

Reactive Policing

Most crimes that come to the attention of the police are reported by the crime victims themselves. According to many surveys, people who reported crimes to the police were most likely to say they did so because they hoped to recover stolen property, because "the offence was a crime," or because they wished to avoid being further victimized by the offender. The 2004 GSS found that many victimizations are not reported to law enforcement agencies. Sexual assault is the crime least likely to be reported: police officers were not informed of

88 percent of sexual assaults; in contrast, only 60 percent of non-sexual assaults went unreported. The criminal event most likely to be reported in 2004 was break and enter: 54 percent of these incidents were reported (Gannon and Mihorean, 2005).

The most common reasons given for not reporting criminal victimization were that the victim did not consider the incident important enough to report and that the victim felt that the police could not do anything about it.

Victims may choose not to report because they perceive that the crime was of a personal or private nature. For example, rates of reporting for stranger-perpetrated crimes are, in general, slightly higher than those for crimes perpetrated by someone known to the victim (Gartner and Macmillan, 2000). Sometimes victims are themselves involved in criminal activity at the time of the incident and are therefore reluctant to invite a police investigation (Block, 1974). Other times, they do not report crimes because they have at their disposal other means of dealing with the situation (Kennedy, 1988). For example, a teenage boy who has been assaulted by a peer may be more likely to seek retaliation through personal action than through police intervention.

Members of some demographic groups are somewhat more likely than members of other groups to report crime to the police, although differences in this regard are not especially strong (Gottfredson and Gottfredson, 1988). For example, crimes involving female or elderly victims are more likely to be reported, other factors held constant. Perhaps this is because many women and many elderly have fewer alternative resources at their disposal for dealing with victimization and its consequences (Fattah and Sacco, 1989; Skogan, 1976). People who view the criminal justice system negatively may be more hesitant to contact the police; however, this seems to be a minor factor (Block, 1974; Gottfredson and Gottfredson, 1988).

Available data indicate that reporting decisions are strongly influenced by the characteristics of the criminal event itself. In general, the more serious the event, the more probable that it will be reported to the police. Thus, incidents that involve physical injury, significant property loss, or the use of a weapon, or that occur in or near the victim's residence, are more likely than incidents without these characteristics to be brought to the attention of the police (Du Mont et al., 2003; Gottfredson and Gottfredson, 1988).

WHAT DOES IT MEAN?

Proactive versus Reactive Policing

In proactive policing, the police become involved in incidents as a result of their own investigative or patrol activities, which bring to their attention events that may be designated as crimes. In reactive policing, the police become involved in criminal events when requested to do so by a member of the public.

These findings are consistent with the view that people report crimes to the police when there is good reason to do so, and don't when the costs of reporting outweigh any potential benefits. For victims of sexual assault or wife abuse, fear of retaliation and concerns about stigmatization or mistreatment by police may negate the advantages associated with reporting. In general, the reporting of crime is best viewed as a rational decision-making process that takes into account the crime, the offender, the victim's resources, and the perceived limitations of the police.

Proactive Policing

As the police engage in routine patrol work, they may encounter individuals or situations they define as criminal. Proactive policing is not in any sense a random or arbitrary process. Rather, it is heavily influenced by police priorities, prevailing community concerns, available police resources, and the styles and traditions that characterize police work in given areas (Desroches, 1991). This is exemplified in the modern-day commitment by most Canadian police agencies to community-based or problem-oriented policing (see Chapter 11). Ericson (1982) reports that police officers who are engaged in patrol activities use cues that structure their proactive work. For example, their attention may be attracted by individuals who appear in particular places at particular times of the day. Conversely, events that could be defined as crimes are not labelled as such because the police choose not to stop and question a suspect.

The line between reactive and proactive police mobilization is often unclear (Ericson, 1982). Citizens may decide to mobilize the police reactively as a result of police-sponsored crime prevention campaigns that encourage them to do so. Conversely, widespread public concern about specific crime problems may influence police to adopt a proactive mobilization strategy. Desroches (1991) reported on a police investigation of sexual behaviour in public washrooms, known as "tearooms." Evidence was gathered through police surveillance techniques, which suggests a proactive police stance on the problem. However, Desroches indicates that this police involvement was largely a response to requests from citizens or businesses for more aggressive enforcement.

Police Involvement in Defining Criminal Events

The type of mobilization—that is, proactive or reactive—does not indicate how the police will intervene in a particular event. Officers' actions depend on a variety of factors, including the characteristics of the incident, the behaviour of the participants, and the nature of the requests being made of the police (Gottfredson and Gottfredson, 1988; Mastrofski et al., 2000).

Police tend to respond officially to events that they perceive as conforming to legal definitions of serious crimes (Black, 1970; Gottfredson and Gottfredson, 1988; Gove, Hughes, and Geerken, 1985). Also of importance in determining police response is the relationship between the victim and the offender. According to Black (1970), the more distant the relationship between victim and offender, the more likely the police are to regard the incident as criminal. This observation is consistent with the often cited tendency of police officers to process crimes "unofficially" when the disputants are family members (Bell, 1987). However, Dawson (2004) has argued that the situation is actually a lot more complicated in that not all intimate relationships are treated the same way by the police. While police might appear to treat offenders more leniently in the case of intimate partners, they do not necessarily do so in the case of victims and offenders who might be described as "friends."

The characteristics of victims and offenders influence police decisions. In an American study of police responses to interpersonal violence, Smith (1987) found that police officers are less likely to employ legal solutions in situations that involve African-American or female victims. In contrast, Boritch (1992) reports that the criminal justice system deals more harshly with female offenders than male offenders—especially when the former deviate from accepted standards of femininity. Violence between males is more likely to result in arrest than is violence between a male and a female, which tends to be resolved through less formal means, such as the physical separation of the disputants. Police decision making is also influenced by the demeanour and preferences of the event participants (Smith, 1987) and by the seriousness of their previous contacts with the police (Carrington and Schulenberg, 2004). Police are more likely to label an event as a crime when the complainant is deferential to them or requests that they take official action (Black, 1970; Gove, Hughes, and Geerken, 1985).

Not surprisingly, the elements of the event itself can also be an important determinant of police action. In general, the more serious the incident, the more likely the police are to take it seriously. In a study of police charging practices with respect to Canadian youth, Carrington and Schulenberg (2004) concluded that the likelihood that the police would charge a youth formally depended in part on whether the incident involved multiple offenders, a weapon, or serious injury.

The community context also matters. Policing traditions or levels of community tolerance for certain kinds of offences could affect the degree to which police feel decisions to intervene (or not intervene) officially have wider social support. The important role played by community context was supported in a study by Jennifer Schulenburg (2003) of policing decisions and crime rates in 447 Canadian communities. Her results suggest that the tendency of the police to charge youth was affected by the size of the community and the level of social disorganization.

Also important in influencing police decision making regarding crime are the organizational constraints that police face in responding to calls for service. As police discovered that they were unable to respond quickly to all 911 calls, they began to develop response priorities based on the seriousness of the crime. Alternatives that were offered to callers included registering complaints at community police stations, calling 311 (community service lines), and seeking resolution through informal means. It is not clearly understood what impact this decision to prioritize police responses (ranging from immediate to day-long delays) has had on actual crime rates. However, a study in Edmonton by Kennedy and Veitch (1997) makes a strong case for the importance of these organizational changes in driving down reporting of less serious crimes.

In contrast to the situation where police are redirecting some minor crimes to community stations or alternative means of resolution, police discretion in especially sensitive areas—such as family violence—is being removed. In most jurisdictions, police officers are now required, through a **mandatory charge rule**, to make an arrest when they have physical evidence that an assault has taken place, even if the victim is reluctant to have them do so (Johnson, 1996). This practice was established in part as a response to the finding (Sherman and Berk, 1984) that arrest is the most effective way to deter violence among intimates and that mediative techniques do not curtail repeat offences. Several studies of policing suggest, however, that the existence of statutory regulations does not mean that police are unable to exercise discretion. Data collected during the 2004 General Social Survey revealed that police officers who attend scenes of spousal assault may take highly variable actions. In about two-thirds of the cases, victims reported that the police gave the abuser a warning, and in less than half of the cases the police actually removed the abuser from the home. In slightly more than one-third of these events, victims reported that the police made an arrest or laid a charge against their partner (Mihorean, 2005).

Some observers contend that removing police discretion reduces the chances that police bias will influence decisions about the seriousness of certain violent acts. Others argue that it deprives the police of the opportunity to defuse situations before they become dangerous. Research has found that

Mandatory charge rule
Legal or procedural regulation that requires the police, in domestic violence cases, to make an arrest when they have physical evidence that an assault has taken place.

arrest may actually increase the likelihood of violence in domestic situations (Sherman, 1992). It has also been argued that bringing individuals into an overburdened court system that is ill-equipped to handle their problems merely creates new problems.

Some critics of mandatory charging contend that this policy disempowers some women instead of empowering them (Loseke, 1989). For example, a woman who does not want her husband arrested, but only wants the police to talk to him, may be reluctant to call the police if arrest is the inevitable outcome. Similarly, some women of colour maintain that because their husbands cannot always expect fair and equitable treatment from the police, they are reluctant to report incidents of marital violence. In situations such as this, the removal of discretion may act against women's interests.

THE SETTING OF CRIMINAL EVENTS

The Social Setting

To suggest that a relationship exists between criminal events and the places in which these events occur is to imply that location involves something more than happenstance. In other words, place matters. Something about particular types of locations increases—or decreases—the likelihood that criminal events will unfold (Graham et al., 2002). Any attempt to investigate these issues is plagued by the fact that particular types of places are intricately linked to particular types of activities. People who live in the centre of a major city may structure their activities differently from those who live on the suburban fringe. Those who do not live in the downtown core may occasionally journey there in search of "excitement," but for rest and relaxation they head for the countryside. People shop at malls, drink in taverns, perform occupational tasks at work, and read or study at the library. We might ask why some of these places host more criminal events than others. Is it because certain types of people tend to be attracted to these settings? Does the physical character of a place make criminal events more or less likely? Are the activities associated with a particular setting more or less likely to lead to criminal events? We discuss these issues in greater detail in later chapters. It is useful at this point to review some of the empirical evidence about the locations of criminal events.

The Community Setting

According to data collected by police and by researchers through surveys, rates of many types of crimes tend to be higher in urban centres than in rural areas

(Brantingham and Brantingham, 1984; Felson, 2002; Fischer, 1995). The 2004 GSS revealed significant differences between urban and rural areas in rates of victimization. In the case of violent crime, the urban rate was 112 per 1,000 people while the rural rate was 84 per 1,000. Household victimization also differed by location. Urban residents reported having their households victimized at a rate of 269 per 1,000 households; for rural residents, the rate was only 164 per 1,000 households (Besserer and Trainor, 2000).

In urban centres, crime rates vary across neighbourhoods (Bursik and Grasmick, 1993). A study of the spatial patterns of crime in Winnipeg, for instance, revealed important differences between high-crime and low-crime neighbourhoods. The most important of these factors was the level of socio-economic disadvantage. Residents of neighbourhoods with social and economic disadvantages experienced higher levels of both property and violent crime. Research into the factors that characterize high-crime neighbourhoods sometimes produces conflicting evidence (Brantingham and Brantingham, 1984), but the data generally indicate that these areas are likely to be poor and densely populated and to have transient populations.

Even in cities or neighbourhoods characterized by high crime rates, most locations are crime-free (Eck, 2001). For example, while we may think of subway stations as dangerous places, Normandeau (1987) found that most subway stations in Montreal had relatively low rates of crime, with only a few stations accounting for most of the crimes in the system. This point is more generally illustrated in Sherman, Gartin, and Buerger's study (1989) of the locations of requests for police assistance in the city of Minneapolis over a one-year period. This study revealed that a handful of "hot spots" accounted for the majority of service calls; specifically, only 3 percent of the locations in the city (addresses or street intersections) accounted for 50 percent of the 323,979 calls. With respect to predatory crimes, robberies occurred at 2.2 percent of these locations, rapes at 1.2 percent, and automobile thefts at 2.7 percent.

The Physical Setting

Data from the 2004 GSS found that about 40 percent of the violent victimization incidents that respondents described to interviewers took place in or around commercial or public institutions (Gannon and Mihorean, 2005). A further 26 percent took place on a street or in some other public place. Twenty-nine percent occurred in the home of the victim or in another private residence.

What are the characteristics of the locations of criminal events? With respect to some types of crimes, important factors are the physical design of

BOX 2.4

Provincial Differences in Crime Rates

Crime rates vary from province to province. While the pattern is not perfect, there is a general tendency for rates of both violent and personal crime to increase from east to west and from south to north.

Figure 2.2

	Violent Crime Rate	Property Crime Rate
N.L.	917	2,738
P.E.I.	799	3,505
N.S.	1,190	3,894
N.B.	937	3,003
Que.	726	3,202
Ont.	755	3,013
Man.	1,602	5,699
Sask.	2,006	6,238
Alta.	1,087	5,064
B.C.	1,195	6,763
Yukon	3,236	6,341
N.W.T.	6,865	7,414
Nvt.	7,884	6,959
Canada	946	3,991

Source: J. Sauvé, 2005. "Crime Statistics in Canada 2004." Statistics Canada, *Juristat*, No. 85-002-XPE, 25(5): 18. Used by permission.

Defensible space

The physical design of a place that may deter an offender.

places and the existence (or not) of **defensible space** (Newman, 1972; Taylor and Harrell, 1996). In the case of property crime, settings that offer concealment in the form of poor street lighting, large bushes or shrubs, or hidden alleyways may make a target more attractive to an offender. Similarly, a convenience store located near a vacant field may be more vulnerable to robbery than one located on a busy city street (Sherman, Gartin, and Buerger, 1989). This approach has been applied to contemporary thinking about the opportunities for crime that arise in day-to-day life and designing ways to remove or reduce the attractiveness of these opportunities through situational crime prevention (Felson and Clarke, 1998). Farrington and Welsh (2002) illustrate how this works in their study of the impact that street lighting has on crime prevention. In their meta-analysis of research on this relationship, they reported significant (up to 20 percent) reductions in crime in areas with improved street lighting.

In a somewhat different way, patterns of family violence may be related to some elements of physical design. Violence between husbands and wives typically occurs in private settings. In 2004, for instance, 93 percent of family-related homicides occurred in a private dwelling—usually the home of the victim and accused (Dauvergne, 2005). The growth of single-family homes not shared with boarders, lodgers, or servants—coupled with the widespread cultural under-standing that the home is a private setting closed to neighbours, friends, or even other family members, except by invitation—helps ensure the concealment of such violence (Gelles and Straus, 1988). Within the home, not all locations are equally risky. According to Gelles and Straus (1988), violence occurs most often in the kitchen, followed by the living room and the bedroom, although the latter place tends to be the setting for the most violent confrontations:

> A fight that erupts in the bedroom, in the early morning, constrains both parties. It is too late to stalk out of the home to a bar and too late to run to a friend or a family member. The bed and the bedroom offer no protection and there are precious few places to flee or take cover (Gelles and Straus, 1988: 94).

In contrast, the bathroom is relatively free of spousal violence, in part because such rooms are small, have locks, and are understood to be places of individual privacy.

The Temporal Setting

Criminal events are more likely to occur in particular places; they are also more likely to occur at particular times (Cohen and Felson, 1979; Bursik and Grasmick, 1993). In other words, crime is no more randomly distributed in time than it is in space. Clermont's analysis (1996) of the crime of robbery found that this offence was more likely to occur at night. Miethe and McCorkle (1998) contend that evenings and weekends are the peak times for most vio-lent and property crimes because darkness brings with it certain other social conditions. At night, there tend to be fewer people out and about who can provide each other (and each other's property) with adequate protection. The night also provides greater anonymity and greater cover for crime commis-sion. Also, people are more likely to engage in drug and alcohol consumption in the evening and on weekends, and this may render both potential offenders and potential victims more susceptible to engagement in criminal events.

Criminal events are also unevenly distributed over the calendar year. For instance, Clermont's study of robbery found that financial institutions were most likely to be robbed in the month of January and that individuals and res-idences are more vulnerable during the summer months. In one way, it should

Figure 2.3

Crime Rate by Type of Offence, Canada, 1962–2004

Rate per 100,000 population

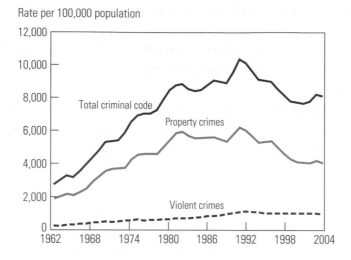

Source: J. Sauvé, 2005. "Crime Statistics in Canada 2004." Statistics Canada, *Juristat*, Catalogue No. 85-002-XPE, 25(5): 4. Used by permission.

not surprise us that criminal events have a temporal structure. Our jobs, our families, and our social commitments greatly influence how we spend our time (Felson, 2002). Moreover, within a given society there is a pattern to people's occupational, family, and leisure commitments. This is why we find ourselves in rush hours on weekday afternoons and on crowded beaches on summer weekends. The temporal structure of our daily activities reflects the rhythms and tempos of social life, and these rhythms and tempos influence not only where but also when the principal players in criminal events find each other.

Criminologists are especially interested in the long-term trends in crime levels. Figure 2.3 shows that crime rates peaked in the early 1990s and have been falling ever since. While the number of homicides and drug incidents increased in 2004, most crimes were still on the decline. Explaining why crime rates rise (Cohen and Felson, 1979) and fall (Kennedy and Veitch, 1997) when they do, and as sharply as they do, is a major task of criminology.

Social Domains

Social domains
Major spheres of life in which we spend most of our time and energy.

Social domains can be thought of as major spheres of life in which we invest most of our time and energy. In Chapters 8, 9, and 10, we focus on the three most important social domains: the family and household, leisure, and work. Each domain is distinguished by particular locations and patterns of activity (Lynch, 1987). People differ with respect to the amount of time they spend in each of these domains. For the elderly retired person, the social domain of the household may be of greatest importance. Children spend much of their time at home, but during the teenage years, involvement in this social domain declines and involvement in the workplace and in leisure activities outside the home increases.

Social domains differ in terms of their private or public character (Anderson and Meier, 2004). The household is the most private of settings, and the people we encounter there are generally better known to us than those we encounter at work or at leisure outside the home. While we tend to think of private domains as safer places than public domains, concern is increasing about the prevalence of criminal actions that were once seen as private acts. The definition of privacy is changing, and so are the ways in which the law and the police treat privacy. Criminal events that once went undetected in the "privacy" of the home are now more likely to attract public attention and police action. Private affairs in the business setting are also attracting more attention; awareness is increasing of the need to prosecute white-collar criminals whose socio-economic status once put them beyond the reach of the law.

The distinctions we make among social domains may not apply equally to all individuals. Some people work at home; others restrict their leisure activities to the household; still others perceive the workplace as a leisure setting—providing an opportunity to gossip with co-workers. Despite these complications, the identification of distinct social domains helps us clarify differences in patterns of criminal events.

The social activities that occur in these social domains, the people we encounter in them, and the relationships we have with those people strongly influence the kinds of criminal events that take place in a given social domain, as well as reactions to them. According to a number of victim surveys, people who report that they often go to bars in the evening also report higher rates of victimization (Felson, 2002). Police data and other observations of barroom behaviour suggest that taverns are the site of a disproportionate amount of crime (Engs and Hanson, 1994; Graham and Wells, 2003).

Many types of criminal events develop in leisure settings. Much juvenile crime—including drug use, vandalism, and fighting—resembles leisure pursuits (Agnew and Peterson, 1989). Also, juvenile crime is most likely to occur when youths are engaged in unsupervised peer activities such as "hanging out" (Kennedy and Baron, 1993; Osgood et al., 1996). Many forms of sexual assault, especially "date rape," occur in leisure environments rather than in more structured environments (DeKeseredy and Kelly, 1993; Johnson, 1996). Similarly, homicides are most likely to occur when the participants are engaged in recreational pursuits in informal settings (Luckenbill, 1977).

Other types of criminal events are more closely related to non-leisure activities. For the organized criminal, crime is a form of work. For the white-collar or corporate criminal, the offending behaviour may simply be an extension of his or her legitimate business practices. Often, there is a direct relationship between a person's job and the risk of criminal victimization (Block, Felson, and Block, 1984; Kennedy and Sacco, 1998). For example, people who handle money, who work in an environment that is open to the public, or who travel from one worksite to another are especially vulnerable to many forms of victimization (Collins, Cox, and Langan, 1987; Mayhew, Elliott, and Dowds, 1989). Partly for these reasons, taxi drivers, police officers, and nurses experience relatively high rates of violence (Block, Felson, and Block, 1984). In still other cases, an *absence* of activity is related to the occurrence of criminal events. With respect to breaking and entering, for instance, households that are unoccupied for long periods of time are at greater risk of victimization than are households that have higher and more regular occupancy rates (Cohen and Cantor, 1981; Cromwell, Olson, and Avary, 1991).

The role played by social domains in criminogenic and victimogenic processes is quite complicated and only inadequately understood. Why should particular kinds of social domains host particular kinds of criminal events? These are important theoretical and research questions. A recent study by Amy Anderson and Robert Meier (2004) suggests even greater complexity. They have agued that the effects of social domains may somehow "interact" in their effects on criminal events. In other words, for instance, particular kinds of family settings might combine with particular kinds of school settings to dramatically increase the probability of criminal events occurring.

STUDYING THE CRIMINAL EVENT

Precursors
Situational factors that bring people together in time and space.

Transactions
The interactions between individuals that have led to the outcome of a crime being committed.

Aftermath
Events that occur after the committed crime.

When studying criminal events, it is important to develop explanations that move beyond the motivations of offenders and the responses of victims. A more comprehensive view considers the precursors of the event (such as the locational and situational factors that bring people together in time and space); the transactions (which tell us how the participants' actions define the outcomes of the event); and the aftermath (including the report to the police, their response, the harm done, the redress required, and the long-term consequences of the event in terms of public reactions and the changing of laws). Figure 2.4 shows a model of the criminal event and its key components.

Figure 2.4

Model of the Criminal Event

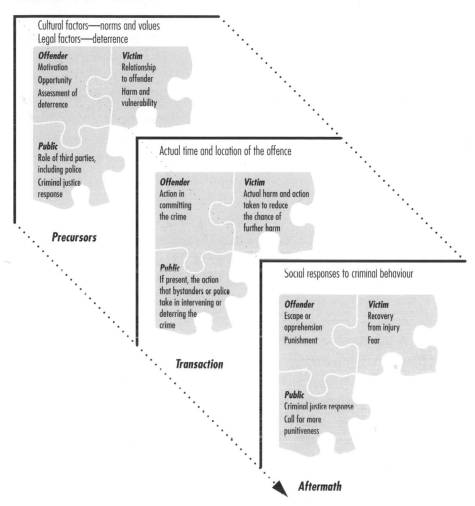

Precursors

As criminologists, we are interested in more than just the motivation of the offender and the actions of the victim that led up to the criminal act. These elements come together in a transaction that increases the likelihood that a crime will take place. Once we understand that criminal events derive from predisposing conditions, it is easier for us to separate the social behaviour that is criminogenic (that is, that breeds crime) from that which does not.

HOW DO WE DEFINE IT?

The Criminal Event

The criminal event consists of its precursors, including the locational and situational factors that bring people together in time and space; the transaction, including how the inter-actions among participants define the outcomes of their actions; and the aftermath of the event, including reporting the event to the police, their response, the harm done, the redress required, and the long-term consequences of the event in terms of public reactions and the changing of laws.

Studying the precursors of criminal events also allows us to see that behaviour that is defined as, or that evolves into, criminality in one situation may not have the same consequences in other situations. The relationship between participants, the interpretation of the harmfulness of the acts, the anticipated responses to certain behaviour, the nature of the location—all may or may not combine to create a criminal outcome.

In determining the precursors of crime, we must reconstruct criminal events using information that may have been distorted by faulty memories, rationalizations, and so on. But it is exactly this process that the courts use to establish guilt or innocence. In order to reflect legal as well as social reality, criminologists must incorporate a similar process in their approaches to crime.

Transactions

In studying transactions, we are assessing the circumstances, incidence, and frequency of certain types of crimes. As we will see in Chapter 3, different data sources (e.g., uniform crime reports, victim surveys, self-report studies) tell us about different aspects of the event, or at least provide different perspectives on such events.

Here we are interested in the particular groups that are affected by different types of crime. In this context, we are able to examine changes in offender behaviour and in the extent of victimization. We are especially interested in viewing the criminal event not in isolation but rather as it relates to social events and to other criminal events. Discerning trends in these events helps us understand the extent to which we need to respond to them. We also want to understand how trends in crime patterns coincide with shifts in social and economic conditions, resources for policing, and so on. The explanations that these types of analysis provide throw light on the vulnerability of certain groups to social change, and on the extent to which legal intervention can work to deter or alter criminal behaviour.

Earlier, we discussed the problems associated with defining (or not defining) certain events as criminal. Victims may not immediately appreciate that they have been victimized; offenders may rationalize their behaviour as something other than criminal. The strict definition of criminality derives from the actions of the police, who certify criminality by initiating a legal process— that is, by either naming an event as criminal or arresting an offender.

What about the events that do not come to the attention of the police but that we could nevertheless define as criminal? This question has important implications for how we define criminal events and for the processes by which the police target certain victims or offenders. Clearly, criminal events are dynamic, not only in terms of their responsiveness to interactional factors in the environment but also in terms of the claims that are made about them by interested parties. These claims are constantly changing in response to changing political and cultural values.

The Aftermath

The extent to which we can develop an integrated perspective depends heavily on the types of crime information to which we have access. We are concerned not only with the actual event but also with the reactions by the police, victims, and others. As we will see, a robbery, rape, fraud, or illegal drug deal can generate "a series of ripples emanating from the crime scene to many individuals, places and situations" (Ramos, 1998: 291). In considering the aftermath of an event, we are interested in the degree to which the victim has been harmed and in the resources needed to aid in his or her recovery. We are also concerned with whether the offender feels that he or she can repeat the offence with impunity. With respect to punishment, has there been sufficient certainty, severity, and celerity (speed of response) to deter a repeat occurrence? Questions such as this frame a great deal of the discussion about how we are managing our crime problems. Lending focus to this debate are the responses to different types of crime. We need to understand that our responses to criminality are strongly affected by the reasons we assign for its occurrence. Moreover, our responses will influence the types of crime that we will experience in the future.

SUMMARY

A criminal event is a social event. Like all other social events, it has a beginning and an end. Criminal events are social in that they involve interactions among people. The nature and form of this interaction shape the course of the event, determine the stages through which it proceeds, and define how serious it is judged to be in terms of harm done. Many different types of actors are involved in these events.

Criminal events are complicated. In this chapter, we have discussed their basic dimensions, and in so doing have raised questions about who participates in these events, when and where they occur, and why they elicit particular forms of societal reaction. In order to understand a criminal event, we need to understand how each of its elements combines and interacts with the others. For example, we cannot address the issue of sexual assault by reducing the problem to a single question: Why do some men commit sexual assaults? Instead, we need to put this question in an appropriate context that also asks why some women are more likely than others to be victimized by sexual assault, when and where such assaults are most likely to occur, and why police, lawmakers, and members of the public think about sexual assault the way they do.

The most obvious participant is the offender. Offenders tend to be young, disadvantaged males. In the case of many "white-collar crimes," the typical offender is an older and better-off male. While women are committing property crimes, offending in general is very much a male activity.

Much attention has been directed at trying to understand the motivations, as well as the group pressures, that influence the behaviour of criminals. The study of offender perceptions provides an important source of information about the pressures that direct individuals to behave in certain ways. Offenders may choose to deal with their blameworthiness by rationalizing their crimes.

Victims of crime, like offenders, tend to be young and, for many crimes, male. That being said, other groups are heavily victimized in particular types of crime. Sexual assault and family violence are disproportionately directed against women. The nature of victims and their relationship to offenders, then, is very much a function of the type of event that has occurred and is governed by location and circumstance. Like offenders, victims may redefine the event as harmless, or at least not criminal. Victim definitions can be very important in influencing the actions taken by criminal justice agencies in criminal events.

Bystanders and witnesses also have a role in defining and interpreting the social events that become crimes. They may defuse a violent situation, or they may actually promote violence through their actions. While bystanders can be helpful in clarifying what actually occurred during a criminal event, their accounts often prove to be inaccurate.

The police play a major role in criminal events. They have the power to certify an event as a crime by assessing the match between the event as they have come to understand it and their knowledge of what the law disallows. In reactive policing, the police respond to reports from citizens, who may be either victims or bystanders. In proactive policing, certain groups or communities are targeted for police attention as a way of preventing criminal events.

With respect to intervention, the police are heavily influenced by their perceptions of what they can do to reduce crime. Police use a great deal of discretion in their work—discretion that can be used negatively to discriminate against certain groups. Police discretion in family violence cases is increasingly being removed.

One other important aspect of criminal events is the conditions under which they occur. The different social dimensions of people's lives invite different types of behaviour and offer circumstances that may or may not give rise to criminal events. It is useful to think about certain patterns of these conditions as "social domains." These domains imply both a location and a set of activities. The major social domains include the family and household, the workplace, and leisure.

We concluded by arguing that any comprehensive view of the criminal event must consider three key components: precursors of the crime, the transaction itself, and the aftermath.

QUESTIONS FOR REVIEW AND DISCUSSION

1. How do offenders see their actions relative to their victims and to the situations in which they find themselves?
2. What do we mean when we say that crime is a social event that takes place in time and space?
3. What role does the legal system play at each stage of the criminal event? Is it always the same agency that deals with the precursors, the transaction, and the aftermath?
4. When does a social event become a criminal event?
5. What does it mean when we say that a criminal event takes on the character of a transaction?

RECOMMENDED READINGS

Felson, M. 2002. *Crime and Everyday Life*. 3rd ed. Thousand Oaks, CA: Sage Publications.

Meier, R.F., L.W. Kennedy, and V.F. Sacco (eds.). 2001. *The Process and Structure of Crime: Criminal Events and Crime Analysis*. Vol. 9, Advances in Criminological Theory. Piscataway, NJ: Transaction Publishers.

Miethe, T.D., and W. Regoeczi. 2004. *Rethinking Homicide: Exploring the Structure and Process Underlying Deadly Situations*. Cambridge: Cambridge University Press.

Wilcox, P., K.C. Land, and S.A. Hunt. 2003. *Criminal Circumstance: A Dynamic Multi-Contextual Criminal Opportunity Theory*. New York: Aldine de Gruyter.

INFOTRAC® COLLEGE EDITION

Explore InfoTrac® College Edition, your online university library, which includes hundreds of popular and scholarly journals in which you can find articles related to the topics in this chapter. Visit InfoTrac® through your web browser (**www.infotrac-college.com**) or through this book's website (**www.criminalevent-4e.nelson.com**).

WHAT'S ON THE WEB?

For chapter links and quizzes, check out the accompanying website at **www.criminalevent-4e.nelson.com**.

LEARNING OBJECTIVES:

- distinguish between observations of crime and reports of crime as methods of gathering empirical information
- describe the Uniform Crime Reporting system that is the basis of "official" crime data
- describe the method and utility of victimization survey data
- discuss crime reports provided by offenders
- discuss the limitations and complementarity of various crime measurement techniques
- consider some problems relating to the measurement of crimes involving women and racial/ethnic minorities
- discuss how crime rates are computed and how they are used

INTRODUCTION

A central concern of modern criminology—and a focus of several of the chapters in this book—is to explain the form, content, and distribution of criminal events. To this end, we need to address several important questions: Why do particular types of events occur? When and where do they occur? Why do they unfold in the way they do? Why are some people more likely than others to be involved in these events, as offenders or victims? In this chapter, we take up a related issue: How are the questions raised by criminological theory to be answered?

In assessing the validity of dominant explanations of criminal events, criminologists do not rely on idle speculation. Rather, they seek to determine the extent to which these explanations are consistent with the empirical evidence that describes these events. In other words, they have more confidence in a given theory if it is able to organize and make sense of the "facts of crime" as revealed by research data.

Of course, our questions about crime have practical dimensions as well. Canadians spend billions of dollars every year in their collective efforts to "do something" about the problem of crime. But which crime prevention or crime control policies should we pursue, and which should we discard? As in the case of our theoretical questions, we seek answers that have a firm empirical base. In this respect, in 2002, the Auditor General of Canada (2002: 25) pessimistically stated:

> Building and maintaining an effective criminal justice system requires reliable national information on the nature of crime, on crime trends, and on what actions work. We are concerned that the existing data are not adequate to this task and can be misinterpreted if not used with caution. Moreover, we are concerned that the national capability to collect and analyze data on the criminal justice system is inadequate.

Thus, for both academic and policy reasons, we need to concern ourselves with the quality of crime data (Mosher et al., 2002). We begin by addressing two very general types of crime information: observations and reports.

OBSERVING CRIME

Direct Observation in Naturalistic Settings

At first glance, the study of criminal events might seem a relatively straight-forward matter. If researchers wish to investigate criminal events, why do they not just position themselves so as to observe these events directly?

Observation can be accomplished in several ways. The researcher can covertly observe a setting in which criminal events are known to occur with some frequency; *or* attempt to gain access to police or private security surveillance videotapes in order to monitor the action in a high-crime setting; *or* associate with people who engage in offending behaviour in order to observe their actions and the actions of those with whom they interact; *or* obtain permission from the local police to join patrol officers for tours of duty on city streets (Ericson, 1982; Ferraro, 1989).

Such methods of learning about crime events seem to have an obvious advantage, in that they allow researchers direct access to the types of information in which they are interested. But they also have serious limitations. *First,* they may not be very efficient, because

HOW ARE THEY USED?

Observations versus Reports

Without question, most criminological research proceeds through the use of reports rather than observations.

crimes—especially the most violent and most serious crimes that interest people most—are statistically rare events (Harding et al., 2002). Thus, even if one conscientiously observes a high-crime setting, criminal events will occur only infrequently. Similarly, when one associates with chronic offenders, it becomes obvious that much of their time is spent in crime-free activity. Thus, researchers would have to expend a considerable amount of time and energy to amass a sufficient number of observations to allow something meaningful to be said about offenders or offending.

Second, criminal behaviour is usually secretive behaviour. Those who are engaged in such conduct generally do whatever they can to ensure that observers (including criminologists) do not have as good a view as they might like.

Third, observation methods raise ethical issues. We should be concerned about the legal and moral obligations of the researcher who observes a crime in progress. We also should be leery of modes of data collection that involve researchers covertly observing people who are going about their business, or misrepresenting themselves to people who take them into their confidence.

Fourth and finally, the data yielded by **direct observation** are limited with respect to the types of questions they can answer. Direct observation may allow us to observe criminal events, but it does not necessarily tell us much about why the events occur where they do, or why some people are more likely than others to be participants. For example, the systematic observation of a high-crime subway platform might provide an opportunity to witness a number of minor thefts or assaults. However, these observations will not tell us how this subway platform differs from others where the crime rate is much lower. Similarly, observations (by whatever means) of juvenile misconduct tell us very little about why some juveniles engage in law-violating behaviour while others do not. And while police ride-alongs increase the researcher's exposure to particular types of events, they do so in a way that is subject to many limitations. As we have mentioned in previous chapters, the police generally become involved in criminal events after being called in by victims or bystanders. Thus, while police ride-alongs may do much to increase our understanding of the role of the police in criminal events, they tell us little about what happened before police assistance was sought.

In sum, observation alone generally does not tell us much about how offenders, victims, and other event participants perceive their own actions and the actions of others. We cannot glean from observation why the offenders act the way they do, how they perceive their victims, why they are willing to risk

Direct observation
A technique in which an investigator attempts to develop a theory through exploration, or confirm hypotheses through direct participation in and observation of the community or other social grouping being studied.

punishment, and what they believe the rewards of their actions to be. Through observation, answers to questions such as these can only be inferred.

Experimental Observation

A second observational approach involves experimentation. Instead of waiting for things to happen, the researcher interested in exploring some aspects of criminal events arranges for them to happen. **Experimental observation** allows for controlled observation of behaviour. Also, by varying experimental conditions, researchers can study the relationship between different conditions and event outcomes.

The experimental approach has characterized much of the research into the effect that violence in the media has on behaviour (Howitt, 1998). In several classic experiments, the researchers were able to observe aggressive behaviour in children after they had watched a film or cartoon that contained significant violent imagery. Critics of such research charge that because the experimental situations are artificial, they tell us very little about real-life criminals (Surette, 1992). The essence of this charge is that there is a huge difference between the violence willingly carried out in an experiment—when it is encouraged and does no real harm to anyone—and the types of criminal violence that concern the criminal justice system and so many members of the public.

In one well-known experimental study, Shotland and Straw (1976) intended to shed light on how bystanders respond when a man attacks a woman. Subjects in the experiment were told that they were taking part in an "attitude study." Each subject was directed to a separate room, where a questionnaire was to be completed. Shortly after beginning work, the subject heard a loud verbal argument between a man and a woman in the hallway. After approximately 15 seconds of heated discussion, the man physically attacked the woman, violently shaking her while she struggled, resisting and screaming. The screams were loud, piercing shrieks, interspersed with pleas to "get away from me" (Shotland and Straw, 1976: 991). What the experimental subjects did not know was that the assailant and the victim were drama students who were confederates of the researchers. Shotland and Straw's study revealed that subjects were more likely to intervene when they believed that the attack involved strangers rather than a married couple.

Another kind of approach takes the researcher into the real world in an attempt to impose experimental rigour on people and behaviour in more natural settings. For instance, several researchers have taken advantage of changes

Experimental observation
An experimental method, often used in laboratories, in which the experimenter creates the conditions necessary for observation rather than searching for naturally occurring situations.

in laws in an effort to determine whether a certain kind of prohibited behaviour is less likely to occur when the laws are strengthened. For example, if the laws against impaired driving are made tougher, does the rate of impaired driving decline (Ross, 1982)? These "quasi-experiments" have both advantages and disadvantages. In the former sense, they avoid the artificial setting of the laboratory. On the negative side, it is much more difficult to impose experimental control in such real settings.

A recent "natural experiment" was reported by Addington (2003). She was interested in trying to determine whether high-visibility events involving school violence contribute to general levels of fear of victimization in the population. The occurrence on April 20, 1999 of the Columbine school shootings in Littleton, Colorado allowed a "natural" opportunity to explore this question. In the Columbine incident, two heavily armed students shot and killed 12 of their colleagues and one teacher and wounded 21 others before taking their own lives. The incident was very extensively covered by news media, and in time the word "Columbine" became a kind of shorthand term for school violence. Much of the news coverage focused on the ways in which the incident was thought to have created fear of school violence. Addington argued that a kind of experimental situation was created by the fact that a national study of fear and victimization was, coincidentally, conducted prior to, during, and after the Columbine episode. It would be possible, therefore, to compare levels of fear among those interviewed after April 20th with those interviewed before that date. Since the respondents were selected randomly, it could reasonably be inferred that whatever differences occurred might be attributable to the publicity surrounding Columbine. Contrary to expectations, Addington found that students who were interviewed after the incident were only slightly more likely to indicate fear of victimization than were those who had been interviewed before the incident.

Tracy and Fox (1989) designed an experiment investigating automobile insurance fraud, a type of white-collar crime that does not often come to the attention of law enforcement officials. The researchers were interested in discovering whether auto repair shops tend to give higher estimates for bodywork on insured vehicles. To investigate this, drivers who were confederates of the researchers presented assigned cars to randomly selected body shops across the state of Massachusetts. The analysis, which took the amount of damage and several other variables into account, revealed that on average, estimates for insured vehicles were 32.5 percent higher than estimates for uninsured vehicles—a difference that the researchers concluded was unrelated to the extent of the damage, the sex of the driver, or the location of the body shop.

As these examples illustrate, experiments may provide a valuable means for answering some types of questions about criminal events. Still, this method presents some major problems, and its use by criminologists has been limited. Most of the experimental work that has been done has not focused on what many consider to be the vital roles in criminal events: offender and victim. Instead, as in the case of the Shotland and Straw study, experiments have been used to study the reactions of witnesses or bystanders to contrived situations (Farrington et al., 1993; Frinell, Dahlstrom, and Johnson, 1980; Shotland and Goodstein, 1984).

Experiments that seek to entice people into criminal conduct or that feign the victimization of unsuspecting experimental subjects pose obvious ethical dilemmas. In some circumstances, experiments such as these place not only the study subjects but also the researchers at risk of physical or emotional harm.

REPORTING CRIME

The Crime Funnel

The data used most often by criminologists interested in the study of criminal events come not from direct observation but from the reports of those who have direct knowledge of those events—principally the police, victims, and offenders. Criminal justice agencies aside from the police (e.g., courts and prisons) can also be important sources of information about criminal events. After all, these agencies are in the "crime business" and keep records of people who are arrested, cases that go to trial, and the number of people incarcerated.

If our interest centres on the criminal event, the data made available by the various criminal agencies differ in terms of their value. In part, this is because different agencies have different needs and therefore do not all collect the same type of information. Of equal importance is the fact that criminal justice agencies are connected to one another in a "volume-reducing system" (Reiss, 1986). In other words, there is a high level of attrition as cases travel through the various stages of the criminal justice system. Not all criminal events that come to the attention of the police result in an arrest, not all arrests result in a trial, and not all trials result in a conviction. Some writers have described this attrition process as a **crime funnel** (Silverman, Teevan,

Crime funnel
A "volume-reducing system," meaning that there is a high level of attrition as cases travel through various stages of the criminal justice system.

BOX 3.1

The Crime Funnel and the UCR

Many crimes may occur

Husband assaults wife

Does wife define it as a crime?

If so, does she call police?

Are police dispatched to the scene?

If so, police can exercise discretion

Event may be handled "unofficially": no record is kept and no crime reported

Event may be handled "officially" and a record is made and should be entered

Due to data mismanagement, some case reports go missing

Remaining records form the basis of the UCR

Only a small proportion of the crimes are defined and recorded and then reported

- Events occur which have the potential to be defined as crimes—e.g., a husband physically assaults his wife.
- Many women, in a manner consistent with dominant cultural understandings, do not define the event as a crime. However, other women, often in consultation with others, do define the event as a crime.
- Of those who define the event as a crime, a smaller proportion call the police.
- Depending on the nature of the call, the police do or do not dispatch officers to the scene.
- If dispatched, police must decide how to handle the situation. Despite the existence of regulations which require official action, police still exercise discretion in deciding how the event will be handled.
- If the event is handled "unofficially," no record might be kept, and no further action might be taken. In a formal sense, for the purpose of official records, no crime can be said to have been committed.
- If the event is handled officially, a completed report is written, with the intention that it be entered into the police information system.
- As a result of data mismanagement, some case reports go missing.
- The cases which remain form the basis of the Uniform Crime Report (UCR).

and Sacco, 2000). For example, according to government estimates (Canada, 1982), in the early 1980s:

- about 60 percent of all break-and-enter incidents were reported to the police;
- 10 percent of all break-and-enter incidents eventually resulted in someone being charged with the crime (17 percent of all of those reported to the police); *and*
- 5.8 percent of all break-and-enter incidents resulted in a conviction (60 percent of those incidents that resulted in a charge).

Dutton (1987) argued that as cases of wife assault move through the criminal justice system, a "winnowing process" occurs. He found that the probability of wife assault being detected by the justice system was about 6.5 percent. Once detected, the probability of arrest was about 21.2 percent. Not all of those arrested were convicted. Dutton concluded that offenders in cases of wife assault had only a 0.38 percent chance of being punished by the courts. In their study on attrition rates in sexual assault cases, Lea, Lanvers, and Shaw (2003) examined all cases of sexual assault or attempted sexual assault reported to police in England during a five-year period from January 1996 to December 2000. They found that of the 379 reported cases of sexual assault or attempted sexual assault, 61 percent were dropped, or NFA'd (classified No Further Action) by the police. Only 11 percent of these cases resulted in a conviction of some kind (Lea, Lanvers, and Shaw, 2003: 592). However, only 5 percent of these cases actually resulted in a conviction of sexual assault. The main reason given for crimes not progressing through the system or not resulting in a conviction was "lack of evidence."

Police Reports

For the purpose of studying criminal events, the data contained in police records are quantitatively and qualitatively superior to those maintained by the courts and correctional agencies. In a quantitative sense, police data encompass a larger number of criminal events. In a qualitative sense, police data are not directly subject to the various sorting procedures whereby cases may later be processed out of the system in a non-random manner.

Police crime data are based on criminal events about which the police have knowledge. You will recall, however, that any measure of "crimes known to the police" cannot be expected to be synonymous with all crimes that occur, because many crimes—especially less serious ones—are not reported to the police. Data discussed in previous chapters indicate that more than 50 percent of the crime reported by victims to survey interviewers may not be reported to the police.

You will also recall that proactive policing results in the discovery of relatively few crimes. Thus, the types and number of crimes about which the police have knowledge depend mainly on the reporting behaviour of members of the public.

Furthermore, not all criminal events that come to the attention of the police become part of the official record. In Edmonton, Kennedy and Veitch (1997) found that the huge number of calls to the police (through both 911 and the complaint line) was leading to congestion in the communication centre. In 1991, the number of calls to that centre, including calls to both 911 (serious injury accidents, alarms, and in-progress criminal occurrences) and the complaint line (non-emergency), peaked at 485,309. Over 100,000 of these callers hung up before getting a response, as it was taking 81 seconds on average to answer a non-emergency call. Kennedy and Veitch suggest that the actual number of crime occurrences may have been higher than reported, as complainants grew frustrated because they couldn't get through to the communication centre and simply stopped trying to report these crimes. The Edmonton Police Service changed its phone system, mainly by directing complaints to four new divisional stations and twelve community stations. By 1994, the average speed of answer of calls had been reduced to 55 seconds, and the number of abandoned calls to 50,000.

Getting through to the police does not guarantee that a crime will be recorded. When a citizen calls the police to report a crime, it does not necessarily follow that a car will be dispatched or that any subsequent action will be taken (Gilsinan, 1989). Even when the police do show up at the scene, they may decide to treat the matter unofficially or as something other than a crime.

Some event characteristics increase the likelihood that a crime will be recorded (Gove, Hughes, and Geerken, 1985). Events with elements that suggest a high degree of legal seriousness are more likely to be recorded as crimes (Gottfredson and Gottfredson, 1988). Also, when strong physical evidence or compelling testimony indicates that a crime has occurred, the event is more likely to enter the official record. An event is also more likely to be treated as a crime when the person who makes the complaint to the police urges that official action be taken (Black, 1971; Mastrofski et al., 2000).

Recording rates reflect not only the characteristics of the event but also the characteristics of the policing agency. Specifically, highly professional police departments are more likely to officially record crimes (Gove, Hughes, and Geerken, 1985), in part because these departments tend to make greater use of crime data in developing departmental priorities and deploying resources.

Highly professional departments also rely more heavily on existing official records in the processing of citizen complaints, because there is a stronger incentive at all departmental levels to "write up" a larger number of police–citizen interactions (Skogan, 1977).

The descriptions of events that are officially labelled as crimes by the investigating officer often undergo significant changes as they move through the internal bureaucracy of the police department. As information travels from the line officer through the communications section to the records division, offences may be shifted from one category to another, downgraded, or ignored (Skogan, 1977). In sum, the amount of crime recorded by the police department is affected by the internal organization of the department and by the bureaucratic procedures by which information is processed (McClearly, Nienstedt, and Erven, 1982).

The Canadian Centre for Justice Statistics (CCJS) (1990) attempted to determine the extent to which differences between Edmonton and Calgary crime levels could be accounted for by differences in record-keeping practices. Edmonton has always had a higher crime rate than Calgary—a difference that has never been adequately explained by social and demographic factors usually associated with higher crime rates (e.g., high unemployment, interprovincial migration). The CCJS study found that data "leakage" in the stages between the original call to the policing agency and the processing of information in the records section was greater in Calgary than in Edmonton. In Calgary, about 80 percent of cases reached the records section, compared to about 94 percent in Edmonton. To some degree, then, Edmonton's higher crime rate in the late 1980s was attributable to differences in how agency data were collected.

Uniform Crime Reporting system (UCR)
The UCR is a survey collated by Statistics Canada based on crime reports from police departments nationwide. The information is available to the government, criminologists, politicians, and the mass media.

The Uniform Crime Reporting System

In Canada and the United States, crime data gathered by the police are collected and processed as part of what is known as a **Uniform Crime Reporting system (UCR)**. Canada's UCR was developed through the joint efforts of Statistics Canada and the Canadian Association of Chiefs of Police, and has been operating since 1962. Its stated objective is to provide police departments with a consistent set of procedures for collecting information relevant to crimes that come to the attention of the police (Haggerty, 2001).

WHAT IS IT?

Uniform Crime Reports

In Canada and the United States, crime data gathered by the police are collected and processed as part of a uniform crime reporting system (UCR). The UCR's stated objective is to provide police departments with a consistent set of procedures for collecting information relevant to crimes that come to the attention of the police.

Aggregate UCR survey
Records the total number of crime incidents reported to the police.

Clearance status
A judgment made by the police based on identification of at least one of the offenders involved in an offence.

In simple terms, the UCR is a survey. Police departments across the country report crime information in a standardized format to the federal statistical agency (Statistics Canada), which collates that information and makes it available to interested data users, including government departments, criminologists, politicians, and the mass media. Since 1982, the Canadian Centre for Justice Statistics—a division of Statistics Canada—has been responsible for collecting information from police departments, which regularly respond to the survey. Currently, the UCR survey collects information at two levels of detail (Sauvé, 2005; Tremblay, 2000).

The **aggregate UCR survey** records the total number of incidents reported to the police. It includes counts of the reported offences, the number of offences that have clearance status, and the number of "actual offences." With respect to persons accused, it only includes information about gender and the adult or youth status of these persons. **Clearance status** refers to a judgment made by the police as to whether they can identify at least one of the offenders involved in the offence. If this person is formally charged with the crime, the offence is "cleared by charge." However, if circumstances do not allow a charge to be made, the police count the incident as "cleared otherwise." This might happen, for instance, if a victim refuses to sign a complaint, or if the offender dies before he or she can be charged.

The aggregate UCR survey classifies incidents according to the most serious crime which occurs in the incident. In this process, violent offences always take precedence over nonviolent. One implication of this practice is that less serious crime tends to be under-represented in this survey. No information is collected about the victims of crime.

The aggregate UCR also counts violent incidents differently than it counts other kinds of incidents. In violent incidents, one crime is counted for each victim. So if one person attacks three people, that incident would be counted as three crimes. However, if three people attack one person, that would be counted as one crime. In the case of nonviolent crimes, one crime is counted for each separate and distinct occurrence (Sauvé, 2005).

For the past several years, however, a revised UCR survey (*UCR 2*) has been carried out, with the goal of correcting deficiencies in the original survey (Silverman, Teevan, and Sacco, 2000). This survey collects detailed information on individual incidents which come to the attention of the police. This information includes details about the accused, the victims, and the incidents themselves. In 2004, a total of 120 police services in eight provinces supplied data for the UCR2 survey. This represents about 58 percent of all the crime reported to the police in Canada.

UCR 2 resolves many of the problems that plagued UCR 1. Most importantly, because the kinds of information collected by the survey have been expanded and because the system is incident-based, it will be possible to use UCR data to consider a wide array of questions that could not be addressed previously. These include questions about the characteristics of victims of crime, the location of criminal events, the differences between stranger and intimate violence, and the relationship between weapon use and level of injury.

While UCR 2 will greatly enhance the quality of police data about criminal events, it leaves unaddressed many other questions about those crimes which never come to the attention of the police in the first place.

Victim Reports

Reports from victims of crime are a second major source of information about criminal events. In **victim reports/surveys**, victims may be asked to describe what transpired during the event, how they reacted, whether the police were summoned, and what costs—physical or psychological—they may have sustained as a result of the incident. Data from victims of crime are usually collected in the context of victimization surveys. These are large-scale studies that ask randomly sampled members of some larger population about their experiences with crime. To date, several major victimization surveys have been conducted in Canada. The first, the Canadian Urban Victimization Survey (CUVS), was undertaken in 1982 in seven major Canadian urban areas (Solicitor General, 1983). A second major study, the Violence Against Women Survey (VAWS), was undertaken in 1993 (Johnson, 1996; Johnson and Sacco, 1995). Four other studies have been undertaken as part of the Canadian General Social Survey (GSS). These national surveys were conducted in 1988 (Sacco and Johnson, 1990), 1993 (Gartner and Doob, 1994), 1999 (Besserer and Trainor, 2000), and 2004 (Gannon and Mihorean, 2005). The plan is to continue to conduct the GSS victimization survey regularly, at roughly five-year intervals. Canada has also participated in the International Crime Victimization Survey, which so far has been conducted five times (see Box 3.2). As well, several researchers have conducted individual victimization surveys in order to investigate particular research problems in which they are interested (Eisler and Schissel, 2004; Rinfret-Raynor et al., 2004).

Because criminal victimization is a statistically rare event, a large number of interviews must be conducted if such surveys are to yield a sufficient number of cases for analysis. The

Victim reports/surveys
Large-scale studies that ask individuals about their experience with crime.

WHAT ARE THEY?

Victimization Surveys

Victimization surveys are large-scale studies that ask randomly sampled members of some larger population about their experiences with crime.

BOX 3.2

The Victimization Survey in International Context

In 2000, Canada participated in the International Crime Victimization Survey for the fourth time. This survey, which is coordinated by the Ministry of Justice in the Netherlands and the UN Interregional Crime and Justice Research Institute, is intended to provide comparable information on victimization in several different countries around the world.

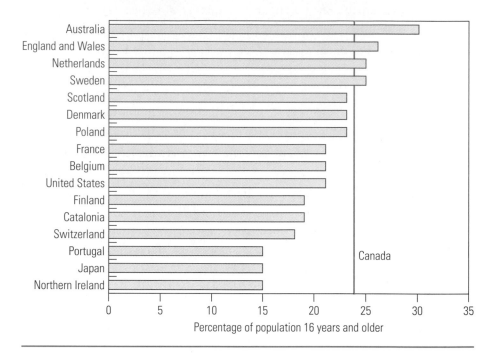

Percentage of population 16 years and older

CUVS gathered data from roughly 60,000 urban Canadians; the 2004 GSS employed a sample of about 24,000. Because of these large sample sizes, victimization surveys are very expensive (Strike, 1995).

To improve the efficiency of the undertaking, it is common in victimization research to conduct interviews by telephone. When this approach is taken, researchers often use sampling procedures to generate a sample of telephone numbers to be called. These procedures restrict data collection to households with working telephones. This may not be as serious a bias as it might at first appear: households without telephones account for less than 2 percent of the target population (Besserer and Trainor, 2000).

In a typical victimization survey, respondents are asked about a range of crimes against the person (e.g., sexual assault, assault, robbery, personal theft) and against property (e.g., break and enter, theft of household property, vandalism). Since these studies focus explicitly on victimization, they usually restrict themselves to the study of crimes involving a direct victim. Special topic surveys, such as the VAWS, may even further restrict the range of victimization experiences about which respondents are asked.

Victimization interviews usually have two parts. First, all respondents (whether they have been victims of crime or not) are asked questions from a "screening questionnaire." Some questions gather basic information on the gender, age, and other social and demographic characteristics of the respondents; others ask respondents about their fear of crime or their attitudes toward the criminal justice system. More importantly, the screening questionnaire is used to identify those respondents who have experienced one or more of the types of victimization that are of interest to the researchers.

Respondents are asked whether they have been victimized. Those who say yes are usually asked a detailed series of questions about the victimization incident. Questions of this type make up the second major part of the interview. Victims may be asked questions about the location and circumstances of the crime or their relationship to the offender. They may also be asked about the financial losses they sustained or about the level of physical injury they suffered. Information may also be gathered regarding whether the victim reported the crime to the police or took any other action in the aftermath of the victimization episode.

As valuable as they are, data from victimization surveys, like UCR data, have been subject to criticisms relating to their methodology (Miethe and Meier, 1994; Mosher et al., 2002; Skogan, 1986). Chief among these are the following:

- Certain crimes are thought to be under-counted (e.g., domestic violence offences).
- Under-counting may result because people forget things that happened to them—a phenomenon especially likely if the crime was a relatively minor one or—perhaps worse—if the individual is especially accustomed to being victimized.
- People may forget or misrepresent the time frame of their experiences and report crimes that are actually outside the time reference of the study. This inflates incidence rates.
- Respondents may lie to please the interviewer (that is, respondents may fabricate crimes in order to provide data).

BOX 3.3

GSS (2004) Property Victimization Screen Questions

The next questions ask about things which may have happened to you during the past 12 months. Please include acts committed by both family and non-family members.

1. During the past 12 months, did anyone deliberately damage or destroy any property belonging to you or anyone in your household (such as a window or a fence)?

2. [Other than the incidents already mentioned,] during the past 12 months, did anyone take or try to take something from you by force or threat of force?

3. [Other than the incidents already mentioned,] did anyone illegally break into or attempt to break into your residence or any other building on your property?

4. [Other than the incidents already mentioned,] was anything of yours stolen during the past 12 months from the things usually kept outside your home, such as yard furniture?

5. [Other than the incidents already mentioned,] was anything of yours stolen during the past 12 months from your place of work, from school or from a public place, such as a restaurant?

6. [Other than the incidents already mentioned,] was anything of yours stolen during the past 12 months from a hotel, vacation home, cottage, car, truck or while traveling?

7. During the past 12 months, did you or anyone in your household have a motor vehicle such as a car, truck, motorcycle, etc?

8. [Other than incidents already mentioned,] did anyone steal or try to steal one of these vehicles or a part of one of them, such as a battery, hubcap or radio?

9. [Other than the incidents already mentioned,] did anyone deliberately damage one of these vehicles, such as slashing tires?

10. [Excluding the incidents already mentioned,] during the past 12 months, did anyone steal or try to steal anything else that belonged to you?

Source: *Canadian General Social Survey.* 2005. Statistics Canada, Family, Household and Social Statistics Division. Used by permission of Statistics Canada.

Those who believe that victimization surveys are valuable offer several reasons. *First*, because victimization surveys collect information directly from victims of crime, they can tell us about crimes that have not been reported to the police. Thus, they provide a more valid estimate of the actual crime rate (Fattah, 1991).

Second, because victimization surveys use samples drawn from the general population, data are collected from both victims and non-victims over a given period. This allows researchers to compare the two groups and to analyze which social and demographic groups face the greatest risks of victimization and how these risks are affected by particular kinds of behaviours such as drinking alcohol and living alone. These data can help us develop theoretical models linking victim involvement in criminal events to factors of this type (Hindelang, Gottfredson, and Garofalo, 1978; Miethe and Meier, 1994).

Third and finally, victimization surveys enable us to investigate the consequences of victimization and the ways that victims cope with these consequences.

Offender Reports

Interviews with offenders can give us important insights into their behaviour, attitudes, and motivations. We can learn why they commit certain types of offences, how they feel about their victims, and how they assess their risk of being apprehended by the criminal justice system (Junger-Tas and Marshall, 1999).

Reports from Known Offenders

Perhaps the most obvious form of **offender report** makes use of data gathered from a sample of known offenders such as prison inmates or those who have been convicted of an offence and are awaiting sentence (Baunach, 1990; Mosher et al., 2002). Surveys of this type can shed light on a range of subjects, including the use of weapons by offenders (Wright and Rossi, 1986) and the characteristics of offenders' victims (Innes and Greenfeld, 1990). Understanding these things gives us useful insights into how offenders regard their own actions and those of other event participants.

Offender reports
Data gathered from a sample of known offenders, such as prison inmates.

One major concern with surveys of known offenders relates to the generalizability of the findings (Flowers, 1989). Many offenders are not captured, and many of those who are captured are not convicted or sentenced. As a result, what we learn in interviews with convicted offenders may not be representative of the larger offender population.

Ethnographic Research

Ethnographic research is another means for gathering information from known offenders. As a research strategy, ethnography moves beyond the use of structured interviews; the researcher attempts not only to speak with but also to observe directly and to interact with the people being studied (Wright and Bennett, 1990). The researcher gathers offender accounts by informally participating in and developing some intimate knowledge of the social world of the offender (Fleisher, 1995).

Ethnographic research
Studies in which the researcher attempts to directly observe and interact with the people being studied in a naturally occurring context.

This approach rests on the assumption that formal interviews with offenders yield very limited research data. Researchers often find it difficult to gain access to members of "outlaw" motorcycle gangs (Wolf, 1991), organized crime groups, and professional thieves through conventional means (Ianni and Reuss-Ianni, 1972; Wolf, 1991). However, if researchers are able to cultivate informal relationships with offenders, they may be able to penetrate their social worlds and thereby learn much that would be invisible to outside researchers.

Researcher Cindy Ness spent a year doing ethnographic fieldwork with low-income female adolescents in West and Northeast Philadelphia in order to better understand how they use and understand acts of physical violence. In order to make sense of the types and levels of violence in which young girls engage, Ness spent a considerable amount of time with 15 girls, two of whom she "hung out with several days each week in their West Philadelphia neighborhood" (Ness, 2004: 35). As well, she spent numerous evenings in "ride-alongs" with the police in order to observe interactions between officers and female youth. Her analysis is revealing. Ness concluded that in order to understand the widespread occurrence of violence among young females, it is necessary to recognize the instrumental function that violence has for them and the ways in which it offers a venue for the attainment of self-esteem in a setting largely devoid of legal avenues of achievement. However, Ness argues, when these girls are simply labelled delinquent, the larger and more socially significant functions of violence go unnoticed.

Ethnographic studies of street gangs (Baron, 1997; Kennedy and Baron, 1993; Baron, Kennedy, and Forde, 2001), violent criminals (Fleisher, 1995), and male prostitutes (Calhoun and Weaver, 1996) have provided insights that could not have been gleaned from police statistics or victim surveys. Chambliss (1975), a proponent of this method of urban ethnography, contends that the data on organized crime, professional theft, and other presumably difficult-to-study events are much more available than we usually think. "All we really have to do is get out of our offices and onto the streets. The data are there; the problem is that too often the sociologist is not" (39).

Self-report studies
Respondents' reports about their involvement as offenders.

WHAT IS IT?

Self-Report Study

Instead of being asked about their involvement in criminal events as victims, respondents are asked about their involvement as offenders. Like victimization surveys, self-report studies are intended to uncover crimes that have not been reported to the police (as well as to elucidate those that have).

Self-Report Studies

Self-report studies predate victimization surveys, having become popular in the 1950s and 1960s (Mosher et al., 2002). Like victimization surveys, **self-report studies** gather

BOX 3.4

Self-Reported Crime among Criminologists

Mathew Robinson and Barbara Zaitzow (1999) attempted to use the self-report method to determine the degree to which "crime experts" commit crimes. The study was conducted through a mail survey of a sample of members of the American Society of Criminology. Anonymous questionnaires were sent to a random sample of 1,500 members of the ASC. Respondents were asked if they had engaged in a variety of criminal offences "ever" and "within the past (six or) 12 months." In all, 522 surveys were returned. Major findings of the study included the following:

1. Not surprisingly, more respondents admitted having engaged in the less serious crimes about which they were asked. For example, 92 percent and 88 percent reported driving above the speed limit "ever" and in the previous 12 months respectively.

2. Fifty-five percent admitted to committing theft "ever"; however, only 7 percent admitted to having done so in the previous 12 months.

3. A rather large percentage of respondents admitted committing a violent offence. Thirty-six percent reported that they had verbally threatened another person "ever," and 15 percent indicated that they had done so in the past six months. Twenty-five percent said that they had "physically attacked another person" "ever," and 2 percent had done so in the previous six months.

4. Two-thirds of the respondents (66 percent) reported that they had driven under the influence of drugs or alcohol at some point in their lives, and 35 percent indicated that they had done so in the previous six months.

5. The only sexual offence that more than 10 percent of the respondents admitted that they had committed was adultery (defined as "sexual relations with a person not your spouse"). Twenty-three percent reported "ever" having done so, and 16 percent reported having done so in the previous year.

6. Nearly one in five (19 percent) admitted to committing tax fraud at some point, and 7 percent admitted to having done so in the previous year.

---

data from the members of some large population. However, instead of being asked about their involvement as victims in criminal events, respondents are asked about their involvement as offenders. Like victimization surveys, self-report studies are intended to uncover crimes that have not been reported to the police (as well as to elucidate those that have). Also like victimization surveys, self-report studies allow the sample to be broken up into respondents who have and who have not been involved in criminal events over a specified period. This enables the researcher to compare offenders and non-offenders in terms of social and lifestyle characteristics that might be useful in testing explanations of criminality (Mosher et al., 2002).

Self-report research has most often been used in the study of juvenile crime, although there is nothing in the approach that prevents it from being applied to adult crime (Maxfield, Weiler, and Widom, 2000) or to "non-traditional" offences such as computer crime (Sacco and Zureik, 1990). The emphasis on juveniles has largely been a matter of convenience: juveniles, in the context of the school classroom, represent a captive audience for the researcher (Chilton, 1991). Once a sample of respondents has been selected, the data about self-reported delinquency are collected in one of two ways (O'Brien, 1985). Some researchers use a questionnaire that includes a checklist of delinquent acts. Subjects are asked to indicate whether they have committed each of the acts and, if so, how often over a given period. Alternatively, researchers may ask respondents about their delinquent conduct in face-to-face interviews (Teevan and Dryburgh, 2000). Each approach has its advantages. Questionnaires make it easier to ensure the respondent's anonymity. Interviews, however, allow for more detailed questioning about the circumstances surrounding the delinquent conduct (Gold, 1970).

The Limitations of Crime Reports

Much of what we know about criminal events is based on the reports provided by offenders, victims, and the police. In addressing the limitations of these data, two issues require consideration: the type of event that is captured by each method of data collection, and the perspective brought to bear on those events that are captured.

What Type of Event?

Each of the methods we have discussed in this section is somewhat restricted in terms of the kinds of criminal events it illuminates. Victimization surveys usually ask respondents only about those events that have a direct and immediate victim. Because they are household surveys, they tend to exclude crimes that victimize businesses or the wider community (e.g., vandalism of public property). Victimization surveys also exclude victims to whom access is limited, including children, the homeless, and residents of psychiatric or other institutions (Weis, 1989).

Self-report studies have been used mainly to obtain information about the "common delinquencies" of youth. They have been criticized for excluding the more serious but less common types of delinquency (e.g., extreme forms of violence), while emphasizing non-serious forms of behaviour (e.g., "cutting classes," "disobeying parents") (Gove, Hughes, and Geerken, 1985; Junger-Tas and Marshall, 1999). When students in criminology classes are asked to demonstrate with a show of hands whether they have committed any of the "crimes" listed in the self-report questionnaires, a large number always respond in the affirmative. Even political leaders have admitted to experimenting with marijuana as youths. A loose interpretation of these data can make it seem that everyone is a criminal. More realistically, these data do support the idea that criminal offending (even of the more serious variety) is far more common than official statistics would lead us to believe. By implication, distinctions between "offenders" and "everyone else" are made only with great difficulty (Felson, 2002; Gabor, 1994).

The police reports that form the basis of the UCR are in some ways the most comprehensive data source. Unlike victimization surveys, the UCR includes crimes without direct victims, as well as crimes committed against businesses, the community, and those individuals who are unlikely to appear in surveys (Biderman and Lynch, 1991). A limitation of the UCR system is that the data it collects are based only on crimes the police know about.

Whose Perspective?

The issue of perspective is central to any attempt to make proper use of crime report data. Each method offers a limited perspective, since it elicits information from only some types of event participants. As we saw in Chapter 2, event participants' understanding of criminal events may differ quite markedly. We expect, therefore, that their reports will reflect these differences.

Victimization data rely on victims' perceptions of criminal events. As such, their quality is subject to whatever distortions—intentional or not—characterize these perceptions. Also, respondents' reports are subject to many compromises. For example, respondents may fail to disclose experiences in which the researcher is interested (Skogan, 1986). If someone is victimized during the course of an illegal activity, he or she may not want to tell the researcher about it. If the event is of minor significance, it may be forgotten by the time of the interview; this may be a particular problem when the reference period about which the respondent is asked is very long. The opposite problem involves **telescoping** (Gaskell, Wright, and O'Muircheartaigh, 2000). In such cases,

Telescoping
Reporting a crime as occurring during the reference period when it actually occurred at an earlier time.

WHAT DOES IT MEAN?

Telescoping

Crimes that the victim regards as significant life events may be brought forward in time so that the respondent reports them as having occurred during the reference period when they actually occurred at an earlier point in time. Telescoping is most likely to be a problem in the study of serious violent crimes.

crimes the victim regards as significant life events may be reported as having occurred during the reference period, when in fact they actually occurred earlier. Telescoping is most likely to be a problem in the study of serious violent crimes.

In many cases of serious victimization, the victim may be reluctant to report the event to a researcher—for instance, in cases of family violence or sexual assault when the victim feels ashamed or embarrassed or believes that reporting the event may put him or her at risk (Johnson, 1996).

Victims' perspectives are limited in other ways. If respondents cannot or do not define an event as a crime, they are unlikely to tell a researcher about it (Block and Block, 1984). In some situations, people may be victimized but not realize it; many forms of fraud are intended to have precisely this outcome. Similarly, if a purse is stolen but the victim believes that she has lost it, she will not report it to a researcher who asks her a question about theft. Much of the criminal harm that is perpetrated by corporations and governments is not readily apparent, even to those who are directly affected; as a result, victims may have no idea that they have been victimized (Walklate, 1989).

Respondents are also likely to differ in their views as to what level of violation constitutes a crime (Gove, Hughes, and Geerken, 1985). For instance, some studies show that highly educated people are more likely to report being the victim of an assault. This finding is most reasonably interpreted in terms of class differences in the definition of injury or in the willingness to tolerate violence, rather than in terms of the greater threats of criminal violence faced by more highly educated respondents (Skogan, 1990a).

Self-report studies allow us to understand criminal events from the perspective of the offender. Yet the offenders who have the most to hide may be the least willing to participate in the research (O'Brien, 1985). Moreover, some offenders may exaggerate their wrongdoings (perhaps as a show of bravado), while others may be reluctant to admit to involvement in criminal activity (Wright and Bennett, 1990). When the latter do report, they may be more willing to admit to trivial rather than serious offences (Jupp, 1989).

Regarding the UCR system, the organizational perspective of policing agencies determines the rules for collecting data. Administrative and political pressures may dictate that certain kinds of criminal events (e.g., impaired driving) be policed more stringently than others (e.g., "soft" drug use) (Jackson, 1990; O'Brien, 1985; Schneider and Wiersema, 1990). Police practices, public tolerance for particular kinds of behaviour, and the needs of the agency for particular kinds of data all influence the ways in which data are collected (Savitz, 1978).

Reiss (1986) contends that the perspective implicit in police data offers a distinct advantage over self-report and victimization data. The latter two data sources reflect the views of highly self-interested parties; in contrast, police data allow for a more balanced picture. Police reports of criminal events are based on a wider variety of information sources, including victims, offenders, bystanders, and witnesses. Also, police data usually are collected closer in time to the actual event than is the case with victim and offender surveys. As a result, police data are less likely to be influenced by the selective effects of memory.

In a similar vein, Gove, Hughes, and Geerken (1985) suggest that compared to other data sources, official statistics provide more rigorous criteria for defining criminal events. They argue that victimization surveys give us only the victim's perspective, which is insufficient in determining whether a crime has in fact occurred. In order to make this judgment, we also need to know the offender's intention, the circumstances surrounding the event, and the condition of the victim.

Criminal events that are recorded in official statistics have passed through two filters. *First,* they have been judged sufficiently serious to be worth reporting to the police. *Second,* they have been certified by the police as serious events deserving of criminal justice intervention. According to Gove, Hughes, and Geerken (1985), the reports contained in the UCR provide a good indicator of "the extent to which citizens feel injured, frightened, and financially hurt by a criminal act" (489). However, we should not conclude from this that discrepancies between police and other forms of data should be resolved in favour of the former. Police records, like other official records, are not always accurate. Too often they are "misplaced, haphazard, and/or incomplete" (Fleury et al., 1998).

These different perspectives have very important implications for how criminal events are understood. For example, if an individual gets into a fistfight with a drinking buddy, that event might be understood differently within the context of different data collection systems. If the individual is asked in a victimization survey whether anyone has hit him or threatened to hit him, and he responds honestly, he is likely to be counted as a victim. If he is asked in a self-report survey whether he has hit anyone, and he answers honestly, he is likely to be counted as an offender. If the police are summoned, they may, because of the circumstances and the relationship between the parties, screen the event out so that it never enters the official record.

We do not necessarily expect reports from different event participants to tell us the same things. Victimization surveys and UCR data may disagree because they employ different criteria in determining the types of events that are to be included (Blumstein, Cohen, and Rosenfeld, 1992; Menard and Covey, 1988; O'Brien, 1986). Thus, if researchers undertook a victimization survey in a given community and then compared the survey rates with the UCR rates for that same community, several sources of variation would be apparent. The UCR measures would encompass crimes committed against businesses, institutionalized people, and individuals who do not have a permanent residence; the victim survey would probably omit such crimes. The UCR rates would include crimes committed within the policing jurisdiction, irrespective of victims' place of residence. Thus, the UCR might include crimes committed against tourists who were visiting the community, as well as crimes against commuters who work in the community but live elsewhere. In contrast, the victimization study, because it usually involves a household survey, would restrict attention to crimes committed against community residents, whether or not the crime occurred in the local community or elsewhere.

Similarly, the descriptions of offenders that emerge from police reports of crimes serious enough to have passed through citizen and police filters cannot be expected to concur with offender profiles that emerge from self-report studies that focus on non-serious delinquency (Loeber, Farrington, and Waschbusch, 1998).

For decades, criminologists have been intensely debating the relative value of specific crime measures. Clearly, no single data source can answer all of the questions we have about crime events (Jackson, 1990; Menard and Covey, 1988). Because our data sources tell us different things, it does not really make sense to think about one data source as *better* than another. Later chapters will rely extensively on data derived from a variety of sources, and it will be important for us to approach these data cautiously and critically. Two controversial issues require further comment at this point. The first concerns the ways in which crime statistics portray the problem of crime against women. The second relates to the relationship between various indicators of race or ethnicity on the one hand and crime on the other.

Measuring Women's Victimization

Do men or women face the greatest risk of criminal victimization? The answer depends on which crimes we focus attention on and on which data sources we use. According to the 2003 UCR 2 survey, 86 percent of victims of sexual assault were women. But at the same time, 73 percent of adult homicide victims were men, and so were 66 percent of adult victims of robbery. With respect to non-sexual assault, the percentage difference between female and male victims was much less disproportionate (46 versus 54) (Canadian Centre for Justice Statistics, 2004).

The 2004 GSS indicates that the rates for robbery are much higher for men than for women (13 incidents per 1,000 versus 8 per 1,000), as are the rates of assault (91 per 1,000 for males and 59 per 1,000 for females). Regarding sexual assault, the rate for women is four times the rate for men (35 incidents per 1,000 versus 7 per 1,000) (Gannon and Mihorean, 2005).

Findings like these strongly influence how the public agenda is formulated; they also tend to legitimize some social problem "claims-makers" at the expense of others. Feminist social critics who attempt to raise public awareness of the problem of crime against women are often opposed by those who claim that women's fear of victimization is an irrational reaction to a world that threatens men more than it does women (Fekete, 1994). For their part, some feminist researchers have generated research findings that offer estimates of female victimization that are wildly at odds with the data yielded by more traditional measures (Gilbert, 1997).

Patterns of Female Victimization

All of this points to a need to understand the patterns of female victimization revealed by police data and victimization surveys. The logical starting point in such an exercise is to determine areas of agreement across methodological approaches to women's victimization. Two such patterns are consistently reported by the advocates of both traditional and more critical research approaches (Boritch, 1997; Gartner and McCarthy, 1996; Tjaden and Thoennes, 1998). The first pattern is that women are more likely than men to be victimized by people they know or with whom they have some ongoing relationship. The second (which is related) is that women have a greater tendency than men to be victimized in private settings (most notably the home) rather than public settings.

These patterns are easy to detect as they relate to the crime of homicide. Women are more likely than men to be murdered in the home, and are more likely to be murdered by a relative. In 2003, 78 people in Canada were killed by a spouse. Sixty of these victims were female, and 14 were male. As well, a larger proportion of separated women were killed by a spouse as compared to separated men (25 percent versus 11 percent). However, a larger proportion of males (54 percent) were killed by common-law partners as compared to females (35 percent) (Beattie, 2005).

Domestic and Sexual Assault

The two types of assault we associate most closely with the victimization of women—domestic assault and sexual assault—also illustrate the private and intimate character of female victimization (Comack et al., 2000). To understand why official data and victimization surveys portray female victimization as they do, we need to consider how well these measure crimes that are committed in private places and that involve offenders and victims who are intimately related.

As already noted, many women who are abused in the context of marital relationships do not define what is happening to them as criminal (Johnson, 1996). Several cultural factors encourage these women to view such incidents as normal and to blame themselves for the violence (Ferraro and Johnson, 1983). Even the fact that a woman phones the police to report an attack by a spouse does not necessarily mean that she defines the event in criminal terms; her action may have less to do with "reporting a crime" than with trying to obtain immediate assistance in order to prevent injury. Victims of spousal assault give as a common reason for phoning the police, a desire to "stop the violence and receive protection" (Mihorean, 2005). And even if women do define such events as crimes, they may choose not to phone the police for a variety of reasons (Johnson, 1996; Mihorean, 2005). They may perceive that taking such action places them at greater risk, or they may be concerned that the police or other criminal justice agents will not take them seriously.

The appearance of the police at the scene of a domestic violence incident does not always mean that the event will be counted as a crime. If there is no clear evidence of physical harm, the police may engage in mediation—that is, attempt to cool the parties down, listen to their respective accounts, or issue stern warnings (Bell, 1987; Kantor and Straus, 1987). The victim may be given information or advice or referrals instead of being treated like a complainant in a criminal matter.

In many domestic disputes, the police view the law as a means for dealing with the disorderly situation rather than as a means for addressing the problem of wife assault (Gondolf and McFerron, 1989). As a result, often no legal action is taken because the situation is not seen as warranting a legal response. Even situations that do involve a legal resolution do not necessarily require that official note be taken of the fact that a woman has been victimized. O'Grady (1989) discovered that in Newfoundland, many instances of domestic violence were legally recorded not as assaults but as "weapons" or "drunk and disorderly in the home" offences.

As we pointed out in Chapter 1, many jurisdictions have attempted to reduce the use of police discretion in the handling of domestic assaults by passing laws that make arrest mandatory in these situations. However, these laws do not completely prevent the police from engaging in discretionary decision making. Data from the 2004 General Social Survey indicate that despite the existence of mandatory or pro-charging policies, the police use considerable discretion in spousal assault cases (Mihorean, 2005).

Victims of sexual assault, like victims of domestic violence, may be reluctant to apply a criminal label if the offender is an acquaintance. Using U.S. national victimization data, Lizotte (1985) reported that the factors that make a strong case for prosecution are closely related to women's reporting decisions. Women are less likely to report an incident to the police when they are unmarried, when the offender is not a stranger, or when the offender has a right to be in the location in which the offence occurred. Thus, the UCR measures sexual assaults for which the legal evidence is relatively clear but which are not necessarily typical of women's sexual victimization (Du Mont et al., 2003).

Though it is often claimed that victimization surveys broaden the search for incidents of women's victimization, these surveys also clearly exclude many types of events. Most notably, they under-count crimes that involve intimates—precisely the types of crimes that disproportionately victimize women. Moreover, victimization surveys usually ignore victimization in the form of obscene phone calls, exhibitionism, and sexual harassment in the workplace (Gillespie and Leffler, 1987; Junger, 1987).

The Canadian Violence Against Women Survey was one of the most ambitious and sophisticated attempts ever made to investigate the problem of violence against women (Johnson, 1996; Johnson and Sacco, 1995). Because the survey included only female respondents, it did not allow us to compare directly the experiences of men and women. However, it did represent an attempt to focus on the specific problem of male violence against women in a way that took into account the limitations that have hampered many previous efforts. The survey methodology reflected extensive consultations with government officials, academics, and women's groups directly involved in the problem of violence against women. Careful testing of survey questions, multiple measures, selection and training of interviewers, and lifetime victimization rates were all incorporated into the design of the survey (Johnson and Sacco, 2000). The survey design was especially sensitive to the ethical and safety problems that could be created if those being interviewed might still be living with their victimizers. The survey yielded a wealth of valuable data and has become the model for similar surveys in the United States and elsewhere (Tjaden and Thoennes, 1998). Moreover, much of what was learned in the VAWS survey was incorporated into the design of later versions of the General Social Survey victimization studies in 1999 and 2004.

Obviously, claims that women experience low rates of crime must be assessed with extreme caution. This is not because the research is done crudely or carelessly, but because all research approaches have limitations.

Race/Ethnicity and Crime

Another controversial question concerns the appropriateness of collecting crime data information relating to the race or ethnicity of offenders and victims. With the exception of an "Aboriginal identifier," such information is currently not gathered and made available to policy planners, academics or others interested in crime in Canada (Kong and Beattie, 2005). In 1990, the Canadian Centre for Justice Statistics planned to routinely gather such data; however, these plans were scrapped when objections were raised from several quarters (Johnston, 1994).

Those in favour of collecting such information argue that the policy is justified because the data would be of real value in the planning and implementation of crime prevention and crime control policies (Gabor, 1994). In other words, the problems which different cultural communities have with crime may require solutions that take the unique character of those cultural communities into account. So, to ignore, for example, that the Asian community in some major city is disproportionately affected by some kind of extortionate crime makes about as much sense as ignoring the fact that sexual assault is more likely to victimize women than men.

Those against the collection of such information raise a battery of objections (Roberts, 1994). Most generally, critics suggest that whatever benefits might be said to derive from the collection of such information is more than offset by the harm that such a policy would promote. If the data show, for instance, that some groups appear to more frequently offend than do members of other groups, they give comfort to racist views which see crime as somehow in the "natural" character of the members of certain ethnic groups.

Perhaps most fundamentally, those who are critical of the collection of race/ethnicity crime data ask, "What exactly do the terms race or ethnicity mean in this context, and who is going to be responsible for the classification of victims or offenders?" Of course, the term "race" has no clear meaning. While it is commonly used to denote skin colour, this is a rather vague basis for classification of supposedly "scientific" information. How many racial categories are there? Is the category "white" or the category "black" to be understood as internally homogeneous?

Many people would argue that the term "ethnicity" might be preferable because it evokes culture rather than skin colour or some other characteristics. However, who is to make the determination regarding the classification of people as one ethnicity or another? In the context of the UCR, we would assume that this is a judgment police officers might make, based on some formal classification scheme. In the victimization or self-report survey, we would assume that respondents would classify themselves. There is, of course, reason to be skeptical of all of these methods. Whether done by a police officer on the scene, or as part of a self-description, decisions about ethnicity are most often only made with great difficulty (Hatt, 1994). As the criminologist Julian Roberts (1994: 176) noted:

> I am a white, Anglophone, Canadian resident of British ancestry, born and raised in a black African country, carrying a European community passport and Canadian citizenship. If I am charged with armed robbery, whose crime statistics should go up? Whites? Kenyans? Immigrant Canadians? Anglophones?

Probably the most controversial arguments about race/crime statistics relate to the charge of racial profiling on the part of the police. Such charges have loomed large in the daily newspapers and newscasts of Canadian cities in recent years. In short, it is claimed that due to systemic biases on the part of policing agencies, the members of racial and ethnic minorities are targeted for high levels of proactive policing. A major consequence of this style of policing would be to create an image of those minority members as being more likely than others in society to be engaged in crime. Any attempt to keep official crime statistics in ways that revealed the race or ethnicity of offenders would really just end up recording police biases. As a result, the victims of police profiling would end up being blamed for the crime problem.

In 2002, a Toronto newspaper (the *Toronto Star*) ran a series of articles in which it was claimed that the Toronto police tend to treat minority group members much more harshly than whites. The series made use of data from the Toronto CIPS (Criminal Information Processing System). This data set contained information on more than 480,000 incidents in which an individual was charged with a crime or ticketed. The series included a number of interviews with black community leaders whose testimony lent credibility and human interest to the charges. The articles not only polarized public discourse but also to some degree the discourse of criminologists whose work was focused on the relationship between "race" and crime (Gold, 2003: Melchers, 2003). Much of the debate hinged on some relatively complex methodological issues and varying opinions of the degree to which the data could be trusted to make the inferences which were made (Gabor, 2004; Wortley and Tanner, 2005).

Another kind of study of police profiling was undertaken in the city of Kingston, Ontario between October 2003 and September 2004 by criminologist Scott Wortley. Unlike other studies, which focused only on incidents already in the police information system, this study collected information at the point of initial police contact. For purposes of the study, police officers were required to fill out a "contact card" which included the age, gender, and race of the person stopped, as well as the location, reason, and outcome of the stop (Wortley, 2005).

Of the 10,114 stops for which racial information was available, 2 percent (219) involved blacks. According to the 2001 census, there were 685 black people living in Kingston. Wortley suggests that when the proportion of stops of black people is divided by the proportion of blacks in the Kingston population, the resulting ratio is 3.5. In other words, blacks were more than 3 times more likely to be stopped by the police. In the case of younger blacks, the ratio was even higher.

Once again, critics found fault with the study on several counts. University of Ottawa criminologist Ron Melchers, for instance, has argued that the ratios constructed by Wortley really prove nothing unless we know how crime is distributed (McMahon, 2005). In other words, if blacks are more heavily involved in crime, the ratio may suggest prudent police work rather than racial profiling. In addition, it was argued that the study may have underestimated the number of blacks living in Kingston and that even more liberal estimates of the number are too small to allow meaningful analyses to be done (Porter, 2005). Clearly, much more research needs to be done before we arrive at any definitive answer regarding the potential relationship between police profiling and an over-representation of ethnic or racial minorities in Canadian crime statistics.

The Problem of Hate Crime

Questions about race and ethnicity are not restricted to offenders. Some criminologists argue that there is reason to be attentive to the relationship between measures of race and ethnicity on the one hand and the experience of being a victim on the other. The basic point is a simple one. Cultural groups might differ in the ways in which they experience the pains of victimization. It has been argued, for instance, that women of colour who experience wife assault may be reluctant to telephone the police because they are afraid of the manner in which the spouse (or even they themselves) might be treated. In a historical context, it has been argued that some groups—for instance, Italian-Canadians or Chinese-Canadians—have been very suspicious of state authority and have always been reluctant to mobilize the police or other formal social controls.

Controversies surrounding the race or ethnicity of victims is brought into sharpest relief in the case of "hate crimes." In Canada, the definition of hate crime has emerged out of the Criminal Code sections on Hate Propaganda and the Principles of Sentencing. Hate crimes are "offences motivated by bias, prejudice or hate based on race, national or ethnic origin, language, colour, religion, sex, age, mental or physical disability, sexual orientation or any other similar factor" (Criminal Code of Canada, Part XXIII, section 718, a(i)). In the case of sentencing, hate motivation can be considered as an aggravating circumstance.

Counting hate crimes presents an even more complicated scenario than does the counting of more garden variety crimes. Essentially, two kinds of approaches have been utilized. One involves the methodologies of victimization surveys. In other words, respondents to victim surveys might be asked if they think that crimes that have been committed against them are the result of hate motivation. Using this approach, the 1999 General Social Survey found that during the 12 months preceding the survey, about 4 percent of criminal incidents were considered by victims to be motivated by hate (Silver et al., 2004). The rate of self-reported hate crime was three times greater among people who described themselves as members of visible minorities than among other respondents to the survey.

The survey approach to the study of hate crime presents several problems. First, because such surveys tend to involve individuals, we never learn anything about hate crimes which might involve corporate victims—for instance, the desecration of a synagogue or graveyard. Second, the numbers of particular subgroups in even the largest samples might be too small to allow any kind of meaningful statistical analysis to be performed. Finally, survey approaches rest exclusively on the beliefs and perceptions of the respondents. This means that the only guide we have to the presence of hate motivation is the victim's perception. It is not difficult to think of situations in which this might prove less reliable than we would like. Unlike other kinds of victimization questions, victims are not being asked about their own feelings but about those of their offenders.

BOX 3.5

Measuring Hate Crime in a Victimization Survey

The 1999 General Social Survey asked respondents about their experiences with eight different kinds of victimization—sexual assault, robbery, assault, break and enter, theft of personal property, theft of household property, theft of motor vehicle and motor vehicle parts, and vandalism. When respondents indicated that a victimization had taken place, they were asked if they believed the crime could be considered a hate crime (Silver et al., 2004). The question was prefaced with the statement:

> There is a growing concern in Canada about hate crimes. By this I mean crimes motivated by the offender's hatred of a person's sex, ethnicity, race, religion, sexual orientation, age, disability, culture or language.

Respondents were then asked:

> Do you believe that this incident committed against you could be considered a hate crime?

If the answer was "yes," a subsequent question was asked:

> Was this because of the person's hatred of your sex, ethnicity, race, religion, sexual orientation, age, disability, culture or language?

Using such a measure, the GSS results indicated that during the 12-month period preceding the survey, 4 percent of the incidents were considered hate crimes by the victims. According to the victims, 43 percent of these incidents were related to race/ethnicity, and 18 percent each involved sex and culture. The remaining categories were collapsed into a general "other" category which accounted for 37 percent of the total. About three-quarters of the hate crimes in the GSS were personal crimes, and almost half were assaults.

A second approach to measuring hate crime could involve the use of police-generated data. In this model, the UCR information system could capture data regarding the presence or absence of an offender's hate motivation. As with all kinds of police-recorded data, this approach could only tell us about crimes which have come to the attention of the police. A more complicated issue relates to the need in the case of hate crimes for the police officers to render a judgment about the offender's motivation. While officers would have access to protocols for this purpose, it would be reasonable to expect a considerable amount of variability with respect to how this judgment is made. Motivations, after all, do not come one to a customer, and the identification of "hate" as the only source or an important source of criminal motivation cannot be done easily.

BOX 3.6

Calculating Crime Rates

To calculate a crime rate, we require three quantities. The first is a count of the number of crimes. In the expression (m/P)k, this is the quantity m. Based on data collected in the 2004 UCR, it has been estimated that in 2004 there were 2,690,719 Criminal Code violations.

Next we need a measure of the population that could have been involved in these crimes as victims or offenders. In the expression (m/P)k, the measure of the at-risk population is P. Based on census data, we estimate the 2004 population of Canadians to be 31,946,316.

Finally, in the expression (m/P)k, we need a constant, k, which will allow us to express the number of crimes that occur per k members of the population.

Putting all of the above together, we can calculate the rate of Criminal Code violations per 100,000 Canadians as follows:

$$\frac{2{,}690{,}719}{31{,}946.316} \times 100{,}000 = 8{,}423 \text{ criminal code violations per 100,000 population}$$

As this definition suggests, computing crime rates is fairly straightforward. First we develop some estimate of the numerator (m)—that is, some count of criminal events. We have already discussed the major forms of such counts—crimes recorded by the police or reported in victimization surveys or self-report studies. Next we select a measure of the denominator (P). This is generally thought of as a measure of the population that is exposed to the events, or is at risk of being involved in the events, as offenders or victims. The number we obtain when we divide the number of criminal events (m) by the measure of exposure or risk (P) is multiplied by some constant (k), so that the rate can be expressed per k units of exposure. The selection of the constant is largely arbitrary, but rates are traditionally expressed per 1,000 or per 100,000 units of exposure.

Using this approach, a pilot study 12 major Canadian police forces reported 928 hate crime incidents between 2001 and 2002 (Silver et al., 2004). The study also found that over half of all the hate crime incidents (57 percent) involved race/ethnicity. Of these incidents, blacks were most likely to be victimized (30 percent), followed by South Asians (18 percent), Arab/West Asians (14 percent), East and Southeast Asians (9 percent), and whites (9 percent).

CRIME RATES

The form in which we most often encounter reports of criminal events is the crime rate—a widely used measure in criminology. Although journalists and politicians, among others, often issue declarations about rates of crime, we are seldom encouraged to think critically about what crime rate measures really are.

The Nature of Crime Rates

Crime rate

A measure that calculates the amount of crime relative to the occurrence of some count of events, conditions, or people.

What are **crime rates**? As defined by Nettler (1984), "a rate compares events during a specified time against some base of other events, conditions or people. It takes the form $(m/P)k$, where m is a measure of some occurrence, P is a population count (or tally of some other condition of interest), and k is a constant" (47).

Some Uses of Crime Rates

The value of crime rate measures is that they allow us to develop some relative sense of the risks that crime poses. This relative character gives the crime rate an advantage over other kinds of indicators of the crime level which are sometimes referred to by journalists or members of the general public.

For instance, sometimes people make arguments about the seriousness of the crime problem through the use of raw numbers. We can note that in 2003, there were 549 homicides in Canada. In 2004, there were 622. The raw numbers have a certain power. In stark form, they describe a large amount of human suffering and loss in each year. Moreover, the situation seems to have deteriorated from 2003 to 2004. Seventy-three more people were killed in 2004 than in 2003. When we examine the homicide rates for the two years, however, the situation is largely unchanged; in each of the years, the homicide rate is 2 per 100,000 population. This is because the increase in homicides from 2003 to 2004 was accompanied by an increase in the size of the Canadian population (from 31,660,466 to 31,946,316).

Another form of presentation that often misleads the consumer of crime data is the crime clock. This is a device which is intended to show the frequency of crimes per unit of time. To present the homicide data for 2004 in the form of a crime clock, we begin by calculating the number of seconds in a year:

365 days $\times$ 24 hours $\times$ 60 Minutes $\times$ 60 seconds $= 31,536,000$

Then we divide the number of seconds by the number of homicides:

$31,536,000 \div 622 = 50,701$

This means that we can expect a homicide to occur every 50,701 seconds or every 845 minutes or every 14 hours.

For 2003, of course, we calculate the number of seconds in the same way:

365 days $\times$ 24 hours $\times$ 60 Minutes $\times$ 60 seconds = 31,536,000

However, the number of homicides is 549. The calculation for 2003 then is:

31,536,000 $\div$ 549 = 57,443

In other words, the 2003 crime clock suggests that in that year we would have expected a homicide every 57,443 seconds, every 957 minutes, or every 16 hours.

These figures, like the raw numbers, suggest that the situation has worsened from 2003 to 2004. However, as noted above, the rate has remained unchanged. The crime clock is misleading because it is presenting raw numbers in ways that seem to suggest they have somehow been standardized. The reason is simple. While population size is a variable which can change from one year to the next, the number of seconds in a minute or a year is a fixed number which does not really standardize the frequency with which crimes occur.

As criminologists, we make extensive use of crime rates when investigating criminal event patterns. By analyzing these rates, we can assess the value of particular theoretical arguments as to how and why these events occur. Crime rates are also used by non-criminologists for a variety of other purposes. One of the most popular is as a "social barometer" that indexes the quality of life (Bottomley and Pease, 1986). Just as the GNP is employed as an indicator of our collective economic well-being, crime rates are often read as indicators of our social well-being (Waller, 1982).

At a personal level, we may factor information about crime rates into our decisions about whether we will buy a home in a particular neighbourhood, vacation in a particular place, or allow our children to attend a particular school.

Crime Rates as Measures of Risk

Usually we are interested in crime rate measures to the extent that they are measures of risk. When we are told that "the rate of violence is much higher in the United States than in Canada," we are being led to believe that when differences in population sizes are taken into account, the risk of becoming a victim of violence is much greater south of the border than north of it. Similarly, when we are told that the neighbourhood to which we are thinking

BOX 3.7

Crime Rates as News

How do crime rates and other crime statistics become news? Vincent Sacco (2000) attempted to answer this question by examining news reports about crime statistics that appeared in the English-language print media during the calendar years 1993 and 1994. This investigation was organized around two broad issues.

The first concerned the means by which crime statistics become part of the news flow. To whose statistics are journalists attentive, and what are the "news hooks" on which stories featuring rates, trends, and percentages hang? The analysis of press coverage revealed that crime statistics become news in basically three ways:

- Most commonly, through a "data release" in the form of a press conference, the release of a new study, or the periodic release of data by some state agency.
- Through some form of "debunking"—that is, journalists (or those whom they cite) call into question what earlier statistics are leading audiences to believe.
- Through the use of statistical information as "background" with respect to some more substantive theme.

The second major issue addressed by the study involved the steps journalists took to turn "dry" and "boring" statistics into news. The analysis found that there was considerable journalistic energy invested in efforts to present statistics in ways that emphasized humour, drama, and the public interest.

---

of moving has a much higher crime rate than the neighbourhood in which we currently live, we may want to reconsider our decision.

How adequate are crime rates as measures of risk? The answer to this question depends on how much confidence we have in the numbers that are used in calculating the crime rate. We have already discussed the many problems that confound our tallies of criminal events (that is, the numerator m of the crime rate equation). However, we also should be concerned about crime rate denominators (P) (Andersen et al., 2003; Sprott and Doob, 2003).

In selecting a crime rate denominator, the usual practice is to use the total population residing within the jurisdiction in which the count of events has taken place. Such measures are usually referred to as **crude crime rates** because they provide only a very general assessment of the level of risk (Silverman, Teevan, and Sacco, 2000). They do not take into account the demographic characteristics of the population, or the empirical fact that different segments of the population are involved in criminal events with different levels of frequency. This problem is sometimes countered through the use of a denominator that better reflects the population at risk. When **age-specific crime rates** are

Crude crime rate
A crime rate measure which employs as a denominator the total population in some jurisdiction and thus which takes no account of the demographic structure of the population.

Age-specific crime rate
The crime risk for a certain age group.

calculated, the base number may include only people aged 18 to 24. However, the difficulties inherent in determining a number that accurately reflects particular subpopulations sometimes leaves such rates open to charges of inaccuracy.

Crime rates also are used to assess the effectiveness of community-based crime prevention programs such as Neighbourhood Watch and Operation Identification, as well as a large number of other criminal justice interventions (Gabor, 1990). As well, changes in crime rates are often used to evaluate the quality of police services.

Claims-making activities often include organized efforts to produce and publicize crime rate data that "document" the issues to which the claims-makers wish to draw attention (Best, 2001; Gilbert, 1997). According to Gilbert (1997), these efforts "embody less an effort at scientific understanding than an attempt to persuade the public that a problem is vastly larger than is commonly recognized" (63). Best (1988) and Hotaling and Finkelhor (1990) have written about how "advocacy numbers" have been used in defining the problem of missing children. They suggest that "guesstimates" of the number of children abducted by strangers have greatly overestimated the prevalence of the problem. Best maintains that the use of crime data for political purposes generally proceeds from three basic assumptions: big numbers are better than small numbers; official numbers are better than unofficial numbers; and big official numbers are best of all. As a result, data collection agencies, official or otherwise, may experience more pressure to keep numbers high than to keep them accurate (Reuter, 1984a).

Crime rates provide us with an important means for comparing crime incidence across jurisdictions and across groups. In this context, they have been offered as a way of measuring individual risk of crime victimization.

Nonetheless, we can reasonably argue that a more refined measure would take into account the differential risks faced by distinct segments of the population. Thus, since most of the crimes counted in crime and victimization rates involve young males, it may make more sense to standardize the level of risk in terms of the proportion of young males in the population rather than in terms of the total population. This is because a shift in the size of this segment of the population will more strongly affect the overall crime rate than will shifts in other segments of the population, such as elderly women.

HOW DO THEY DIFFER?

Crude versus Age-Specific Crime Rates

In selecting a crime rate denominator, the usual practice is to use the total population residing within the jurisdiction in which the count of events has taken place. Such measures are usually referred to as "crude crime rates." Age-specific crime rates use a denominator that better reflects the population at risk, such as individuals 18 to 24.

Ecological position
Incorporates geographic and economic relationships within a community into the analyses of crime rates.

Not only the demographic composition but also the location of communities may be relevant to an understanding of crime rates (Gibbs and Erikson, 1976; Stafford and Gibbs, 1980). The concept of **ecological position** refers to geographic and economic relationships that link the community for which the rate is being calculated, to nearby communities.

Ecological analyses help explain how two communities can have populations of similar size and demographic composition but differing crime rates. Say, for example, that Community A is a considerable distance from neighbouring communities so that the residents of those other communities do not commute to Community A, either for employment or for recreational purposes. In other words, the members of the neighbouring communities are not regularly available as offenders or victims in Community A. When the official crime rate of Community A is calculated in terms of the population residing within Community A, most of the at-risk population will be taken into account.

Say that, in contrast, Community B is a "central city" within a larger metropolitan area. Members of neighbouring communities travel to and spend most of their working days in Community B. As well, residents of these satellite communities regularly shop or attend cultural events in the central city. When the residents of the satellite communities commit crimes or are victimized as they visit Community B, these crimes are counted in the official crime rate of the central city. However, because these individuals are not residents of Community B, they are not counted in the denominator. If we fail to account for the differences in the ecological positions of Communities A and B, we may be at a loss to explain why the latter community has a generally higher crime rate.

The CCJS study (1990) that we mentioned earlier in this chapter suggests that some of the variation in the crime rates of Edmonton and Calgary may be attributable to differences in ecological position. Calgary has no significant suburban population; in contrast, around 100,000 people live in the suburbs surrounding Edmonton. When the rates for the two communities were recalculated on the basis of the metropolitan area rather than on the basis of city populations, the total Criminal Code rate for Edmonton was 8.2 percent lower, while the corresponding decrease in Calgary was only 0.43 percent.

At a more basic level, it is reasonable for us to ask whether population measures are adequate indicators of risk in the calculation of crime rates. Population measures suggest how many people expose themselves to risks (of offending or victimization), but they do not tell us *how frequently* they expose themselves. Populations differ not only with respect to demographic structure but also with respect to members' potential for victimization. For example, communities in which people regularly spend a great deal of time engaged in evening activities outside the home may have very different rates for some types of crimes than communities in which most people stay at home most of the time. The risky lifestyles that characterize the former communities make their members more vulnerable to victimization (Baron, 1997; Kennedy and Forde, 1990).

Many sociologists are now contending that we need to measure risk more directly (Balkin, 1979; Fattah and Sacco, 1989; Stafford and Galle, 1984). For instance, the elderly may have lower rates of victimization because they expose themselves less often to the risk of victimization; if their victimization rates were to be adjusted in this light, they might more closely approximate those of younger people (Lindquist and Duke, 1982). Efforts to examine such hypotheses have had only limited success (Clarke et al., 1985; Fattah and Sacco, 1989). Before we can investigate these issues comprehensively, we will need to considerably refine our definition of "exposure."

SUMMARY

Research data are indispensable to our understanding of criminal events. They allow us to test theoretical ideas; they help us to chart the dimensions of criminal events for policy purposes; and they provide us with indicators of the quality of life. Data about criminal events can be derived from many different sources, but tend to be generated by one of two basic investigative strategies: observation and reports.

Criminal events can be directly observed in naturalistic settings or in the context of field or laboratory experimentation. Much can be learned about criminal events by waiting for them to happen (as in field studies) or by making them happen (as in experiments), but most contemporary research depends on information revealed by reports about crime.

The reports used most widely are generated by those who are most active in criminal events: police, victims, and offenders. UCR data, which are collected by the police, describe a wide range of crimes and provide a continuous national record. Recent revisions to the UCR survey are likely to increase the value of UCR reports for both academic and policy purposes. The major limitation of UCR data relates to the fact that any police-based information system can tell us only about crimes that come to the attention of the police in the first place. Crimes that the police do not learn about—and there are a significant number of them—are not included in the UCR system.

Surveys of victims and offenders are intended to illuminate those crimes which are not recorded by the police. These surveys provide valuable information; they are also subject to all of the problems that characterize all surveys. Victims and offenders are not always as accessible as we would like them to be, and we cannot always be sure that they will not—intentionally or not—distort the truth in response to questions about their involvement in criminal events.

The problems associated with these major sources of crime data—police, victim, and offender reports—do not suggest a lack of knowledge or awareness on the part of those who collect the data. Rather, they alert us to the fact that any attempt to investigate complex social phenomena is fraught with inherent difficulties. The ways in which crime data construct our statistical images of crimes involving women and ethnic/racial minorities make this point.

Crime information can be presented in more and less responsible ways. Crime rates are intended to take into account characteristics of the population within which the crimes occur. Crime clocks and other rhetorical devices seem to resemble crime rates, but what they tell us is not all that useful.

No single data source is likely to answer all of our questions about criminal events. The major data sources tell us quite different things because they capture different types of events and bring different perspectives to bear on those events. For this reason, it is unproductive to engage in endless debates about the superiority of one data source over another. The usefulness of any data source depends heavily on how well it helps us address particular questions.

We should not dismiss crime data just because our data sources are flawed and less comprehensive than we would like. If we use them wisely, we can learn a great deal from crime data. Even when we know that our data are problematic, we often know *how* they are problematic. The errors that characterize our efforts at data collection are often systematic rather than random; when we know the sources and consequences of these systematic errors, data are more valuable than they might otherwise be.

QUESTIONS FOR REVIEW AND DISCUSSION

1. How useful are crime rates as a measure of our "quality of life"?
2. UCR crime data often figure prominently in press reports of crime trends. What does the informed news consumer need to know about these rates?
3. What types of data collection problems do victimization studies and offender self-report studies share?
4. What are some of the more important ethical problems confronting researchers in criminology?

5. Why is it too simplistic to claim that victimization surveys and self-report studies of offending are "better" than UCR reports?

6. Do the major forms of crime measurement support or dispute the popular notion that there are "lies, damned lies, and statistics"?

RECOMMENDED READINGS

Best, J. 2000. *Damned Lies and Statistics: Untangling Numbers from the Media, Politicians and Activists.* Berkeley: University of California Press.

Haggerty, K.D. 2001. *Making Crime Count.* Toronto: University of Toronto Press.

Kennedy, L.W., and V.F. Sacco. 1996. *Crime Counts: A Criminal Event Analysis.* Toronto: Nelson.

Mosher, C.J., T.D. Miethe, and D.M. Phillips. 2002. *The Mismeasure of Crime.* Thousand Oaks, CA: Sage Publications.

INFOTRAC® COLLEGE EDITION

Explore InfoTrac® College Edition, your online university library, which includes hundreds of popular and scholarly journals in which you can find articles related to the topics in this chapter. Visit InfoTrac® through your web browser (**www.infotrac-college.com**) or through this book's website (**www.criminalevent-4e.nelson.com**).

WHAT'S ON THE WEB?

For chapter links and quizzes, check out the accompanying website at **www.criminalevent-4e.nelson.com**.

Part 2

Theories of Crime

Chapter 4 | Psychosocial Conditions and Criminal Motivations

LEARNING OBJECTIVES:

- review what is meant by theoretical explanation
- discuss the intellectual origins of contemporary criminology and the enduring legacy of classical and positivist thought
- review and critically evaluate biocriminological accounts of criminal conduct
- describe the evolution theories which focus on the role of social conditions in criminal motivation
- examine the relationship between crime and social strain
- examine the relationship between culture and crime

In this chapter, we begin our review of the theories that have been used to explain crime. We focus on attempts to answer this question: Why are some people more inclined than others to behave in ways that violate the law? To this end, we examine the sources of offender motivation, including physiological and psychological deficiencies, troublesome social conditions, and the offender's commitment to cultural beliefs that condone criminal conduct.

INTRODUCTION

What are criminological theories, and why do we need them? In day-to-day conversation, we tend to use terms such as *theory* and *theoretical* to describe things that may be interesting but are irrelevant, unimportant, or impractical. We often dismiss what someone tells us with the retort, "That may be true in theory, but it doesn't have much to do with reality!" Students of criminology need to recognize that far from being irrelevant, theories can be extremely useful and practical analytical tools.

Criminological theories can be understood as generalized explanations of criminal phenomena (Bohm, 1997). They provide potential answers to questions about why crimes occur, why some types of people are more likely than others to be involved in crimes (as offenders or as victims), why crimes are more likely to occur in certain places and at certain times, and why agencies of social control respond to crime as they do.

Criminologists are not alone in seeking answers to these questions. Angry newspaper editorials offer seemingly reasonable accounts of why crime rates are rising. On any given Sunday morning, television preachers explain crime and associated problems in terms of evil forces at large in the world. Crime victims may ask what they did that led to their victimization. Though not always recognized as such, these accounts of why and how crimes occur represent a kind of theoretical thinking. However, we expect more from criminological theories than from the many "folk theories" that are part of our conventional wisdom.

First, criminological theories—at least of the type discussed in this book—are intended as general explanations rather than specific ones. Put another way, such theories are usually not interested in why one particular offender committed a particular crime; rather, they try to explain the patterns that characterize criminal phenomena in general. For example, we want our theories to tell us why males are more likely than females to commit a violent offence, why the chances of victimization are reduced as people grow older, and why crime rates shot up in the 1960s.

Second, we expect our theories to be consistent with—and help make sense out of—the *facts* of crime as revealed to us by research. The gross facts of crime, as we currently understand them, are often consistent with a variety of different theoretical perspectives. As a result, the evidence sometimes seems to support, at least partially, apparently competing views. For example, why do we find higher rates of many types of theft in bigger cities? Some sociologists have argued that large cities undermine the social controls that might discourage people from stealing (Wirth, 1938). Others have suggested that bigger cities are more likely to be home to the kinds of people (e.g., young, unmarried males) who tend to steal no matter where they live (Gans, 1962). Alternatively, we might argue that the city provides a setting that accommodates an elaborate

Criminological theories
Generalized explanations of why, how, and with what consequences crimes occur.

WHAT ARE THEY?

Criminological Theories

Theories provide us with answers to questions about why crimes occur, why some types of people are more likely than others to be involved in crimes as offenders or as victims, why crimes are more likely to occur in certain places and at certain times, and why agencies of social control respond to crime as they do.

network of thieves, targets, and fences and thereby turns theft into a profitable and enduring activity (Fischer, 1975; 1995).

On the surface, each of these theories of crime and urban life seems equally viable, since each is consistent with the general patterns of empirical data. This suggests that in order to assess the relative value of these theories, we need more detailed empirical knowledge about the relationship between crime and urban settings. As empirical data accumulate, we would hope to discover that one of the theoretical positions better accounts for the patterns we are observing.

This brings us to a *third* requirement of criminological theories: like all scientific theories, they must be falsifiable. That is, they must be stated in terms that allow us to test them, so that we can discover which theories provide false accounts of the phenomena we are observing. A theory that cannot be rejected no matter what we discover is of little use to us.

Criminological theories are not intellectual abstractions without real-life implications. On the contrary, they are often highly practical, especially when we use them as guides in our efforts to deal with crime as a social problem. Obviously, how we understand the causes of a problem has important consequences for what actions we take to resolve it.

The field of criminology has never been short of theories about crime. To the uninitiated, the choice of explanations can be bewildering: theories often seem to contradict or at least compete with one another. Our review focuses on several types of theoretical questions. The first question concerns the behaviour of offenders, discussed in this chapter and in Chapter 5. Why are some people more inclined than others to behave in ways that violate the law? In Chapter 6, we turn to another type of theoretical question. How do we understand the situations that allow offenders to act on their propensities? As we will see, an emphasis on situations and opportunities complements the more traditional motivational theories of crime. In Chapter 7, we examine theoretical explanations of what occurs in the aftermath of crime.

The Intellectual Origins of Criminology

The "founder" of criminology was an Italian philosopher named Cesare Beccaria, who wrote in the late 1700s about the need to take into account the psychological reality of the offender. The state, he contended, needs to use the fear of pain to control behaviour. Beccaria called for reform of the repressive and barbaric laws of the eighteenth century, an era when justice was administered in arbitrary and abusive ways. The offender's standing in the community had a direct impact on the treatment he or she could expect from the courts; justice in this sense was relative, rather than absolute.

According to Beccaria, the degree of punishment should be sufficient to outweigh the pleasure derived from the criminal act (Martin, Mutchnick, and Austin, 1990: 8). Beccaria's views, and those of Jeremy Bentham after him, heavily influenced modern thinking about deterrence and punishment. According to this **classical school** of thought, the "rational man" would act to avoid punishment. Thus, it was important that laws be clear about both how one should act and what the costs of deviating from this lawful behaviour would be (Bohm, 1997).

Beccaria is better described as a social reformer than as a criminologist in the modern sense of the term. He was more interested in changes that would make the criminal justice system effective and fair than he was in explaining the causes of crime. Beccaria was critical of the criminal justice systems of Europe for their use of torture and secret trials. He was especially troubled by the widespread and apparently random utilization of the death penalty. As well, judgeships were often auctioned to the highest bidder, and those who were accused of crimes did not have regular access to due process. Abuses of this type, Beccaria argued, violated both the freedom of individuals and the social contract that individual citizens made with the state. Laws, he argued, must be clear, simple, and directed only at those behaviours which actually threaten society.

Implicit in Beccaria's view was a model of what offenders are like and why they offend. For Beccaria, the offender's behaviour could be understood in terms of **hedonism**. In short, he saw the offender as a kind of rational calculator seeking to maximize pleasure and minimize pain. It follows that a person commits crime when the pleasure promised by the offence outweighs the pain that the law threatens.

The classical model of "rational man" led to a view that the law could be used as an instrument of control. This assumed, however, that men and women were not only free to act but also equal in their ability to do so.

Despite the insightful nature of Beccaria's work, he was not universally acclaimed. Indeed, the Catholic Church placed his classic work, *On Crimes and Punishment,* on the list of prohibited books. However, the legacy of the classical school remains powerful in the modern era. Much popular thinking about the "causes of crime," for instance, is consistent with the view that offenders offend because they somehow *choose* to do so. Our justice system assigns criminal responsibility largely on the basis of this assumption and

Classical school
A set of theories that views the offender as a "rational person" who would be deterred only by the threat of sanction.

Hedonism
The principle that the seeking of pleasure and the avoidance of pain are the ultimate aims and motivating forces of human action.

proceeds from the related assumption that legal threats are important in the control of criminal conduct. More central to our interests, we will discuss in Chapter 5 a group of theories that can be said to derive from some of the major theoretical assumptions of the classical school.

In the late 1800s, Cesare Lombroso began to question many of the views of the classical approach (Ferracuti, 1996). The century following the publication of Beccaria's work was marked by rapid and significant scientific progress. This period witnessed the birth of oceanography, the development of Darwinian theory, and early attempts at dating geological formations. In direct opposition to Beccaria's assumption that people have free will, Lombroso believed that human behaviour was *determined*. For Lombroso, individuals responded to their surroundings in predetermined ways, and some were born with behavioural deficiencies that led to criminality. In other words, heredity was a principal cause of criminal tendencies (Martin, Mutchnick, and Austin, 1990: 29). These assumptions led Lombroso to argue that "criminal types" existed.

Atavism
The theory that offenders are less likely to conform to the demands of contemporary social life because they reflect a more primitive evolutionary condition.

For Lombroso, one important type was the "atavistic criminal." Atavism suggests a throwback to an earlier period in human evolution. In other words, Lombroso's atavistic criminals were less likely to conform to the demands of contemporary social life because they reflected a more primitive human condition. Lombroso believed that the physical signs of atavism could be described and measured scientifically. Born criminals not only acted in a particular way but *looked* a particular way. The atavistic criminal often had ears of unusual size, fleshy lips, pouches in the cheeks, and a head of unusual size and shape (Vold, Bernard, and Snipes, 1998).

Lombroso was not suggesting that these physical characteristics directly caused criminal behaviour; his point was that they were indicators that the person was more likely to behave criminally.

Positivist school
The philosophical position, developed by Auguste Comte, that scientific knowledge can come only from direct observation, experimentation, and provision of quantitative data.

Lombroso is important not because of his specific theories, but because of how he approached the problem of crime generally. Unlike the classical writers who preceded him, he did not see crime as a product of free will; instead, he belonged to the positivist school, which considered crime in terms of causes and effects. For Lombroso, the science of criminal offending was not a matter of philosophical speculation but rather a research problem. He collected evidence by taking physical measurements of convicts and comparing them with measurements of (what he believed to

WHAT DOES IT MEAN?

Classical versus Positivist

Classical criminology views the offender as rational—that is, as deterred by the threat of legal sanction and responsive to social control. Positivists contend that criminal behaviour has causes outside those who perpetrate it, and that these causes can be studied using scientific principles.

be non-criminal) soldiers. While most of the specific ideas advanced by Lombroso were discredited (while he was still alive), the general approach endures. For many criminologists, the key to unlocking the puzzle of crime rests with the careful and systematic collection of research evidence, which will allow us to understand how those who commit crimes differ from those who do not.

Consistent with the views of the positivist school, the theories which we examine in this chapter encourage us to consider the factors that push or pull people into or away from criminal conduct. In contrast, the classical legacy is linked to theories that emphasize the factors constraining people from developing or acting on criminal motivations. As we will discuss in Chapter 5, when these constraints are weak, people have more freedom to do as they please—which sometimes means behaving criminally. As you will soon see, these ideas are not necessarily contradictory.

For all their differences, the various theories that fall within these two schools of thought share a fixation on criminality rather than on crime. That is, they focus on the offender rather than on the situations and broader social contexts within which offenders act.

EXPLAINING OFFENDER BEHAVIOUR

Classical and positivist perspectives differ in terms of the prominence they attach to the role of "will" in human affairs. Theories that derive from the classical school conceptualize criminal behaviour as willful and purposeful. Theories that derive from the positivist school perceive will as a less significant characteristic of criminal behaviour, and seek instead to understand how social and other factors compel—or at least encourage—criminal conduct. With respect to positivist theories, the focus of this chapter, three broad subthemes can be identified. The first views criminal motivation as resulting from deficiencies in the offender's physiological or psychological makeup. The second views offenders as a product of troublesome social conditions that propel them toward crime. The third views motivation as arising from the offender's commitment to cultural beliefs that condone criminal conduct.

BIOCRIMINOLOGICAL EXPLANATIONS OF CRIMINAL MOTIVATION

As we noted, modern scientific criminology is rooted in the work of the nineteenth-century biological positivist Cesare Lombroso and his students. Lombroso was interested in trying to understand how physical characteristics and evolutionary anomalies could explain why some people acted in ways that were prohibited by law. In the 1930s, interest began to shift away from the study of biological causation and toward the study of social causation. Almost from the start, criminology seems to have treated biological explanations with considerable suspicion (Wright and Miller, 1998: 14).

Recently, however, there has been a resurgence of interest in biological accounts of criminal offending. To a considerable degree, this reflects a growing tendency to view criminology as an "interdisciplinary" field. This development has been spurred by the publication of a large number of reviews and analyses of published research. These reviews and analyses have helped make the findings of biological research on crime more accessible to scholars who have not received biological training (Wright and Miller, 1998) (see Box 4.1).

The more recent biological theories differ from earlier ones in a number of ways (Cullen and Agnew, 1999; White and Hanes, 2000). *First*, as will become clear, recent theories focus on a range of biological factors, including genetic inheritance, and on a range of environmental factors, including diet and birth complications. *Second*, they do not argue that biological factors lead directly to crime; rather, they tend to argue that biological factors affect those developmental processes that result in conformity. *Third*, they usually argue that the impact of biological factors is mediated by the social environment. In other words, biology "interacts" with the social environment.

Genetics

Genetics
In criminology, a field of study that attempts to determine how certain presocial factors such as family ties and blood relations influence criminal outcomes (often in conjunction with environmental factors).

In recent years, there has been a renewed interest in the influence of **genetics** and physiology on the creation of criminal offenders. This school of thought argues that certain individuals are more likely to commit crimes due to faulty genetic programming (Mednick, Moffitt, and Stack, 1987).

The genetic approach has been taken in an effort to determine the importance of family ties or blood relations to individual deportment. It is argued that violent crime, in particular, can be explained in terms of genetics. For instance, individuals with intimate family ties offer the same protection from harm to family members as animals offer to their blood connections. In contrast, individuals with less intimate ties (e.g., adopted children) are more likely to be subject to violence from non-blood relations (e.g., stepparents) (see Daly and Wilson, 1988). Ellis (1982) conducted a review of genetic explanations of crime. Genes influence behaviour through the nervous system. Humans may be so similar genetically that we cannot explain differences in behaviour by genetic variation; forces outside the individual must

BOX 4.1

Biology and Crime

A useful summary of much of the empirical research on the relationship between biological factors and crime has been provided by Patricia A. Brennan, Sarnoff A. Mednick, and Jan Volavka (1995). Their review of a large number of studies reaches the following conclusions:

On Genetics
"Criminal behavior in parents increases the likelihood of nonviolent crime in the offspring. The relationship is due, in part, to genetic transmission of criminogenic characteristics. This genetic effect is stronger for females and is especially important for recidivistic crime."

On Perinatal Factors
"Delivery complications are associated with juvenile and adult violent crime. The effect of delivery complications on crime is stronger in more unstable families."

On Neuropsychological and Neurological Factors
"Frontal lobe dysfunction has been found to be associated with adult violent crime. Left hemisphere front-temporal dysfunction is related to a wide variety of antisocial outcomes."

On Neurochemical Factors
"Reduced cerebrospinal fluid 5-hydroxyindoleacetic acid (a metabolite of serotonin) levels have been found in individuals exhibiting impulsive aggression, especially those with a history of alcohol abuse."

On Psychophysiology
"Antisocial individuals evidence reliably reduced levels of autonomic reactiveness and poor conditioning of autonomic responses. Prospective studies reveal a relationship between EEG slow alpha activity in childhood and arrests for property crime in adulthood."

On Biosocial Interactions
"Biosocial factors have been found to be especially likely to predict criminal outcome when combined with adverse social environments."

count for more. So how do nature (genes) and nurture (environment) influence human behaviour, and criminality in particular? The debate on this question is old and heated. The effects of the two forces have been studied in four different ways: general pedigree studies; twin studies; karyotype studies; and adoption studies.

General pedigree studies
A non-experimental approach to the study of intergenerational transmission of genetically predisposed behaviour between related individuals.

As Ellis (1982) explains, **general pedigree studies** involve establishing the extent to which people who are related also behave similarly. This approach is non-experimental, because it is difficult to control the effects of common genetic background versus environmental influences. Parents share both genetic and environmental factors with their children; it follows that if both parents and children are criminal, it is likely because of these shared factors rather than some environmental factor they do not share. The evidence shows that 30 to 45 percent of individuals with criminal records had one or more parents with criminal records. But knowing about "crime in the family" does not really make it easier for us to use genetics in explaining criminality. This is because it is almost impossible to detach family biology from environmental factors (including family socialization) (Curran and Renzetti, 2001).

Twin studies
A non-experimental study designed to research and compare criminal predispositions between dizygotic and monozygotic twins.

The second type of non-experimental design is the **twin study**. According to Ellis (1982), this design allows us to compare the two types of twinning that occur in humans. Most often, twins are the result of two ova fertilized by two separate sperm. These dizygotic (DZ) twins share 50 percent of genetic programming. In contrast, if a single fertilized ovum splits very early in its development, monozygotic (MZ) twins, who share 100 percent of genetic programming, are formed. A key concept in twin studies is the notion of "concordance." Concordance is a quantitative measure of the degree to which the observed behaviour or trait of one twin matches that of the other (Akers, 1994). Of central interest for our purpose is the degree of concordance regarding criminal behaviour.

Twin studies show a higher level of concordance between MZ twins in their criminality than between DZ twins. This has led some researchers to conclude that genetic commonalities are the key contributory factors (Katz and Chambliss, 1995). However, because of the strong similarity in their appearance, MZ twins elicit common responses from others more than do DZ twins. This similarity in treatment—a factor in the socialization of MZ twins—may be more important in guiding behaviour than the fact that they share genetic programming. Twin studies also seem to show that the inherited factors associated with crime are more powerful among women than among men (Hodgins, 2000). Like other genetic studies, twin studies are characterized by a large number of methodological problems—for instance, wide variation in the ways in which

DO THEY EXIST?

Crime Genes

Until we can improve our methods, we have no real scientific basis for arguing for (or against) the existence of a "crime gene."

criminality is defined and in the methods according to which zygosity is determined (Curran and Renzetti, 2001).

The third type of study discussed by Ellis (1982) involves genetic karyotypes. **Karyotype studies** compare the size, shape, and number of specific chromosomes in individuals. Some researchers report that in criminal males, the Y chromosome has a higher than expected probability of being larger. Also, research shows that some offenders have an unusual number of chromosomes—that is, a number other than the 23 pairs typical in humans. XYY karyotype males are rare among the criminal population, but they are still more likely to be encountered there than among the general population. The research in this area suffers from small samples and inconclusive explanations. The correlations that exist are not readily interpreted as causative factors.

Karyotype studies
These claim that an individual's chromosomes—that is, their size, shape, and number—are a causal factor in criminality.

A related idea that has attracted the attention of the mass media, the public, and some academics is the premenstrual syndrome (PMS) hypothesis. Like the XYY argument, the PMS argument derives from the idea that the origins of crime and violence can somehow be found in gender-based genetic differences (Katz and Chambliss, 1995). Explanations attributing causal significance to PMS imply that women—like men—may do things the law disallows because of hormonal imbalances. However, as with the XYY argument, the attention paid to the PMS theory probably outstrips whatever explanatory value the idea may have. Many feminists contend that the PMS hypothesis lends a scientific gloss to the old stereotype that women are emotional prisoners of their biology.

The fourth design is based on **adoption studies**. As Ellis (1982) points out, we can contrast the behaviour of near-birth adoptees (people adopted by non-relatives shortly after birth) with that of both their genetic and their adoptive parents. If the behaviour is due to genetics, adoptees should more closely resemble their genetic parents (whom they have never seen) than their adoptive parents. Of course, identical twins would be ideal for such studies, but it is unusual for such twins to be separated, so research of this type is rare (Coleman and Norris, 2000). Still, properly executed adoption studies offer a powerful experimental design for isolating the influences of genetic factors from the influences of socialization and other environmental effects. For example, if some individuals exhibit criminal tendencies that are consistent with their birth parents but not with their adoptive parents, it is assumed that this behaviour is due to genetic programming.

Adoption studies
The behavioural comparison of near-birth adoptees to their genetic and their adoptive parents.

In the research to date, the efficacy of using *genotypes*—that is, genetic makeups—to identify likely candidates for criminal behaviour is not very well established. The most credible research is provided by adoption studies; these have in fact reported fairly low rates of concordance between the offending patterns of identical twins who were separated at birth and raised with different families (Mednick, Moffitt, and Stack, 1987). Adoption studies offer little evidence that genetic differences explain differences in criminality.

Walters and White (1989: 478) summarized the problems of genetic-based research as follows:

> Genetic factors are undoubtedly correlated with various measures of criminality, but the large number of methodological flaws and limitations in the research should make one cautious in drawing any causal inferences at this point in time. Our review leads us to the inevitable conclusion that current genetic research on crime has been poorly designed, ambiguously reported, and exceedingly inadequate in addressing the relevant issues.

Until these deficiencies are addressed, there is no real scientific basis for arguing for (or against) the existence of a crime gene.

Crime gene
The sociobiological perspective that certain genes may be linked to criminality.

DNA

An interesting new debate is developing around the use of genetic profiling using DNA in criminal proceedings. In many countries, extensive programs have been developed to create DNA archives using material acquired from convicted felons. This information, it is argued, is not only helpful in establishing guilt or innocence of offenders but can also provide important bases for profiling criminals and preventing crime. In the U.S., the FBI DNA database, CODIS, includes a compilation of data acquired from state level archives. This information includes only information on those who have been convicted, but there is interest in expanding this program to include information on those who are arrested. In the United Kingdom, a similar initiative to add arrestee information to DNA databases developed by the Home Office has generated a great deal of debate, as there is concern that this practice will impinge on the genetic privacy of individuals not actually convicted of a crime. In Britain, the agencies involved in collecting DNA material point to the real progress that has been made in crime investigations with the help of genetic profiling (Home Office, 2005).

The role that DNA has played in bringing stronger investigative tools to crime control is indisputable. The questions about privacy raise some important issues about how we might use these data in a way that does not prejudge court cases. In addition, there will be a temptation to start using these databases to begin profiling genetic characteristics of offenders. In other words, the genetic matches for individuals that assist in determining the identity of offenders in particular crimes can be aggregated to build profiles of certain types of genetic patterns that connect to certain types of crimes. This will bring progress in our study of the links between genetics and crime but may pose some interesting ethical issues, as well. For example, suppose that we find that there is a preponderance of specific genetic patterns in sexual offenders? Do we sample everyone's DNA to determine whether or not individuals share these patterns and, if they do, preclude them from certain activities, for example, teaching in schools or running day care centres?

Constitution

Biological approaches have also focused on the constitutional structure (that is, the body types and psychological propensities) of offenders. After reviewing research by Garofalo (1914) on Italian convicts and studies by Sheldon (1949) on incarcerated juveniles, Wilson and Herrnstein (1985) concluded that certain physiological similarities can be detected among offenders. For example, short, muscular young males are more likely than others to appear in prison populations. According to Wilson and Herrnstein (1985: 103), "The biological factors whose traces we see in faces, physiques, and correlation with behaviour of parents and siblings are predispositions towards crime that are expressed as psychological traits and activated by circumstance."

The difficulty with the constitutional approach is that knowing about body type doesn't tell us much about a person's propensity to act criminally; it merely tells us (and only if we believe the research) that some inmates happen to be short and muscular. Moreover, body typing ignores the fact that one of the most popular activities in men's prisons is weightlifting. It also fails to consider the fact that in a violent encounter, the less muscular combatant will tend to lose the contest and end up in the hospital, while the more muscular participant will emerge as the victor and end up in prison. Furthermore, this approach doesn't address other important factors related to crime, including the circumstances in which a motivated offender comes to participate in criminal activity.

In defending the constitutional approach to criminality, Wilson and Herrnstein (1985) borrowed from classical criminology to argue that crime is

Constitutional structure
Predispositions toward crime are claimed to be expressed by biological factors, such as phenotypes (body types) and psychological propensities.

Body type
In order to determine the relationship between physique and criminality, Sheldon categorized ("somatotyped") three basic types of body build—endomorphic, ectomorphic, and mesomorphic—that are associated with a particular type of temperament.

BOX 4.2

Body Type and Criminal Behaviour

In a famous study, William Sheldon (1949) tried to determine the relationship between physique and the tendency to engage in criminal behaviour. Sheldon used a method called somatotyping to categorize three basic types of body build—endomorphic, ectomorphic, and mesomorphic. Each of these, he argued, was associated with a particular type of temperament.

As pictured in Figure 4.1, the body types represent extreme forms. Most individuals are a combination of all three types.

Having compared a sample of known delinquents with a control group of students, Sheldon concluded that delinquents were more likely to have mesomorphic physiques and the accompanying temperament, which emphasized risk-taking, adventure, and an interest in physical activity.

Figure 4.1

Sheldon's Somatotypes in Relation to Physique and Temperament

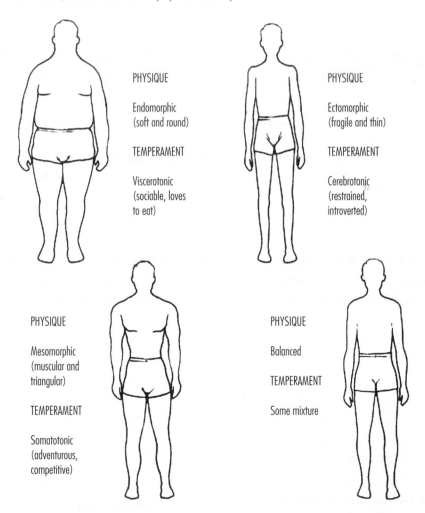

PHYSIQUE

Endomorphic
(soft and round)

TEMPERAMENT

Viscerotonic
(sociable, loves
to eat)

PHYSIQUE

Ectomorphic
(fragile and thin)

TEMPERAMENT

Cerebrotonic
(restrained,
introverted)

PHYSIQUE

Mesomorphic
(muscular and
triangular)

TEMPERAMENT

Somatotonic
(adventurous,
competitive)

PHYSIQUE

Balanced

TEMPERAMENT

Some mixture

Source: Bartol, Curt R. 1991. *Criminal Behaviour: A Psychosocial Approach*. 3rd ed. Englewood Cliffs, NJ: Prentice-Hall.

a rational act based on a calculation of potential gain versus loss. Through this process, individuals weigh the probabilities that they will succeed or fail in their endeavours. Individuals may discount potential costs through a process whereby immediate gratification becomes the paramount concern. This choice is not really a free choice, however, as it is predetermined by poor socialization and constitutional deficiencies. The short time horizons possessed by individuals with these deficiencies distort how they make their decisions about benefits and costs. These individuals will tend to involve themselves in criminal activity for short-term gain. According to Wilson and Herrnstein, they represent criminal types who need to be isolated and subjected to high levels of deterrence. Thus, the state's role is to set up contingencies that will reduce the benefits and increase the costs of misbehaviour.

The deterministic nature of constitutional theories firmly establishes them in a positivistic framework that maintains there is little offenders can do to change their propensities to act criminally. From this perspective, we need to reduce the likelihood of criminal activity by isolating individuals who are likely to be problem offenders.

Diet

Some researchers are interested in the degree to which diet can affect behaviour. Strong scientific evidence supports the idea that certain individuals are more prone to hyperactivity or aggressive behaviour following a sudden intake of sugar (hypoglycemia) (Dorfman, 1984). In a famous case, a San Francisco city supervisor attributed his 1978 murder of the mayor and a fellow supervisor to his diet of Twinkies and other "junk food." His lawyers were able to use what has come to be known as the Twinkie defence to convince a jury that their client suffered from "diminished mental capacity" and was therefore not guilty of murder.

Some researchers contend that food allergies—for instance, to milk, eggs, or chocolate—can lead to aggressive or violent behaviour (Wright and Miller, 1998). The idea that diet can be a major cause of violence seems questionable; that being said, it is clear that a change of diet can have a dramatic effect on the behaviour of prisoners. In a study of detention homes in California, it was established that when the diet of 276 juveniles was revised—mostly by reducing sugar intake—antisocial behaviour declined by 48 percent, incidents of theft by 77 percent, incidents of

Diet
The concept that the behaviour of certain individuals can be affected by their diet.

Twinkie defence
When a defendant experiences diminished mental capacity and is therefore not guilty of criminal behaviour due to an over-consumption of junk food.

WHAT IS IT?

The Twinkie Defence
The argument that due to the over-consumption of junk food, a defendant experienced "diminished mental capacity" and is therefore not guilty of criminal behaviour.

assault by 82 percent, and refusal to obey orders by 55 percent (Kinderlehrer, 1983: 143). Similar results were obtained when supplies of orange juice were increased—a finding that has led some researchers to attribute the former negative behaviours not to excessive sugar content but rather to vitamin and nutrient deficiencies in prisoners' diets (Dorfman, 1984). A study of a British prison, conducted in 2003, showed a 25 percent difference in antisocial behaviour among prisoners who were provided daily capsules of vitamins, minerals, and essential fatty acids compared to those who received a placebo capsule that contained no supplements (Lawson, 2003).

Research recently discussed in *The Economist* suggests that the intake of omega-3 acid that is derived from eating seafood has an important long-term effect on the health and behaviour of children. The study, on 14,000 pregnant women, was conducted in the United States by Joseph Hibbeln, a researcher at America's National Institutes of Health. Hibbeln said that the study produced "frightening data," showing that 14 percent of those seven-year-olds whose mothers had had the lowest intake of omega-3s during pregnancy demonstrated antisocial behaviour, compared with 8 percent of those born to the highest-intake group. Hibbeln stated, "This is particularly worrying in the light of work which shows that pathological behaviour in childhood is a good predictor of a lifetime of aberrant behaviour" (The Economist, 2006). These findings raise some interesting questions about the connection of diet to long-term delinquent behaviour. The caution that is needed in looking at these results relates to the connection that is made between what is considered aberrant behaviour and delinquency.

The focus on nutrients has led to research on the relationship between trace element patterns and a predisposition to violence. One study compared 24 pairs of violent and nonviolent brothers; a second study matched 96 violent males of mixed age and background with 96 nonviolent males who served as a control group. The research revealed that the violent subjects fell into two groups: type As, who tested high in copper and low in sodium and potassium and who were episodically violent, and type Bs, who were the reverse and who displayed consistently antisocial behaviour. As the type A pattern tends to fade with age, parole boards could use hair analysis (a procedure for tracking trace elements) to predict, on the basis of the mineral content in the subject's body, when episodic violence will likely cease (Dorfman, 1984: 46).

The applicability of these findings to offenders outside institutions is impossible to determine. They do provide some interesting suggestions as to how lifestyle—especially diet—influences our actions. They do not tell us

Trace elements

Mineral content in the subject's body which determines episodic violence or antisocial behaviour.

much about what situations elicit violence, or about what social factors (e.g., early childhood socialization, peer pressure, or fear of stigmatization) may play a role in deterring it.

The ingestion of substances other than food has attracted a great deal of attention in criminological analyses. Drugs, including alcohol, are present in many criminal events. The criminality that surrounds the illicit sale and purchase of drugs makes their use of interest to us. As with dietary factors, it is unclear how important drugs are in explaining criminality. Their presence in criminal situations may be related to but not central to explanations of criminality. Many people use (and abuse) alcohol without becoming violent and attacking other people. Yet, as evidenced by the many bar fights that occur, alcohol sometimes seems to fuel violent attacks.

Explanations based on genetics, constitution, and diet can be summed up this way: if one accepts that crime is a cultural and social concept, defined through custom and law, it seems unlikely that such a thing as a "criminal type" or a "crime gene" exists whereby behaviour is preprogrammed to deviate from this social construct—or, indeed, that certain people with particular body types or particular diets will generally offend. These explanations, while interesting, seem to be more useful for describing the conditions of incarcerated offenders and assisting in controlling their behaviour than for predicting the likelihood of criminality in the first place.

Intelligence And Crime

Neuropsychological Theory

There has been an upsurge in interest in the relationship between IQ and behaviour (see Murray and Herrnstein, 1994). It has long been recognized in criminological research that a correlation exists between IQ and delinquency. According to one well-known expert:

IQ
A measure of intelligence derived from standardized testing procedures that compare individuals' mental and chronological ages.

> After sex and age, the single most firmly established psychological fact about the population of offenders is that the distribution of their IQ scores differs from that of the population at large. Instead of averaging 100, as the general population does, offenders average about eight points lower (Herrnstein, 1995: 49).

What remains in doubt is the meaning of the "weak to moderate negative correlation between IQ (intelligence quotient) and delinquent behavior" (Akers, 1994: 77). Some researchers contend that the relationship between IQ

Neuropsychological theory
The theory that people with identical IQ scores can have very different patterns of mental strengths and weaknesses (e.g., verbal skill, spatial perception) that can influence behaviour.

and crime may be indirect—that IQ affects school performance and delinquency results from these problems in school (Hirschi and Hindelang, 1977). Moffitt, Lynam, and Silva (1994) argue that one way to approach this issue is to look beyond IQ by applying neuropsychological theory, according to which people with identical IQ scores can have very different patterns of mental strengths and weaknesses. Moffitt, Lynam and Silva claim that IQ offers limited information about which of these strengths or weaknesses influences behaviour. The IQ test compresses an aggregate measure of abilities (notably verbal skills and spatial perception) into a single composite indicator of performance. Most neuropsychological test batteries include a standard IQ test, which measures verbal and spatial functions very accurately, but they also add more tests to cover functions such as memory, motor skills, and mental self-control. A battery of neuropsychological tests can reveal, for instance, that children with identical low IQ scores may be suffering from different and relatively isolated problems such as impulsive judgment, weak language processing, poor memory, or inability to match visual information with motor actions. Each type of deficit could be more accurate than the overall IQ in predicting delinquency, but each would contribute to delinquency through a unique theoretical causal chain (Moffitt et al., 1994: 279).

IQ continues to attract a great deal of controversy when discussed in the context of crime. The researchers who advocate this approach point to the fact that while IQ is considered a weak indicator of antisocial behaviour, it has been embraced by the United States Supreme Court in its judgments about whether on not to ban execution for low-IQ offenders (Sailer, 2006).

Learning Disabilities

Learning disabilities
Difficulties faced by children and youths such as dyslexia, dysgraphia, aphasia, perceptual and motor deficits, poor intersensory integration, and minimal brain dysfunction.

Culliver and Sigler (1991) provide an extensive review of the relationship between learning disabilities and juvenile delinquency. Learning disabilities are defined as problems faced by children and youths such as dyslexia, dysgraphia, aphasia, perceptual and motor deficits, poor intersensory integration, and minimal brain dysfunction. Although these disabilities are often difficult to detect, it is strongly believed that they are directly related to delinquent behaviour in youths.

Culliver and Sigler report that five hypotheses have been used to study this relationship:

School failure hypothesis
The theory that self-perpetuating academic failure resulting from learning disabilities causes frustration and aggressive behaviour.

- The school failure hypothesis argues that academic failure results from learning disabilities and that this failure becomes self-perpetuating. Because they are frustrated by their failure, students become more aggressive and are in turn labelled as troublesome. This leads to rejection from teachers and administrators, which in turn leads these youths to withdraw from mainstream activities and become involved in inappropriate behaviour, and, ultimately, delinquency.

- The susceptibility hypothesis contends that learning disabled students have unique characteristics, such as impulsiveness, inability to anticipate future consequences, and irritability. In acting out their feelings, they are more likely to become delinquent.

- The differential arrest hypothesis posits that learning disabled students are more likely to be apprehended by police because they are less able to conceal their activities than are their non-learning-disabled peers. This hypothesis also suggests that learning disabled students cannot effectively interact with police because of their abrasiveness and poor social perception and are therefore more likely to be arrested.

- The differential adjudication hypothesis argues that delinquents with learning disabilities who are arrested and charged are more likely to be convicted of crimes due to their inability to cope with the process of criminal justice adjudication. "Moreover, learning disabled students are unable to vindicate their feelings and concerns regarding the criminal charges" (Culliver and Sigler, 1991: 125).

- The differential disposition hypothesis argues that learning disabled delinquents face a higher chance of receiving harsher sentences than do non-learning-disabled delinquents.

Culliver and Sigler report that while the potential link between learning disabilities and delinquency has generated much interest, research results "tend to create more confusion and uncertainty than fact upon which sound theories can be built and effective programs developed" (1991: 125). This same conclusion is reached by Cornwall and Bawden (1992) in their assessment of the link between reading disabilities and aggression. As Skaret and Wilgosh (1989) state, the problems with the research should lead us to deal with the effects of learning disabilities on delinquency in a different way. Instead of struggling to provide definitive findings supporting a causal relationship, perhaps we should pay attention to the fact that adolescents with learning disabilities seem to be at relatively high risk for delinquency. "Sound remedial education practices, including counselling and other support systems will improve academic achievement and social skills, and *may, possibly*, lead to some reduced delinquent behaviour" (Skaret and Wilgosh, 1989: 121). This is the

Susceptibility hypothesis
The theory that learning disabled students have unique characteristics, such as impulsiveness and irritability, and thus are more likely to become delinquent.

Differential arrest hypothesis
The theory that learning disabled children are more likely to be apprehended by the police since they are less likely to conceal their activities.

Differential adjudication hypothesis
The theory that delinquents with learning disabilities who are arrested and charged are more likely to be convicted of crimes due to their inability to cope with the process of criminal justice adjudication.

Differential disposition hypothesis
The theory that learning disabled delinquents have a higher chance of receiving harsher sentences than other delinquents.

same prescription offered by Moffitt, Lynam, and Silva (1994) in their conclusions about the remedial effects of using psychoneurological testing in assessing propensity toward delinquency.

Psychopathology

Psychopathology
Study of abnormal behaviour.

Psychopathy
A sociopathic disorder characterized by lack of moral development and the inability to show loyalty to others.

For the most heinous crimes, such as sexually motivated murders and serial murders, we often apply the label of **psychopath** to the perpetrator.

Psychopaths are often described as aggressive, insensitive, charismatic, irresponsible, intelligent, dangerous, hedonistic, narcissistic, and antisocial. They are perceived as superb manipulators, and as capable of pretending to possess "normal" human emotions even while remorselessly carrying out their personal agendas. They are outwardly normal but are famously unable to maintain long-term commitments to people or programs.

It is believed that psychopaths are more dangerous than other criminals, and that they behave criminally consistently over their lifetime. It has been argued that psychopathy results from a number of environmental causes; it has also been argued that biological factors play a role in producing psychopathy. For example, Hodgins (2000: 225) states that there is indeed evidence that a genetic factor contributes to psychopathy. Because of differences in their autonomic nervous systems, psychopaths may be less responsive to incoming stimuli that would normally produce a fear reaction. If it is correct that psychopaths possess a nervous system that dampens stimulation, they may be suffering from a kind of "stimulation hunger" that causes them to seek out stimulation even while simultaneously failing to learn from the aversive conditioning to which they are subjected (Katz and Chambliss, 1995). Jeffery (1990: 364) suggests that we look at psychopaths in terms of how the nervous system functions in times of threat. As Jeffery points out, psychopaths do not become anxious or fearful in the presence of punishment or danger because their autonomic nervous systems are not aroused by danger. Also, because psychopaths are unable to anticipate the consequences of their actions, they make little attempt to avoid punishment or pain.

Sociopathy
Antisocial personality disorder involving a marked lack of ethical or moral development.

According to Hickey (1991), the term *psychopath* is used to describe a wide range of individuals who have been determined by societal and medical standards to possess antisocial qualities and characteristics. Hickey adds that the label of psychopath is used interchangeably with that of **sociopath**. Furthermore, because the term is so general, the psychopath "often turns out to be exactly what we want him or her to be" (1991: 50). In other words, the concept of the psychopathic personality is so broad that it could apply to almost anyone who breaks the law (Akers, 1994). Psychopathic characteristics such as irresponsibility, untruthfulness, and a lack of guilt associated with antisocial conduct are just as discernible in successful corporate executives, athletes, and even national leaders as they are in criminals. Not surprisingly, estimates of the number of psychopaths in the population vary wildly, from 10 percent to 80 percent depending on the definition of psychopath being employed.

For criminological researchers, the dilemma in all of this is that psychopaths can hide their symptoms while leading "normal" lives. We only learn about their tendencies after they act out their antisocial fantasies. Often it takes some time to uncover these individuals' acts, as shown by the long crime sprees of serial murderers. Paul Bernardo and his wife Karla Homolka were convicted in the 1990s for the torture-murder of two Ontario schoolgirls; they were regarded by many of their neighbours as normal members of the community.

SOCIAL CONDITIONS AND CRIMINAL MOTIVATION

It has been argued that people's social circumstances can make it difficult for them to be law-abiding. Criminal behaviour can thus be understood as the means people resort to in attempting to deal with the problems and frustrations they encounter in their lives.

From this perspective, many types of crime and delinquency can be understood as forms of "problem solving" (Brezina, 2000). That is, individuals commit crimes in order to adapt to conditions and situations that threaten them in some way. Criminals are not sick and are not the victims of faulty genes; rather, they are rational actors whose behaviour is goal-oriented. This perspective encourages us to understand that crime often has a real appeal for the offender.

Frustrated Ambitions

People who aspire to goals they cannot realistically attain may feel pressure to behave criminally. This pressure is most likely to be felt by those who occupy disadvantaged positions in the social structure. Perhaps the best-known version of this argument was articulated in the late 1930s by the sociologist Robert Merton, who was trying to explain how particular forms of social organization create the strains that lead to nonconformity.

Using American society as an example, Merton (1938) argued that if everyone is encouraged to pursue material success, those who do not have access to legitimate means for achieving that success will be frustrated by their lack of opportunity. Those at the bottom of the social hierarchy—the poor, ethnic minorities, recent immigrants—do not have easy access to inheritance, quality education, or other means for realizing the American Dream. Since success is still important to them, they must find ways to adjust to the social strain society places on them. These adjustments may often involve criminal conduct.

BOX 4.3

Merton's Paradigm of Deviant Behaviour

Robert Merton (1938) argued that nonconformist behaviour results when people are encouraged to pursue cultural goals that prevailing social arrangements do not allow them to achieve. These individuals may have internalized these goals, but they also lack legitimate means for achieving them. As a consequence, they must adjust their behaviour to accommodate the gap between the goals and the means. Merton identified five adaptations in the goals–means relationship.

1. Conformity   Individuals who make this adaptation accept as legitimate both the goals and the means for achieving them. This is the adaptation most people make.
2. Innovation   Innovation involves accepting the goals but rejecting the means of goal attainment. For example, a person who embezzles accepts material gain as a legitimate goal but rejects the culturally prescribed means for achieving it.
3. Ritualism   This adaptation involves accepting the means for achieving the goal but rejecting the goal itself. Individuals who engage in ritualism simply "go through the motions" without coming any closer to the goals they supposedly seek.
4. Retreatism   Here, both means and goals are rejected. At least in terms of what the culture prescribes, those who opt for this adaptation can be described as dropouts.
5. Rebellion   Like retreatism, this form of adaptation involves rejecting both goals and means. Rebellion differs from retreatism in that it involves substituting other goals as well as other means by which they might be achieved.

Merton presented his five adaptations in schematic form as follows (where + means accept and − means reject).

	Goal	Means
Conformity	+	+
Innovation	+	−
Ritualism	−	+
Retreatism	−	−
Rebellion	−	−
	(+)	(+)

In his **anomie theory**, Merton proposed that frustration and alienation develop when individuals who aspire to society's economic goals (including upward social mobility) lack access to the means for achieving those goals. That is, a gap exists between expectations and opportunity. In responding to the anomie that develops due to this gap, they adapt in certain ways. One such adaptation involves resorting to crime to achieve conventional goals such as wealth. Blau and Blau (1982) argued that it is not absolute but relative deprivation that results in frustration and a sense of personal injustice; this, in turn, leads to criminal activity.

Anomie theory
Theory that says anomie occurs when there is a lack of integration between the cultural goals which people are encouraged to pursue and the legitimate means available for achieving those goals.

Consider the gangster Al Capone. Arguably, the goals to which he aspired did not differ significantly from the goals pursued by "legitimate" business-people. Capone sought wealth, power, and celebrity. He differed from conventional entrepreneurs with respect to the means he employed to achieve these objectives but not with respect to the objectives themselves. Seen in this way, the behaviour of gangsters, thieves, and other goal-oriented criminals is best understood as the product not of a pathological personality but of social arrangements that create a gulf between what people aspire to and what is actually available to them.

Status Deprivation

Several years after Merton published his work, Albert Cohen followed a similar line in his investigation of gang delinquency among working-class juveniles. In Cohen's view (1955), much juvenile crime was rooted in the problems experienced by disadvantaged youths. These youth aspired to middle-class status, but were often judged inadequate by a school system that dispensed status rewards on the basis of middle-class criteria. In other words, children from the working class typically found that their socialization experiences had not prepared them to compete effectively for status in the classroom; as a result, they came up short when they were assessed by the school's **middle-class measuring rod**. According to Cohen, working-class youths often felt frustrated and inadequate when they confronted middle-class expectations regarding punctuality, neatness, and the need to postpone gratification.

Middle-class measuring rod
The middle-class ethic, which people use to compare and determine their status, that prescribes an obligation to strive, by dint of rational, ascetic, self-disciplined, and independent activity, to achieve worldly success.

Middle class youths may then reject the source of their problem—namely, the middle-class value system of the school. In this way, delinquent subcultures emerge through "a process of adaptations by youth to what they perceive as blocked access to middle-class

WHAT DOES IT MEAN?

Middle-Class Measuring Rod
Working-class youth may feel frustrated and inadequate when they confront middle-class expectations regarding punctuality, neatness, and the need to postpone gratification.

status" (Vowell and May, 2000: 45). Delinquency may signal such a rejection, especially if it celebrates standards that run directly counter to those of middle-class society. Delinquency that seems intended to offend members of conventional society rather than to achieve some specific goal may serve this purpose. Cohen found that much delinquency has an "in your face" quality precisely because it is meant to signify a rejection of middle-class values. According to Tanner (2001: 63), aggressive and destructive delinquency often appears senseless to others, but to the delinquents themselves "it is a powerful way of hitting back at a system that has done them no favours."

Strain and Delinquency

Richard Cloward and Lloyd Ohlin (Cloward, 1959; Cloward and Ohlin, 1960) borrowed heavily from Robert Merton to demonstrate that a comprehensive theory of delinquency must explain not only why juveniles engage in delinquency but also why they engage in some types of delinquency and not others. Like Merton, they argued that the motivation to delinquency can be located in the discrepancy between the goals to which lower-class youths aspire and the means available to achieve them. Cloward and Ohlin were also influenced by Merton's view that not everyone in society finds the **legitimate means** to conventional ends equally available. For some people, the legitimate means of obtaining success goals, such as education or a good job, are out of reach; it is precisely this lack of legitimate opportunity that creates the pressure to deviate in the first place.

Legitimate means
Widely accepted routes of achieving cultural goals through institutions.

However, Cloward and Ohlin extended Merton's theory by arguing that it is important to recognize that illegitimate means are also structured. Opportunities to be criminal are no more evenly dispersed in society than are legitimate means to achieve success goals. Building on this logic, Cloward and Ohlin theorized that the kind of delinquent a youth becomes depends on the kinds of opportunities he or she has to be delinquent.

Illegitimate means
Two aspects of the delinquent opportunity structure: opportunity to learn and to play the delinquent role.

Cloward and Ohlin (1960) used the term **illegitimate means** to encompass two major aspects of the delinquent opportunity structure. The *first* is the opportunity to learn a delinquent role. As Sutherland (1947) noted, learning how to be delinquent and why it is acceptable to be delinquent are necessary precursors to being delinquent. The *second* is the opportunity to actually play a delinquent role. An individual can become a member of a drug network or stolen-car ring only if such organizations exist in his or her social environment. For Cloward and Ohlin, then, a central theoretical problem was to understand how particular types of community organizations make particular types of delinquent opportunity structures possible. Their analysis identified three forms of delinquent opportunity structures, each of which was associated with particular types of social conditions.

The first form, the **criminal pattern**, is characterized by a rational delinquency oriented toward the pursuit of monetary objectives. The prime examples of this are organized theft and the sale of drugs or other illicit goods or services. Delinquency of this type is most likely to emerge in lower-class neighbourhoods where a stable adult criminal world exists and where the criminal and conformist sectors of the community are highly integrated. When such integration exists, the "cop on the beat" is willing to look the other way, and the "honest" storekeeper is occasionally willing to fence stolen goods. The presence of a stable adult criminal world provides a structure for recruitment and upward mobility for juveniles who perceive criminality as a possible career.

Neighbourhoods that give rise to the criminal pattern can be described as socially organized; we expect a different pattern to emerge in neighbourhoods that are socially disorganized. Socially disorganized slums lack a stable adult criminal world and thus an established criminal structure. This situation can be doubly frustrating for neighbourhood youths who have already encountered the disparity between legitimate goals and legitimate opportunities. Moreover, as Shaw and McKay (1942) pointed out, these areas lack the social controls that might contain the behavioural manifestations of this frustration. For these reasons, Cloward and Ohlin discerned in socially disorganized areas a **conflict pattern** of delinquency. The conflict pattern is characterized by gangs who express their frustration by fighting over contested neighbourhood turf.

Finally, Cloward and Ohlin maintained, it is unwise to assume that everyone who engages in criminal or conflict opportunities will be successful. We are not all cut out to be drug dealers or gang warriors. Cloward and Ohlin used the term *double-failures* to describe people who are unable to succeed through either legitimate or illegitimate means. Double-failures tend to become involved in a **retreatist pattern** in which delinquency is organized around the consumption of drugs.

Recent Versions of the Strain Argument

A General Strain Theory

Strain theory is no longer a dominant view in criminology; however, interest in it has been reviving recently (Menard, 1995). For instance, Agnew (1992) has proposed a **general strain theory**, which extends the logic of the argument well beyond what was originally proposed by Merton. According to Agnew,

Criminal pattern
A rational delinquency oriented toward the pursuit of monetary objectives, exemplified by organized theft and the sale of illicit goods or services.

Conflict pattern
A pattern of delinquency that occurs in socially disorganized neighbourhoods, where youth often experience the disparity between legitimate goals and legitimate opportunities, and this leads to aggressive behaviour.

Retreatist pattern
Pattern exhibited by people who are unable to succeed through either legitimate or illegitimate means (double-failures), and who resort to delinquency organized around the consumption of drugs.

Strain theory
The theory that the constant emphasis on success in society and its possible attainment consistently contradicts the actual opportunity facing people—especially at the bottom of society, where the greatest amount of crime occurs.

General strain theory
A focus on negative relationships between people that promote anger, fear, and frustration, which may lead to delinquency.

strain theory focuses on negative relationships with others. In negative relationships, individuals are not treated the way they would like to be treated; such relationships promote anger, fear, and frustration, which may lead to delinquency.

With specific reference to juvenile offending, Agnew argues that there are three main types of strain. The *first* type results when we believe that others are preventing us or threatening to prevent us from achieving what we want to achieve. This type is most familiar because it is very similar to the type of strain described by Merton. In less abstract terms, we might think about this kind of strain resulting from unemployment or feelings of exploitation in the labour market (Baron, 2002). The *second* type of strain results when we believe that others have removed or are threatening to remove what we already possess and what we value. This might include the loss of a boyfriend/girlfriend, a move out of one's neighbourhood, or the death of a parent. The *third* type of strain results when our relationships with others cause us to experience negative life events. This type might include negative relationships with teachers, abuse by parents, or bullying by peers.

As individuals attempt to cope with the negative emotions that these relationships cause them to experience, they may explore delinquent solutions. Depending on the type of strain being experienced, drug use may be a means of escape, violence may be a way to get even, and theft may allow the acquisition of material goods that are not otherwise available. Several tests of the revised general strain theory have provided empirical support for the argument and helped us understand better how strain and delinquency are related (Brezina, 1996; Paternoster and Mazerolle, 1994). Agnew and White (1992) found that the various types of strain have a significant impact on delinquency and that the effects are most visible among adolescents who lack self-efficacy and who have delinquent friends. More recent tests have suggested that the processes linking diverse types of strain to delinquent outcomes may be even more complicated. For instance, Paul Mazerolle and his colleagues found that the motivating influence of strain may vary from one type of crime to another (Mazerolle et al., 2000). These researchers analyzed data collected from a sample of high school–aged youth, and found that strain seems to have a direct effect on violence; however, its effect on other types of delinquency (e.g., drug use) depends on the presence of other factors such as relations with deviant peers.

More recently, Stephen W. Baron (2004) investigated some of the implications of general strain theory among a population that has often been neglected by criminological researchers—homeless youth. Baron interviewed a sample of young people who were living on Vancouver streets with the intention of determining how, and the extent to which, several different kinds of social strain increased the likelihood of deviant conduct. The types of strain included various kinds of abuse and victimization, as well as several kinds of economic insecurity. Following from Agnew, Baron reasoned that anger would be a key variable which linked these various forms of abuse to criminal outcomes. Baron found that while all forms of strain were related to criminal behaviour, anger was not always the lynchpin. Baron also found that the kinds of effects which these various types of strain had upon crime depended on the influence of other factors, such as self-esteem and whether or not the youths had deviant friends or held deviant attitudes.

General strain theory has an important place in contemporary criminology, but there are many questions which deserve greater attention. Perhaps the most important one concerns the ways in which the relationship between crime and strain varies for males and females. Of course, traditional criminology has tended to be inattentive to gender differences and has assumed that whatever explains male crime should explain female crime as well. Modern theory construction is more sensitive to these issues, and with the development of sophisticated research techniques, it is possible to try to make sense of the ways in which criminogenic influences are conditioned by gender.

Robert Agnew and Lisa Broidy (1997) attempted early on to try to make some theoretical sense of the relationships involving strain, crime, and gender. They argued that for it to be truly useful, general strain theory must be able to address two issues. First, it should be able to explain why, in general, males offend at much higher rates than females. Second, it should help us to understand why females offend at all. With respect to the first question, they argued that while males and females experience comparable levels of strain in their lives, it is possible that males respond differently to the strain they experience. They cite research which suggests that men might be more likely to respond to strain with anger or that they might be more likely to turn their anger outward.

With respect to the second question, Agnew and Broidy argue that the general strain theory is perfectly compatible with a central argument in the feminist literature—that female crime is rooted in the oppression of women. They argue that, as compared to males, females are likely to experience strains in their personal networks of friends and family, gender discrimination, excessive demands from others, and low levels of prestige in their work and family roles. The anger that females experience is more likely to express itself in various kinds of "self-deprecating" reactions. Crime and various forms of deviance can

BOX 4.4

Celebrity and Strain

Most interpretations of Merton's argument about the relationship between social strain and crime emphasize the importance of material success. In other words, it is the inability of people who seek wealth and power that is experienced as the strain which results in various forms of rule-breaking. Merton's thinking was, of course, influenced by the economic ravages of the Great Depression. Contemporary society, however, is different in many relevant ways from the one which Merton's theorizing reflects. Despite high levels of poverty and inequality, contemporary North American societies are characterized by higher living standards and by omnipresent media. Is it possible to reformulate Merton's arguments in ways that take these differences into account?

One reformulation asks if it is fame rather than material success which constitutes a dominant cultural goal (Parnaby and Sacco, 2004). It can be argued that fame is highly desirable and that to a degree, access to the means of becoming famous is not readily available to everyone. Can this circumstance result in a situation in which people turn to various forms of crime and deviance in order to achieve notoriety?

It is easy to think of examples which are consistent with this view. The gangsters Al Capone and John Gotti both appeared on the cover of *Time* magazine. Gangsterism has always been a route to fame, available to those who might find other ways of becoming famous unavailable. Serial killers have fan clubs, and their memorabilia sells online at astronomical prices (Schmid, 2005). Social critic Neal Gabler (1998: 183) observes:

> John C. Salvi III, who was accused (and later convicted) of murdering two receptionists on December 30, 1994 at two different abortion clinics, told his attorney that he wanted to be interviewed by Barbara Walters . . . The so-called Unabomber, who killed three and wounded twenty-three in sixteen separate bombing attacks, not only delivered a manifesto to the *New York Times* and *Washington Post* that he demanded be published—else he would kill again—but was clearly concerned about his image, confiding to his journal that if he were caught . . . he would be wrongly dismissed as a "sickie."

A particularly vivid example of this phenomenon occurred in January of 2006 when it was discovered that best-selling author James Frey was discovered by the investigative website thesmokinggun.com to have largely fabricated his autobiography. His book, A *Million Little Pieces,* which described a life of horrendous crime and addiction, was composed mainly of exaggeration, hyperbole, and outright fabrication. An official choice of the Oprah book club, the volume was second only to Harry Potter in sales in 2005. The author achieved fame and celebrity through the creation of a fictional life of crime.

One final irony in this case is worth noting. Once the deception was exposed, the publicity surrounding the real "crime" of lying to readers moved the book back to number one on several bestseller lists.

still be the result. They end up concluding that general strain theory could prove as useful an explanation of female as of male delinquency but that a great deal of research would be necessary to bear this conclusion out.

Researchers have begun to investigate these issues using a variety of complex statistical techniques. A study by Piquero and Sealock (2004) provided mixed results. Male and female adolescents in their study did not differ with respect to the amount of strain they experience. However, in response to strain, females reported higher levels of both anger and depression than did males. The researchers concluded that while the theoretical process by which strain leads to delinquency may be the same for males and females, it is still important to understand how each phase of the process is experienced and interpreted by men and women. The findings of other researchers have also tended to lend at least partial support to the argument made by Agnew and Broidy with respect to strain, gender, and delinquency (Eitle, 1998; Hoffman and Su, 1997; Mazerolle, 1998).

Crime and the American Dream

Even more recently, Messner and Rosenfeld (1997) have elaborated on Merton's argument to explain why the United States has such high rates of serious crime relative to other industrialized nations. Like Merton, they suggest that the root of the problem is the American Dream, which they define as a commitment to the goal of material success that everyone in society pursues in conditions of open, individual competition. As a result of widespread allegiance to the American Dream, many people adopt an "anything goes" mentality as they chase their personal goals.

According to Messner and Rosenfeld, the problems created by the American Dream are magnified because the economy and the lessons that it teaches dominate other social institutions, such as the family and the school. They note, for instance, how family activities and routines are required to conform to the schedules and rewards of the labour market, and that, despite much rhetoric about "family values," it is the homeowner and not the homemaker who is admired and respected. In a similar way, the school is not a setting that produces model citizens but one that teaches competition for grades as students prepare for labour force participation.

This institutional balance of power, they argue, has two important consequences. *First*, it allows the competitive and individualistic message of the American Dream to diffuse to other settings. *Second*, because the lessons of the economy override the lessons taught in other institutional environments, the social control that we expect the school or the family to exert over criminal behaviour is undermined. Both conditions are conducive to high rates of crime. Canadian studies of crime have suggested that Canadian society is able to protect those who fall out of the race for the "dream" through social assistance programs and strong community support—although with changes in government policies, these programs and supports may be falling away (Papadopoulos, 1997). The increasing strength of the competition model in Canadian society may lead us to parallel the American experience in promoting individual success; as a result, elements of the strain evident in parts of the American population may appear in Canada as well. What this means for Canadian crime rates remains unclear.

CULTURE AND CRIMINAL MOTIVATION

Another important approach locates the origins of criminal motivation in the cultural worlds to which offenders have been exposed. The cultural milieu in which we are socialized provides us with our ideas of right and wrong, moral and immoral, appropriate and inappropriate. When our socialization is successful, we internalize these views and try to behave in ways that conform to the cultural standards we have learned. It follows that if we are exposed to beliefs and ideas that support behaviour the law defines as criminal, we may be more likely to behave like criminals.

Like strain theories, cultural accounts of crime present a "normalized" picture of the offender. In other words, offenders are not necessarily pathological; they merely have learned a particular set of cultural lessons. Their behaviour is normal within a particular cultural context.

Differential Association

Differential association
The theory that criminal behaviour is learned in the process of interaction with intimate groups.

Cultural approaches focus not only on criminal behaviour as norm violation but also on criminal behaviour that is normative (Alarid, Burton, and Cullen, 2000). One of the pioneers of this perspective was Edwin Sutherland, who in the 1930s proposed a cultural theory of crime that he called the **theory of differential association**. Against the prevailing wisdom of his day, Sutherland (1947) maintained that crime is a learned behaviour. In the process of interacting with people whose views support criminal conduct, a person can learn to be a criminal just as another person can learn to be a mechanic, a stamp collector, or a lover of classical music. According to Sutherland, the differential rate at which people associate with the carriers of criminal values determines the differential rate at which they engage in criminal conduct.

For Sutherland, differential association involves two important types of learning. *First,* one must learn the actual techniques of crime commission. Sometimes these techniques are very simple and do not differ markedly from law-abiding behaviour. For example, stealing a car when the owner has left the keys inside is not so different from driving one's own car. Other times, specialized skills are required—for instance, stealing a locked car when the keys have not been left inside.

Sutherland emphasized that knowledge or technical skills alone are insufficient to explain criminal behaviour. Everyone has some idea of how to commit a wide variety of crimes. Yet although most of us could figure out how to murder or assault someone, we refrain from committing such acts. So *second,* aside from technical knowledge, one must have exposure to the "specific direction of motives, drives, rationalizations and attitudes" (Sutherland, 1947: 6). Stated differently, to behave criminally, one must learn that crime is an acceptable type of behaviour.

Consistent with the principles of the theory of differential association, Desroches (1995) found that half of the bank robbers he studied became involved in that type of crime as a result of their association with other offenders. Typically, they learned this skill from more experienced criminals, who convinced them that bank robbery is both fast and easy. Through this process of differential association, they learned not only how to rob banks but also how to justify the crime and to view it as a low-risk offence.

A study of delinquency among Chinese-Canadian youth living in Winnipeg also made use of the differential association argument. Wong (1999) discovered that youth who adhered closely to the tenets of Chinese culture were less likely to engage in delinquent conduct. In part, this may be because Chinese culture places high value on factors such as family solidarity and respect for authority. He found that youth who were, according to a variety of measures, acculturated to Chinese culture had lower rates of delinquency than youth who were acculturated to "North American culture." At the same time, those youths who reported having delinquent peers were more likely to engage in delinquent conduct. As Wong argued, these findings are consistent with the theory of differential association.

Subcultural Explanations of Criminal Motivations

In complex, highly differentiated societies such as our own, cultural "pockets" exist in which groups of people are engaged in intensive interaction and confront common problems or share common interests. It is in this sense that

BOX 4.5

The Tenets of Differential Association Theory

Edwin Sutherland was one of the few criminologists to formulate a theory in terms of an interrelated set of propositions. The following summary of his arguments by Traub and Little (1980) refer to the process by which a particular person comes to engage in criminal behaviour:

1. Criminal behaviour is learned. Negatively, this means that criminal behaviour is not inherited as such.
2. Criminal behaviour is learned in interaction with other people in a process of communication. This communication is mainly verbal, but also includes gestures.
3. Most learning of criminal behaviour occurs within intimate personal groups. Negatively, this means that the impersonal agencies of communication, such as movies and newspapers, play a relatively unimportant role in the genesis of criminal behaviour.
4. When criminal behaviour is learned, this learning includes (a) techniques of committing the crime, which are sometimes very complicated, sometimes very simple; and (b) the specific direction of motives, drives, rationalizations, and attitudes.
5. The specific direction of motives and drives is learned from definitions of the legal codes. In some societies, an individual is surrounded by people who invariably define the legal codes as rules to be observed; in other societies, he or she is surrounded by people whose definitions are favourable to the violation of legal codes.
6. A person becomes delinquent because of an excess of definitions favourable to violation of law over definitions unfavourable to violation of law. This is the principle of differential association. It refers to both criminal and anti-criminal associations and has to do with counteracting forces. When people become criminal, they do so because of contact with criminal patterns and also because of isolation from anti-criminal patterns.
7. The process of learning criminal behaviour by association with criminal and anti-criminal patterns involves all of the mechanisms involved in any other learning. Negatively, this means that the learning of criminal behaviour is not restricted to the process of imitation. A person who is seduced, for instance, learns criminal behaviour by association, but this process would not ordinarily be described as imitation.
8. Though criminal behaviour is an expression of general needs and values, it is not explained by those general needs and values, since non-criminal behaviour is an expression of the same needs and values. Thieves generally steal in order to secure money, but likewise honest labourers work in order to secure money. The attempts by many scholars to explain criminal behaviour by general drives and values—such as the happiness principle, striving for social status, the money motive, or frustration—have been futile and must continue to be so, since they explain lawful behaviour as completely as they explain criminal behaviour.

All of this suggests that cultural knowledge and beliefs exist that promote criminality; however, only a few of us are offered sustained exposure to that knowledge or those beliefs. Sutherland's approach has been especially helpful in explaining why normally law-abiding individuals commit crimes at work. According to Sutherland (1961), white-collar crime occurs because people have learned how to commit it and because they have learned from others that it is acceptable.

we speak of subcultures of rap music fans, marathon runners, or the police. Participants in these worlds are also participants in the larger culture shared by the rest of us; in that sense, these **subcultures** are both part of and distinguishable from the larger culture. It can be argued that subcultural involvement promotes criminal behaviour when the subcultural values in question are inconsistent with the conformist values enshrined in law.

Subculture
A group of people in a dominant culture with different values, evident in their expression of deviant behaviour.

Thorsten Sellin (1938) suggested that the high rates of crime among immigrant groups can be understood with reference to the culture conflict that ethnic subcultures encounter. His view acknowledged that when people migrate from one country to another, they carry with them considerable cultural baggage. We recognize this fact when we visit a restaurant in Little Italy or attend a cultural festival in Chinatown. This cultural baggage often also includes ways of acting that, although not considered criminal in the country of origin, are defined as such in the host country. By way of illustration, Sellin (1938) tells the story of a Sicilian father in New Jersey who "killed the 16-year-old seducer of his daughter, expressing surprise at his arrest since he had merely defended his family honour in a traditional way" (68).

Like Sellin, anthropologist Walter Miller (1958) attempted to understand how the cultural values of a particular group can increase the likelihood of criminal conduct. Miller studied lower-class life in a large eastern American city in an effort to identify the distinct character of lower-class culture. He was especially interested in how this subculture related to the delinquencies of lower-class male youths. He argued that life among the lower class was organized around six **focal concerns**:

Focal concerns
Concerns around which life in the lower class is organized: trouble, toughness, smartness, excitement, fate, and autonomy.

1. Trouble   Life is a series of troublesome episodes: trouble with the police, with the welfare officer, with one's neighbours, and so on.
2. Toughness   "Machismo" is widely prized in lower-class areas as an interactional style.
3. Smartness   This refers not to intellectual ability, but rather to the ability to live by one's wits.
4. Excitement   Life is best described as boring and monotonous, punctuated occasionally by thrill-seeking behaviour. Excitement might include bouts of drinking or fighting.

WHAT DOES IT MEAN?

Subculture of Violence

A powerful cultural emphasis on social honour and on the need to save face when a threat to one's honour arises in a public setting means that a derogatory remark made about one's character may be seen as sufficient reason to engage in physical battle. To argue that violence, in this sense, is subcultural is to argue that it is "normative."

BOX 4.6

Rap Music and Deviant Behaviour

Does rap music encourage criminal and deviant behaviour among its listeners? Certainly many members of the general public blame acts of highly visible violence among urban youth on the influence of rap lyrics (Kohler, 2005). As well, according to some social critics, the explicit attention to thuggery, the overt misogyny, and the celebration of violent forms of conflict resolution lead inevitably to troublesome behaviour. The "code of the street," about which Elijah Anderson has written, is said to have been given a life of its own, so that the code spreads to places in society such as white middle-class suburbs which have material conditions very unlike the inner-city areas which gave birth to rap. Perhaps the most widely known critic of the spread of this "code of the street" through rap music has been comedian Bill Cosby (Dyson, 2005).

The question as to whether rap music leads to specific kinds of criminal outcomes is an empirical one. Dave Miranda and Michel Claes (2004) argue that while some studies have found effects of this type, such studies are highly problematic. First, in investigating the effects of rap music, these studies fail to take into account the influence of peers and of other forms of violent media. Second, these studies fail to specify how much of the effect of rap music is attributable to the lyrics themselves. Finally, these studies treat rap music as a homogeneous entity and fail to distinguish among types of rap music.

To investigate these issues, Miranda and Claes sought to understand the effects of rap music on 348 French-Canadian students in the city of Montreal. Students were asked to complete a questionnaire which asked about self-reported delinquent behaviours, the deviant behaviour of peers, the importance given to lyrics, and preferences for particular types of rap music.

The study found that rap music as a whole was significantly linked to deviant behaviour of various kinds. However, the relationship differs depending on the type of music preferred. Adolescents who preferred French rap music were more likely to engage in violence, gang behaviour, and mild drug use, while the preference for gangsta rap was more closely related to thefts. Such effects were observable even when account was taken of peers' involvement in deviance, attention to other violent media, and attention to lyrics. Interestingly, the preference for American-style gangsta rap was not related to self-reported gang behaviour.

---

5. **Fate**   Life is largely seen in terms of good luck and bad luck.

6. **Autonomy**   There is a general desire to be free of the control of police, landlords, welfare workers, and others who might seek to regulate life.

For Miller, these focal concerns were problematic in themselves because they suggested a value orientation at odds with the legal code. People who live their lives in terms of these focal concerns are likely, sooner or later, to end up in trouble with the law. For Miller, the problem was aggravated by the fact that the slum areas he was investigating were conducive to the emergence of juvenile gangs. In these gangs, he suggested, the focal concerns of the lower class were exaggerated as youths attempted to model what they understood to be adult behaviour. The result was a kind of overconformity to a value scheme that promoted behaviour likely to invite legal sanction.

Other theorists have applied similar logic to explain patterns of homicide and assault. Noting that much interpersonal violence is concentrated socially (e.g., among young members of the urban underclass) or regionally (e.g., in the American South), they argue that offenders (and often their victims) may behave as they do because they are immersed in a **subculture of violence** (Felson et al., 1994; Rice and Goldman, 1994; Wolfgang and Ferracuti, 1967). This subcultural orientation, it is argued, requires that some kinds of transgressions be resolved in a violent fashion.

Subculture of violence
A subculture in which disproportionate rates of criminal violence are the product of a group's commitment to subcultural values and norms that condone violence as an acceptable means of resolving interpersonal conflict.

Much assaultive violence seems to originate in what many would consider minor or trivial altercations. An exchange that begins with a stare, a jostle, or an insult may end with one of the parties seriously injured or dead. Subcultural theorists maintain that patterns like this only make sense when we recognize the underlying powerful cultural emphasis on social honour and the need to save face. Given this emphasis, a derogatory remark made in a public setting may be enough to provoke physical retaliation.

To argue that violence, in this sense, is subcultural is to argue that it is normative. In other words, the physical defence of one's honour is not merely what one *can* do but what one *must* do to retain the respect of other participants in the culture. Because the violence is normative, the person who behaves violently is unlikely to feel shame or embarrassment for doing so.

In the context of the subculture-of-violence argument, it is the particular cultural interpretation given to an affront to character—not the affront per se—that is the source of the violence. Precisely because cultural environments differ, a sneer is less likely to provoke trouble in a university faculty club than it is in a lower-class bar.

A recent and influential version of the subculture-of-violence argument was developed by American anthropologist Elijah Anderson (1999). Based on his ethnographic analysis of inner-city neighbourhoods in Philadelphia, Anderson argued that the public sphere of inner-city life is dominated by a "code of the streets" which has formed in reaction to both the status insecurity and the constant threats of violence that characterize ghetto life. Even those youths who may not be inclined to behave in violent ways may feel a need to demonstrate bravado and a low level of tolerance for disrespect since the failure to do so could result in further victimization. Anderson is not arguing that this code is somehow a personality characteristic of most people who live in the disadvantaged urban areas. Rather, it is better understood as a set of normative rules that pertain mainly to life on the street. In addition, it is the most alienated members of these communities who are most likely to rely on this street code (Brezina et al., 2004). To some degree at least, the code of the street is reflected in the lyrics of many "gangsta" rappers such as Tupac Shakur or 50 Cent, for whom themes of violence and respect have been prominent.

A weakness of the subcultural approaches is that they tend to infer rather than identify independently the differences between subcultural values and subcultural behaviours. Hagan (1985) argues that there is little empirical evidence to suggest that groups adhere to deviant subcultures in which violence is considered integral to the group's functioning. The violence is more likely to be a consequence of situational factors such as opportunity and circumstance rather than a specific group goal.

Is Mainstream Culture Criminogenic?

Subcultural arguments generally proceed from the assumption that it is useful to distinguish between a subculture that somehow promotes criminality and a conformist mainstream culture (that is, the one reflected in criminal law). Yet not all theorists who have examined the relationship between crime and culture share this assumption. Some contend that the "conformist" culture may itself promote criminal behaviour.

For instance, it can be argued that violence against women is greatly encouraged by broad patterns of cultural belief. According to many feminist writers, sexual assault and wife abuse have less to do with the subcultural orientation of a deviant minority than with pervasive cultural representations of women in the entertainment and advertising media. When slasher movies, television dramas, and sexually explicit, over-the-counter magazines and videos portray women as willing or deserving victims of violence, it is not surprising that the message is picked up and acted on by some in society.

Culture of competition
A cultural atmosphere in which crime is promoted by competition that defines wealth and success as central goals of human activity.

In a similar vein, Coleman (1987) argues that the behaviour of white-collar and corporate criminals is in many ways promoted by a culture of competition that defines wealth and success as the central goals of human action. He asserts that criminal action in the support of either profit margins and bottom lines or personal success clearly reflects the influence of pervasive cultural beliefs. "[The] fear of failure is the inevitable correlate of the demand for success, and together they provide a set of powerful symbolic structures that are central to the motivation of economic behaviour" (Coleman, 1987: 417).

One of the most influential statements concerning the relationship between criminal behaviour and mainstream culture was provided by David Matza and Gresham Sykes (1961). Their analysis of juvenile delinquency led them to conclude that much youthful crime is better said to reflect **subterranean values** than subcultural values. Subterranean values are not (as subcultural values are) part of the belief system of some identifiable criminal minority. Rather, they are values that are held by many in society, although they may be in conflict with other cherished values. The concept of the subterranean value has never really been fully developed, and only rarely has it been investigated empirically (Hagan et al., 1998).

Matza and Sykes suggested that although many researchers have identified values such as "disdain for work" and "search for kicks and thrills" as subcultural values of delinquency, considerable evidence indicates that these value orientations are much more widely held. Middle-class conformists and juvenile delinquents may express their disdain for work or search for kicks in very different ways, but the value orientations held by both groups seem to have much in common. Anyone who has seen *Kill Bill* or *The Devil's Rejects* or similar movies would be hard-pressed to make the case that violence does not have a wide cultural appeal.

According to Matza and Sykes (1957), the rules of conventional society are rarely as inflexible as subcultural theories make them out to be. In fact, those who learn the lessons of mainstream culture understand that although criminal behaviour is *usually* wrong, it is not *always* wrong. Conventional morality prohibits us from acting criminally, but it also provides us with reasons why it is sometimes all right to do so. Matza and Sykes term these culturally derived justifications of criminal conduct "techniques of **neutralization**" and argue that in a very real way, they make offending possible.

Matza and Sykes (1957) identified five neutralization techniques used by juvenile offenders. *First,* offenders deny responsibility and contend that their crimes resulted not from ill will but from circumstances and conditions beyond their control. *Second,* they deny injury, claiming that the crime did not harm others. *Third,* they deny the victim, accepting

Subterranean values
Values that are held by many in society, although they may conflict with other cherished values.

Neutralization theory
The view that delinquents often use linguistic constructions (that is, excuses or rationalizations) to reduce the guilt resulting from their delinquent behaviour.

WHAT DOES IT MEAN?

Techniques of Neutralization

First, through *denial of responsibility,* offenders express their belief that their crimes resulted not from ill will but rather from circumstances and conditions beyond their control. Second, through *denial of injury,* offenders reject any claim that the crime resulted in harm to others. Third, through *denial of the victim,* offenders accept responsibility for their actions and acknowledge the harmful consequences, but suggest that the victims were to blame for what happened to them. Fourth, offenders argue back at the negative evaluations others make of them by *condemning the condemners.* Fifth, by *appealing to higher loyalties,* they maintain that their actions were necessary in order to meet obligations to family and peers.

responsibility for their actions and acknowledging the harmful consequences but also suggesting that the victims were to blame for what happened to them. *Fourth,* they condemn the condemners and argue against the negative evaluations that others make of them. *Fifth,* they appeal to higher loyalties and maintain that their actions were necessary in order to meet obligations to family and peers.

The central point of the neutralization argument is that knowledge of neutralization techniques precedes and makes possible involvement in criminal activity. In other words, people are able to break the law because they define the law as irrelevant to their own behaviour. People acquire knowledge of neutralization techniques as they gain knowledge of the cultural environment to which they are exposed. As a result of this process, they come to view criminal acts as acceptable, and this gives them the freedom to commit such acts. Once vandalism is redefined as a "harmless prank," assault as "getting even," and theft as "borrowing," there is a loosening of the moral inhibitions that might normally prohibit these behaviours.

Later research has not provided unequivocal support for Matza and Sykes's claim that neutralization precedes rather than follows involvement in crime (Agnew and Peters, 1986; Hamlin, 1988). Most studies have found that those who use neutralization techniques are more likely to engage in crime and deviance, but this correlation tends to be weak (Costello, 2000). Some researchers have tried to account for the complexities of neutralization processes by arguing that neutralization is a "hardening process" (Minor, 1981). In other words, over time, criminal behaviour and techniques of neutralization become mutually reinforcing; attempts at neutralization both precede and follow criminal involvement. As a result, the commitment to both the behaviour and the cultural definition of the behaviour intensifies. Thus, the employee who steals at work may define the pilfering as a legitimate substitute for unpaid overtime or, alternatively, as a harmless activity (given that the costs are covered by insurance). The resulting behaviour may reinforce itself over time as the commitment to the act and to the morality of stealing develop in a mutually supportive fashion.

SUMMARY

Criminological theories are general explanations intended to make sense of the empirical facts of crime. To ask "What causes some people to behave criminally?" is to ask a question which reflects the influence of the positivist school of criminology. Criminal behaviour is understood as the product of causal forces working within or upon the offender. Sociobiologists have argued that some individuals are genetically programmed in such a way that they are more likely to commit crimes. Wilson and Herrnstein (1985) claim that one can detect certain physiological similarities among offenders. In their view, offenders' constitutional deficiencies lead them to discount the costs of crime through a process whereby immediate gratification becomes a paramount concern. This discounting can also be the result of physiological episodes brought about by problems with diet, drugs, alcohol, and so on.

A strong and consistent sociological tradition in criminology emphasizes social conditions as a major influence on motivations to offend. This perspective views criminal behaviour as the means by which some people attempt to deal with the frustrations they face in day-to-day life. The frustrated ambitions of individuals who aspire to achieve legitimate success but who lack the means to do so result in anomie, which can lead to criminal innovation.

According to Merton, criminogenic conditions reside in the gap between ambition and legitimate means, as dominant **cultural goals** both inspire and frustrate members of society (Cernkovich, Giordano, and Ruddolph, 2000). This gap can widen as a result of the economic deprivation resulting from unemployment, especially for young people. Most crime is committed by individuals in the lower socio-economic groups, and prisons are most likely to be filled with individuals from these groups. Some criminologists have argued, however, that this is the case not necessarily because these groups are more delinquent, but rather because they are easy targets for the police, who expend more effort on street crime than they do on white-collar crime.

Cultural goals
Legitimate objectives held by all or by diversely located members of society.

The focus on frustration has led criminologists to look at gang delinquency among working-class juveniles. According to Cohen, much juvenile crime is rooted in the difficulties experienced by disadvantaged youths who aspire to middle-class status but are judged inadequate by a school system that assigns status rewards on the basis of middle-class criteria. Rejection of this value system may signal delinquency.

According to cultural theorists, the criminogenic conditions that influence individual behaviour emerge from the milieu in which offenders operate (Alarid, Burton, and Cullen, 2000). There is not necessarily anything pathological about offenders; they may merely have learned a particular set of cultural lessons on how to act criminally. Their behaviour, then, is normal within their particular cultural context, and explicable given that they have been thrust outside the normal operations of society. The same process that ostracizes offenders also strengthens the bonds among insiders, as sanctions are applied against norm violators.

So it is possible to look at criminals as outsiders who are punished for failing to conform to the explicit norms of the dominant culture. It is also possible to look on certain criminal behaviour as normative. Sutherland's differential association theory proposes that crime is learned behaviour. For Sutherland, the differential rates at which criminals associate with the carriers of criminal values determine the differential rates at which they engage in criminal conduct. This perspective allows us to account for the fact that certain cultural insiders, while adhering to the law in their personal lives, commit crimes in the context of their working lives.

The idea that there may be more than one set of values in society raises the possibility that mainstream culture is itself criminogenic. Matza and Sykes contend that those who learn the lessons of mainstream culture learn that criminal behaviour is usually wrong, but not always. Some acts can be rationalized or neutralized with explanations that find their basis in the tenets of mainstream society.

QUESTIONS FOR REVIEW AND DISCUSSION

1. What types of diet are more likely to make people criminal? Is the link between poor diet and criminality a direct one?
2. Can you think of exceptions to the body-typing predictions, some exceptions to the rule that some crimes that are not likely to be committed by people with particular body shapes?
3. Why do you think we pay so much attention to explanations of violent behaviour that emphasize "psychopathology"?
4. How is crime learned from others?
5. Why do individuals need to neutralize their feelings about the victims of their crimes?

RECOMMENDED READINGS

Anderson, E. 2000. *Code of the Streets: Decency, Violence and the Moral Life of the Inner City*. New York: W.W. Norton Company.

O'Kane, J.M. 1992. *Crooked Ladder: Gangsters, Ethnicity and the American Dream*. New Brunswick: Transaction Press.

Passas, N., and R. Agnew. 1997. *The Future of Anomie Theory*. Boston: Northeastern University Press.

Rowe, D.C. 2001. *Biology and Crime*. Los Angeles: Roxbury Publishing Company.

INFOTRAC® COLLEGE EDITION

Explore InfoTrac® College Edition, your online university library, which includes hundreds of popular and scholarly journals in which you can find articles related to the topics in this chapter. Visit InfoTrac® through your web browser (**www.infotrac-college.com**) or through this book's website (**www.criminalevent-4e.nelson.com**).

WHAT'S ON THE WEB?

For chapter links and quizzes, check out the accompanying website at **www.criminalevent-4e.nelson.com**.

LEARNING OBJECTIVES:

- explore the general logic of theories which emphasize the role of social control rather than unique motivation as explanations of crime
- examine theories which focus on the individual level, most notably the general theory of crime, power–control theory, and interactional theory
- discuss theories which suggest that too much control can also be a source of problems
- consider the theoretical synthesis provided by control balance theory
- examine other forms of social control explanation, including those which focus on the life course, the community, and decision-making processes

INTRODUCTION

The theories discussed in the previous chapter seem to suggest that since criminal behaviour has unique characteristics, it requires unique motivations. However, in putting so much energy into determining the unique cultural and social arrangements driving crime, motivational theories risk losing sight of a basic question: Is motivation sufficient or necessary to explain offending? Just because individuals are moved or inclined to behave in particular ways, does this mean they will? Motivational theories assume that it is the propensity, desire, or willingness to offend that separates offenders from non-offenders.

Many theorists argue that the motivation to behave criminally is probably much more widespread than actual criminal behaviour (Agnew, 1993). We can all think of times when lying, cheating, or stealing might have been the most effective way of achieving our goals. According to critics of motivational theories, what separates the offender from the non-offender has less to do with the presence of motivation and more to do with the ability or willingness to act on this motivation. This position acknowledges that we are not always free to act in ways consistent with our motivations.

In this chapter, we consider how informal and formal social controls influence criminal offending. The underlying significance of these perspectives is that criminal behaviour may not require a distinct or unique criminal motivation. Instead, people may offend when the social pressures that would prevent them from doing so are weak or absent. Thus, criminal behaviour is not so much the product of criminogenic forces as it is a rational choice made by individuals who feel no constraints about engaging in it.

It will become clear as we proceed that these theories, much more so than the theories discussed in the previous chapter, reflect a legacy of classical thought. In other words, they are generally strongly connected to concepts such as choice and rational action. Their assumption typically is that people commit crimes when they are free to do so or when they see doing so as consistent with their self-interests. These are assumptions with which Cesare Beccaria, the founder of the classical school, would be very comfortable.

As we will see, however, some theorists interested in social control argue that it is too much—rather than too little—control which is an important source of the problem of crime. In this chapter, we consider these kinds of theories as well.

SOCIAL TIES AND CONFORMITY

Social Controls and the Individual

It has been argued that many important social controls are informal social controls, in the form of relationships with people who support and promote the values of conformity. Many theorists contend, for instance, that strong social ties between juveniles and their (conformist) teachers, parents, and peers discourage involvement in delinquency. Strong ties to parents make effective adult monitoring and supervision of juvenile leisure activity possible (Alarid, Burton, and Cullen, 2000; Gottfredson and Hirschi, 1990; Wells and Rankin, 1991). Parent–child relationships characterized by caring, trust, and intimate communication offer support to adolescents who might otherwise choose delinquent reactions to the problems that face them (Patterson and Dishion, 1985).

Informal social control
Casual methods of coercion employed by community members to maintain conformity.

As an explanation of crime, these ideas have a very long pedigree. In his famous study of the social causes of suicide, the famous French sociologist Emile Durkheim identified a type of suicide which he labelled "anomic." The designation was intended to describe the ways in which people can become disconnected from others and as a result may be more likely to take their own lives. Durkheim was struck, for instance, by the fact that rates of suicide went up in times of rapid economic decline *and* in times of rapid economic growth. While the former might be explained in terms of increases in the level of poverty, surely the latter could not be. Durkheim attempted to show that both situations share a common sociological feature. In times of both boom and bust, large numbers of people are displaced from the customary ways in which they have been living their lives. In other words, as they become disconnected from others, the social regulation of their goals and desires, which gives their lives a sense of meaning and proportion, ceases to operate. Of course, the point is generalizable—social life to some considerable degree requires the external regulation of behaviour, not only for the sake of others but for one's own sake as well.

Early advocates of the application of such logic to the problems of crime and delinquency included Albert Reiss (1951) and F. Ivan Nye (1958). Reiss argued that juveniles are more likely to engage in delinquent conduct when the external and internal controls which are expected to regulate their behaviour are not working well. For Reiss, external controls include those exerted by the community, the church, the school, and the family. Internal controls refer to the mechanisms which have been internalized and which operate from the inside out.

In a similar way, sociologist F. Ivan Nye argued that delinquency can largely be understood with reference to the absence of effective controls rather than the presence of powerful motivations. Importantly, for him, it is the family which is the locus of much of this control. Nye theorized that family controls are of four types: (1) direct control—this refers to the relatively immediate effort to regulate behaviour through, for instance, the application of punishment; (2) internalized control, which operates from within and which we recognize as *conscience*; (3) indirect control—this refers to the ways in which behaviour is regulated as a result of emotional relationships with people who would condemn an individual's delinquency; and (4) families' role in "need satisfaction"—in other words, when families are able to allow young people to meet their needs, they render less attractive the option of meeting these needs in a delinquent way.

Containment theory
Theory, based on control theory, that youth are insulated from delinquency by inner and outer containments that constrain nonconformist behaviour.

Containment Theory

The criminologist Walter Reckless (1967) developed **containment theory** to try to explain how even in areas characterized by high rates of delinquency, many youths seem to be law-abiding. Like many of the theorists discussed in the previous chapter, Reckless recognized that many factors can "pull" and "push" people into crime—for example, they can be pulled into crime by the attraction of what they see as "easy money," or pushed by the frustration resulting from blocked opportunity. However, what interested Reckless most was the fact that many more youths seemed to experience these motivational pushes and pulls than engaged in delinquent conduct.

Using the logic of **control theory**, Reckless reasoned that youth are insulated from delinquency by "**inner**" and "**outer**" **containments** that constrain nonconformist behaviour. Outer containments are those aspects of the individual's social environment which help ensure that delinquent behaviour does not occur. Most importantly, these include relationships with family members and with members of other primary groups. These groups set standards for individuals, teach and reinforce appropriate conduct, and provide a sense of belonging. Inner containments are those elements which are part of the individual's psychic makeup; for Reckless, these containments were the more important of the two. Inner containments are the products of effective socialization and the successful internalization of rules of acceptable behaviour. Reckless concluded that the most important element of inner containment is self-concept. A "good" self-concept implies an ability to tolerate frustration, a strong sense of responsibility, and a clear orientation toward future goals. Most important, the containment value of self-concept implies an ability to think of oneself as a "law-abiding person." Such a view of self can be an effective buffer against pressures to deviate.

Theory of the Bond

The most influential statement of the relationship between social ties and social control is Travis Hirschi's **theory of the bond**. Hirschi (1969) argued that the causes of juvenile delinquency are not located in some type of unique delinquent motivation, but rather in the weakness of the **social bond** linking delinquent adolescents to the world of conformist others. Weak bonds allow individuals to formulate behavioural intentions that reflect narrow self-interest. Lying, cheating, and stealing are often the outcome.

According to Hirschi, the bond to conformist society has four distinct strands. The first strand, **attachment**, refers to the degree to which children are sensitive to the expectations

Control theory
A group of theories which proceed from the assumption that criminal behaviour emerges in the absence of controls (internal or external) that might check or contain it.

Inner containments
The products of effective socialization and the successful internalization of rules regarding acceptable behaviour.

Outer containments
Aspects of the individual's social environment (e.g., primary groups) that help ensure that delinquent behaviour does not occur.

Theory of the bond
Theory that strong social bonds insulate youths against the delinquent environment.

Social bond
In social control theory, the strength and quality of the relationships that link potential offenders to conformist others and that serve to insulate them from criminal influences.

Attachment
The degree to which children are sensitive to the expectations of parents or teachers.

WHAT ARE THEY?

Inner and Outer Containments

Inner containments represent the products of effective socialization and the successful internalization of rules of acceptable behaviour. Outer containments are those aspects of the individual's social environment that help ensure that delinquent behaviour does not occur.

BOX 5.1

Depression and Delinquency

What role do psychological conditions play in the development of delinquency? One answer to this question stresses the relevance of social bonds. A research project undertaken as part of a much larger study of crime and delinquency in the city of Chicago (called the Project of Human Development in Chicago Neighborhoods) investigated this question by interviewing almost 800 adolescent girls (Obeidallah and Earls, 1999). The researchers found that mildly to moderately depressed girls may be at risk of engaging in delinquency. More specifically, the researchers found the following:

- Although 40 percent of non-depressed girls engaged in property crimes, 68 percent of girls who were mildly to moderately depressed did so. Furthermore, 42 percent of girls who were not depressed engaged in crimes against other persons, compared to 82 percent of mildly to moderately depressed girls.
- Fifty-seven percent of mildly to moderately depressed girls engaged in higher levels of aggressive behaviour, compared to only 13 percent of those who were not depressed.

All of this suggests that depressed adolescents tend to lack self-esteem and to drift toward delinquent peers. However, one interpretation stresses the role of social control factors:

> Some research suggests antisocial youth have weakened attachments to pro-social institutions. Because depression promotes a lack of interest and difficulty in concentrating, youth may withdraw from pro-social activities and institutions (e.g., schools, athletics), thus attenuating their attachment to these institutions and increasing their likelihood of engaging in antisocial behaviours (Obeidallah and Earls, 1999: 3).

of parents and teachers. When children are sensitive to expectations, they must take the potential reactions of conformist others into account when contemplating delinquency. When youths care about the views of their parents and teachers, they define delinquency as a less attractive option.

The second strand, commitment, refers to the amount of time and energy youths invest in conventional activities such as obtaining good grades. The more juveniles invest in such things, the less likely they are to engage in behaviours that jeopardize them.

The third strand, involvement, refers to participation in the world of conformity—jobs to be done, projects to be undertaken, goals to be achieved, and deadlines to be met. In short, involvement in the world of conformity leaves little time for involvement in delinquency. This reminds us of the adage that "idle hands are the devil's workshop."

Commitment
The size of the investment of time and energy that a youth has made to a conventional activity, such as getting good grades.

Involvement
Participation in the world of conformity so that little time is left for delinquency.

The fourth strand is **belief**. Hirschi diverges from subcultural theorists in that he does not believe that delinquents are committed to a set of distinctly delinquent values. Rather, they vary in the extent to which they believe that the conformist values of parents, teachers, and others are worthy of respect.

Strong social bonds—defined by Hirschi as high levels of attachment, commitment, involvement, and belief—insulate youths against delinquent involvement. To explain why some youths are delinquent while others are not, we must focus on the weakness of delinquents' bonds rather than on the factors that motivate them to behave in a criminal fashion.

General Theory of Crime

More recently, in collaboration with Michael R. Gottfredson (Gottfredson and Hirschi, 1990), Hirschi has proposed a general theory which he argues is applicable to all forms of crime, including white-collar and organized crime. Unlike some theorists, Gottfredson and Hirschi argue that there is no need to offer distinct explanations for distinct types of criminal conduct. This is because, despite their differences, many types of crime can be defined as "acts of force or fraud undertaken in pursuit of self-interest" (1990: 15). Even many crimes which we might not think of as being linked to low self-control fall under the purview of the theory. Higgins (2005) for instance, suggests that even relatively gentle crimes such as software piracy may be linked to levels of self-control. Some researchers have even shown that low self-control is related not only to various forms of deviant risk taking (such as dangerous driving) but also to socially approved forms of risk taking, such as bungee jumping and whitewater rafting (Jones and Quisenbery, 2004).

This is because, Gottfredson and Hirschi argue, the acts we call crimes and analogous behaviours share many common elements:

- They provide immediate gratification of desires.
- They are exciting, risky, or thrilling.
- They provide few or meagre long-term benefits.
- They require little skill or planning.
- They can result in pain or discomfort for the victim.

In short, they argue, crime as a type of activity appeals to people who are impulsive,

---

Belief
The degree to which youths believe that the conformist values of parents and teachers are worthy of respect.

General theory of crime
The theory that criminal activity appeals to people who are impulsive, short-sighted, physical, risk-taking, nonverbal, and, most importantly, low in self-control.

WHAT DOES IT INCLUDE?

The Theory of the Bond

The first strand, attachment, refers to the degree to which children are sensitive to the expectations of parents and teachers. Commitment, the second strand, refers to the amount of time and energy youths invest in conventional activities such as obtaining good grades. The third strand, involvement, refers to their degree of participation in the world of conformity. The fourth strand, belief, refers to the degree to which youths believe that the conformist values of parents, teachers, and others are worthy of respect.

short-sighted, physical, risk-taking, and nonverbal. They use the term low self-control to describe this propensity, and maintain that people who are attracted to crime will also be attracted to other, analogous activities, such as drinking and driving (Keane, Maxim, and Teevan, 1996) and drug use (Sorenson and Brownfield, 1995).

What are the sources of low self-control? For Gottfredson and Hirschi, it originates in child rearing. Child rearing that is effective in discouraging delinquency requires that parents monitor their child's activity, recognize deviant behaviour when it occurs, and punish such behaviour when it does occur. Low self-control results when this process goes awry. Parents may not care what their children do, and even if they are concerned, they may be unable to supervise their children effectively or to punish the offending behaviour.

For Gottfredson and Hirschi, low self-control is the key cause of criminality (Arneklev, Grasmick, and Bursik, 1999; Piquero, MacIntosh, and Hickman, 2000). As such, it explains why some people rather than others are likely to behave in a criminal fashion. However, they also recognize the need to distinguish between criminality as a propensity and crime as a social event. Crimes occur when individuals with low self-control encounter situations and opportunities that are conducive to offending.

Since the publication of Gottfredson and Hirschi's *A General Theory of Crime* (1990), a number of studies have been undertaken to assess its central argument. Several of these studies report results consistent with the theory (Burton et al., 1998; Higgins, 2002; Keane, Maxim, and Teevan, 1996; Chapple, 2005; Pratt and Cullen, 2000; Sorenson and Brownfield, 1995); others are more critical.

Some writers have argued that although the theory is valuable, it must be used in conjunction with other theoretical arguments that emphasize the importance of criminal opportunity (LaGrange and Silverman, 1999; Longshore, 1998; Longshore and Turner, 1998), social learning (Pratt and Cullen, 2000), external social control (Brannigan et al., 2002; Nakhaie, Silverman, and LaGrange, 2000), or social strain (Peters et al., 2003). In a study of Vancouver street youth, for instance, Baron (2003) found that while measures of self-control were related to a range of criminal behaviours, as well as to other undesirable outcomes such as homelessness and having deviant peers, factors associated with other theories (such as general strain) were also of value.

While the general theory of crime assumes that the self-control is a stable characteristic of people, this has not been adequately demonstrated. In an important examination of this question, Turner and Piquero (2002) report that data from several different waves of youth surveys suggest that the measurement of self-control at different stages of the life cycle did not consistently support or refute Gottfredson and Hirschi's stability hypothesis.

Some critics draw attention to what they see as the methodological limitations of the argument. Self-control is a concept which is not easily conceptualized for research purposes. As Marcus (2004) argues, there is considerable debate in the research literature with respect to the degree to which self-control can be measured separately from the behaviours which it is supposed to explain. The tendency in the research literature to confuse causes and effects can result in circular argument. Stelios Stylianou (2002) has argued that too often tests of the theory have confused statistical significance with substantive significance. In other words, just because a piece of research meets the scientific criteria of "proof" does not mean that it has shown that the real-world effects demonstrated in the research are important.

As well, some writers argue that there is a need to pay more attention to the social and historical contexts within which offending occurs (Simpson and Piquero, 2002). Davis Redmon (2003), for instance, examined lewd behaviour during the Mardi Gras in New Orleans. He suggests that while those who might expose themselves in public or engage in some other form of drunken conduct score lower on measures of self-control, the reasons why they do what they do are complicated. A simple explanation would have us believe that low self-control causes the lewd conduct. It might be, Redmon maintains, that life in a society which demands high levels of self-control, people will try to find situations and contexts in which they can free themselves from that control. Mardi Gras, like Halloween and other carnival occasions, provides these opportunities in the context of repressive societies.

The general theory of crime has been criticized for its relative inattention to gender differences in the development of self-control (Higgins, 2004; Miller and Burack, 1993). It is well known that females generally offend less frequently and less seriously than males, and it would follow that self-control is stronger for women than for men. However, why this should be the case is less clear in the context of the theory. Some writers, such as Blackwell and Piquero (2005), have argued that insights derived from power–control theory might be helpful in answering this question.

Power–Control Theory

Power–control theory, which was developed by John Hagan, A.R. Gillis, and John Simpson (Hagan, 1989; Hagan, Gillis, and Simpson, 1979; Hagan, Simpson, and Gillis, 1987, 1988), provides another example of how family

Power–control theory
The theory that due to differential control (that is, girls are subject to greater control than boys) within the patriarchal family, males have a higher propensity to engage in risk taking and delinquent behaviour.

relationships permit or discourage delinquency. Of central interest to these researchers is the fact that males are much more delinquent than females. Hagan, Gillis, and Simpson try to explain this fact in terms of the family's differential ability to control male and female children.

Consistent with the general social control argument, power–control theory argues that social control is stratified within the family setting (Tibbetts and Herz, 1996). In traditional patriarchal families, which accept a cultural claim to male dominance, girls are subject to greater control than boys. Also, mothers are assigned greater responsibility for controlling dependent children. This position has two important implications. First, the informal social control processes in which family members are involved affect female more than male family members. Mothers are more likely to be the subjects and daughters are more likely to be the objects of this control. Second, as a result of these differences, male children are considerably freer than female children to engage in a wide range of risk-taking behaviour, some of which involves delinquency.

The power–control argument assumes that we must situate family relations of control in the broader context of economic and occupational stratification. Thus, parents who have more authority and more autonomy in the workplace are less likely to be strict disciplinarians at home. Moreover, these parents are more likely to encourage entrepreneurial forms of risk taking among their children. In this way, relations of authority in the workplace are mirrored in parent–child relations.

A recent revision to power–control theory tries to account more precisely for how parents—and especially mothers—affect the delinquency of their children (McCarthy, Hagan, and Woodward, 1999). In particular, it argues that in less patriarchal homes, mothers may be more likely to exert somewhat greater control over their sons. For instance, they may encourage their sons to reject the cultural claims to male dominance and risk taking that promote delinquent conduct. At the same time, they may control their daughters less and thereby encourage female risk taking and, it follows, greater delinquency. Because family control relations reflect occupational and economic conditions, it can be expected that changes in the gendered nature of workplace authority will have important implications for changes in the gendered character of delinquency (Uggen, 2000).

Interactional Theory

Terence Thornberry (1987) and colleagues (Thornberry et al., 1991) have proposed an **interactional theory of delinquency** that shares, at its core, the assumptions of control theory. However, Thornberry attempts to link the logic

Interactional theory of delinquency
The theory that weak ties to conventional others increase the likelihood of delinquent behaviour, but that these ties can be strengthened over time in response to changing circumstances.

of control theory to the insights derived from arguments stressing the role of cultural learning and peer influence. Like Hirschi, Thornberry argues that adolescents are at risk of engaging in delinquent behaviour when they have low levels of attachment to parents, of commitment to school, and of belief in conventional institutions and people. However, Thornberry emphasizes that the weakness of the ties to conventional others does not make delinquency inevitable, although it does make it more likely.

Furthermore, Thornberry argues, it is too simplistic to assume—as many theorists seem to do—that social ties to the world of conformity are unchanging. On the contrary, they may strengthen or weaken over time in response to changing circumstances. Most notably, while weak social bonds to parents or teachers may make delinquency possible, delinquency that has already occurred may further affect these relationships. Consider the example of a youth whose weak bond to her parents contributes to her engagement in delinquent activities. When the parents learn about the delinquency, they may react by rejecting her or by subjecting her to severe punishment. These reactions may further undermine the relationship between daughter and parents, thus making delinquency even more possible. In terms of illuminating the criminal event, the real strength of Thornberry's argument is that it attempts to come to terms with the dynamic and fluid character of criminality.

How Much Control Is Enough?

Most theories which focus on social control maintain that involvement in offending increases when social control is lessened. However, some theories take a different view and suggest that the problem might not be too little control but too much control.

The most venerable theory to make this argument is what is known as "labelling theory." While proponents of punishment or rehabilitation contend that when offenders are apprehended, the criminal justice system can play an important role in discouraging further offending, labelling theorists argue that the frustrations and problems associated with social control can actually increase the risk of criminal behaviour (Becker, 1963; Gibbs, 1966; Kitsuse, 1962; Rubington and Weinberg, 1987).

Labelling theory
The theory that frustration created by particular social arrangements, such as identifying a person as a criminal, may motivate criminal behaviour.

WHAT IS IT?

Labelling

A label is a form of stigma that makes it difficult for those on whom it has been imposed to lead normal lives. An individual who has been labelled a criminal, thief, delinquent, or troublemaker often finds it difficult to obtain employment or to maintain friendships with others, who tend to react to the powerful emotional content of the label. People who have been labelled can easily become frustrated by their personal circumstances or come to perceive as hypocritical the responses of those who condemn their conduct. Increasingly, legitimate associations become less available, and illegitimate associations more available.

Thus, they seek to understand how the control responses to even minor and sporadic criminal acts can create conditions that make crime more probable.

Labelling theorists strongly emphasize how the responses of the police and the criminal justice system to people identified as offenders create problems for those who must bear the label of "criminal." Such a label can be understood as a form of stigma that makes it difficult for those on whom it has been imposed to lead normal lives. An individual who has been labelled a criminal, thief, delinquent, or troublemaker often finds it difficult to obtain employment or to maintain friendships with others, who tend to react to the powerful emotional content of the label. People who have been labelled can easily become frustrated by their personal circumstances or come to perceive as hypocritical the responses of those who condemn their conduct. Increasingly, legitimate associations become less available, and illegitimate associations more so.

Labelling theorists contend that societal reactions have a strong impact on how labelled people see themselves. Feedback that consistently sends the message that one is a disreputable person may eventually lead to acceptance of that definition. This can create a criminal self-identity—that is, **secondary deviance** (Lemert, 1951). The problems created by the labelling process increase the likelihood that the labelled person will develop a stable pattern of criminal behaviour. Labelling theory describes a kind of **self-fulfilling prophecy**: people who are treated as if they are beyond redemption will come to act as if they are. The police and other criminal justice agencies are supposed to reduce involvement in crime; labelling theory suggests that they very often have the opposite effect.

Criminologists have criticized the labelling approach for redirecting attention from the individual onto the agencies of social control, and for failing to develop a body of supporting empirical evidence (Gove, 1975; Sagarin, 1975; Wellford, 1975).

A somewhat different understanding of how control might encourage offending has been investigated by Pogarsky and Piquero (2003). They note that several studies seem to show that people who have been punished may be more likely rather than less likely to offend as we might expect to be the case. They suggest that the research evidence provides some support for two competing explanations of this phenomenon. The first type, which they refer to as the selection account, suggests that the people who get selected out for

Secondary deviance
The idea that feedback that consistently sends the message that one is a disreputable person may eventually lead to the acceptance of the definition.

Self-fulfilling prophecy
The theory that people who are perceived as beyond redemption will come to act as if they are.

punishment by the criminal justice system are more likely to be chronic offenders than to be unlucky one-time offenders. Chronic offenders can be expected to underestimate the chances of getting caught anyway, so even if they are punished, they are still more likely to offend again. The other type of account, called the resetting account, is akin to what is sometimes called the "gambler's fallacy." In short, people think of the chances of getting caught as being interconnected. As a result, they might think that when they get caught, they have gotten their bad luck out of the way. Therefore, they commit more crimes and thus increase their chances of getting caught, on the assumption that their risk of getting caught in the future has been lowered. In the same way, gamblers who lose several bets in a row might increase their bets, on the assumption that the time for winning is now ripe.

Differential Coercion Theory

Mark Colvin (2000) has proposed a theory which also seeks to understand how the application of control intensifies rather than discourages criminal behaviour. For Colvin, the key concept is coercion, which he understands as being of two types. Direct or interpersonal coercion involves the use or threat of force and intimidation to create compliance through fear. Impersonal coercion refers to the pressures which arise from structural arrangements and circumstances that seem beyond individual control, such as the economic or social pressure associated with unemployment or poverty. Colvin recognizes that he is not the first to theorize about the relationships between coercion and crime, and he is careful to show how frequently coercion (or something like it) shows up in the criminological literature. What Colvin attempts to do, however, is to combine many of these insights in a theoretically systematic way.

Colvin argues that there are two dimensions to coercion. The first refers to the strength of the force—from no coercion to full coercion. The second refers to the consistency with which coercion is applied. Individuals differ in the degree to which they are exposed to coercion, which is why the explanation is referred to as a theory of differential coercion. Colvin's general argument is that exposure to coercion is related to criminal offending.

For Colvin, coercion creates social psychological deficits which are conducive to delinquent behaviour. People who are exposed to coercion are more likely to have higher levels of anger, lower self-control, weaker social bonds, and a higher level of "coercive ideation" (Unnever et al., 2004). The concept of coercive ideation refers to a world view which emphasizes coercive threats, which can in turn only be overcome with other coercion. In general, Colvin maintains:

> Predatory street criminals emerge from an experience of erratic coercion during socialization processes in families, in schools, among peers, in workplaces, and in the bureaucracies of welfare and criminal justice agencies. Both cultural norms and economic conditions influence the levels of coercion in these sites (Colvin, 2000:141–142).

Critics have suggested that the theory has several problems. Alexander and Bernard (2002) suggest, for instance, that the argument lacks the degree of specific detail necessary to allow for useful empirical tests. As well, they maintain that the argument might be better understood as a kind of strain theory rather than as a separate type of explanation. They speculate that, on its own, coercion might not prove to be a very powerful factor in the explanation of crime. Revisions to the theory by Colvin and his colleagues (2002) have stressed the role played by social support in alleviating the pressures created by coercion.

Control Balance Theory

In 1995, criminologist Charles Tittle proposed an influential new argument which he has labelled "control balance theory." Tittle argued that this explanation represented a new form of theoretical synthesis.

At the centre of this theory is the notion of a control ratio. This refers to the amount of control that each of us is subject to relative to the amount of control that each of us is able to exercise over others. Of course, in both cases, control is understood as a variable. We differ from each other with respect to what we can do to limit the ability of others to achieve their goals and with respect to the ability of others to prevent us from achieving our goals. Tittle argues that when the ratio is evenly balanced, we can expect conformity rather than rule-breaking. Departures from this position of balance in one direction or the other make deviance more likely. If there is a control deficit (that is, when the amount of control to which the individual is subject is greater than the amount of control which the individual can exercise), we can expect repressive forms of deviance to emerge. These include predation, defiance, and submission. When there is a control surplus (that is, when the amount of control the individual can exercise is greater than the amount of control to which the individual is subjected), we might expect more autonomous forms of deviance to emerge. These include exploitation, plunder, and decadence. As the control ratios grow more unbalanced, the kinds of deviance we experience can be expected to become more serious. The forms of deviance are themselves attempts to restore balance.

Tittle also argues that for deviance to occur, individuals must be motivated. In this respect, his approach differs from that of many other social control theorists (Tittle, 2004). The sources of this motivation can be quite varied. An important source of motivation can occur in the context of specific situations, when individuals are reminded of their specific control imbalances. Insults, mistreatment, or exploitation might remind individuals of the extent to which others exert control over their lives.

Like other recent theories, control balance lends itself to relatively sophisticated empirical examination, and a large literature has begun to develop (DeLisi and Hochstetler, 2002; Hickman and Piquero, 2001; Higgins and Lauterbach, 2004; Savelsberg, 1999). In response to the empirical and theoretical questions others have raised about the control balance argument, Tittle has attempted to reformulate the position in a way that speaks to these criticisms (Tittle, 2004). One such refinement is the introduction of the concept of "control balance desirability." In brief, this concept is defined in terms of the potential of a deviant act to alter "a control imbalance in a favorable way" in the long run and in terms of the indirectness or impersonality of the act. Tittle suggests that this concept of control balance desirability is useful in explaining why people choose to commit one deviant act rather than another.

Life Course Perspective

Another version of social control that pays explicit attention to change over time is the **life course perspective** (Laub, 2004; Laub and Sampson, 1993). Life course explanations differ markedly from explanations such as the general theory of crime discussed earlier. Explanations such as the general theory assume that perhaps one particular factor, such as low self-control, exerts rather constant effects on crime over the life cycle; in contrast, life course arguments seek to understand how and why different factors matter at different times (Bartusch et al., 1997; Paternoster and Brame, 1997).

Sampson and Laub tried to reconcile two contradictory sets of research findings. One body of research indicates that adult criminality is strongly influenced by patterns of childhood behaviour (Wilson and Herrnstein, 1985). This research suggests that people embark on criminal paths long before adulthood, so the characteristics of adults' social roles (such as unemployment) are largely irrelevant as causes of crime. Yet another body of research indicates that changes in people's lives (such as getting or losing a job, getting married, or

Life course perspective
Adult criminality is strongly influenced by patterns of childhood behaviour, and changes in people's lives affect the likelihood of involvement in crime.

having children) affect the likelihood of involvement in crime. According to Sampson and Laub, most criminologists focus their attention on the study of teenagers, and as a result little research has been done regarding whether the propensity to commit crime changes or remains stable over the life course.

Sampson and Laub's life course perspective makes an important distinction between "trajectories" and "transitions." **Trajectories** are the pathways on which people are located and the directions in which their lives seem to be moving. **Transitions** are specific life events—such as a first job or a marriage or the birth of a child—that may or may not alter those trajectories (Fleisher and Krienert, 2004). For example, a juvenile who is actively involved with delinquent peers, who lives in an abusive home, and who is failing at school may be on a criminal trajectory. However, suppose that in his late teens he begins a romantic relationship with someone who is nurturing and supportive, and the two decide to get married and raise a family. As he develops a deep commitment to the relationship and begins to plan for the future, his involvement in crime diminishes. In the life course framework, the marriage is a transition that alters his criminal trajectory.

For Sampson and Laub, trajectories change when transitions alter the nature and number of social bonds that help ensure conformity. However, it is not simply the occurrence of particular life events that brings these changes about. Rather, it is the "social investment" in the institutional relationship that dictates the importance of informal social control.

Sociologist Mark Warr (1998) argues that life course transitions involve much more than changes in the amount and types of informal social control. Major life changes such as moving to a new residence or starting a new job strongly affect relationships with delinquent peers. Warr suggests that marriage often replaces involvement with criminal peers with "preoccupation with one's spouse and family of procreation" (1998: 209). He concludes that life course theory must take greater account of delinquent "peer careers" in explaining why criminal involvement changes over the life course. In a manner consistent with this view, Wright and Cullen (2004) argue that finding a job might steer young people away from crime but not because of the strength of the employer-employee relationship. Rather, the workplace more likely provides the setting in which a group of delinquent peers is replaced by a group of conformist ones.

The interpretative value of the life course perspective extends beyond the level of individuals. For instance, Macmillan (1995) has used life course theory to explain increases in Canadian rates of property crime over the past several

Trajectories
In the life course perspective, these describe the directions in which lives seem to be moving.

Transitions
In the life course perspective, specific events that may or may not alter trajectories.

decades. Over this time, he argues, young people were more likely to leave their parental homes earlier, to marry later, and to wait longer for parenthood. With respect to life course theory, the implication is that young people—especially young males—were less likely to make those transitions that would have connected them to networks of informal social control. Possibly, this led to an increase in the pool of potential criminal offenders. Macmillan's analysis suggests that changes in crime rates may be related to structural changes in the life course.

Life course approaches are useful in looking at a variety of problems in criminology (Farrington, 2003). Kazemian and LeBlanc (2004) have shown how the life course approach can be combined with the study of criminal events to demonstrate how patterns of crime perpetration change from adolescence to adulthood. Their analysis suggests that changes in crime patterns across the life course have more to do with the opportunities and situations which confront individuals than with their innate propensities to commit crime.

Social Controls and the Community

Other theorists have considered the roles played by informal social controls at the level of the neighbourhood or local community. According to Wirth (1938), the larger, the more densely populated, and the more heterogeneous the community, the more accentuated are the characteristics associated with urbanism, including isolation and social breakdown. Urbanism brings together individuals who have no sentimental or emotional ties to one another. From this emerges a spirit of competition, self-aggrandizement, and exploitation. To counteract this spirit, society reverts to **formal social controls**.

People who are in frequent social contact with strangers and acquaintances develop a reserve toward one another. The strong family and friendship ties that are necessary for intimate communities disappear in cities; the result is higher levels of alienation, anomie, and delinquency. As a result, says Wirth, crime rates in urban areas are higher than those in rural areas, where informal social controls between intimates still operate.

Some urban neighbourhoods are more successful than others at constraining the delinquent inclinations of youths. Clifford Shaw and Henry McKay (1942), two sociologists associated with the University of Chicago, wanted to understand why some parts of their city had consistently high rates of crime, delinquency, and other social problems. It intrigued them that rates of delinquency remained high and steady even in neighbourhoods where the "turnover" of residents was rapid and there were significant changes in the

Formal social controls
Conventional methods of technology and physical coercion, such as the police force, used to maintain social order.

ethnic and demographic mix. They associated urban variations in rates of crime with the social context of urban areas rather than with the specific characteristics of the populations who lived in them.

Social disorganization
Long-term, widespread deterioration of social order and control in a population.

Shaw and McKay found that high-crime areas are characterized by a high degree of **social disorganization**—that is, the residents of these areas were unable to achieve common values or solve their common problems (Kornhauser, 1978). The researchers argued that areas characterized by high levels of social disorganization tend to be economically disadvantaged, to have high rates of population turnover, and to be racially and ethnically diverse. In such areas, the informal social controls that might constrain delinquency are ineffective. As predicted by Wirth (1938), local friendship networks are less likely to develop, and levels of participation in formal or voluntary organizations are low. As a result, adults in these communities may be ineffective in their attempts to supervise and control teenage peer groups that are likely to become involved in delinquency (Sampson and Groves, 1989).

The logic of the social disorganization argument is manifested in the many forms of crime prevention that attempt to develop a sense of community in high-crime neighbourhoods. Neighbourhood Watch and similar programs seek to increase levels of interaction among residents; at the same time, they encourage neighbours to develop a sense of responsibility for one another.

After a long period of dormancy, interest in social disorganization theory is surging (Oberwittler, 2004; Sampson, Raudenbush, and Earls, 1997; Veysey and Messner, 1999). In an important restatement of this perspective, Bursik and Grasmick (1993; Bursik, 1999) distinguish three types of social controls; all three are less effective in areas characterized by high levels of social disorganization. "Private" controls are associated with family and friends and with other groups with which individuals are intimately linked. "Parochial" controls are somewhat broader and are exerted by local schools, stores, churches, and voluntary organizations. "Public" or external controls relate to the local community's ability to mobilize sources of control that originate beyond its boundaries. Local communities are not equally successful in their attempts to get urban bureaucracies to allocate funds to neighbourhood projects and to get the police to take neighbourhood problems seriously.

Bursik and Grasmick contend that when these controls are operating, they discourage crime by discouraging both criminal motivation and the opportunities for crime. They also note that these controls do not appear instantaneously; rather, they develop slowly over time as residents associate with one another and establish relationships. Factors that contribute to neighbourhood instability undermine the processes that lead to effective community controls and thus make higher rates of crime and delinquency more likely.

In another influential reworking of the social disorganization paradigm, Sampson and Groves (1989) argued that certain structural characteristics of neighbourhoods—such as low socio-economic status, residential mobility, and racial heterogeneity—disrupt local social organizations. As a result, local social networks become unstable, the level of participation in community

---

BOX 5.2

Crime and Social Capital

Much of the recent research into the relationship between social disorganization and crime makes use of the concept of "social capital." The term social capital is used in a wide variety of ways in the social sciences, but in general it relates to the ways in which the social relationships which people have allow them to accomplish what they could not accomplish on their own. The idea of social capital can be distinguished from physical or human capital. Physical capital refers to real objects (tools, factories, properties) that can make one more productive. Human capital refers to the characteristics of people (such as their skills, abilities, or training) which could increase productivity. Social capital refers not to the tools people own or their personal characteristics but to the connections that exist between people. The basic point is that "social networks have value." In other words, the networks in which we are involved make resources available to each of us which can provide both individual and collective benefits. The substance of social capital involves the sharing of information, mutual trust, mutual obligations, and shared norms about appropriate behaviour.

So, how does the concept of social capital amplify our understanding of social disorganization? In simple terms, social capital can be seen as an important factor which intervenes between the structural aspects of social disorganization (poverty, population turnover, etc.) and informal social controls at the community level. In neighbourhoods where social capital is plentiful, neighbours share information about local problems and common rules about what kinds of behaviour can and cannot be tolerated. Also in such neighbourhoods, parents may assume responsibility not only for their own children but for others' children when they see them misbehaving in public. In a review of relevant research, Charles E. Kubrin and Ronald Weitzer (2003) conclude that while relatively few studies have focused on these relationships, those which do provide support for the general argument.

Of course, social capital also has a "negative" side (Halpern, 2005; Putnam, 2000). Organized crime—one of the kinds of crime we will discuss in Chapter 10—can be seen as a clear example of such "negative social capital." In other words, organized crime networks are effective precisely because of the social capital to which network members have access. In a very insightful analysis of the Sicilian Mafia, for instance, Diego Gambetta (1993) shows how it is the resources inherent in the relationships that Mafioso have with their clients, politicians, and colleagues that allows the organization to accomplish what individuals alone cannot accomplish.

groups declines, and teenage gangs go unsupervised. The end result is communities which are unable to exert control over the kinds of behaviour that residents find threatening. Tests of the argument (Lowenkamp et al., 2003; Sun et al., 2004; Veysey and Messner, 1999) have generally been supportive of the theoretical model.

Social disorganization theories, both older and newer ones, are usually perceived as relating specifically to city life. But they may be more general than this. For example, Osgood and Chambers (2000) found that in several American states, rates of juvenile arrests for violent crime in rural areas and small towns were related to such "urban" variables as residential instability, family disruption, and ethnic heterogeneity. Also, there is no theoretical basis for the idea that primary, parochial, and public controls have less to do with rural life than with life in major urban areas.

THE POWER OF LAW: THE DETERRENCE DOCTRINE

Specific and General Deterrence

Deterrence
Theory of prevention in which the threat of punishment or retribution is expected to forestall some act from occurring.

Specific/special deterrence
The ways in which individuals are deterred from offending or reoffending by receiving punishment.

Punishment
Confinement, restriction of activities, infliction of pain, and other measures taken to exact retribution, to enforce compliance, or to bring about behavioural changes.

General deterrence
The ways in which individuals, on seeing offenders receiving punishment, will be deterred from breaking the law themselves.

Severity
With reference to deterrence, the perceived or actual seriousness of the penalty for a legal infraction.

Laws threaten penalties for their violation. **Deterrence** theories are concerned with how these threats are communicated to potential offenders. The belief that legal deterrence is a valuable mechanism of crime control continues to dominate criminal justice philosophy and practice (Maxwell and Gray, 2000). Deterrence theories attempt to determine whether the threat of penalties decreases the likelihood of offending. **Specific or special deterrence** refers to how individuals are deterred, through **punishment**, from offending or reoffending. Suppose you break into a house, are apprehended, and then are sentenced to prison for a period of time. If the prison term discourages you from committing another such crime, we can say that it is a specific or special deterrent. According to the principle of **general deterrence**, individuals are deterred from breaking the law when they watch others who have done so receive punishment. Thus, friends who watch you receive punishment for breaking the law will desist from breaking and entering.

Deterrence of any kind has three properties. The first is the **severity** of the penalty. Does the law threaten prison, or only a fine? Are offenders likely to be sentenced if they are caught, or are they likely to be released with a warning? The Criminal Code states clearly the punishment attached to each crime, and sentencing guidelines are set for judges to apply in the cases that come before them.

It is assumed that all individuals in society are aware of the law's prescriptions about punishment and are deterred in direct proportion to the escalating threat of this punishment. So it should be widely understood that the most severe punishments are reserved for the most serious crimes. Sentencing guidelines at the provincial and federal levels change fairly often; presumably, this reflects changes in society's sense of the seriousness of various offences.

The second property of legal threats is the certainty of punishment. Regardless of what the law threatens, how likely is it that the offender will be apprehended and sentenced? Many research studies have found that with respect to deterrence, certainty is a more important factor than severity. In other words, a high likelihood of being punished is more important than being punished in a specified manner.

Certainty
With reference to deterrence, the likelihood (perceived or objectively measurable) that an offender will be apprehended or punished.

As we saw in earlier chapters, most of the crimes that are known to the police were brought to their attention by the public. For various reasons, however, many crimes go unreported. Furthermore, many crimes that are reported remain unsolved. In both situations, the offender "gets away" with the crime. The rational offender calculates the certainty of risk and then acts on this calculation. When risk of apprehension and conviction is high, the crime is less likely to occur.

The third property of legal threats is the celerity (swiftness) of punishment (Clark, 1988). When justice is delayed, the perception may arise either that the punishment is unfair or that it will have a diminished impact on the offender. Concerns have been raised that delays in the justice process may unfairly stigmatize individuals who are in fact innocent. Court backlogs that lead to trial delays of a year or more have led some to argue that cases should be dismissed without guilt or innocence being determined. The message conveyed by such dismissals would be that the criminal justice system is incapable of handling cases swiftly. This would cast doubt on the system's ability to handle them at all.

Celerity
With reference to deterrence, the swiftness (perceived or objectively measurable) with which an offender is apprehended and punished.

Mark Stafford and Mark Warr (1993) have questioned the distinction most researchers make between general and specific deterrence. In their view, the distinction is false. To assume that general deterrence is effective is to assume that those who form the audience have no direct knowledge of the punishment in question. Yet some of those who learn about the punishment of others have committed the same kind of act for which the punishment is being meted out, although they themselves did not get caught. In other words, they have experience with

WHAT DOES IT MEAN?

Specific versus General Deterrence

Specific deterrence refers to how individuals are deterred from offending or reoffending by receiving punishment. With general deterrence, individuals who see offenders receiving punishment will be deterred from breaking the law themselves.

"avoiding punishment." Similarly, in the case of specific deterrence, it is usually assumed that the punishment the individual experiences will affect the likelihood of subsequent offending. At the same time, the individual who is being punished may have knowledge of others who committed similar acts and didn't get caught. Thus, Stafford and Warr maintain, the distinction that is usually made between general and specific deterrence rests on a number of simplifying assumptions that distort empirical realities. They suggest that instead of speaking of general and specific deterrent effects, it makes more sense to speak of indirect and direct experience with punishment and punishment avoidance. An empirical test of this view with respect to the deterrence of drinking and driving found that offending decisions are indeed affected by both personal and vicarious experiences, and that such decisions are also influenced by knowledge about both punishment and punishment avoidance (Piquero and Paternoster, 1998).

Legal versus Informal Sanctions

Some researchers suggest that in emphasizing the importance of penalty characteristics, deterrence theories have adopted too narrow a view of how legal threats discourage crime. Williams and Hawkins (1986) assert that the deterrent effects of legal sanctions may be supplemented by at least three other types of sanctions: commitment costs, attachment costs, and stigma of arrest. **Commitment costs** refer to the possibility that arrest may jeopardize people's investments in some legitimate activity. The greater a person's investment in some conformist line of activity, the more he or she will be discouraged from offending. Commitment costs include concerns about education prospects and future employment. **Attachment costs** refer to the costs associated with the loss of valued relationships with friends and family members. The belief that arrest will weaken these ties may make arrest a fearsome prospect. The **stigma of arrest** refers to the belief that apprehension by the police may harm one's reputation. It is important to distinguish this fear that others will learn about one's arrest from the fear that they will learn that one has committed the act. Williams and Hawkins point out that generally, less stigma is associated with driving while impaired than with being arrested for this crime. In the case of homicide, however, the stigma associated with arrest may not be much greater than the stigma associated with the commission of the act. Williams and Hawkins contend that commitment costs, attachment costs, and the stigma of arrest are forms of informal social control that are activated by formal controls, and so should be viewed as part of the deterrence process.

Commitment costs
The possibility that arrest may jeopardize people's investments in some legitimate activity.

Attachment costs
The costs associated with the weakening of ties to loved ones that may make an arrest a fearsome prospect.

Stigma of arrest
The belief that apprehension by the police may harm one's reputation.

Arguments about the deterrent properties of legal sanctions do not assume that potential offenders are accurately informed about the risks they face. How accurate their perceptions are is itself an excellent question (Henshel and Silverman, 1975). We suggest that in terms of whether an individual will offend, what the law actually threatens is less significant than what people believe the law threatens. As well, decisions to offend or not offend reflect not just the threats of the law but also the individual's own history of offending. What we believe about the risks of getting caught is to some degree at least conditioned by whether we have been caught in the past (Pogarsky et al., 2004).

Situational Deterrence

Criminologist Maurice Cusson (1993) has criticized deterrence theory and research for failing to address the specific character of the situations in which crimes occur. A typical research project might ask respondents how likely it is that they would be apprehended if they attempted to steal a car. Too often, however, the context of the automobile theft is not specified. Obviously, how risky one perceives car theft to be depends greatly on the specific circumstances in which the theft is attempted. Study respondents will make certain private assumptions in order to provide an answer to the researcher's question; thus, the answers may have little to do with the actual assessment of risks that an individual makes in any specific situation.

Cusson notes also that when researchers ask survey subjects to calmly assess the risks of apprehension, they are ignoring the emotional character of the deterrence process. Deterrence, he argues, is not about the cold and rational calculation of risks but about fear. A burglar who breaks into a house may rationally believe that the chances of getting caught are low, but may still panic when he hears a noise. Fear can override rational calculation and make the deterrence process look quite different in reality than it appears in theory. For these reasons, Cusson suggests that we must consider deterrence as a situational factor. **Situational deterrence** emphasizes how the offender's fear of apprehension is related to the specific circumstances of the criminal event.

Situational deterrence
The ways in which the offender's fear of apprehension are related to the specific circumstances of the criminal event.

According to Cusson, potential offenders face two types of danger in the pre-criminal situation. The first type is immediate: a robber worries that the victim may fight back or be armed; a burglar worries that a barking dog may bite. The second type of danger has to do with subsequent harm relating to some

WHAT IS IT?

Situational Deterrence

Situational deterrence emphasizes how the offender's fear of apprehension is related to the specific circumstances of the criminal event.

BOX 5.3

Closed Circuit Television and Deterrence

In recent years, especially since the events of September 11, 2001, closed circuit television systems have been seen as a potentially useful means of dealing with crime (Walby, 2005). To date, CCTV has been more popular in European than North American nations. According to Welsh and Farrington (2003), during the 1990s, Britain spent three-quarters of its crime prevention budget on CCTV. In North America, the technology has been used principally in private places such as schools and hotels. The current trend is to place surveillance cameras in more public settings.

Of course, the real utility of CCTV depends on the correctness of a deterrence model of criminal behaviour. In other words, a major reason to invest in this approach is the belief that rational offenders will perceive an increase in the probability of apprehension. As a result, their criminal behaviour will be effectively discouraged. Of course, it is also argued that the use of cameras allows for a greater likelihood of identification of those who are "caught in the act." But even in these cases, the hope of crime prevention planners is that higher rates of apprehension will produce more significant general deterrent effects.

How effective is CCTV in preventing crime? To date, this is not a question that yields a simple answer. Part of the reason for the confusion is the fact that the research intended to evaluate the effects of CCTV has not been rigorous enough to allow definitive statements to be made. There are several problems in this respect. For one thing, if CCTV encourages more reporting of crime, then crime rates might actually go up rather than down after the technology is introduced. In addition, crime prevention measures often come in packages, so it might be difficult to determine whether any increases we observe are attributable to CCTV or some other measure which is also underway (or even a combination of the two).

Reviews of several studies of CCTV (Deisman, 2003; Eck, 1997; Welsh and Farrington, 2003) suggest that:

1. CCTV can achieve overall decreases in crime, but such decreases are likely to be quite small.
2. The effects of CCTV on crime are highly variable and depend not only on the type of crime but also on the type of setting in which the cameras are located.
3. The strongest effects are associated with crime against property which occur in car parks.
4. The effects of CCTV can be magnified by widespread publicity announcing the installation and operation of surveillance cameras.

It is important to point out that the debate over CCTV is not narrowly focused on questions of effectiveness. Many social critics worry about the threats which this technology poses to civil liberties and the ways in which it can worsen problems relating to racial and other forms of social profiling.

element in the pre-criminal situation. A television monitor in the convenience store about to be robbed does not threaten the robber directly, but it may eventually if it leads to the robber's apprehension.

Cusson notes that the risks facing offenders before and during the commission of the offence do not guarantee that the offender will be deterred. Offenders differ in terms of the level of courage they can muster in particular situations and also in terms of their ability to manage the fear they do experience. Also, some crimes—such as joyriding and vandalism—may be attractive precisely because they have an element of danger.

Cusson's analysis forces us to recognize that deterrence effects are not embodied solely in abstract legal threats; they are also found in the risks that offenders understand themselves to be facing in the settings in which criminal events actually occur.

Ambivalence about Crime and Deterrence Strategies

Deterrence arguments figure quite prominently in many public policy debates. Despite the perception that there is widespread consensus on the need to crack down on crime, public attitudes toward crime and its prevention suggest a strong degree of ambivalence, which has many sources. First, Canadians are concerned that the law is not being adequately enforced (Currie, 1985). Also, they feel that the law generally reflects their values (Tyler, 1990), and they obey the law because they believe it to be right. At the same time, they are critical of how justice is presently being dispensed. Many believe that the law favours the rich and the powerful and that the legal process is too slow. The system as a whole is seen as ineffective in deterring serious crime, especially in terms of the punishment that is administered (Brillon, 1985; Baron and Hartnagel, 1996).

Yet there is no consensus in the research literature regarding the effectiveness of punishment in reducing criminal behaviour. Cook (1977) reviewed the literature on deterrent effects (including the impact of capital punishment on violent crime) and concluded that there is little persuasive evidence that deterrence works or even exists. This undermines proposals for strict punishment regimens, especially if they are contrary to our views of what is humane and just.

Second, as Braithwaite (1989) points out, confusion has developed over what is perceived as a conflict between crime control and respect for civil liberties. Some express concern that too much informal social control impedes individual freedom—neighbours spying on neighbours can be a real threat to personal privacy. However, punishment delivered by formal agents is ineffective

BOX 5.4

Does the Law Deter Impaired Driving?

The first federal law against impaired driving was passed in 1921. By enacting this law, the Canadian Parliament made driving while intoxicated a summary offence. In 1969, major changes to the law were made. At that time, the 1921 law was repealed, and a 1951 law, which prohibited "driving while impaired," was maintained. However, the 1969 revisions defined this condition as driving while blood alcohol concentration exceeded .08%. It also prohibited the refusal to provide a breath sample for an "approved instrument." Have these laws been effective in reducing the number of highway accidents caused by impaired driving?

Figure 5.1 shows a general decline in the number of impaired driving incidents between 1977 and 2002. But how much of this decline is attributable to the law? Even more specifically, has the law reduced the number of fatalities associated with impaired driving? An answer to the second question has been provided by Mark Asbridge and his colleagues in the Department of Community Health and Epidemiology at Dalhousie University (Asbridge et al., 2004).

The researchers note that many studies have suggested that laws of this type produce short-term effects only. In other words, the publicity which surrounds the introduction of new laws causes drivers to recalculate the chances of getting caught. Over time, though, the average driver realizes that the chances of getting caught are still quite low, and as a result, the offending behaviour returns to its old levels. However, these investigators sought to determine what the effects of the impaired driving law would be over the longer term.

In order to investigate the relationship between the legal innovations in 1969 and the number of fatalities, it was necessary to employ some sophisticated time-series analyses which would control the influence of other factors that might also contribute to any observed decrease. Such factors included, for instance, the passage of the mandatory seatbelt law and the founding of Mothers Against Drunk Driving.

Focusing on the province of Ontario, the researchers found that over the period 1969 to 1996, drinking-driving fatalities decreased by 18 percent. However, how do we reconcile the finding of a long-term decline with other studies which found the decline to be only short-term? Asbridge and his colleagues suggest that different social processes might be operating over the longer term to produce this decrease. For one thing, the marshalling of resources to actually enforce new laws might take a considerable amount of time, and thus the effect of actual enforcement might not be apparent over the short term. In addition, it is over the longer term that the law is likely to affect moral judgment. This means that the law does not only deter crime by scaring people; it also encourages them to think differently about the threatened behaviour. Once again, we would not expect these changes in moral judgment to occur over the short term.

Figure 5.1

Rates of impaired driving incidents, Canada, 1977–2002

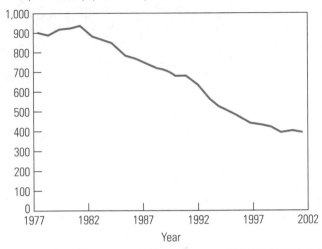

Rate per 100,000 population 16 years and older

Source: Janhevich, D., M. Gannon, and N. Morisset. 2003. "Impaired Driving and Other Traffic Offences 2002." *Juristat.* 23(9): 3.

unless it is combined with informal social sanctions (that is, shaming). When the risk of arrest is perceived as low and the severity of punishment is minimal, individuals can still be prevented from committing crimes by the stigmatizing reactions of others.

Third, there is a lack of consensus over the usefulness of incarceration (Miller and Anderson, 1986). At the same time, we are uncomfortable with leaving reintegration to communities. Few communities are ready to receive criminals as they begin their transition to "normal" life. In fact, some communities are actively blocking the return of released offenders, especially those who were imprisoned for sex crimes. Offenders need to be reintegrated into society and kept from reoffending, but few communities are doing much to take this job over from formal agencies.

Fourth, Canadians are ambivalent about crime because they are in awe of it. The reality of violent crimes is usually horrific, yet in the media such crimes are presented as titillating, thrilling, and addictive. It is no easy task to promote pro-social behaviour in a society in which criminals are often depicted as folk heroes (Phelps, 1983). The **folk hero syndrome** may be on the decline (see Skipper, 1985); that being said, there still exists in our society a residual belief that criminals should be admired for resisting convention.

Folk hero syndrome
A residual belief that the criminal should be admired for expressing some degree of resistance to convention.

Rational choice theories
These focus on the offenders' actions and decisions as they are based on perceived benefits rather than on precipitating or psychological factors.

RATIONAL CHOICE THEORIES

Like deterrence theories, **rational choice theories** have their roots in the classical tradition (Piquero and Tibbetts, 2002). However, rational choice theories take a somewhat broader perspective than deterrence theories. They recognize the role that legal threats play in deterring offending but also argue that other factors—such as the potential gains that might be derived from the commission of crimes and the ease with which they can be committed—are also important.

The increasing popularity of rational choice theories can be seen at least in part as a product of the dissatisfaction of many criminologists with more traditional motivational theories (Fattah, 1993). Theories that emphasize strain or cultural learning, for instance, are seen as creating false distinctions between criminal and non-criminal activity. Rational choice theories argue that both types of behaviour are oriented toward the same kinds of ends (e.g., money, self-gratification); therefore, criminal behaviour may not require a unique motivation (Cornish and Clarke, 1986). Also, traditional motivational theories really only explain why some people may be predisposed to commit crimes—not why or how crimes are committed. Because crimes are events that occur in specific places at specific times, motivational theories can be faulted for not paying enough attention to the situational context of criminal events.

Rational choice theories focus on offenders' actions based on perceived benefits rather than on precipitating social or psychological factors (Clarke and Felson, 1993; Nagin and Paternoster, 1993; Tibbetts and Gibson, 2002). As offenders seek benefits and attempt to avoid losses, they make decisions and choices that can be understood as reflecting rational thought. Rational choice theorists argue that instead of considering which broad social factors (strain or cultural values) influence offending behaviour, we should really be studying how offenders make decisions. How do burglars decide on their targets? How do they decide which specific house to break into? How do they decide what to do if they see a window sticker indicating that the home is protected by an alarm system? The answers to questions such as these allow rational choice theorists to develop an understanding of criminal events and of the role that offenders play in those events (Tunnell, 1992). Unlike traditional motivation theories, rational choice theory is interested in the situational character of crime (Birkbeck and LaFree, 1993).

Rational choice theories do not assume that offenders operate in a purely rational fashion. Rather, it is assumed that offenders usually proceed from a "limited rationality." In other words, they may inaccurately perceive the benefits of committing particular crimes; they may lack the time to weigh the possible outcomes; or they may have access to only limited information with which to make their decisions.

Rational choice theorists contend that because specific situational factors are important and because offender decision making varies across situations, it makes little sense to develop a generic theory of crime. The choices involved in robbing a convenience store are very different from the ones involved in stealing a car or defrauding a bank (Clarke, 1992). Clarke has described these choices as consisting of five separate elements, which can in turn be used to develop strategies for situational crime prevention. These include increasing the effort the offender must expend; increasing the risks the offender must face; reducing the rewards or benefits the offender expects to obtain; removing offenders' excuses or rationalizations for their actions; and reducing or avoiding provocations that may tempt or incite offenders to criminal actions (Center for Problem Oriented Policing, 2003). Clarke has formulated these elements in terms of specific recommendations that could prevent crime; the recommendations cover topics ranging from identifying targets to reducing emotional arousal. Connecting specific behavior to specific responses has made situational crime prevention particularly interesting to police and private security agencies which are working on ways to manage environments in a way that reduces the likelihood of crime.

SUMMARY

Critics of motivation theories argue that many people contemplate breaking the law but do not follow through. Formal and informal social controls may block them from acting in rational but criminal ways. Building on earlier contributions, Hirschi argues that delinquency emerges when controls diminish through the weakening of the social bonds that link adolescents to conformist others. Strong social bonds, which are based on high levels of attachment, commitment, involvement, and belief, and which are built into the socialization that individuals experience at home and at school, insulate youths from delinquent involvement. These bonds are subject to pressure from changes in the ways in which families function. They are also influenced by the degree of social disorganization experienced in communities, disorganization that can lead to weakening social ties and increased levels of criminality.

At the same time, it is possible to argue that too much control—like too little control—can cause problems for social order. Labelling theories and coercion theory seek to understand this issue. In a more integrated way, control balance theory attempts to understand the problems of too much and too little control in an integrated way.

The purpose of deterrence strategies is to communicate to individuals the threat that punishment will follow delinquent acts. Deterrence does not result if the law is not imposed in a quick, certain, and severe way. But deterrence depends on many factors, including the fear of punishment, the perception of risk, and so on. It has been suggested that what the law actually threatens is less relevant to the decision to offend than what people believe it threatens. Perceptions of deterrence are also affected by widespread public doubts regarding the likelihood and efficacy of punishment.

Some criminals make rational choices to involve themselves in crime—that is, they weigh the benefits of crime involvement against the costs of apprehension. This may mean that certain individuals are more likely to live a life of crime. Career criminals follow a path toward heavy involvement in crime, even when they have not actually made a deliberate choice of crime as a career. There is evidence that a small number of individuals commit a disproportionate amount of crime.

QUESTIONS FOR REVIEW AND DISCUSSION

1. What factors do you think strengthen the social bonds between parents and children? What weakens those bonds?
2. How effective are various legal and informal sanctions in deterring crime? Is the threat of jail the only form of punishment that is effective in stopping crime?
3. If crime is so profitable, why don't we all commit crimes?
4. If most crime is committed by a small number of people, why can't we simply focus on that small group and make sure they are constrained from acting in criminal ways?
5. Discuss some of the ways in which "too much social control" might actually result in more crime.

RECOMMENDED READINGS

Bursik, R., and H.G. Grasmick. 1993. *Neighborhoods and Crime: The Dimensions of Effective Community Control.* New York: Lexington Books.

Colvin, M. 2002. *Crime and Coercion: An Integrated Theory of Criminality.* New York: St Martin's Press.

Gottfredson, M., and T. Hirschi. 1990. *A General Theory of Crime*. Stanford, CA: Stanford University Press.

Piquero, A.R., and S.G. Tibbetts. 2002. *Rational Choice and Criminal Behavior*. New York: Routledge.

Putnam, R.D. 2000. *Bowling Alone: The Collapse and Revival of American Community*. New York: Simon and Schuster, Chapter 18.

INFOTRAC® COLLEGE EDITION

Explore InfoTrac® College Edition, your online university library, which includes hundreds of popular and scholarly journals in which you can find articles related to the topics in this chapter. Visit InfoTrac® through your web browser (**www.infotrac-college.com**) or through this book's website (**www.criminalevent-4e.nelson.com**).

WHAT'S ON THE WEB?

For chapter links and quizzes, check out the accompanying website at **www.criminalevent-4e.nelson.com**.

Chapter 6 — Opportunities, Lifestyles, and Situations

LEARNING OBJECTIVES:

- understand that the victim, and not just the offender, needs to be at the centre of criminological analysis
- explore opportunity theories, with specific reference to explanations focusing on lifestyle and routine activities
- discuss recent refinements of opportunity arguments
- discuss how crimes can be understood as interactions rather than just actions

INTRODUCTION

The fact that offenders are ready and willing to engage in criminal conduct—because of their personalities or backgrounds or views of the law—does not in and of itself explain how criminal events occur. Potential offenders must also encounter opportunities that allow them to pursue their criminal inclinations. This is equally true of other events: an inclination to learn the saxophone, go to graduate school, or become a skydiver does not ensure that these things will happen. In such cases, as in the case of criminal events, it is useful to consider how opportunities allow individuals to act on their inclinations. It is important, as well, that we understand precisely what happens when offenders and opportunities meet. How do offenders offend, and how are victims victimized? In this chapter, we consider how contemporary criminologists theorize about these and related questions.

We are concerned in this chapter with the study of actual and potential crime victims. A criminal event perspective encourages us to recognize that in many situations victims are as important to the occurrence of crime as offenders. Often, crimes happen not only because offenders are present and behave in particular ways, but also because victims are present and behave in particular ways. The study of criminal offenders is, as we have seen, at least several centuries old; criminological interest in the study of victims is much more recent. It was really only in the 1960s and 1970s that scholars, building on the pioneering work of earlier writers, began to move the study of crime victims to the centre of criminological analysis (Fattah, 1976; Kennedy and Sacco, 1998).

At least three factors account for the emergence of "victimology" as a field of study. *First,* some of the most important theoretical ideas in offender-centred criminology—such as Merton's strain theory, Sutherland's differential association theory, and social disorganization theory—were developed in the 1930s. After three decades or so of theoretical testing, in the 1960s and 1970s, some criminologists began to question the utility of these accounts and to search for more novel approaches to the problem of crime. Several theoretical developments during this period, such as labelling theory and conflict theory, reflect this widespread desire to inject new life into the criminological enterprise. In a similar way, many criminologists became more and more interested in how an emphasis on the role played by victims might reorient the analysis of crime.

Second, in the 1970s, the first major advances were made in the development of victimization surveys. In the United States, for instance, the National Crime Survey began to make available on a regular basis vast amounts of data about the nature, causes, and consequences of criminal victimization. This encouraged researchers to ask and answer empirical questions about why some people rather than others become victims of crime, and about the role played by victims in victimization processes.

Third, in the 1960s, Canada—and to an even greater extent the United States—experienced a dramatic rise in levels of predatory crime (Cohen and Felson, 1979). The increase in victimization levels gave birth to a powerful victims' movement that demanded governments take seriously the pain, suffering, and rights of crime victims (Weed, 1995). Governments were compelled to respond to the demands of victim organizations; this made social scientific knowledge about crime victims especially timely.

In the past few decades, the study of crime victims has revolved essentially around two key issues. The first has to do with "victimization opportunity." In short, we ask why some people are more at risk of victimization than others, and how relative risk is affected by what people do. The second issue relates to the notion of "victim–offender interaction." In this respect, we seek to discover how the actions of victims combine with the actions of offenders to produce criminal outcomes. This chapter considers both issues.

OPPORTUNITY THEORIES AND VICTIMIZATION

Lifestyle Exposure

Cloward and Ohlin's analysis of criminal behaviour (see Chapter 4) extended the range of relevant theoretical questions beyond the search for motivational factors. Their theory alerts us to this cogent fact: it is not enough to understand why some people are motivated to break the law (since answers to this question generally do not explain why some laws and not others end up being broken); it is also necessary to understand how criminal inclinations are channelled by opportunities to be criminal.

Since the late 1970s, the study of criminal opportunities has been dominated by researchers interested in victimization events. Their explanations, which are known as lifestyle exposure or routine activities theories, focus on how spatial and temporal variations in crime are related to variations in the opportunities to commit crime.

> **Lifestyle exposure theory**
> Focuses on patterned ways in which people with certain demographic characteristics distribute their time and energies across a range of activities, and the relationship of these patterned ways to the risk of victimization by motivated offenders.

The **lifestyle exposure theory** of criminal victimization was developed by Michael Hindelang, Michael Gottfredson, and James Garofalo in their 1978 book *Victims of Personal Crime*. Their theory, which is grounded in the data of victimization surveys, seeks to explain what it is about being male, young, single, or poor that increases the chances of being victimized. The linchpin of their argument is the concept of lifestyle. In general terms, *lifestyle* refers to the patterned ways in which people distribute their time and energies across a range of activities. We have no trouble recognizing that the lifestyle of a teenage male differs markedly from that of an elderly female. These differences relate to how and where one spends one's time, with whom one associates, and what types of leisure pursuits one enjoys. These lifestyle differences are not merely a matter of personal choice; they also reflect the social roles one is required to play and the various types of social constraints to which one is subject.

Where and how people spend their time is related to their risk of victimization. Engaging in evening activities outside the home increases an individual's chances of becoming a crime victim (although it is evident that the home is also a location of a fair amount of violent crime). Research also suggests that crimes are more likely to occur in some places and in the course of some activities than in others.

Hindelang, Gottfredson, and Garofalo (1978: 251–64) offer the following eight propositions about victimization. These summarize the link between

BOX 6.1

Victimization Risk and Evening Activities outside the Home

Ever since the earliest victimization studies, it has been clear that the risks of victimization increase as one engages in higher numbers of activities outside the home. Data from the 2004 General Social Survey illustrate the strength of this relationship.

Rates of Violent Crime per 1,000 Canadians

Number of Evening Activities per Month	Total Violence	Sexual Assault	Robbery	Physical Assault
Less than 10	44	8	f	33
10 to 19	77	14	5	59
20 to 29	104	21	11	72
30 and more	174	36	20	118

f—too unreliable to publish

Source: Gannon, M., and K. Mihorean. 2005. "Criminal Victimization in Canada 2004." Juristat 25(7): 23.

lifestyle and key demographic variables such as age, sex, marital status, family income, and race:

1. The more time individuals spend in public places (especially at night), the more likely they are to be victimized.
2. Certain lifestyles make it more likely that individuals will frequent public places.
3. Individuals tend to interact with people who share their lifestyle.
4. The probability that an individual will be a victim increases with the extent to which he or she and the offender belong to the same demographic category.
5. The proportion of time that an individual spends in places where there are many non-family members varies according to lifestyle.
6. The chance that an individual will be the victim of crime (especially theft) increases with the amount of time he or she spends with non-family members.
7. Lifestyle differences are related to the ability of individuals to isolate themselves from those with offender characteristics.
8. Lifestyle variations influence the convenience, desirability, and ease of victimizing individuals.

BOX 6.2

Robbery Incidents and Time of Day

Crimes vary in space and also in time. The graph below shows how robbery incidents are distributed over the hours of the day. The pattern for these crimes, which occurred in Winnipeg in 2001, shows that the fewest incidents occur in the morning hours, and incidents peak in the evening before midnight.

Total number of reported incidents by hour in 2001

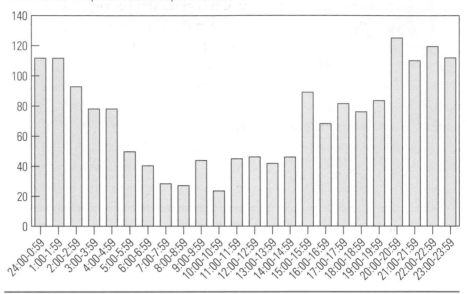

Source: Fitzgerald, Robin, Michael Wisener, and Josée Savoie. 2004. *Neighbourhood Characteristics and the Distribution of Crime in Winnipeg.* Ottawa: Canadian Centre for Justice Statistics, Statistics Canada. Page 30.

According to this argument, rates of personal victimization are relatively high for young minority males because these individuals tend to associate with people who are likely to offend (that is, with other young minority males) and because they tend to frequent places (e.g., bars) where offending often occurs. In contrast, elderly females are likely to associate with other elderly females (whose level of offending is very low) and to avoid high-risk settings. In a sense, lifestyles structure victimization opportunities. In explaining empirical variations in levels of personal crime, Hindelang and colleagues contend that these opportunity structures, not offender motivation, are a central theoretical issue.

Routine Activities

Cohen and Felson (1979) note that traditional motivational theories in criminology are unable to explain why rates of many crimes increased so dramatically

✳ **Routine activities theory** ✳
A theory which proposes that the presence of a motivated offender, the presence of a suitable target, and the absence of capable guardianship are vital to the completion of a crime.

in Western nations in the postwar period. Many criminological theories (e.g., those emphasizing explanatory factors such as poverty, unemployment, and size of inner-city population) suggest that crime rates should have been falling during this period, not climbing. How, then, can the problem of rising crime rates be reconceptualized?

According to Cohen and Felson, the presence of a motivated offender is only one of the necessary preconditions to an assault, a sexual assault, a homicide, a break and enter, or some other "direct-contact predatory violation." For crimes such as these to occur, two other conditions must be met. There must also be a "suitable target" against which the criminal motivation can be directed (e.g., a home to break into, a person to assault, goods to steal). Furthermore, there must be an "absence of capable guardianship." In sum, a motivated offender must meet a suitable target in the absence of anything (or anyone) that might prevent the crime from occurring.

Cohen and Felson suggest that variations in crime levels are determined not only by the numbers of people willing to commit crimes but also by the numbers of suitable targets and by the levels of guardianship that are routinely exercised over these targets. Even where the numbers of suitable targets and the levels of guardianship are stable, higher crime rates can be expected if the tempos and rhythms of social life affect the rate at which motivated offenders encounter suitable targets in the absence of capable guardianship. For Cohen and Felson, illegal activities must be understood as behaviours that depend on, and feed off, the population's "routine activities." As the structure of routine activities changes, so does the frequency with which crimes occur.

How does all this help explain why crime rates changed as they did after the Second World War? Cohen and Felson contend that changes in patterns of routine activities made it far more likely that offenders would encounter suitable targets in conditions of weak guardianship. This period witnessed a broad shift in the locus of routine activities. More and more women, whose lives had previously revolved around the household, entered or returned to the paid labour force or school. Also, vacations became longer, and travel became cheaper, so holidays were more likely to be spent away from home. The frequency with which people dined at restaurants increased; this gave rise to a booming fast-food industry. At the same time, divorce rates increased, and people who were single were waiting longer to get married; both

WHAT DOES IT INCLUDE?

Routine Activities Theory

First, there must be a motivated offender. Second, a suitable target against which the criminal motivation may be directed must be available. Third, there must be an absence of capable guardianship.

BOX 6.3

Repeat Victimization

Studies of crime victims tell us that some people are more likely than others to be victimized; they also tell us that those who have been victimized once are more likely to be victimized again. The likelihood of repeat victimization, however, varies by type of offence. This is illustrated in the table below, which shows the findings relating to property and violent crime from the 2004/2005 British Crime Survey.

PROPERTY CRIME			
Crime Type	Once	Twice	Three or More Times
Vandalism	70	17	14
Burglary	86	9	5
All Vehicle Thefts	81	13	6
Bicycle Thefts	88	9	3
Thefts from the Person	94	4	2
Other Thefts of Personal Property	89	7	4
VIOLENCE			
Common Assault	71	15	5
Wounding	81	9	10
Robbery	93	4	3

Source: Nichols, S., D. Povey, A. Walker, and C. Kershw. 2005. *Crime in England and Wales 2004/2005*. London: Home Office Statistical Bulletin. http://www.homeoffice.gov.uk/rds/

changes pointed to a significant rise in the number of smaller, single-person households. As a result, leisure interests previously pursued at home were now being pursued elsewhere, among non-family members.

Not coincidentally, this period also witnessed "a revolution in small durable product design" (Cohen and Felson, 1979: 500). A general increase in the standard of living, combined with technological advances, resulted in a wide range of lightweight, durable consumer goods flooding the consumer market. The demand for tape recorders, television sets, and stereo equipment increased, as it did later for products such as personal computers, CD players, and VCRs (Felson, 2002).

According to Cohen and Felson, all of these changes had a profound impact on the rates of direct-contact predatory crime. By increasing the number of suitable targets and reducing guardianship levels, these changes provided criminals with greater opportunities; as a result, crime rates rose quickly. The shift in routine activities away from the home exposed more people to criminal dangers from which they previously had been insulated. Moreover, more people were leaving their homes unoccupied for longer periods of time, thus depriving their homes of capable guardianship. At the same time that guardianship was being reduced, homes were being stocked with more highly desirable durable consumer goods that were easy to steal, carry, and sell or use. One need not agonize over the question of criminal motivation, Cohen and Felson conclude, in order to understand an increase in crime over the period.

Advances in the Study of Victimization Opportunity

In the past several years, a large body of research has been published regarding the questions raised by opportunity theories of victimization (Felson, 2002; Kennedy and Forde, 1990; Skogan and Maxfield, 1981; Tremblay and Tremblay, 1998; Wilcox et al., 2003). As a result, the field has grown in a number of distinct ways.

Theoretical Refinements

Terance Miethe and Robert Meier (1994) have refined and modified the theoretical approach to the study of victimization opportunity. They have proposed a "structural-choice model of victimization." Building on the work of earlier writers (Cohen, Kluegel, and Land, 1981), they maintain that opportunity theories highlight the importance of four factors: the physical proximity of targets to a pool of motivated offenders; the target's exposure to high-risk environments; target attractiveness; and the absence of guardianship. They also contend that current theories of victimization opportunity suggest two propositions. *First,* routine activities or lifestyles foster a structure of criminal opportunity by enhancing the contact between potential offenders and potential victims. *Second,* the subjective value of a person or of property, and the level of guardianship exerted over a person or property, determine which targets are chosen for victimization. Thus, their model implies that while patterns of routine activities expose some people or property to greater risks, which specific targets are selected by offenders will depend on the rewards and risks associated with those specific targets. For Miethe and Meier, then, proximity and exposure are "structural" factors because they predispose people to differing levels of risk. In the same vein, target attractiveness and guardianship are "choice" components because they determine which targets are selected, in contexts characterized by particular levels of risk.

Hot spots
High-crime locations.

Some elaborations of opportunity theory focus on how arguments about criminal opportunity are compatible with arguments about the spatial distribution of crime. In Chapter 2, we discussed the research on "**hot spots**" undertaken by Lawrence Sherman and his colleagues (1989). In their analysis of calls for police service in Minneapolis, they found that a relatively small number of urban locations (addresses and intersections) hosted relatively large amounts of crime. Their explanation of this pattern emphasizes the need to focus on the routine activities of places. In other words, crime rates are high at specific locations because of how those locations are used by the people we find at them. Similarly, most interpretations of social disorganization emphasize how neighbourhood disorganization affects offending; yet it is equally reasonable to assume that social disorganization affects levels of criminal opportunity (Bursik and Grasmick, 1993; Smith, Frazee, and Davison, 2000).

Marcus Felson (2002), one of the architects of routine activities theory, has written recently about the relationship between the character of communities and levels of criminal opportunity. Of special interest to Felson is the urban form he describes as the "metroreef." These "communities" emerge when "metropolises themselves begin to fuse into a single organism, a seemingly endless suburban sprawl at moderate or low metropolitan density" (1998: 87). We might recognize the concentration of population in southern Ontario spreading out from Toronto in all directions as a clear example of such a "metroreef." According to Felson, metroreefs promote crime because of the way they "unpack" everyday activities.

For example, in the metroreef, the reliance on cars has reduced the connections people have to their immediate environment, and perhaps the interest they have in it. People are willing to travel farther to work, shop, and socialize. Felson notes as an example that the corner grocery store has been replaced by the mega-supermarket. The former would have attracted local residents, who most likely would have walked there; the latter attracts strangers from a much wider area, who almost certainly drove there. Felson's analysis points out how the social organization of everyday life in the metroreef makes available a large number of criminal opportunities to those who are inclined—for whatever reason—to take advantage of them.

Kennedy and Forde (1999) have developed what they refer to as "routine conflict theory." This argument seeks to understand the social roots of violence by integrating routine activities theory with arguments about how violent responses to conflict situations are learned. For Kennedy and Forde, it is meaningful to speak of "routine conflict" in two respects. *First*, the conflict situations—often potentially criminally violent ones—in which individuals find themselves emerge out of the routine interactions in which they engage. These conflicts may involve a fight over money, sex, or drugs, or they may involve trivial disagreements arising from perceived slights. They may lead to threats or to physical harm or to a parting of the combatants before real trouble begins. Conflicts may have long histories—which suggests that the combatants have been feuding for years—or they may spark between strangers who have never met before (Kennedy and Forde, 1999: 9). *Second,* how an individual responds to a conflict situation is a function of the "scripts" that individual has learned as part of the socialization process. In other words, when we find ourselves involved in conflict, we rarely understand what is happening as a "completely new situation" involving a "completely novel solution." More typically, we draw on our past experiences with conflict; our actions are informed by our sense of what has worked in the past and therefore is likely to work again. In sum, Kennedy and Forde argue that violent routines are available to people based on what they have learned and on what they expect to happen in particular situations.

This theory maintains that individuals come to situations with a predisposition to behave in particular ways. Moreover, individuals learn "repertoires" for managing their daily lives, much as they learn other aspects of their lifestyles. These repertoires include guidelines regarding how routinely encountered conflict situations should be managed. Kennedy and Forde also note that individuals learn how to act when confronted by the actions of others; they also learn that reactions to perceived threats are tempered by the situations in which they find themselves. Certain environments (e.g., bars, sporting events) may be more likely than others to encourage routine acts of violence.

Several writers have suggested that perhaps both offender and victim processes can usefully be understood with reference to the same kinds of theoretical explanations. For instance, it has been suggested that the general theory of crime might prove to be a useful explanation of victimization as well as of offending (Schreck, 1999; Stewart et al., 2004). Why should this be?

A person who scores low on self-control is likely to lack empathy, to have a "here and now" orientation, to have a low level of tolerance for frustration, and to have other characteristics that could be linked to higher levels of victimization. Christopher Schreck argues that many of the behaviours associated with low self-control can produce higher risks of victimization as a by-product:

Heavy drinkers, for example, are less able to defend themselves or guard their belongings. Criminal behaviour, another indicator of low self-control, frequently involves untrustworthy associates who try to double-cross one another, especially if some of the conspirators take no precaution against betrayal (Schreck, 1999: 635).

In a related way, Piquero and Hickman (2003) have argued that Tittle's control balance theory might also provide a helpful model for thinking about victimization. They suggest that people who have balanced control ratios are least likely to experience victimization. It will be recalled that individuals who have control deficits experience more control than they exert. Such individuals may not have the confidence and skills to defend themselves against those who seek to victimize them. In contrast, individuals with control surpluses can indirectly place themselves at risk for victimization because they perceive relatively few constraints on their actions. Further, the ability to "get away" with controlling others can produce a profound insensitivity to the absence of autonomy among those whom they control. Individuals with the most control surplus, then, can be said to enjoy almost total freedom to exercise control over others and to act as the mood strikes without concern for counter-control. As a consequence, they may place themselves in situations that increase their vulnerability to victimization.

In the opposite way, other writers (Osgood et al., 1996; Riley, 1987) have argued that offending (like victimization) can itself be understood as a function of routine activities. In other words, the routine activities that people engage in increase or decrease the likelihood that they will find themselves in situations that encourage or allow offending behaviour. Osgood and colleagues argue that for a range of criminal and deviant behaviour, situations conducive to offending are especially prevalent when routine activities often place people in unstructured social activities with peers in the absence of authority figures. The lack of structure leaves time available for deviance. Also, when peers are present, various types of crime and deviance are not only easier to accomplish but also more rewarding. Finally, the absence of an authority figure (such as a parent or a teacher) means that it is less likely that anyone will assume responsibility for the social control of the offending behaviour.

Broadening the View of Risk

Traditionally, researchers interested in the factors that place people at increased risk of victimization have focused on a relatively narrow range of "lifestyle factors," including alcohol consumption, frequency of nighttime activities outside the home, and a range of demographic indicators such as sex, age, and social class. All of these are thought to be indicative of differences in the kinds of roles people play in society. More recently, some researchers have begun to argue that it is important to extend the range of lifestyle risk factors. Two such variables are of particular interest: offending behaviour and prior victimization experience.

With respect to offending behaviour, several studies have shown that an important, if imperfectly understood, relationship exists between offending and victimization (Dobrin, 2001; Jensen and Brownfield, 1986; Sampson and Lauritsen, 1990; Richie, 2000). In short, people who engage in offending behaviour face an increased risk of criminal victimization. There are two very reasonable explanations for this. *First*, as lifestyle models argue, people tend to associate with those who are socially and demographically like themselves. By implication, offenders tend to associate with other offenders. Moreover, offenders often victimize those who are most accessible to them, so it should come as no surprise that those who tell researchers they have offended are also likely to tell them they have been victimized. A *second* explanation emphasizes the character of offending behaviour itself rather than the social demographic characteristics of those who engage in it. Those who engage in prohibited behaviour often make perfect victims because they are unlikely to want the police to be involved in any investigation of their activities. In this sense, offending behaviour can be seen as increasing one's vulnerability to predatory crime (Kennedy and Baron, 1993).

Data relating to homicide in Canada in 2004 show the significance of this pattern (Dauvergne, 2005). In 2004, police homicide information revealed the murder of 18 prostitutes. Moreover, this was the third year in a row in which the statistics reflected the ongoing investigation into the serial killing of sex workers in Port Coquitlam, British Columbia. An additional 100 homicides were committed against persons working in other illegal "professions," including drug dealing, organized crime, and various street gang activities.

For many people, this link between offending and victimization greatly complicates the understanding of crime. In popular discourse, we are encouraged to think of "criminals" and "victims" as two separate categories of people who differ not only behaviourally but also morally. Yet the empirical evidence suggests that the picture is not so straightforward. Victims and offenders share many characteristics in common—both, for instance, are typically young and typically poor. Moreover, offending is not only a risk factor for victimization; victimization is a risk factor for offending (Agnew, 1992; Fleisher, 1995; Widom, 1995). In other words, for a wide variety of understandable reasons, people who have been criminally exploited by others may be more likely to engage in certain types of criminal behaviour themselves. Clearly, the relationship between offending and victimization is very complex and does not conform neatly to our idealized moral vision of how the world *should* look.

A *second* factor that is generating strong interest among those who study victims is "prior victimization" (Farrell and Pease, 2001; Gabor, 2004; Wittebrood and Nieuwbeerta, 2000). Analyses of victimization data suggest that much victimization is multiple victimization. Stated differently, people who have been victimized once are more likely to be victimized again. There are some crimes—for example, wife assault—for which we are not surprised to learn this. Yet several studies suggest that the phenomenon may be somewhat more widespread than this. An initial act of victimization seems to increase the risk of later victimization, for both property and personal crime.

Ken Pease and Gloria Laycock (1996) use the term "hot dot" to refer to a victim who is repeatedly victimized. In a sense, hot dots are the ultimate hot spots. In their review of the problem of repeat victimization, Pease and Laycock maintain that available research supports the following conclusions:

- An individual's past criminal victimization is a useful predictor of his or her subsequent victimization.
- The greater the number of previous victimizations, the greater the likelihood that the individual will experience victimization in the future.
- High-crime areas differ from low-crime areas at least in part because in high-crime areas a small number of victims are victimized at excessive rates.
- When victimization recurs, it tends to do so soon after the prior occurrence.
- The same offenders seem to be responsible for the bulk of repeated offences against a victim.
- Many factors, from policing styles to the nature of criminal justice information systems, inhibit a more detailed understanding of how repeat victimization contributes to the crime problem.

Two general kinds of explanations can be offered for patterns of repeat victimization. One argument suggests that the social or demographic characteristics that put people at risk for the first victimization may continue to place them at risk after that first victimization. The other maintains that there may be something in the victimization experience itself that increases the risk of further victimization. We might assume that an offender who has burglarized a house once would not want to do so again, yet this may not be the case—a house that has recently been burglarized successfully may be an even more desirable target for a second run. After all, the offender probably has some prior knowledge about when the house is unoccupied and how easy it is to gain access. Also, the burglar can safely assume (given the empty cardboard boxes on the front lawn) that the stolen television and DVD player have been replaced by new equipment. There is research evidence to support the conclusion that both prior risk factors and increased vulnerability due to the victimization experience may be important sources of repeat victimization (Wittebrood and Nieuwbeerta, 2000).

The Problems of Special Populations

Theories of victimization have tended to try to understand how the risk of becoming a crime victim is distributed in the general population. To some degree at least, this kind of theoretical development has reflected the types of data which have been available for analysis. Large general population surveys have encouraged thinking about the "average" victim of crime.

However, there are groups within the population whose relatively unique experiences with crime may not be very adequately captured by such surveys. For example, while a couple of decades of research have shown us (as we saw in Chapter 3) that the victim experiences of women can be very different from the victim experiences of men, there are subgroups to which our general theories might not apply as well as we would like to assume. These groups might include, for instance, Aboriginal women (Brownridge, 2003), immigrant women (Brownridge and Hali, 2002), or women who are members of military families (Harrison, 2002).

Another such group is the homeless (Eisler and Schissel, 2004; McCarthy et al., 2002). The reliance on sampling and interviewing methods, which make use of the telephone, largely exclude this group from consideration. However, given the unique problems faced by individuals who lack a permanent domicile, there is little reason to assume that the crime problems they face are the same as those faced by the rest of the population.

The particular problems faced by homeless youth have been demonstrated in research which has examined offending and victimization within this population (Tyler and Johnson, 2004). Stephen Baron (1997) conducted detailed interviews with 200 male street youth about a variety of issues but especially their involvement in criminal events as offenders and as victims. His findings were illuminating in several respects. First, he found that almost all of the interviewees had suffered some kind of criminal victimization, and most had been victimized repeatedly. Second, the analysis revealed a strong relationship between offending and chronic victimization. The more violent crimes the offender had committed, the more likely the offender was to report having been victimized. It is quite likely, Baron reasons, that the "capricious nature" of these crimes left the offender vulnerable to serious physical injury. Also, offenders who behave violently are often themselves at risk of violent retribution at the hands of those they have victimized. Third, and perhaps less obvious, Baron found that violent offending can sometimes deter victimization. Those who are themselves not inclined to behave violently may be reluctant to try to steal from someone who is known to have no such inhibitions. Fourth and finally, youths from abusive families are more likely to be victimized. Perhaps their experiences in those domestic settings have encouraged them to develop provocative and belligerent interactional styles that make them likely targets for victimization. Baron concluded that it is important to focus future analytical attention on the relationship between offending and victimization—especially as such issues affect those, such as homeless youth, who are at high risk of both.

Specifying the Offender's Role

In a very basic way, the ideas generated by opportunity theory have reoriented criminologists' thinking about the causes of crime. Opportunity theories have provided an additional piece to the puzzle as to why and where criminal events occur. A major limitation of these theories is that they have tended to pay little attention to the role of the offender or to the relationship between offender and victim. Rather, it has been assumed that probabilities of offending can be worked out on the basis of sets of conditions relating to opportunities.

What is the nature of the relationship between offending and opportunity? The view of the offender that is generally considered most consistent with opportunity theories of victimization derives from the classical school of criminology (see Chapter 5). In one sense, opportunity theories reflect key assumptions of the social control and deterrence arguments. The suggestion that crimes are less likely to occur when capable guardianship is present is consistent with such arguments. In a related way, opportunity theories are perfectly compatible with rational choice theories of the offender (Clarke and Felson, 1993; Nagin and Paternoster, 1993). It is assumed that offenders make rational decisions about criminal action based on the offending opportunities that the environment presents to them.

Recent attempts to arrive at a neoclassical version of rational choice theory recognize that the rationality of criminal offenders is often compromised.

For example, many offenders make decisions about crime commission while under the influence of drugs or alcohol. As well, the fear that a criminal opportunity might slip away may encourage them to make their behavioural choices quickly or in the absence of detailed information (Wright and Decker, 1994). Given contingencies such as this, modern rational choice theorists often speak of a "limited" rather than a "pure" rationality (Cromwell et al., 1991).

CRIME AS INTERACTIONS

An important theoretical question in the study of criminal situations relates to how these events unfold over time. They are set in motion by offenders who are inclined to make use of available criminal opportunities. To explain why they follow their particular courses of action, we must consider the specific behavioural choices that offenders, victims, and others make in the situations in which they find themselves. It is especially important to understand how the choices each participant makes influence the choices made by others. Victims and offenders act and react, and in so doing exert mutual influence. Stated differently, crimes have an interactional character: what any one participant does depends on what others do. Interactional dynamics have not attracted as much attention as issues such as offender motivation; even so, a general appreciation of how criminologists attempt to understand these interactions is necessary.

Victim Precipitation

One of the concepts most often employed in the study of crime dynamics is that of victim precipitation, according to which the opportunity for crime is created by some action of the victim. In an early and influential study of 588 criminal homicides in Philadelphia, Marvin Wolfgang (1958) reported that about one-quarter of the time, the victim could be said to have precipitated his or her own murder. In these cases, Wolfgang noted, it was the eventual victim who—often under the influence of alcohol—was the first to brandish a weapon or threaten deadly force. The eventual offender, fearing for his or her own safety, either intentionally or unintentionally reacted to the threat in a way that proved fatal for the victim. In a stereotypical case, an altercation between two individuals at a bar escalates to the point where one of the parties produces a gun or a knife or a broken bottle and says to the other party, "I'm going to kill you." The other party responds

Victim precipitation
Occurs when the opportunity for crime is created by some action of the victim.

> ### WHAT DOES IT MEAN?
>
> #### Victim Precipitation
> This occurs when the opportunity for crime is created by some action of the victim.

with haste and force, and suddenly the person who uttered the threat is lying dead on the barroom floor.

The concept of victim precipitation encourages us to understand the outcome of a crime situation as the joint product of the behaviours of the offender and the victim, rather than simply in terms of the offender's motivation. In the case of the barroom encounter, the killing can be said to have resulted not from the killer's actions but from the killer–killed interaction. It is important to point out that what people *intend* their words or their actions to mean in cases like this is much less important than *how the words are interpreted* by others in the interaction. The person who brandishes a broken beer bottle and threatens death to a disputant may be expressing mere bravado rather than serious intent to harm the other party. To the disputant, whose judgment is clouded by alcohol and who believes the threat to be real, other interpretations of the situation are well out of reach. With respect to cases like this, we have little trouble understanding the explanatory value of the concept of victim precipitation. The homicide would probably not have occurred, we can conclude, if the victim had not initially behaved in an aggressive fashion; thus, the victim was an active contributor to his or her own violent demise.

To what degree can the explanatory logic of victim precipitation be generalized to other types of events? In theoretical terms, this is a tough question. For instance, is it reasonable to argue that crimes such as robbery, theft, and sexual assault can also be victim precipitated? In events such as these, does it make sense to argue that victims actively contribute to their own victimization?

Amir (1971) concluded from a study of over 600 rape cases in Philadelphia that about one case in five was victim precipitated. Amir classified rapes as victim precipitated if the victim "actually, or so it was deemed, agreed to sexual relations but retracted before the actual act or did not react strongly enough when the suggestion was made by the offender" (266).

We might be inclined to agree that victims who initially threaten their offenders in some sense precipitate a homicide; we would not agree that victims who initially say yes to sexual relations precipitate rape if they subsequently say no. For one thing, the assumption in the latter case seems to be that the female rather than the male is responsible for the level of male sexual arousal and that if that arousal is not satisfied, the female must bear the violent consequences. Also, it seems to imply that a subsequent decision not to engage in sex, when there has been some initial agreement to do so, is appropriately understood as precipitous of violence. Finally, homicide and sexual assault differ in a fundamental way that is obscured by the haphazard application of the concept of victim precipitation. The types of homicides described by Wolfgang involve events in which victims threaten their offenders with deadly force and are repaid in kind. In the cases of rape described by Amir, the victim was not behaving in a threatening or aggressive fashion, and the violence exhibited by the offender could not have been understood as "payment in kind."

Amir's study illustrates a serious concern that many people have with the concept of victim precipitation: it is difficult to separate the moral dimensions of the concept from its explanatory dimensions. The claim that victims precipitate victimization seems uncomfortably close to the suggestion that victims should be blamed for their victimization. Many criminologists contend that victim blaming should be avoided at all costs (Timmer and Norman, 1984). At the same time, most people can express some degree of empathy for the battered wife who, after years of being subjected to violence, kills her abusive husband. To call a killing of this type "victim precipitated" does not usually elicit a charge of victim blaming.

For some criminologists, the solution is to recognize that crude attempts to sort crimes into precipitated and unprecipitated categories are doomed to failure. Victims and offenders may contribute to the unfolding of a criminal event in a variety of ways, and thus a broader taxonomy of victim and offender roles is necessary (Fattah, 1991; Karmen, 2001). Another solution involves recognizing that it is often inappropriate to speak of victim and offender roles, since doing so minimizes our understanding of how the actual circumstances of criminal events determine who shall bear what label. In other words, there is a need to move beyond the study of victim precipitation to "the full round of interaction," which involves not only the eventual victims and offenders but also other event participants (Luckenbill, 1984).

The Situated Transaction

Goffman (1963) defines a situated transaction as a process of interaction involving two or more individuals. To understand criminal events as situated transactions, we must focus on what goes on between the participants rather than on what any one of them does individually. According to Goffman (1959), human behaviour is acted out as if it was part of a theatrical performance. What's important in the interaction is the impression the actor gives to

Situated transaction
Process of interaction involving two or more individuals that lasts as long as they find themselves in one another's presence.

WHAT DOES IT MEAN?

Situated Transaction

This refers to a process of interaction involving two or more individuals that lasts as long as they find themselves in one another's presence. If we are to understand criminal events as situated transactions, we need to emphasize the study of what goes on between the participants rather than what any one of them does.

BOX 6.4

Stages in the Situated Transaction

David Luckenbill has argued that homicide can be understood as a situated transaction. It is a transaction in that "an offender, victim and possibly an audience engage in an interchange which leaves the victim dead," and it is situated in that the "participants interact in a common physical territory" (1977: 196). Based on an analysis of 70 homicide events in a California county, Luckenbill contended that these incidents typically move through six stages:

- Stage 1   The opening move in the transaction is an action undertaken by the (eventual) victim and defined by the (eventual) offender as an offence to "face." For example, the victim says, "Get lost" or "What are you staring at?"
- Stage 2   The offender interprets the victim's words or actions as personally offensive.
- Stage 3   The offender makes an opening move in salvaging "face" or protecting "honour"—in short, the offender retaliates verbally or physically.
- Stage 4   The victim responds in an aggressive manner. His or her actions suggest a working agreement that the situation is suited to violent resolution. By cheering or heckling, onlookers may encourage the movement toward violence. They may also block a convenient exit for one or both parties, or prevent others from breaking up the fight.
- Stage 5   There is a physical interchange, typically brief and precise.
- Stage 6   The brief battle is over. At this point, the offender flees or remains at the scene, either voluntarily or as a result of force applied by bystanders.

---

others. Based on this impression—which generally involves the playing out of a particular role in a specific situation—individuals extract information about others in the interaction. When enough information has been obtained for each individual to define the situation to his or her satisfaction, the roles can be properly acted out (Martin, Mutchnick, and Austin, 1990: 332). With these definitions in hand, individuals are able to sustain and complete a number of transactions throughout their daily lives. But these transactions do not always have positive outcomes.

In his analysis of 70 homicides in California, Luckenbill (1977) utilized an approach that draws on **symbolic interactionism**. Like other researchers, he reported that these murders tended to occur in informal settings and generally involved people who knew each other. What distinguishes his approach, however, is his view that homicide is a product of situated transactions rather than of the behaviour of individual participants. For Luckenbill, situated transactions should be viewed as "character contests" in which efforts by the disputants to "save face" result in deadly combat.

Symbolic interactionism
The role of linguistic interaction in developing a social identity and functioning according to shared norms and values.

This perspective on criminal events is not meant to imply that situated transactions are restricted to one type of crime. The kinds of transactions that result in acquaintance rape differ from those that result in homicide. And even with homicide, some transactions are more "situated" than others (Williams and Flewelling, 1988). For example, it is incorrect to argue that the victims of mass murderers or serial killers are combatants committed to battle. (This is not to deny that such crimes also have situational dynamics.)

Often, transactions are so complex that they blur whatever distinctions we try to make between victims and offenders or between different types of offenders. Frequently, the interaction that the eventual victim and eventual offender are engaged in determines the character of the outcome (Felson and Messner, 1996: Miethe and Drass, 1999). How useful is it for us to say that individuals are of a certain "criminal type" when we know that their behaviour can be affected so strongly by the situations they face and the roles they believe they must play? We do not—as we do in cases of victim precipitation—look to the victim for the causes of the violence, but rather to the victim–offender exchange. With respect to the homicides described by Luckenbill, it should be clear that up until the moment of battle, either party could have pulled out of the exchange or responded differently, and the results would have been quite different. Questions about who should have done what (and when) to prevent the violence are likely to elicit more than one answer. In his study of street youth, Baron confirmed the importance of transactions in determining who is the victim and who is the offender. He reported that the more violent the altercations street youths participated in (as offenders), the greater their risk for violent victimization.

The Social Organization of Crime and Deviance

Joel Best and David Luckenbill (1994) have attempted to develop a comprehensive typology of criminal transactions. These transactions, they argue, differ in a number of ways from one another. Some last only seconds (a mugging); others can last several days or even weeks (blackmail). Some involve people in face-to-face contact; others involve people separated by great distances. Some involve only one or two individuals; others involve a great many more.

Best and Luckenbill identify three main categories of transactions. The first, *individual deviance,* consists of one individual playing a deviant or criminal role—for example, a person involved in illicit drug taking. The second, *the deviant exchange,* involves two people (or more) playing cooperative roles vis-à-vis each other. Drug dealing, the sale of pornography, and prostitution all involve deviant exchanges. The third, *deviant exploitation,* involves parties in conflict. In deviant or criminal exploitation, at least one individual is performing an offender role and at least one is playing the "target." Like the other forms of deviant transaction, deviant exploitation has some characteristic subtypes.

✻According to Best and Luckenbill, once we recognize that deviant or criminal ✻ transactions are organizationally complex, we gain some distinct analytical advantages. *First,* the classification scheme distinguishes between individual deviance, deviant exchange, and deviant exploitation, and this allows us to see similarities among forms of rule breaking that we might not think had very much in common. Usually, we don't think about what murder has in common with fraud, or what skid row drinking has in common with suicide. *Second,* offenders' careers typically involve several kinds of transactions, each of which has its own properties, which can be distinguished using this scheme. Robbing a store to get the money to buy drugs involves one kind of transaction (exploitation), buying the drugs involves another (exchange), and taking the drugs involves still another (individual deviance). An individual's crimes can be understood as organized in terms of their frequency and the offender's degree of engagement in various types of transactions. Of course, different kinds of transactions carry different kinds of risks and present offenders with different sorts of problems requiring solution.

The Significance of Interactional Issues

The research on victim–offender interactions challenges many of the stereotypes that are inherent in other theoretical approaches. With respect to motivational theories, for instance, we are sometimes led to argue that crimes occur only because criminals are determined to commit them. Theories that focus only on opportunity, if not carefully interpreted, seem to suggest that crimes occur because motivated offenders find the opportunities to translate their inclinations into action.

In contrast, interactional theories suggest that more than motivation and opportunity are needed to understand why and how crimes occur. Crimes are the outcome of social exchanges between people who find themselves in specific circumstances and must make quick decisions about how they should respond to each other's behaviour (Felson and Messner, 1996). A robbery does not occur merely because an offender with an inclination to rob encounters an opportunity conducive to robbery. The potential victim may resist in ways that turn a potential robbery into an attempted murder. The potential victim of an attempted break and enter may "overreact" by killing the offender. Victims of property crimes contribute to interactions through the steps they take—or don't take—to protect their property; their actions, or lack thereof, send a message to the potential offender about the risks of trying to steal the property. In sum, victims are not merely passive objects of an offender's predatory desires; nor are they necessarily active contributors to their own victimization. They are, however, key event participants whose actions shape and constrain event outcomes.

Similar comments apply to other participants. For instance, Luckenbill, in his study of homicide, revealed that the role of bystanders in situated transactions should not be minimized. He found that the presence of bystanders and the actions they took shaped the course of the transaction. In the early stages, they sometimes increased the likelihood of mortal battle by encouraging the offender to interpret an offensive remark as requiring a firm response; in the later stages, they sometimes supplied a weapon or blocked the exit of the potential victim. Of course, just as bystanders may facilitate the occurrence of a crime, they may also prevent crimes or transform one type of crime into another. A bystander who has the presence of mind to call 911 on witnessing an assault or who is familiar with cardiopulmonary resuscitation (CPR) may prevent an assault from becoming a murder.

Much of the material discussed in this chapter recalls the distinction made by Donald Black (1983) between predatory and moralistic crime. The former is rooted in exploitation, while the latter is rooted in conflict (Cooney, 1998; Jensen, 2002). Much crime—especially much violent crime—involves people who know each other and who in many cases have joint histories of conflict. What we simply understand from outside the event as an "assault" or a "homicide" might be understood quite differently by the participants. Often, the person we call the offender sees her or himself as the victim, and what we call the crime is an attempt on the part of the victim to seek justice. While the media emphasize random violent victimization by strangers, the criminologist knows that this stereotype does not fit a majority of cases.

SUMMARY

The pressure to behave in a criminal fashion is not sufficient to explain why people commit one type of crime and not another. Researchers who take a routine activities approach explain variations in levels of crime across places and over time based less on variations in the numbers of individuals motivated to commit crime than on variations in the opportunities to commit crime. The concept of opportunities revolves around the notion that some individuals have certain lifestyles or follow certain routines that make them more vulnerable to criminal victimization. This lifestyle exposure, coupled with the presence of motivated offenders and the absence of capable guardians, makes becoming a victim of crime more likely.

Crimes involve choices—by offenders, victims, and others—all of which affect the outcome. Crimes can thus be said to have an interactional character: what any one participant does depends on what others do. An important consideration here is the role played by the victim, who together with the offender and other main players comes to be involved in what is called a situated transaction. In such transactions, the characteristics of the individuals involved come to define the direction that the crime will take. In the early stages of interactions, it is often difficult to predict who will be the eventual victim and who the offender. It is the actions that occur that clearly define these roles. Harm and guilt are clearly worked out only after the fact, and often depend on the actions of third parties.

Interactional approaches suggest, then, that crimes are the outcome of social exchanges between people who find themselves in specific circumstances and who must make quick decisions about how they should respond to one another's behaviour. Their responses determine the outcomes. These outcomes are not always predictable, in that they can be affected by many factors in the situation. Interactional approaches help us determine the effectiveness of various strategies used by victims or police in deterring or preventing crime.

QUESTIONS FOR REVIEW AND DISCUSSION

1. Why do you think young males are more likely to live risky lifestyles than any other group?
2. What do you think will be the major change in future lifestyles that will make individuals in society more vulnerable (or less vulnerable) to crime?
3. Are there steps that can be taken to reduce the likelihood that individuals who confront each other in an interaction will escalate this dispute to violence?
4. The police play an important role as third parties in defining behaviour as criminal or non-criminal. What are the pluses and minuses of police using more discretion in deciding what should be treated criminally and what should be treated as a non-criminal dispute?
5. Are we likely to see a drop in crime as young people who follow risky routines become older and less likely to be involved in these types of behaviour?

RECOMMENDED READINGS

Coston, C.T.M. 2004. *Victimizing Vulnerable Groups*. Westport, CT: Praeger.

Gannon, M., and K. Mihorean, 2005. "Criminal Victimization in Canada 2004." Statistics Canada, *Juristat*, 25(7).

Kennedy, L.W., and V.F. Sacco. 1998. *Crime Victims in Context*. Los Angeles: Roxbury.

Lamb, S. 1996. *The Trouble with Blame: Victims, Perpetrators and Responsibility*. Cambridge, MA: Harvard University Press.

Miller, Susan L. 2005. *Victims as Offenders*. New Brunswick, NJ: Rutgers University Press.

INFOTRAC® COLLEGE EDITION

Explore InfoTrac® College Edition, your online university library, which includes hundreds of popular and scholarly journals in which you can find articles related to the topics in this chapter. Visit InfoTrac® through your web browser (**www.infotrac-college.com**) or through this book's website (**www.criminalevent-4e.nelson.com**).

WHAT'S ON THE WEB?

For chapter links and quizzes, check out the accompanying website at **www.criminalevent-4e.nelson.com**.

Chapter 7

Crime's Aftermath:
The Consequences of Criminal Events

LEARNING OBJECTIVES:

- discuss reactions to and consequences of criminal transactions
- explore the various individual-level effects of criminal victimization and the means by which victims cope with these effects
- examine the broader effects of crime, especially public fear
- critically investigate more public and more extreme reactions to crime, including "moral panics"

INTRODUCTION

This chapter is concerned with what happens in the aftermath of the criminal event. The issues, theories, and research discussed remind us that for analytical purposes, it makes little sense to say that criminal events end when the thief flees the scene or when the victim of homicide falls to the floor. Just as important is how participants and the rest of us respond to criminal events.

Several of the questions addressed in this chapter relate to the experiences of crime victims. What are the effects of crime on victims? How do victims cope with these losses, and why do some manage better than others?

But we must not restrict ourselves to the event participants. Criminal events elicit responses from many individuals and groups in society. As we will see, **fear of crime** can be a serious problem, especially for some groups in the population such as women and urbanites. Obviously, to some extent the aftermath of criminal events must be seen as an outcome of the event transaction as well as the wider social context in which these events occur. For example, the level of injury experienced by a victim of violence will be related to decisions made by the victim to resist the offender and decisions made by the offender to actively overcome that resistance (Kleck and Sayles, 1990; Ziegenhagen and Brosnan, 1985).

Fear of crime
A concern or anxiety relating to the possibility of criminal victimization and usually assessed in social research through the measurement of attitudes or reported behaviours.

Our analysis indicates that the various parts of the criminal event are related to each other. Particular patterns of transactions produce particular patterns of consequences in the aftermath. For instance, Weaver and his colleagues (2004) use a criminal events approach to try to understand which features of violent encounters produce lethal outcomes and which do not. Not surprisingly, some characteristics of the victim are significant. For instance, older victims and male victims are more likely to die in violent encounters—in the former case perhaps because of greater frailty and in the latter perhaps because males are more likely to resist, thereby leading to an escalation of violence. The character of the transactions also influences the character of the outcomes. For instance, the use of guns or knives increases lethality, as do circumstances relating to drug dealing.

More generally, a "random" murder that is given sensationalist treatment by the mass media will elicit more public fear than a murder involving drinking partners (Best, 1999; Liska and Baccaglini, 1990). In a similar fashion, an offender who is caught selling illegal drugs when society is in a state of panic about drug crimes can expect less sympathy than an offender who is apprehended during a period when the level of concern is lower.

WHAT ARE THE COSTS OF CRIME?

Any attempt to discuss the consequences that crimes have for victims, and victims' efforts to cope with these consequences, is beset by some rather serious research problems. Perhaps the most notable is the "specification problem" (Fattah and Sacco, 1989). In short, it is not always clear what a crime's effects were and what they were not (Cohen, 2005).

Some costs of crime are more obvious than others (Meadows, 1998). With respect to financial loss, it is obvious that the economic cost sustained when someone steals a purse from a victim equals the cost of replacing the purse and its contents. But suppose the victim reacts to the theft by deciding to install deadbolt locks, and to take taxis instead of walking to evening destinations. Suppose as well that she decides that instead of carrying cash she will write cheques for her purchases in the future. Should the costs of the locks, the taxi fares, and the chequing account be considered an economic cost of the crime? This issue assumes even more importance when we recognize that financial losses are perhaps the easiest to calculate, given that there is a convenient standard of measurement (Kennedy and Sacco, 1998).

With respect to physical injury, if the victim sustained a broken arm, that injury clearly should be considered a consequence of the crime. But if stress resulting from the crime aggravated a pre-existing health condition, is it correct to say that the incident caused physical harm even though there were no apparent physical injuries? The problems with efforts to assess the costs of crime for victims emerge logically from the types of research methods applied. Typically, information about victimization outcomes—like other information about victims—comes from victim surveys or from specialized samples of crime victims.

Two general strategies can be used to investigate how victims are affected by crime. *First*, survey respondents can be asked directly about the losses they experienced. These questions—like all questions that ask people to report on past events—are subject to errors as a result of faulty memory, dishonesty, and misunderstanding (Skogan, 1986). Usually, these questions focus on the most obvious losses to the victim, such as injury or stolen or damaged goods. Though these questions are useful up to a point, they focus attention only on what happened during or immediately after the event, and reveal little about longer-term impacts. With victimization surveys, respondents are asked about events that occurred in some specified period preceding the survey (typically a year or six months); therefore, our data about problems that emerge later are often minimal. Respondents can also be asked how they changed or limited their behaviour in response to the victimization. These questions require respondents not only to recall accurately when their behaviour changed but also to understand the causes of their behaviour.

A *second* research strategy involves the researcher rather than the survey respondents making judgments about the effects of the victimization experience. Suppose we are interested in determining whether the victim's involvement in a criminal event increased feelings of anger. Instead of asking victims directly if they are angry about the experience, we might compare victims and non-victims in terms of the responses they give to more general questions about feelings of anger. If we discover that victims are angrier than non-victims, we might conclude that the victimization experience is responsible for some of the difference. This is standard social scientific practice; however, the results may not be clear, since we probably asked the questions about victimization and the questions about feelings of anger in the same interview. So it is impossible to determine what the cause is and what the effect is. It is reasonable to argue that victimization results in feelings of anger; but it may be just as reasonable to argue that people who have an angry demeanour are more likely to become victims of crime.

Financial Consequences

As noted, financial costs are among the most obvious costs associated with victimization. As with all types of costs, these can be direct or indirect. Direct costs include the value of the property stolen or damaged as well as any costs associated with medical care. According to the Insurance Information Centre of Canada, in 2001, the insurance industry paid out $243 million in claims for residential and commercial break and enter offences (Fedorowycz, 2004). There are also indirect financial costs—for example, those reflecting lost work time, child care costs, or expensive lifestyle changes. Also, direct costs do not include any long-term losses arising from criminal victimization.

Physical Consequences

Victimization data allow us to analyze the physical consequences of crime. Data from the 2004 General Social Survey (GSS) tell us that victims sustain physical injury in a minority of violent incidents. In 2004, victims (male and female) were injured in roughly 25 percent of violent incidents.

Victimization studies are quite useful in telling us about the direct injuries incurred from criminal victimization but tell us relatively little about longer-term effects. Although it is not evident in surveys of this type, the injuries that result from physical encounters can lead to a worsening of existing health problems. Also, when the victim's mobility is restricted, he or she may be less able—or even unable—to exercise or to meet nutritional requirements.

Emotional Consequences

More common than physical injuries are a variety of emotional reactions to crime, from mild to extreme (Ruback and Thompson, 2001). These reactions may include shock, mistrust, sleeplessness, anger, stress, depression, and a diminished capacity to enjoy life events (Tjaden and Thoennes, 1998). Victims may also express a sense of guilt—that is, they may blame themselves for what has happened. Figure 7.1 gives the frequencies of various emotional effects reported by victims of violence who responded to the 2004 General Social Survey.

One of the most significant effects that has been associated with victimization is an increase in fear of crime (Johnson, 1996; Keane, 1995; Tjaden and Thoennes, 1998). Serious crimes—especially crimes of violence—may result in a **vulnerability conversion** (Lejeune and Alex, 1973), as victims develop a sudden understanding that they are more susceptible to the dangers of life than they thought.

Vulnerability conversion
Especially for victims of violence, development of a sudden understanding by victims that they are more susceptible to the dangers of life than they thought.

Figure 7.1

Emotional Effects of Violent Victimization, GSS 2004

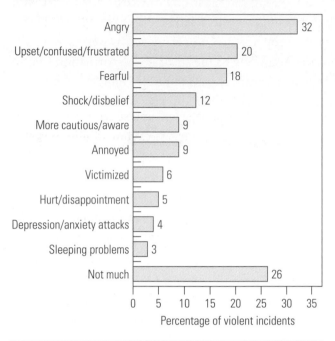

Source: Gannon, M., and K. Mihorean. 2005. "Criminal Victimization in Canada 2004." Statistics Canada, *Juristat*, 25(7): 12. Used by permission of Statistics Canada.

Fear is not the only emotional reaction that victimization elicits. Another common one is anger. Victims of crime often feel outraged that their property or person has been violated by an offender. Interestingly, though researchers have spent a great deal of time and energy researching how victimization promotes fear, we know considerably less about the relationship between victimization and anger. Data from the 2004 General Social Survey indicate that to some crimes, anger is a common response. In about 40 percent of incidents of break and enter, victims expressed anger. In another 22 percent, victims felt upset, confused, or frustrated (Gannon and Mihorean, 2005).

In part, break and enter elicits a strong emotional response because it is viewed as a crime with the potential for violence. Typically, victims are away from home when the offence occurs, but they are still forced to contemplate what might have happened had they been at home. Also, because a burglary could threaten violence against all members of the household, each member of the household may feel concern not only for his or her own personal safety but also for the well-being of other family members. Finally, because burglary represents an invasion of privacy and often involves theft of or damage to objects that have sentimental value, the emotional response can be severe (Hough, 1985).

Janoff-Bulman and Frieze (1983) maintain that serious criminal victimization is stressful in large part because it is unusual and because, unlike more routine stressors, it does not trigger well-developed coping mechanisms. These events make evident people's "psychological baggage" and suggest to them that they need to question not only their assumptions of invulnerability but also other assumptions underlying their day-to-day existence.

One such assumption is that "the world is meaningful." Most of us prefer to go through life believing that things happen for a reason—that good things happen to good people and that bad things happen to bad people. It is comforting to think that all things considered, the world makes sense. We can believe it because we also believe that we can exercise a certain amount of control over what happens to us. A serious, random act of crime can challenge this assumption. In the aftermath of such an event, the world seems to make less sense—we have become victims of misfortune even though we may have tried hard to keep ourselves and our property safe.

Criminal victimization can also undermine an individual's positive self-concept. Victims may develop feelings of weakness and helplessness and believe that they should have done more than they did to avoid being victimized. Traditionally, society has reinforced this view by holding victims responsible for what has happened to them.

It has often been argued that victims' psychological distress can be magnified by social and criminal justice agencies charged with the responsibility of helping them (Rosenbaum, 1987). In particular, the police have sometimes been accused of failing to provide victims with the emotional support they require and often expect (Carter, 1985; Skogan and Wycoff, 1987). The 2004 General Social Survey, like most surveys, indicates that crime victims are less likely to have positive perceptions of the police than non-victims. This is especially true for victims of violence (Gannon and Mihorean, 2005). Even in the case of property crime, victims may feel that the police are not doing enough to help them or to recover their stolen property. When property is recovered, they may wonder why it was not returned to them more promptly.

To some extent, victims' discontent with the police reflects the routine nature of police work. Some victims of even minor crimes expect a rapid response when they phone the police. Yet dispatchers, overwhelmed by calls for service, may assign minor crimes a very low priority. As a result, victims feel let down by the police. Similarly, victims who know they have been victimized may expect the police officer who arrives on the scene to accept their version of the story at face value and then engage in hot pursuit of the offender. For the police officer, the situation may be more ambiguous, and he or she may find it necessary to ask questions in order to make sense of the event. Also, the officer's experience may suggest that "hot pursuit" is pointless because the offender is unlikely to be found in this way, if at all.

Much of the research on emotional reactions to victimization suggests that they are likely to erode slowly over time (Burt and Katz, 1985; Hough, 1985). There is also some evidence that symptoms sometimes persist, or even re-emerge months after the incident (Sales, Baum, and Shore, 1984). These findings imply that the recovery process may not be as linear as is sometimes believed.

The emotional consequences of crime and victimization are not restricted to victims. It has also been argued that members of offenders' families often experience considerable pain and anguish as they attempt to make sense of the offenders' actions (May, 1999). Self-help and counselling groups have been established to help offenders' families cope with the social stigma that derives from being related to an offender. Through their engagement in such groups, members of offenders' families strive to be understood as "the other victims of crime" (Howarth and Rock, 2000).

Behavioural Consequences

Some of the behaviours that result from victimization are directly related to physical injuries or economic losses. For example, victims may need to take time off work for medical care or to repair and replace property. The 2004 GSS found that a significant number of violent crime victims found it difficult to engage in important life activities as a result of the incident. Victims had difficulty carrying out their main activities in about one-quarter of the incidents. This was more likely to be a consequence for victims of robbery than for victims of other kinds of violent crime (Gannon and Mihorean, 2005). Of those who did report trouble carrying out their main activities, 37 percent said it was for only one day. Thirty-nine percent said these limitations lasted for between two and seven days, and 16 percent said the effects were experienced for more than two weeks.

Avoidance behaviour
Behaviour by which victims seek to distance themselves from the kinds of people or situations they perceive as dangerous.

Victims exhibit a variety of behavioural reactions to crime; many of these are intended to make them safer. A common response is **avoidance behaviour**—that is, victims seek to distance themselves from the kinds of people or situations they perceive as dangerous (DuBow, McCabe, and Kaplan,

1979). At an extreme, this may involve changing residences or neighbourhoods (Dugan, 1999). Victims may also try to fortify their homes by installing new locks or an alarm system, or they may purchase firearms or enroll in a self-defence course. Ironically, victims who engage in these behaviours are often less likely than others to feel safer as a result (Lurigio, 1987).

Victims also seek help from others (Ruback and Thompson, 2001). As we noted in Chapter 1, a common response (although less common than many think) is to contact the police. It seems that victims are most likely to do this when they see some practical or tangible reason for it. But even before they contact the police, they often contact friends or family members for advice. Sometimes the victim isn't sure the event was a crime, or that it was serious enough to warrant police intervention. Friends and family members can help clarify matters by reminding the victim of standards against which the event can be judged (Greenberg, Ruback, and Westcott, 1984).

This information-seeking behaviour has two important implications. *First*, it helps explain why—according to some research—victims often wait well over an hour after an incident before notifying the police (Greenberg, Ruback, and Westcott, 1984). *Second*, it demonstrates that the victim's decision is not necessarily an individual one; it often reflects the social influence of others to whom the victim has access immediately following the crime (Greenberg, Ruback, and Westcott, 1984).

In the longer term, victims may engage in some type of collective action (DuBow, McCabe, and Kaplan, 1979). The most obvious form this takes is membership in a community crime prevention group such as Neighbourhood Watch (Rosenbaum, 1988). Or they may involve themselves in one of the many generic or more specialized victims' groups that have proliferated in recent decades (Weed, 1995).

A common reaction is to tell others the story of the crime (Wachs, 1988). The 2004 GSS found that victims of violence are likely to turn to family members, friends, and co-workers to discuss what happened (Gannon and Mihorea, 2005). Lejeune and Alex (1973) reported that this is a near-universal tendency among mugging victims. They observed, as well, that listeners are as interested in hearing the story as the victim is in telling it. Telling the story of one's victimization may have important therapeutic value: when others react in supportive ways or tell similar stories, the victim may find it easier to make sense of the event and to place it in perspective.

The behavioural reactions of victims can be easily overstated, because most people are familiar with someone who has responded to crime in perhaps an

Neighbourhood Watch
A community crime prevention program in which residents monitor neighbourhood life and exert guardianship over each other's property.

BOX 7.1

Assessing the Long-Term Costs of Victimization

Research on the impact of victimization on victims has tended to focus on short-term consequences (Menard, 2002). With respect to financial costs, for instance, victimization researchers have typically equated the cost of being victimized with whatever "out-of-pocket" expenses can be directly attributed to the incident.

But it is obvious that victimization has longer-term effects. This has been powerfully demonstrated by research undertaken by Ross Macmillan (2000). Through a sophisticated analysis of Canadian and American victimization data, Macmillan estimated income losses over the life cycle that are associated with violent victimization. His findings included the following:

- The income losses attributable to violent victimization are "age graded." The greatest costs are associated with victimization incidents that occur in adolescence.
- Criminal violence affects earnings in later life by disrupting processes of educational and occupational attainment. In other words, violent victimization seems to affect the commitment to, and effort put into, education; it also affects academic performance. A major result of decreased educational attainment is a reduction in the status of the occupations the affected individual enters in young adulthood.
- According to data from the 1993 GSS, lifetime loss in income from a violent victimization that occurs in adolescence is a remarkable $237,200. The expected income loss from sexual assault is $241,600, from robbery $262,400, and from assault $212,800.
- The costs of criminal victimization are not borne equally by all in society. The poor and the young have especially high levels of victimization and are most likely to be affected by the costs of victimization. In this way, criminal victimization can be understood as reinforcing the marginalization of the socially and economically disadvantaged.

---

extreme manner. But generally speaking, most crime victims do not make major or basic lifestyle changes (Hindelang, Gottfredson, and Garofalo, 1978). Our lifestyles are a product of our family responsibilities and occupational commitments, so they can't be changed easily.

There is a tendency in the criminological literature to think about such changes as **costs of victimization** that limit behaviour; yet victimization can also have benefits (Ruback and Thompson, 2001). As Skogan (1987) points out, when people change their behaviour in other circumstances in response to negative experiences, we call this "learning." To the degree that such learning makes people less vulnerable without dramatically affecting their quality of life, it may be beneficial.

Costs of victimization
Losses of a physical, financial, emotional, and social nature that can be attributed to the victimization experience.

Coping with the Costs of Victimization

Victims differ in their ability to cope with the costs of criminal victimization (Resick, 1987; Sales, Baum, and Shore, 1984; Skogan, 1987). Victims who are isolated from supportive others may find it more difficult to manage the stresses associated with crime than those whose families and friends are able to lend emotional and/or practical assistance. People with more economic resources may find it less difficult to absorb economic losses and to replace stolen or damaged property. Also important are prior psychological functioning and previous history as a victim. Individuals who are already suffering from depression may respond to criminal victimization more negatively; so may those who have already been victimized by crime.

One way that victims try to cope with the costs of victimization is by re-evaluating the event (Taylor, Wood, and Lichtman, 1983). In so doing, they redefine the situation to make it less threatening to their self-esteem or their future plans. In short, they heed the various cultural adages that advise us to "look on the bright side." Taylor and colleagues suggest that victims follow a number of evaluative strategies to achieve this. For instance, they may compare themselves with less fortunate others. Provided one chooses the criteria for comparison carefully, one can always find examples of people who have lost more or suffered more. Alternatively, despite suffering or loss, the victim may try to discover ways in which the event was beneficial. That is, the victim may say, "I sure learned my lesson" or "I won't ever get myself into that situation again."

Agnew (1985b) suggests that this process resembles the neutralization process that Matza and Sykes (1961) described in their explanation of why offenders commit crime. However, instead of convincing themselves that a particular criminal act was not really wrong—which is what offenders do—victims try to convince themselves that particular criminal acts resulting in their victimization were not really harmful. For instance, they may invoke a "denial of injury" in order to minimize the harm caused. Or they may articulate a "denial of responsibility" to minimize the guilt or shame that accompanies self-blame. These neutralizations, claims Agnew, allow victims to avoid feelings of fear and other negative emotions that sometimes accompany criminal victimization.

The research on victim reactions to crime suggests that victims seek help from a variety of sources as well as the police (Kaukinen, 2002a; 2002b). These other sources include friends, family members, and health care professionals. Those people to whom victims have access and upon whom they can rely

BOX 7.2

Profile of Victim Service Agencies and Clients

A 2002/2003 survey of victim service agencies and their clients undertaken by Statistics Canada provided the following profile:

- Among the agencies that reported to the survey, 42 percent (207) were police-based, 20 percent (97) were community-based, 12 percent (61) were sexual assault centres, 11 percent (52) were court-based, 9 percent (46) were system-based, 4 percent (21) were other types of service agencies, and 2 percent (8) were criminal injuries compensation or other financial benefit programs.
- Services most frequently offered by agencies include: general information (95 percent), emotional support (95 percent), liaison with other agencies on behalf of the client (85 percent), court information (85 percent), information on the criminal justice system structure and process (85 percent), public education (85 percent), immediate safety planning (85 percent), court accompaniment (83 percent), and assistance with victim impact statements (81 percent).

A one-day snapshot of 373 victim agencies servicing 4,358 clients revealed that:

- 77 percent of the clients were female, and 23 percent were male.
- 78 percent of the clients were victims of crimes against the person. Of these, 38 percent were victims of sexual assault, 4 percent were victims of criminal harassment, 2 percent were secondary victims of homicide, 3 percent were secondary victims of other crimes resulting in the loss of life, and 52 percent were victims of other violent offences, including physical assault.
- Of the 1,300 victims of sexual assault, 16 percent had been victimized by a spouse, ex-spouse, or intimate partner, 45 percent by other family members, and 39 percent by others, including friends, acquaintances, and strangers.
- Of the 1,780 victims of other violent offences in which the relationship was known, 68 percent had been victimized by a spouse, ex-spouse, or intimate partner, 11 percent by other family members, and 21 percent by others, including friends, acquaintances, and strangers.
- 45 percent of clients received emotional support, 39 percent received general information, 28 percent received case/trial updates, 26 percent received information on the criminal justice system structure and process, 23 percent received education, prevention advice, or training, and 22 percent received court information.

Source: de Léséleuc, S., and R. Kong. 2004. *Victim Services in Canada: National, Provincial and Territorial Fact Sheets.* Ottawa: Canadian Centre for Justice Statistics, Statistics Canada.

for assistance can be important sources of emotional support and practical assistance. It is important to note that such help-seeking behaviour forces us to recognize that those victims are not just passive objects whom crime acts upon. Rather, they are active agents who struggle with and strive to overcome the obstacles which crime presents to them (Kaukinen, 2002a).

SOCIAL OUTCOMES: INDIVIDUAL, ORGANIZATIONAL, AND GOVERNMENTAL RESPONSES

Crimes have implications not only for those who are directly involved but also for others who have only secondhand knowledge of these events. So criminologists also consider how the public, government officials, and various private interests respond to crime.

Most obvious are the economic costs associated with the operation of the criminal justice system. In 2002/2003, over $12 billion were spent on administering policing, courts, legal aid, prosecutions, and adult corrections in Canada. This represents about $399 for each Canadian. Policing activities represented the largest expenditure at 61 percent. This is followed by adult corrections (22 percent), courts (9 percent), legal aid (5 percent), and criminal prosecutions (3 percent) (Gannon and Mihorean, 2005). In contrast, many critics argue that the funding for agencies intended to assist victims is much lower than it should be (Kaukinan, 2002b). The distribution of justice spending among the sectors has remained relatively unchanged over the past number of years, while the total amount spent on justice services has climbed steadily.

Of course, these costs do not include all of our collective spending regarding crime. Other costs include those relating to insurance and the various tariffs which are attached to a variety of goods and services as a result of higher security costs. A major item in this respect is the growth of the private security and investigation service industry. According to Sanders (2005), the number of people

Figure 7.2

Per Capita Spending on Justice Services, 1990/1991–2002/2003

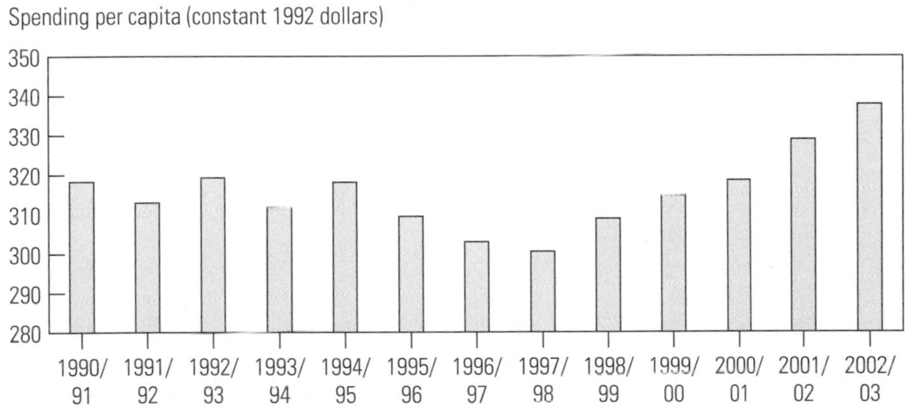

Spending per capita (constant 1992 dollars)

Source: Kong, R. *Criminal Justice Indicators 2005.* Ottawa: Centre For Justice Statistics, Statistics Canada, Catalogue No. 85-227-XIE. Page 51.

employed in this employment sector has increased from 46,651 in 1991 to 78,919 in 2001; and in 2000, the annual revenues for security and investigation services were approximately $2.3 billion. Indeed, there are more people working in private security than there are employed in public policing (Taylor-Butts, 2004).

As difficult as such economic estimates are to derive (and as cold as they might appear), Cohen (2005) argues that they are useful tools in the planning of criminal justice policy. Such estimates are helpful in any effort to characterize the problem and in the development of ways to address it. To mischaracterize the economic costs of crime could mean a misallocation of scarce resources.

Public Fear of Crime

Researchers have been investigating public reactions to crime since the early 1970s. Much of this research has focused on the fear of crime. Surveys indicate that serious crime is statistically rare and that the fear of becoming the victim of a serious crime is much more pervasive. Fear of crime may now be as serious a problem as crime itself. Journalists have taken notice of this, and have covered this issue extensively in recent years.

Typically the fear of crime is investigated through the use of victimization survey methodology. The four cycles of the Canadian General Social Survey victimization survey have all involved questions intended to determine how victims and non-victims feel about crime in Canada. Box 7.3 presents a summary of the findings from the 2004 survey.

BOX 7.3

Fear of Crime Findings from the 2004 Canadian General Social Survey

- About six in ten Canadians believe that crime is lower in their own neighbourhoods than it is elsewhere in Canada.
- About six in ten Canadians believe that crime has been stable in their neighbourhoods over the five-year period preceding the survey.
- Residents of Atlantic Canada are, in general, least fearful of crime.
- The vast majority of Canadians (men and women) indicated that overall, they are satisfied with their personal safety.
- Lower levels of fear are reported by those who frequently walk or use public transportation.
- The fear of crime is higher for those who believe that they live in higher-crime neighbourhoods.
- Fear of crime is higher for women than for men, but it appears that the gap between the two has narrowed somewhat since 1999.

Source: Gannon, M., and K. Mihorean. 2005. "Criminal Victimization in Canada 2004." Statistics Canada, *Juristat* 25(7).

What Is the Fear of Crime?

Even though the term **fear of crime** is widely used in the popular press and social scientific literature, there is little consensus as to what it means (Rader, 2004; Williams et al., 2000; Sacco, 2005). Both *fear* and *crime* are complicated terms. *Fear* typically suggests an emotional or physiological reaction (Dozier, 1999). We recognize that we are afraid when our mouths go dry, our hearts begin to pump faster, and the blood drains from our faces. Criminologists do not employ the term in the same way; after all, they rarely have access to people when they are actually afraid (Mirrlees-Black, Mayhew, and Percy, 1996).

Most research on the fear of crime comes from surveys (often victimization surveys) that ask members of the public about their beliefs or perceptions regarding crime. These surveys usually treat fear as an attitude or a perception rather than as an emotion. Also, criminologists usually treat fear as a personal rather than an altruistic matter, in the sense that they ask people about their worries regarding their own safety or the safety of their property. However, Warr (1991) contends that people often are fearful not for their own safety but for the safety of other family members. For instance, parents may express less fear if asked about their own safety but more fear if asked about the safety of their children. The concern about family members has appeared, as well, in the discussions about how people will react to evacuation orders should there be a terrorist attack on a major city. It is clear that many people will not leave their homes until they know the whereabouts of their immediate family members and know that they are safe.

Skogan (1993) suggests that at least four distinct meanings of fear are reflected in the research literature. The first of these, *concern*, focuses on the extent to which people understand crime to be a serious problem in their communities. Concern is a judgment that people make about the frequency and seriousness of crime in the local environment. Using this definition, it is possible for a person to be concerned about crime without being personally fearful (Furstenberg, 1971).

A second definition of fear emphasizes *risk*. Research that uses this definition employs questions asking respondents how likely they think it is that they will become victims of crime at some point in the future. This definition does not include an explicit emotional dimension; however, the assumption is that

---

WHAT IS IT?

Fear of Crime

Fear is usually treated as an attitude or a perception rather than as an emotion (Gabriel and Greve, 2003). Also, criminologists usually treat fear as a personal rather than an altruistic matter, in the sense that they ask people about their worries regarding their own safety or the safety of their property. However, people often are fearful not for their own safety but for the safety of other family members.

people who perceive their chances of being victims of crime to be high will be more afraid.

Fear can also be understood in terms of *threat*. This definition stresses the potential for harm that people believe crime holds for them. Respondents to surveys are often asked questions along the lines of "How safe do you feel walking alone in your neighbourhood at night? Would you say you feel very safe, reasonably safe, somewhat unsafe, or very unsafe?" Questions like this are asking people how likely they think it is they would be harmed if they were to expose themselves to risk.

Finally, fear can be defined in terms of *behaviour*. Surveys may ask people not how they feel about their safety or how likely they are to be subject to harm, but about what they do (or say they do) in response to crime. For example, respondents may be asked whether they engage in "avoidance behaviour," or about the precautions they take to protect themselves from crime.

In this research, it is not only the concept of fear that is problematic but also the concept of crime. Though it is rarely stated explicitly, the kinds of crime to which reference is made are those of a direct, predatory nature. Respondents are usually asked how much they worry about crimes such as robbery or burglary, or how safe they feel on neighbourhood streets. Less often are they asked how much they fear corporate crime or violence in the family (Warr and Stafford, 1983).

Patterns in Fear

The term *public fear of crime* encourages the view that fear is a problem evenly shared by all members of society (Miethe, 1995). However, as in the case of other social problems, the burden of fear falls more heavily on some than others. Two broad sets of factors have been shown to be related to differences in the fear of crime. One set relates to characteristics of individuals, the other to characteristics of their social environments.

Both sets of factors are important to a comprehensive understanding of fear of crime. The individual-level factors—gender, age, and socio-economic or minority status—are often interpreted as measures of social and physical vulnerability. They explain why some people—women, the aged, the poor, racial minorities—may feel especially susceptible to criminal victimization or less able to cope with the consequences of victimization. In contrast, the environmental factors describe dangers in the environment itself. When crime rates are higher, when public order is tenuous, and when people learn about local crime by talking to friends and neighbours, they define their environments as less safe.

Individual-Level Factors regarding Fear of Crime

Gender

Of all the factors that have been related to fear of crime, the strongest effects are associated with gender (Stanko, 1995). Women are much more likely than men to express anxiety about crime (Johnson, 1996; LaGrange and Ferraro, 1989; Skogan and Maxfield, 1981). For one thing, women are more likely to be smaller and less physically capable than the typical male offender, and to perceive themselves that way (Gordon and Riger, 1989). These physical differences are reinforced by traditional gender-role socialization processes that encourage women to think of themselves as vulnerable to a variety of forms of danger and that discourage them from developing assertive methods for dealing with threatening behaviour (Sacco, 1990).

Another important factor explaining the higher levels of fear among women is the specific fear of rape (Gordon and Riger, 1989; Johnson, 1996). Men are unlikely to express worry about being victimized sexually; yet this crime seems to be at the core of women's fears for their personal safety. Warr (1985) contends that women see rape as both serious in its consequences and frequent in its occurrence. They tend to estimate the risks of rape as relatively high and the consequences as relatively severe, and this has a significant impact on their fear.

Also according to Warr, rape is a "perceptually contemporaneous offence." In other words, it can occur not only as an isolated act but also in connection with other crimes such as robbery and burglary. In other words, these crimes are even more fear-provoking for women because they are associated with sexual danger.

Age

It is widely believed that fear of crime is especially prevalent among the elderly. Despite their lower victimization rates, older people tend to express greater concern for their personal safety (Baldassare, 1986; Garofalo, 1981b; Sacco and Nakhaie, 2001). Journalists, policymakers, and many social scientists often contend that their greater fear has a basis in reality (Cook and Skogan, 1990; Fattah and Sacco, 1989).

It can be argued that older people suffer high levels of fear of crime for much the same reasons women do. Both groups tend to be less physically able, and to have fewer resources for coping with the threat of crime and the consequences of victimization (Yin, 1980).

Many researchers have challenged the idea that the elderly are more afraid of crime (Moeller, 1989; St. John and Heald-Moore, 1996; Yin, 1982). LaGrange and Ferraro (1987) contend that researchers who have found that fear increases in old age tend to measure fear by asking questions about feelings of safety while on the street alone at night. They maintain that though older people are more likely to give answers indicating anxiety about their personal safety, this question really has nothing to do with the day-to-day lives of most older people. For a variety of reasons relating to health, finances, and general lifestyle, older people do not typically find themselves walking alone on the street at night. This means that their answers are more hypothetical than descriptive of the everyday realities of the elderly.

Race and Income

Personal safety is a greater problem for low-income individuals and for visible minorities (Miethe, 1995; Skogan and Maxfield, 1981; Will and McGrath, 1995). The differences are not as great as for gender, but they are significant. Two factors have been advanced to explain why. *First,* income and race are indicators of access to resources. Economic and racial minorities are often less able to take taxis, install alarm systems, and take other measures that might make them feel safer. *Second,* in many cities, there are very clear patterns of racial and economic segregation, and many neighbourhoods with large numbers of low-income or minority residents are also neighbourhoods with very high rates of crime. This means that at the level of individuals, measures of race and income are related to fear because they are "proxy" measures for neighbourhood of residence.

Environmental Factors regarding Fear of Crime

We are more likely to feel anxious about our personal safety in some settings than others (Lane, 2002). Warr (1990) has shown that people are more afraid of crime when they are alone, when they are in an unfamiliar setting, and when it is dark. Other research has shown that people are more likely to feel safe in settings that are open to observation, that offer no hiding places for potential offenders, and that would be easy to escape if necessary (Fisher and Nasar, 1995). All of this alerts us to the fact that fear is not just a social psychological characteristic that some people have and other people do not have; it is also a response to the social contexts in which we find ourselves.

The Community Setting

Generally speaking, fear of crime is a more significant problem in big cities than in small towns (Baumer, 1978; Garofalo, 1981b; Moeller, 1989). The simple explanation for this is that big cities have higher crime rates; urbanites' greater fear is a rational response to the realities of big-city crime.

BOX 7.4

Community Disorder

According to some researchers, including R. LaGrange and colleagues (1992) and Wesley Skogan (1990b), public concern about disorder is usually gauged by asking respondents to indicate how serious a problem various types of disorder are in their neighbourhoods. Typically, people are asked about disorders such as the following:

- trash and litter lying around
- dogs barking loudly or being a nuisance
- inconsiderate or disruptive behaviour
- graffiti on sidewalks and walls
- vacant houses and unkempt lots
- unsupervised youths
- noisy neighbours
- people drunk or high on drugs in public
- abandoned car parts lying around
- kids or adults trespassing in people's yards

But this is not necessarily the whole story. The urban sociologist Claude Fischer (1981) suggested that fear is a more significant problem in cities because the "public world of city life" routinely presents residents with situations that increase their feelings of insecurity. As we travel through urban public places, we are likely to encounter people who are strangers not only in the personal sense but also in a cultural sense. Because cities are hotbeds of lifestyle innovation, Fischer argues, we always run the risk of finding ourselves on the street, in an elevator, or on a subway platform with people whose style of dress or public behaviour strikes us as weird or threatening. Though many of the strangers we encounter are not criminals or delinquents, our unfamiliarity with groups whose lifestyles differ dramatically from our own may undermine our sense of security in cities.

Within communities, levels of fear vary from one neighbourhood to another (Austin et al., 2002). Some of this is of course due to differences in crime rates (Miethe and Lee, 1984). Those who live in neighbourhoods where the levels of crime are higher are more likely to be concerned about their personal safety and the safety of their property.

Levels of fear in a given neighbourhood are also affected by "social disorder" or **incivility** (LaGrange, Ferraro, and Supancic, 1992; May and Dunaway, 2000; Skogan, 1990b). These terms

Incivility
Physical conditions such as abandoned buildings and strewn trash, as well as social conditions such as public drinking or drug use.

WHAT ARE THEY?

Incivilities

Incivilities include physical conditions such as abandoned buildings, unkempt residences, and strewn trash and litter, and social conditions such as public drinking or drug use, panhandlers, and groups of noisy youths.

refer to those low-level breaches of the social order that, while not strictly criminal, often seem to be related to a sense of unease. There are two basic types of incivilities. *Physical incivilities* include conditions such as abandoned buildings, unkempt residences, and strewn trash and litter. *Social incivilities* include public drinking or drug use, panhandlers, and groups of noisy youths. In a study of reactions to disorder in 40 neighbourhoods, Skogan (1990b) found that although disorder tends to be a problem where crime is also a problem, disorder raises the fear to a higher level than would be the case if it was based on the local crime rate alone.

Why does social disorder promote fear of crime? The usual answer is that it signals that local social controls are breaking down. Typically, incivility is seen as an indication that people in the neighbourhood don't care much about themselves or their community. The subtext here is that neighbourhoods that can tolerate incivility can also tolerate more serious threats to person or property (Kelling and Coles, 1996).

The Information Environment

Fear of crime is a reaction to both what we experience and what we see and hear. Since fear of crime is more pervasive than crime itself, it makes sense for us to ask what role various information sources play in promoting crime-related anxieties.

It seems reasonable to assume that the mass media do much to promote fear of crime (Heath and Gilbert, 1996). After all, crime figures prominently in both news and entertainment media, and Canadians are avid consumers of mass media (see Chapter 1).

Yet, despite the apparent logic of this, researchers have had trouble establishing a clear link between people's media diets and their fear of crime (Doob and MacDonald, 1976; Heath and Gilbert, 1996; Sacco, 1995). This is partly because it is hard to research the issue: it is not always easy to determine what people learn from the mass media and what they learn from other sources (Doob, 1982). Most of us not only watch television news and read newspapers but also talk to friends or neighbours about what we hear and read.

Even when we take these limitations into account, the media's effects on fear of crime are not as strong as we might expect. It is too simplistic to argue that people respond in predetermined ways to media messages about crime. People approach the media with their own predispositions, personal histories, and beliefs about media credibility, and all of these affect how they interpret the information they receive (O'Keefe, 1984; Schlesinger et al., 1992).

Although we are heavy consumers of media content, what we learn does not necessarily have much relevance to our judgments about our personal safety. In fact, we seem to base our judgments far more on other sources. It is quite possible that the news about crime that moves through interpersonal channels in the form of gossip and rumour is more likely to induce fear than news that comes to us in broadcast or print form (Bursik and Grasmick, 1993; Skogan and Maxfield, 1981). For example, when we learn about crime by talking to our neighbours, we are learning about victims of whom we may have some personal knowledge. In these situations, we cannot dismiss what we hear by telling ourselves that the victims are nameless and faceless and that they live somewhere else.

In comparison, the average crime story that we read about in the newspaper is stripped of much of its emotional content and is likely to involve victims who are much more anonymous. Moreover, the typical media crime story provides us with so little information about victims, offenders, or the circumstances of the crime that we learn relatively little that will help us assess the risks in our neighbourhoods, our workplaces, or anywhere else our daily routines take us (Gordon and Riger, 1989). Most crime news is "non-local" in character and thus not relevant to the judgments we need to make about the threats we face in local environments. Consistent with this view is the finding reported by some researchers that news coverage is likely to affect fear when the media give prominent treatment to random violent crimes that occur locally (Heath and Gilbert, 1996; Liska and Baccaglini, 1990).

Community Reactions

What implications do individuals' reactions to crime have for their communities? Theorists have provided two general answers to this question. The first, derived from the pioneering French sociologist Emile Durkheim, suggests that public reactions to crime can make important contributions to the cohesion and stability of social life:

> Crime brings together upright consciences and concentrates them. We have only to notice what happens, particularly in a small town, when some moral scandal has just been committed. [People] stop each other on the street, they visit each other, they seek to come together to talk of the event and to wax indignant in common (Durkheim, 1933: 102).

According to this perspective, crime shocks our sentiments and reaffirms our commitment to the common values the crime violated. Our communal opposition to crime unites us: we speak out against crime, we are more vigilant in exercising informal social control, we join concerned citizens' groups, we support the toughening of laws intended to control crime. The overall effect is to strengthen social integration, and to strengthen social control in such a way that crime rates decline or at least stabilize.

In sharp contrast, others have suggested that because crime generates fear, it is more likely to drive people apart (Conklin, 1975; DiIulio, 1989; Goodstein and Shotland, 1982). John Conklin (1975) argues that when people are less afraid of crime, they are more likely to trust others and to think positively about their communities, and less likely to restrict their activities and reduce their social interactions with other community members. In contrast, when levels of fear are high, people are more likely to stay home at night and less likely to get to know or to be interested in their neighbours. Some may even be tempted to flee the community for a safer haven. Overall, then, crime does not build communities up as the Durkheimian model contends; rather, it undermines communities by weakening interpersonal ties. This view implies that public reactions to crime weaken informal social controls. When the streets are empty and people stop caring what happens to their neighbours, potential offenders may feel freer to take advantage of criminal opportunities.

There is research to support both perspectives. But generally speaking, the argument that crime drives people apart seems to have more empirical validity (Skogan, 1981, 1990b). Note that the two arguments are not necessarily inconsistent with each other.

Liska and Warner (1991) apply the routine activities theory of Cohen and Felson (1979) to suggest why elements of both arguments are useful. They contend that the Durkheimian view is correct in claiming that public reactions to crime reassert social controls in ways that stabilize crime rates or push them down. However, their view of the process by which this happens is closer to the position taken by Conklin than to the one advanced by Durkheim. Routine activities theory emphasizes the role that opportunities play in the commission of crimes (see Chapter 6). Social patterns that separate people from their property and from their family members increase the opportunities for crime. Liska and Warner agree that public reactions to predatory crimes (such as robbery) keep people at home and away from strangers. Though this reduces their sense of community, it also allows them to exert greater guardianship over their persons and property. As this happens, opportunities for crime are decreased, and greater control of crime is achieved.

BOX 7.5

Can Crime Cause Crime?

Some researchers have argued that public reactions to rising crime rates can amplify subsequent increases in crime rates. The central mechanism in this process is the breakdown of informal social control at the community level. Lynne Goodstein and Lance Shotland (1982) described the process by which crime rates spiral upward as follows:

> The cycle begins with actual increases in the crime rate or with the occurrence of one or several particularly noteworthy crimes. Such crimes might include an unsolved murder or a series of sexual assaults for which an offender has not been apprehended.
>
> In the next stage, information about these crimes and the threats that they pose to other members of the community is disseminated widely. People learn via the mass media or rumour networks that crimes are increasing and/or that even they might be at risk.
>
> As the information circulates, people begin to fear for their safety. This fear causes them to withdraw from community life. They stay home at night rather than go out, and report that their enjoyment of the community has declined.
>
> As people withdraw from the community, the delicate web of social relations begins to break down, as do the various informal social controls that regulate conduct. Thus, as the streets become less populated, they are subject to less control because citizen surveillance of them is reduced.
>
> As the levels of community control decline, the levels of crime may be expected to rise; and as the levels of crime continue to rise, the cycle begins to repeat itself.

Goodstein and Shotland's argument is consistent with the theoretical view that crime is made more likely by the absence of controls that would check it. As the authors note, empirical evidence supports each of the individual linkages just described. What is less clear is the validity of the overall model, which has not been rigorously tested.

More recently, Bellair (2000) has argued that the relationship between crime and informal social control is extremely complex. Robbery and stranger assault can reduce informal surveillance of the street; but at the same time, informal surveillance of the street can reduce the prevalence of robbery and stranger assault. In other words, the effects flow in both directions. Bellair also reports that though some crimes, such as robbery, may reduce the informal control that residents exert over the street, other crimes, such as break and enter, may increase these controls.

Claims-making

Fear can strengthen the public's concerns about crime. People's reactions to crime can be determined by the actions of special-interest groups. Some writers refer to the processes by which laws are passed and legal reforms are initiated as **claims-making** (Best, 1995; Loseke, 2000; Spector and Kitsuse, 1977).

Claims-making
The making of assertions about the existence of some problem that requires a policy solution.

In the claims-making process, a group offers assertions about the existence of some problem that requires a policy solution. It then attempts to gain public support for its claims and to attract the attention of public officials and the mass media. Becker (1963) describes the claims-maker as a "moral entrepreneur" who is best exemplified by the crusading reformer. According to Becker, there is "some evil which profoundly disturbs" these reformers, to the point that they believe that "nothing can be right in the world until rules are made to correct it" (147–8).

In the early stages, claims may reflect a narrow set of relatively private interests (Pfuhl, 1986; Ross and Staines, 1972). Claims-makers may see themselves as representing those who have been victimized by some condition, or who feel directly threatened by it (Weeks et al., 1986). But claims can also be issued by agencies seeking to expand their mandates, or by professional groups seeking to enhance their status. Researchers have suggested that the pressure for the passage of computer crime laws is largely the result of the crusading efforts of computer crime "experts," who by publicizing the issue gain recognition for themselves and their work (Hollinger and Lanza-Kaduce, 1988).

Best (1990) asserts that with respect to legislative and other policymaking bodies, claims-makers can be either insiders or outsiders. Insiders include political lobbyists, representatives of powerful professional organizations, and members of government, all of whom have relatively direct access to those who make public policy. In contrast, outsiders have no direct access and must rely more heavily on taking their message directly to the public. In so doing, outsiders hope to enlist members in their cause. How a given claims-making process unfolds depends on several factors, two of which require particular attention.

The *first* involves the amount of opposition that claims-makers encounter in their attempts to convince the public and policymakers that a particular remedy is necessary. Some kinds of claims-making are more adversarial than others. Issues that do not have an adversarial quality are sometimes referred to as **valence issues**. Child abuse, crimes against the elderly, and computer crime are valence issues, in the sense that most people would readily agree that they are problems requiring public intervention. In contrast, efforts by claims-makers to organize public support for interventions directed against abortion or pornography are often met by resistance or by counter-definitions of what the problem really is (Ross and Staines, 1972).

Valence issues
Issues that do not have an adversarial quality.

WHAT DOES IT MEAN?

Claims-maker

The claims-maker is a "moral entrepreneur," best exemplified by the crusading reformer who believes that rules must be formulated to combat the evil in the world.

A *second* factor affecting claims-making is the wider social context in which the process unfolds. Prevailing social values and beliefs can facilitate or hinder claims-making. Based on an analysis of many case studies of criminalization, Hagan (1980) argued that successful claims-makers have usually appealed effectively to dominant cultural values. For example, the social problem of crime against the elderly emerged in the 1970s because a "ripe issue climate" existed in which rising crime, the needs of crime victims, and the needs of the elderly were already seen as important problems.

Criminalization is clearly a form of claims-making, yet the passage of a law is not always enough to satisfy claims-makers. Much contemporary claims-making about crime is directed toward changing how behaviour that has already been criminalized is treated by the criminal justice system. The recognition in recent years that crimes against women, victims' rights, impaired driving, crimes against the elderly, stalking, and hate crime are issues requiring more vigorous enforcement or innovative approaches attests to the validity of this observation (Best, 1999).

In general, when we understand responses to crime as the product of claims-making, conflict, and power (rather than of social consensus), this alerts us to the biases of these responses. This in turn casts doubt on the value of approaches that characterize the law as a neutral arbiter that can be understood without reference to the society that produced it.

Extreme Reactions: The Moral Panic

Public reactions to crime can generally be characterized as subtle and routine (Hindelang, Gottfredson, and Garofalo, 1978). Typically, crime dominates neither our personal nor our public agendas. Sometimes, however, the media, the government, and members of the public respond to crime in a much more intense fashion. The sociologist Stanley Cohen (1972) used the term **moral panic** to describe such episodes. Goode and Ben-Yehuda (1994) explain:

> During the moral panic, the behaviour of some members of a society is thought to be so problematic to others, the evil they do, or are thought to do is felt to be so wounding to the substance and fabric of the body social that serious steps must be taken to control the behaviour, punish the perpetrators and repair the damage. The threat this evil presumably poses is felt to represent a crisis for that society: something must be done about it and something must be done now; if steps are not taken immediately, or soon, we will suffer even graver consequences.

Moral panic
The behaviour of some members of society is seen as so problematic, evil, or harmful to the society that it becomes a social imperative to control the behaviour, punish the offenders, and repair the damage (e.g., the Great European witch hunts).

The sentiment generated or stirred up by this threat can be referred to as a kind of fever; it can be characterized by heightened emotion, fear, dread, anxiety, hostility and a strong feeling of righteousness (31).

According to Goode and Ben-Yehuda, moral panics have several distinguishing characteristics:

- A heightened concern over some behaviour or the group that is thought to be responsible for it.
- An increase in hostility toward the individuals in question.
- A substantial or widespread consensus regarding the seriousness and the nature of the problem.
- A public reaction that seems out of proportion to the size of the problem.
- A volatile character such that panics emerge and subside rather suddenly.

In recent years, we have witnessed several episodes that could be described in these terms. The social responses to illegal drugs (Reinarman and Levine, 1989), serial killers (Jenkins, 1994), child abduction (Best, 1988), and random violence (Best, 1999) provide illustrations of this concept.

According to some social scientists, the societal reaction to the problem of juvenile gangs in the late 1990s and early years of the 21st century exhibit many of the characteristics of the moral panic (St. Cyr, 2003). In a large number of cities in Canada and the United States, people have become convinced that such gangs are becoming bigger, better organized, and more violent than ever before. As well, it is widely believed that often the local gangs represent franchises or branch plants of much more powerful, highly centralized gang organizations. Stories about gang violence have become a staple of crime news reporting and circulate regularly within local and national rumour networks.

While the moral panic about youth gangs is promoted in many quarters, this does not suggest a conspiracy of intentions. It is through the process of the social construction of reality that the widespread existence of youth gangs comes to be taken for granted. As police, politicians journalists, educators, victims' groups, and others in society borrow and build on each other's themes, a consensus is built regarding the nature and seriousness of the problem (Meehan, 2000; McCorkle and Miethe, 2002).

Critics point out, however, that in the case of the moral panic over gangs (as in the case of

WHAT IS IT?

Moral Panic

"During the moral panic, the behaviour of some members of a society is thought to be so problematic to others, the evil they do, or are thought to do, is felt to be so wounding to the substance and fabric of the body social, that serious steps must be taken to control the behaviour, punish the perpetrators, and repair the damage" (Goode and Ben-Yehuda, 1994).

moral panics more generally), many of the claims regarding the problem do not stand up terribly well to careful empirical scrutiny. For instance, arguments about the rapid rise in the levels and seriousness of juvenile crime in Canada and the United States in recent years are at best questionable (Doob and Cesaroni, 2004). Moreover, it has been known by criminologists for decades that policing agencies and journalists often tend to exaggerate the degree of organizational sophistication of youth gangs—most of which are best conceptualized as "near groups." It is also evident that as the panic about youth gangs has spread, the terms "gang" and "gang violence" are often used in very casual and non-specific ways. It is true that most juvenile crime is committed in the company of others (Warr, 2002). This, however, does not automatically make it gang crime. Finally, the evidence which is thought to suggest that notorious street gangs, such as the Crips, might be setting up branch plant operations in cities very distant from Los Angeles is subject to more than one interpretation. Instead, local groups calling themselves the Crips might be copying the names or the style, language, and rituals of such celebrity gangs (Best, 1999).

It might be argued as well that after the events of September 11, 2001, much of North America was in the grip of a moral panic relating to terrorism (Roth and Muzzatti, 2004). Governments passed sweeping laws, and many people altered their travel habits and dramatically overestimated the chances of being victims of terrorists. Even more destructively, many people's attitudes toward individuals of Middle Eastern origin were marked by suspicion and distrust. The lack of rationality and proportionality which is evident in the societal response to terrorism is characteristic of moral panics. While about 3,000 people died in the World Trade Center attack, close to 50,000 people die in Canada each year from causes related to tobacco use, yet there is a relatively restrained public response to the harm done by smoking.

According to Goode and Ben-Yehuda (1994), three theories can be used to explain the development of moral panics. The first, the **grassroots model**, views these panics as originating in the mood of the public. The concerns expressed by the mass media and by politicians are a reaction to public sentiment, not the cause of it.

A second theory, the **elite-engineered model**, argues that moral panics are deliberate attempts by economic or political elites to promote public concern about some issue that does not involve the interests of the elites. Moral panics are a means of manipulating consciousness; elites resort to them to divert

Grassroots model
Views moral panics as originating in the mood of the public.

Elite-engineered model
Argues that moral panics represent the deliberate attempt on the part of the economic or political elite to promote public concern about some issue that does not involve the elite's interests.

attention from real social problems, the solutions to which might undermine the interests of the elites.

The third perspective, and the most common, is **interest-group model**. Unlike the elite-engineered model, this perspective does not see the power or resources that create moral panics as narrowly concentrated in the hands of a small group. Instead, power is understood as more diffuse and more pluralistic. The implication is that moral panics are set in motion by the actions of politicians, crusading journalists, or professional associations.

Goode and Ben-Yehuda contend that the elite-engineered model does not seem to explain most moral panics; the other two perspectives are of greater value, especially in combination. The grassroots model allows us to see which fears and concerns are available as the raw materials for moral panics; the interest-group model allows us to understand how these raw materials are intensified and mobilized.

Interest-group model
Argues that moral panics can be set in motion by the actions of small groups, such as politicians, crusading journalists, or professional associations.

SUMMARY

Victimization has financial, physical, emotional, and behavioural costs, and the ability to adjust depends on a number of factors. Victims who are alone may find it more difficult to manage the stresses associated with crime than those whose families and friends are able to lend emotional and/or practical assistance. People with more economic resources may find it less difficult to absorb economic losses and to replace stolen or damaged property. Also important are prior psychological functioning and previous history as victims. Individuals who are already suffering from depression may respond to criminal victimization more negatively; so may those who have already been victimized by crime.

Fear of crime can increase in the aftermath of crime. *Fear* can be approached from at least four distinct angles: "concern," a judgment that people make about the frequency and seriousness of crime in the local environment; "risk," how likely people think it is that they will be victims of crime; "threat," the potential for harm that people believe crime holds for them; and "behaviour," what people do (or say they do) in response to crime.

Public discussion of crime is often fuelled by special-interest groups pushing for stronger interventions by the police and the criminal justice system. These "claims-makers" seek to get certain issues and problems placed in the forefront of the public agenda. Moral panic represents an extreme response: an intense reaction to crime problems that includes strident calls for action, even when the crimes being committed are few in number and not widely threatening to the public.

QUESTIONS FOR REVIEW AND DISCUSSION

1. Are there ways we can properly compensate crime victims for their losses? Should the offenders be involved in this process?

2. Many social critics have argued that "victim," like "offender," is a stigmatized category. Do you agree?

3. Is the fear of crime a realistic assessment of the risk of crime or a reflection of an overreaction to crime?

4. Do you agree that people should not change their behaviour in response to their fear of crime? Does changing behaviour increase people's chances of being victims, or does it keep the chances of victimization the same?

5. Can you identify different moral panics that have occurred and explain what the reactions to these panics have been?

RECOMMENDED READINGS

Conklin, J.E. 1975. *The Impact of Crime.* New York: Macmillan.

Critcher, C. 2003. *Moral Panics and the Media.* Buckingham: Open University Press.

Macmillan, R. 2001. "Violence and the Life Course: Assessing the Consequences of Violent Victimization for Personal and Social Development." *Annual Review of Sociology,* 27: 1–22.

Madriz, E. 1997. *Nothing Bad Happens to Good Girls.* Berkeley: University of California Press.

Ruback, R.B., and M.P. Thompson. 2001. *Social and Psychological Consequences of Violent Victimization.* Thousand Oaks, CA: Sage Publications.

INFOTRAC® COLLEGE EDITION

Explore InfoTrac® College Edition, your online university library, which includes hundreds of popular and scholarly journals in which you can find articles related to the topics in this chapter. Visit InfoTrac® through your web browser (**www.infotrac-college.com**) or through this book's website (**www.criminalevent-4e.nelson.com**).

WHAT'S ON THE WEB?

For chapter links and quizzes, check out the accompanying website at **www.criminalevent-4e.nelson.com**.

Part 3

Domains of Crime

Chapter 8 — Crime and the Family and Household

LEARNING OBJECTIVES:

- begin a discussion of the ways in which criminal events are distributed across different social domains
- explore the characteristics of households which contextualize crime and the victimization which occurs in this domain
- discuss the precursors, transactions, and aftermath of various forms of family violence
- discuss the precursors, transactions, and aftermath of various forms of crime against the household

INTRODUCTION

In Part 2, we presented the theoretical perspectives that criminologists have used to explain criminal behaviour and the evolution of criminal events. Part 3 focuses on how criminal events cluster in particular social domains. Chapters 9 and 10 are concerned with the leisure and work domains. In this chapter, we analyze the domain of the family and the household.

In the three chapters in Part 3, we discuss crime events in an integrated fashion, reviewing what we know from current research about offenders, victims, the circumstances in which these events occur, and so on. As we proceed, we will present the relevant theories that best explain the aspect of the event we are examining. Some theories, especially those that focus on motivation, are more useful when analyzing the precursors of crime events. Generally speaking, transactions are best understood from opportunity perspectives. The aftermath can be analyzed using insights drawn from theories about reactions to crime.

Throughout these chapters, as we discuss specific research findings, we encourage the reader to refer to the theories we reviewed in Part 2. These theories constitute a road map for guiding us through the details of research findings; they help us identify commonalities in social behaviour, and they provide an understanding of the complexities of social interaction. We begin with a description of the family and household domain.

THE FAMILY AND THE HOUSEHOLD

In the literature of social science, the concept of family has several different meanings. A narrow definition views the family as "husband and wife, with or without never-married children of any age, living at home, or a lone parent with or without one or more never-married children at home" (Devereaux, 1990: 33). Broader definitions suggest that the concept of family includes any adult–child grouping (e.g., with lesbian or gay parents) and all intimate cohabiting or consciously committed support groups, including childless couples, communes, and networks of friends (Luxton, 1988).

In general, we understand the **family** as any relatively enduring pattern of social relationships through which domestic life is organized (Miller, 1990). Customarily, the family is seen as a distinct kind of intimate group in that its relationships are based on kinship. However, this definition of a family is as much a matter of culture as it is of **social organization**. For instance, the customary cultural view of the family as a unit of procreation leads many people to define a family in which the father is absent as a "broken" home (Wells and Rankin, 1986).

The **household** is generally understood as the social and physical setting within which family life is organized. Many surveys—such as those used in the census—lead us to equate families with households, but in so doing they may distort the empirical realities of family relations. Family relations often extend beyond a particular household. For instance, husbands and wives who are separated usually maintain separate households, although—perhaps because of dependent children—family relations may be sustained.

From a wealth of demographic data, it is clear that family relations have changed a great deal in recent years (Almey, 2000; Statistics Canada, 2005; Le Bourdais, Neill, and Turcotte, 2000; Milan, 2000). For example:

- In the past few decades, Canadians have seen a decrease in marriages, an increase in common-law marriages, and a rise in the breakup of all types of unions.
- The instability of many common-law arrangements and the rising rate of the dissolution of all types of unions suggest that more people will spend more time living alone or in the context of a larger number of short-term relationships.

Family
Any enduring pattern of social relationships through which domestic life is organized.

Social organization
Coherence and continuity in the social environment, and rational co-operation among individuals and social institutions.

Household
The social and physical setting within which family life is organized.

- In 75 percent of Canadian families with children at home in 2002, a two-parent team was tackling the job of raising children. The remainder had a lone parent in charge—an arrangement that is gradually becoming more prevalent among Canadian families.

- Canadian families now have fewer children living at home than they did in the past. This reflects both a decline in birth rates and an increase in the number of "empty nesters" and in the proportion of couples who have never had children.

- The average age for first marriages is rising steadily for both brides and grooms. In 2000, first-time brides were 31.7 years old, while grooms proclaimed their first marriage vows at an average age of 34.3. Only two decades earlier, women and men were 25.9 and 28.5 years old, respectively, when they got married.

- In Canada, the number of common-law unions has more than doubled since 1981. At that time, there were 357,000 common-law relationships—about 6 percent of all couples. By the 2001 Census, roughly 14 percent of all couples were common law.

- Couples are living longer and living better after their children leave than ever before.

Obviously, the Canadian family is changing. We are witnessing a move away from the conventional single-family unit toward variations that include single parents, multiple singles, and lone individuals. As a result of these varying structures, social relations within families are different from what we would have expected in the past. Also, more and more households are now made up of elderly Canadians living on their own, with the result that this group's dependence on their children is increasing.

FAMILY VIOLENCE

Family violence
Child abuse, wife assault, elder abuse, and other forms of physical coercion that are contextualized by domestic living arrangements.

Our culture's tendency to idealize the family as the most intimate and nurturing of social groups long discouraged research into the extent to which violence is a part of family life (Miller, 1990). Only very gradually, in large part through the efforts of claims-makers, has it come to be recognized that **family violence** is a social problem. In the 1960s, the problem of child abuse emerged as a policy and research issue (Best, 1990; Mann, 1999; Pfohl, 1977). In the 1970s, wife abuse moved onto the agendas of researchers and criminal justice professionals (Loseke, 1989; Tierney, 1982). In the 1980s, elder abuse came to be recognized as a form of family violence requiring attention (Leroux and

Petrunik, 1990). To a far lesser degree, criminologists have also researched and theorized about other forms of family violence, including sibling violence (Hoffman et al., 2005) and adolescent violence toward parents (Brezina, 1999).

Precursors

Any discussion of the preconditions of family violence must begin with a close look at the social organization of families, which contain within them the seeds out of which violent episodes grow.

Characteristics of Families

Interpersonal conflict theory has been used to shed light on how families run into the kinds of problems that lead to interpersonal violence. The following draws on insights provided by Gelles and Straus (1988).

First, family life provides the social setting for omnipresent conflict. Family members spend a great deal of time with one another and interact across a wide variety of dimensions. They also make a great number of decisions, from how to spend money and who will spend it, to where vacations will be spent and how they will be paid for, to who will prepare dinner and what dinner will be. The frequency of interactions like this, coupled with their intensity (often high), sets the stage for conflict. Also, because the family is a heterogeneous social grouping—that is, it includes within it males and females and people of different ages—it also provides the context for the playing out of gender or generational conflicts that have societal origins. Because family members usually know one another well, they are well aware of one another's weaknesses and vulnerabilities. This intimate knowledge makes it easier for conflicts to escalate into violent exchanges.

Second, family life is private life. What happens between family members often takes place behind closed doors. The private character of family life reflects a consensus view that families are different from other social groupings. The privacy of the family has structured how the police and the courts have responded to intrafamily violence (Browning, 2002). Neighbours, friends, and co-workers may not know about violence that occurs between family members, and even if they do know about it, they may regard it as none of their business. Moreover, the view that violence in the home is a family matter may be shared by the victims of violence. All of these factors reinforce the low visibility of violent conflict in the home and suggest the extent to which it is immune from many of the informal social controls that regulate violent behaviour among non-intimates. Those who take a feminist perspective argue that concerns for the privacy of the home simply shield the abuser from the sanctions of the criminal justice system. These concerns, they continue, reflect a bias toward maintaining power relationships in families that favour men, while ignoring the injustices perpetrated against women.

Third, cultural attitudes toward family violence are highly ambivalent. In the family, unlike in the workplace or other more formal settings, physical violence continues to be tolerated. This is most evident with respect to the spanking of children (Davis, 1994). Most parents believe that in certain circumstances it is perfectly appropriate for one family member to use physical force against another family member. This is not to suggest that spanking is necessarily abusive (although it well may be), but rather that rules about violence in the home differ from rules about violence in other social domains. Nor does the tolerance of physical violence extend to dependent children alone. In the recent past, violent behaviour by husbands against wives was tolerated in much the same way that parental violence toward children is tolerated now. Most people still continue to regard violence among siblings as normal and natural and—despite obvious physical consequences—not really a form of violence at all.

Fourth, the family is a hierarchical institution. In other words, some family members have more power than others (Comack et al., 2000; Sagrestano, Heavey, and Christensen, 1999). Obviously, parents are more powerful than children. As power–control theory would predict, in traditional patriarchal family structures, which are characterized by the presence of an adult male authority figure, the husband is assumed to have the right to make decisions that are binding on other family members (Hagan, Gillis, and Simpson, 1985). Such authority relations, which are recognized by law, create a situation that allows those with more power to behave with relative impunity toward those who have less power. Also, the widespread support for existing authority relations allows those with power to believe they have a right to expect compliance from those who are less powerful. Violence can thus be understood as one effective means of gaining compliance.

Inequality in Family Relations

Consensus views of the family have been challenged by those who see that inequalities in family relations render some people more vulnerable than others to intrafamily violence. Our tendency to categorize the major forms of family violence as "wife assault," "child abuse," and "elder abuse" reflects this fact. The consequences of this "hierarchy of family violence" rest most heavily

Figure 8.1

Percentage of Male and Female Victims Reporting Consequences and Outcomes of Spousal Violence, Canadian GSS data, 2004

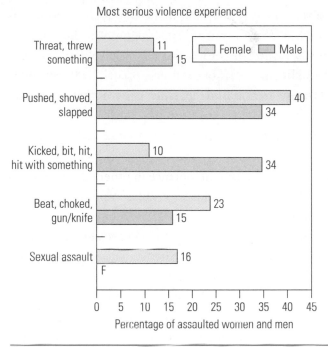

Most serious violence experienced

Percentage of assaulted women and men

Source: K. Mihorean. 2005. "Trends in Self-Reported Spousal Abuse." In K. AuCoin (ed.) *Family Violence in Canada: A Statistical Profile 2005*. Ottawa: Canadian Centre for Justice Statistics, Statistics Canada. Page 15.

on the shoulders of women, who historically have been economically dependent on men. Not surprisingly, as both children and adults, females face a greater risk than males of experiencing violence at the hands of family members. Victimization surveys typically show that the overwhelming majority of victims of partner violence are women (Johnson, 1996). These differences are most pronounced when more serious forms of violence are considered. Data from the 2004 Canadian General Social Survey (GSS) indicate that women are more likely than men to report having been beaten or choked by a partner or having been threatened with a gun or a knife or having had these weapons used against them (see Figure 8.1). Women are also much more likely to report being victims of multiple acts of violence and to report having sustained injuries (Mihorean, 2005).

According to Beattie (2005), spousal homicides accounted for about one in five solved homicides between 1994 and 2003. In 2004, as in other years, women were much more likely to be killed by their partners than were men;

the spousal homicide rate against female victims was five times what it was against males (Dauvergne, 2005).

Some studies have found that within families, women may be as violent as men. This has led some observers to suggest that we need to focus more attention on the "battered husband" (Steinmetz, 1977–78). However, these studies do not indicate the context, motives, or consequences associated with the violent acts (DeKeseredy and Hinch, 1991; Johnson and Sacco, 2000). By most measures of victimization—who initiates the violence, who uses violence offensively rather than defensively, and who suffers the most injury—there is little question that women are more often and more seriously victimized (Johnson and Bunge, 2001).

Patterns of violence against children also reflect patterns of inequality and dependency. Family assaults of children—that is, assaults by either parents or siblings—are alarmingly common. According to 2003 UCR data, six out of ten physical assaults of children under the age of six were perpetrated by a family member. However, as children grow older, the proportion of assaults committed by peers and acquaintances increases (Beattie, 2005). Within families, parents are the most likely perpetrators of violence against children. In 2003, more than six in ten assaults on Canadian youth were committed by a parent, most commonly the father (AuCoin, 2005). Fathers were also most likely to be the accused in cases of family-related sexual assault (AuCoin, 2005).

As with assault, most young homicide victims were killed by a parent—typically the father (Dauvergne, 2005). Between 1994 and 2003, parents committed 90 percent of all family murders; fathers committed about 60 percent, mothers about 30 percent, and other family members about 10 percent.

Another form of abuse that reflects hierarchy and dependency relationships is elder abuse, the victims of which may be infirm and reliant on a spouse or on an adult-child caregiver for the basic necessities of life (Pillemer and Finkelhor, 1988; Quinn and Tomita, 1986). Our understanding of elder abuse as a social problem is much less developed than our understanding of some other forms of family violence, in part because researchers have been interested in such crimes for a much shorter time.

It is perhaps important to recall from Chapter 2 that of all age groups, the elderly have the lowest rate of criminal victimization. This empirical observation emerges when we examine different types of crime data and different types of offences. A study of various forms of elder abuse as recorded in the Uniform Crime Report for 2003 revealed just under 4,000 incidents of violence against older persons (AuCoin, 2005). About 60 percent of these incidents were committed by people who were not family members. Male family members were the accused in the majority (78 percent) of family-related assaults. Sons and husbands made up about two-thirds of the accused offenders, in roughly equal proportions. The average age of spouses accused of victimizing an older person was 66, and the average of the adult male sons was 40.

Isolation and Economic Stress

Conflict, privacy, ambivalent attitudes about violence, and inequality are not the only contributors to violence in the family. When families are isolated from the wider community of kin, friends, and neighbours, the negative effects of privacy can increase (Browning, 2002). In such circumstances, those who behave violently may become increasingly insensitive to prevailing community standards of appropriate conduct. Furthermore, they and their victims may lose or find less accessible the social supports that could be crucial in ending or preventing violence.

Economic stress can also contribute to violent conduct. The Violence Against Women Survey (VAWS) and several other studies have shown that low income is related to wife assault (Kruttschnitt, 2002; Rinfret-Raynor et al., 2004), although some studies suggest that the relationship may be less strong

---

BOX 8.1

Risk Factors for Wife Assault

Victimization surveys are an important source of information about the kinds of factors that put some people at higher risk of particular types of crime. The British Crime Survey (BCS)—like all victimization studies—shows that wife assault does not occur randomly and that various factors put some women at greater risk. These factors include:

- Previous victimization   Being victimized previously by wife assault increases the risk of subsequent victimization.
- Separation   Women who are separated from their partners are at much higher risk of domestic violence than women with other social statuses.
- Gender inequality   Egalitarian relationships place women at lower risk than relationships characterized by greater gender inequality.
- Poverty   Women in economically precarious households are at greater risk than women in more stable economic environments.
- Youth   As women become older, their risk of violent victimization in the home declines.

Source: Walby, S., and A. Myhill. No Date. *Reducing Domestic Violence . . . What Works?* London: Home Office Research. Used by permission.

than previously thought (Mihorean, 2005). Strain theories would predict that a husband or father who is out of work may use violence to compensate for feelings of inadequacy that the perceived failure to play the breadwinner role may promote (Frieze and Browne, 1989). Strain may also arise from non-economic sources such as illness or the death of a loved one. In the case of child abuse or elder abuse, strain may originate in the demands of the caregiving experience itself (Fattah and Sacco, 1989).

Transactions

In general terms, the location and timing of violent events reflect the importance of the precursors discussed earlier. Most violent events involving family members take place in the home. Typically, spousal homicides occur in private residences—most often in the home of the victim (Comack et al., 2000). The reason is fairly obvious: the home is where family members are most likely to confront one another in privacy.

Intrafamily violence is most likely to erupt in the evening or late at night. Arguments that begin in the early evening may turn violent if they are unresolved as the night wears on (Gelles and Straus, 1988). Indeed, an examination of Canadian homicides over a ten-year period found that when police were able to discern the motive, spousal homicides were most commonly found to result from the escalation of an argument (Beattie, 2005). Importantly, the late-night and early-morning hours bring with them a reduction in the options available for resolving conflicts without violence. It is too late to call a family member or to leave the house to visit a friend. Stressful events that fuel tensions or challenge parental or patriarchal authority increase the likelihood of a violent episode involving children. Despite the attention paid to the physical mistreatment of very young children, it seems that much family violence is directed at teenage children, whose various forms of adolescent rebellion may be viewed as requiring strict physical discipline (Pagelow, 1989).

Sometimes the factors that make a violent event more likely come into sharp relief. Gelles and Straus (1988) note that violent events occur with greater frequency during the Christmas and Easter holidays. At these times, the sources of economic and non-economic stress can be especially pronounced. Family members spend more time than usual together and may entertain unrealistically positive expectations about how others will behave. Also, family celebrations may involve drinking alcohol, and this in itself can make violence more likely.

Patterns of Family Violence

Perhaps the most distinctive characteristic of family violence is its repetitive and cyclical character (Williams, 2003). Many other forms of victimization result from chance encounters between victim and offender; in contrast, the intimate relationships in which family members are involved increase the probability that violent events will reoccur or escalate. Minor acts of violence may be self-reinforcing when those who engage in them come to see violence as an effective means of achieving compliance and when they see the use of violence carries few sanctions (Johnson, 1996). Most victims try to resist the physical violence, but their resistance is more likely to be passive (reasoning with the offender, trying to get help) than active (Harlow, 1991). Silverman and Kennedy (1993) note that most spousal homicides are not the result of a sudden "blowup," but rather represent the culmination of serial violence, which is fuelled by drugs and alcohol, a lack of problem-solving skills, and the effects of long-standing quarrels and antagonisms. Data from the 2004 General Social Survey revealed that over half of those who self-reported spousal violence in a current or previous relationship also indicated that the violence had occurred on more than one occasion (Mihorean, 2005). Many cases of family violence escalate into even more serious forms of victimization. At a minimum, the physical violence that does occur is probably part of a much larger pattern involving a variety of forms of emotional and psychological mistreatment. Alcohol, controlling behaviour, and misogynist attitudes can interact with each other in complicated ways to produce injurious and even lethal outcomes (Johnson, 2001; Thompson et al., 2003).

Increasingly, researchers are contending that we must focus on the various contexts in which different types of family violence occur. For example, with respect to partner violence, Johnson and Ferraro (2000) argue that several distinct subtypes can be identified. "Common couple violence" is not part of a general pattern and arises mainly in the context of a specific argument in which one of the partners responds violently to the other. In contrast, "intimate terrorism" involves violence as just one tactic in a general pattern of control. "Violent resistance" refers to the use of violence as a form of self-defence. Finally, "mutual violent control" suggests a pattern in which both husband and wife are controlling and violent in a situation that "could be viewed as two intimate terrorists battling for control" (Johnson and Ferraro, 2000: 950).

The Aftermath

Family violence can have severe physical consequences and even result in death (Federal/Provincial/Territorial Ministers Responsible for the Status of

Women, 2002). Some evidence suggests that violence in the home is more likely to result in injury than other types of violence (Harlow, 1991). This finding can be explained by the repetitive character of family violence and by the relatively limited ability of victims to escape violent encounters.

Short and Long-Term Consequences of Family Violence

Violence has emotional and psychological as well as physical effects. Victims of violence in the home, like other victims of violence, experience many forms of fear, trauma, and stress (Thompson et al., 2003). Indeed, violence in the home may be more likely than other forms of violence to produce these consequences since it usually occurs in environments that are assumed to be "safe" (Burgess, Holmstrom, and McCausland, 1977). Being victimized by an intimate can produce greater stress, since victims have to cope with the fact that the violence was at the hands of someone they trusted (Sales, Baum, and Shore, 1984). Stephanie Riger and her colleagues (2002) have argued that the effects of wife assault can extend well beyond the physical and emotional effects that we usually associate with this kind of victimization. Batterers, for instance, often intimidate the victim's extended family so that many of the services the family members might supply become unavailable. As a result, the victim might lose access to child care, financial assistance, and even a safe haven.

Despite the seriousness of their injuries, victims may decline to seek medical aid so as to avoid having to explain to others the sources of the injury. The stigma of being a victim keeps many from seeking help. And those who do seek help may encounter emergency room personnel who are less than sympathetic. According to Kurz (1987), some ER staff describe abused wives as "AOBs" (alcohol on breath) and as troublesome people who deserve the predicament in which they find themselves.

For similar reasons, victims of family violence may decline to report the incident to the police (Klaus and Rand, 1984). For many female victims of spousal abuse, calling the police is a last resort, even when the violence is severe (Mihorean, 2005). Victimization surveys suggest that the victim's fear that the offender will seek revenge figures largely in the decision not to report. The victim may also fear that an arrest could lead to a loss of financial support.

In the past, police were reluctant to intervene in family situations, and when they did intervene, they were often reluctant to remove the offender (most often the husband) from the situation. More and more, however, the police are enforcing the law as it applies to family violence, and currently all provinces and territories have pro-charging policies in place to better ensure that spousal assault will be treated as a criminal matter (Mihorean, 2005). Williams and Hawkins (1986) contend that applying sanctions to offenders may deter future offending. As we noted in our review of deterrence theories in Chapter 5, there is a strong stigma associated with arrest (Dutton et al., 1992). However, because they do not seek help from the police does not imply that victims seek help from no one. More extensive use might be made of friends' and family members' resources than of justice system resources (Kaukinen, 2002a, 2002b).

There is also a strong sentiment among victims' groups that more must be done to help victims of family violence. The number of safe houses is considered inadequate to meet the needs of women who feel at risk. Between April 1, 2003 and March 31, 2004, more than 95,000 women and children were admitted to 473 shelters across Canada (Taylor-Butts, 2005). At a more basic level, some claim, it is unfair that women have to flee their homes for safety's sake. Moreover, it is not at all clear that leaving a violent home increases the women's safety. One very disturbing finding in the research is that within the context of violent relationships, women who have left their abusers may be at greater risk rather than reduced risk of violence. This is in part at least because offenders are likely to be angered by their spouse's absence (Johnson and Hotten, 2003; Rinfret-Raynor et al., 2004).

Providing resources such as shelters is helpful in managing the more serious forms of violence, but most of the time, the day-to-day problems that people encounter do not come to the attention of the authorities. Many of these problems are, however, known to neighbours, friends, and others. We are becoming increasingly aware of situations of serial violence, eventually resulting in homicide, in which outsiders knew of the conflict for a long time but were either reluctant to intervene or were not taken seriously by authorities when they sought out help to intervene and to stop the violence.

One important issue being considered by researchers interested in the aftermath of family violence is how violent behaviour by one family member promotes violent behaviour by others. The courts are growing more willing to accept the psychological consequences of violence as a defence for killing; in other words, they are beginning to accept that we cannot always rely on the notion of rational behaviour when establishing why people act as they do. Arguments that an act was performed in the "heat of passion" have always been recognized when one partner kills another in a jealous rage. Yet the idea that violence begets violence is only now being taken seriously in the courts. In this context, for example, the courts recognize, in certain circumstances, the

BOX 8.2

Portrait of the Batterer

What are the characteristics of men who violently victimize their female partners? To answer this question, R. Karl Hanson and colleagues (1997) collected a range of information from almost 1,000 male residents of Edmonton. Using self-reporting data, the researchers compared men who did and men who did not behave violently toward their partners. The researchers summarized the profile of the batterer that emerged from the data as follows:

> The portrait of the abusive man suggested by this research is one of a lifestyle characterized by violence, anger and subjective distress. He is likely to have been raised in a violent home in which his parents hit him as well as each other. His own aggressive, disobedient behavior during his youth developed into Antisocial Personality Disorder as an adult. He has a long history of impulsive behavior including motor vehicle infractions, substance abuse and impulsive violence. He feels deeply dissatisfied with himself and his intimate relationships. His feelings of subjective distress are dominated by anger and hostility. He is worried about other men being interested in his partner, and, importantly, feels justified in using force to keep her in line (Hanson et al., 1997: 204).

validity of the battered wife syndrome as a defence against conviction of a violent crime.

Family Violence and Delinquency

The use of physical violence against children may increase the risk that they will themselves behave in violent or nonviolent criminal ways (Fagan, 2003; Hamilton et al., 2002; McMahon and Clay-Warner, 2002; Widom, 1995). Physical punishment may induce conformity in children in the short run; in the longer term, it may create the very problems it is intended to prevent (Straus, 1991).

How does physical violence against children increase the risk of delinquency? *First,* according to social control theorists, the bonds between juveniles and their parents (and other conformist models) provide a certain amount of insulation against involvement in delinquency (Kierkus and Baer, 2002). A high degree of parental attachment means that the parent is better able to teach the positive social skills that will facilitate an individual's success at school and in the workplace (Currie, 1985; Patterson and Dishion, 1985). Obviously, parental abuse may weaken this bond and lessen the degree of juvenile sensitivity to parental expectations of appropriate behaviour (Rankin and Wells, 1990).

Second, when a parent is abusive, the child or adolescent may seek to avoid contact. According to control theorists, delinquency is prevented when parents are able to monitor and supervise the behaviour of their children. So if children seek to avoid contact with an abusive parent, delinquency may well increase (Gottfredson and Hirschi, 1990; Perrone et al., 2004; Thornberry, 1987).

Third, violent delinquency may be a form of acting out on the child's part (Agnew, 1985a). Children may behave violently toward classmates or other acquaintances as a way of expressing their frustration with their abusive home situation. Children may also run away from home or engage in other "escape crimes." Their resulting homelessness, combined with a lack of labour market skills, may increase the likelihood that they will make use of available delinquent or criminal opportunities to support themselves (Herrera and McCloskey, 2003; McCarthy and Hagan, 1991).

Fourth, growing up in a violent home (or a violent neighbourhood) may provide children with lessons in the use of violence as a means of achieving goals and controlling others (Eitle and Turner, 2002; Sprott and , 2000). A child who witnesses spousal violence may come to see it as a legitimate means of resolving conflict (Fagan and Wexler, 1987; McCord, 1991). According to Hotaling, Straus, and Lincoln (1990), homes in which child assault or spousal assault occurs have higher rates of sibling violence and higher rates of violence by the dependent children against children outside the home.

CRIMES AGAINST THE HOUSEHOLD

Crimes against households are very common in Canada. Table 8.1 shows the rates of the various forms of household victimization investigated in the 2004 GSS. The overall rate of reported household victimization is 248 incidents per 1,000 households.

According to UCR data, in 2004, roughly 1.3 million property crimes were reported to the police. Rates for this category, which includes but is not restricted to crimes against households, increased in 2003 after steadily declining since 1991. In 2004, however, the decline resumed (Sauvé, 2005).

Precursors

The routine activities theory of predatory crime (see Chapter 6) explains crimes against the household in terms of how offenders encounter opportunities for offending. Modern lifestyles send people outside the home for long periods of time to work and pursue leisure activities; as a result, many households are left unoccupied and unguarded, which enhances their appeal as targets for crime.

TABLE 8.1

Household Victimization Rates per 1,000 Households, by Selected Household Characteristics, Canada, 2004

	Break and enter	Motor vehicle theft / parts	Theft, household and property	Vandalism	Total household
Type of Incident					
Canada	39	44	88	77	248
Location of Home					
Urban	42	48	96	83	269
Rural	28	29	56	51	164
Household Size					
1 person	37	28	61	53	178
2 persons	33	39	74	73	219
3 persons	43	59	112	103	317
4 or more persons	49	60	123	92	323
Type of Home					
Single detached	38	45	84	80	247
Semi-detached	45	46	131	101	323
Row house/duplex/ apartment	38	43	76	56	213
Other	39	32	82	61	215
Ownership of Home					
Owned	35	43	83	81	242
Rented	49	49	101	68	267

Source: Gannon, M., and K. Mihorean. 2005. "Criminal Victimization in Canada 2004." Statistics Canada, *Juristat* 25(7): 26.

Not all households are equally likely to be victimized. The patterns of household victimization as revealed by victimization surveys and UCR data suggest that opportunities for property crimes are structured. In general, rates of household crime are higher in urban than in non-urban areas (Cohen and Cantor, 1981; Maguire and Bennett, 1982). For example, according to the 2004

GSS, the rates of household theft were 96 and 56 incidents per 1,000 households for urban and rural areas respectively (Gannon and Mihorean, 2005). These differences may arise from the fact that formal and informal social controls are often less effective in urban centres. Alternatively, larger cities may provide a fertile breeding ground for criminal subcultures that provide an intricate network for distributing stolen goods.

On the other hand, there is research to suggest that the effects of an urban setting are not necessarily linear. For instance, in Canada in 2002, urban areas with populations greater than 500,000 tended to have lower rates of break and enter than cities with less than 500,000 (Fedorowycz, 2004).

Not all urban neighbourhoods face the same risk of household crime. Residents of socially disadvantaged areas may face greater risks than those who reside in more affluent areas (Evans, 1989; Maguire and Bennett, 1982). Low-income areas have many characteristics that may increase the prevalence of household crime. The study by Robin Fitzgerald, Michael Wisener, and Josée Savoie (2004) of crime in Winnipeg neighbourhoods revealed that neighbourhoods with higher crime rates also had higher rates of population density, lower levels of residential stability, and less access to socio-economic resources.

Lower income may result in fewer precautions being taken to protect the household (because security costs money). Low-income areas also contain a disproportionate number of single-parent households; this leaves children with generally lower levels of adult supervision (Maxfield, 1987; Smith and Jarjoura, 1989). Mixed land use in these areas may mean the presence of bars and stores that bring a large number of strangers through the neighbourhood. Under such conditions, it may be more difficult to know who does and who does not belong in the area (Lynch and Cantor, 1992). Finally, residential instability and social heterogeneity are greater in poor areas, and this may undermine the development of collective community sentiments and thereby diminish effective informal social control at the local level (Bursik and Grasmick, 1993). In other words, as people become less tied to one another, they have less reason to worry about what others think and to conform to others' expectations.

The fact that poor *areas* have higher rates of household victimization than more affluent ones does not necessarily mean that poorer *households* have higher rates of victimization than their more affluent counterparts (Maguire and Bennett, 1982). This may be because offenders choose the more affluent targets in less affluent areas, or the wealthier homes located near such areas (Waller and Okihiro, 1978; Cohen and Cantor, 1981; Cohen, Kluegel, and Land, 1981).

Victimization research also suggests that some types of housing are more susceptible than others to various forms of household crime (Massey, Krohn, and Bonati, 1989). Most susceptible are dwellings that offer the thief or the burglar easy access or that provide cover during the commission of the crime. Thus, the risk of break and enter is higher when a housing structure offers multiple points of entry, when doors or windows are covered by trees or shrubs, when the house is on a corner or near a major route that allows easy escape, and when neighbours' houses do not directly overlook the target (Bennett and Wright, 1984; Evans, 1989). The 2004 GSS found that household victimization was highest for semi-detached and row houses and for duplexes (see Table 8.1).

Studies in which burglars themselves served as informants have provided information regarding what types of household settings are likely to be "high risk" for this type of victimization (Wright, Logie, and Decker, 1995). For example, Reppetto (1974) interviewed 100 convicted burglars, who identified several characteristics that made a household a more attractive target: ease of access, appearance of affluence, inconspicuous setting, isolated neighbourhood, absence of police patrols, and lack of surveillance by neighbours.

Many studies have found that burglaries are quite likely to occur when houses are empty—often during daylight hours (Nicholas et al., 2005). The rhythms and tempos of family life affect the risk of household crime in other ways. A good deal of traffic in and out of the home is an expected characteristic of large families. Doors are more likely to be left open or unlocked, and property may not always be put away, which makes such homes an attractive target for thieves (Smith and Jarjoura, 1989). Also, the summer months bring warm temperatures, open windows, and houses left empty by vacationers; all of these factors may increase the opportunities for household crime (Sacco and Johnson, 1990).

Transactions

We often think about opportunities for crime as an objective feature of the social environment (an open door invites theft), but the situation is more complicated than this. Criminal opportunities also have a subjective quality. For criminal events to occur, a potential offender must define the open door as an opportunity for theft. One person may see the large shrubs blocking a residential window as nothing more than interesting landscaping; another may see this shrubbery as providing cover during a robbery attempt.

What are the characteristics of the property offender? Like many other types of predatory offenders, these individuals tend disproportionately to be young males, many of whom come from socially disadvantaged backgrounds

(Maguire and Bennett, 1982; Waller and Okihiro, 1978). Data from the 2002 UCR indicate that most break-and-enter offenders were males; 63 percent of the males were adults, and 37 percent were youths aged 12 to 17 (Fedorowycz, 2004).

Professional versus Amateur Thieves

It is useful to distinguish between two broad types of property offenders (Evans, 1989). On the one hand, there is the **professional offender**, who is sometimes characterized as the "good burglar" (Shover, 1973, 1983) and as the "elite of the criminal world" (Cromwell, Olson, and Avary, 1991). These individuals have a considerable degree of technical competence and are connected to a network of other thieves and tipsters, as well as to fences to whom they sell stolen property. Professional thieves think of themselves as "specialists" and understand their offending in occupational terms; they speak of pulling a "job" or "working" a particular area (Maguire and Bennett, 1982). Most of their crimes are carefully planned and involve rational assessments of specific risks and benefits.

Professional offenders
Burglars with considerable technical competence who are connected to a network of thieves, tipsters, and fences.

The professional offender usually figures prominently in media portrayals of household crime and in police rhetoric about the typical offender. However, several researchers argue that popular images of the cool, calculating, highly specialized, and rational property offender may be exaggerated. According to Cromwell, Olson, and Avary (1991), much of what we know about these offenders comes from interviews with offenders or ex-offenders, who may be engaging in **rational reconstruction**. In other words, in recalling their crimes, they may tend to suggest that far more planning took place than was actually the case. Professionals are sometimes said to seek opportunities for crime. But according to Cromwell and colleagues, these offenders do not so much seek opportunities as develop a special sensitivity to the opportunities they happen to encounter.

Rational reconstruction
Occurs when individuals recall their crimes and suggest there was more planning than actually took place.

Hough (1985) suggests that notwithstanding the activities of some unspecified number of professional household thieves, these individuals are probably responsible for only a minority of the crimes revealed in victimization surveys. This speculation is supported by the fact that surveys generally uncover a large number of crimes that point to amateurish offenders with little technical knowledge or experience (Felson, 2002). Many household crimes are committed by unsophisticated offenders, most of whom are probably juveniles. These **occasional offenders** commit crimes when opportunities or situations present themselves (Evans, 1989). Irrespective of the level of professionalism of the offender, property crimes such as break and enter are motivated by instrumental needs (Bennett and Wright, 1984). These crimes do not reflect expressive needs such as anger or revenge; rather, they are prompted by the offender's desire to obtain the property of the victim.

Occasional offenders
Commit crimes when opportunities or situational inducements present themselves.

BOX 8.3

Trends in Break and Enter

In Canada, break and enter is the third largest offence category in that it accounts for one in ten Criminal Code violations and one in four crimes against property. In 2002, there were 274,894 incidents of break and enter. The overall crime rate has been declining since the early 1990s, and the rate of break and enter declined 35 percent between 1996 and 2002, reaching its lowest level in 25 years.

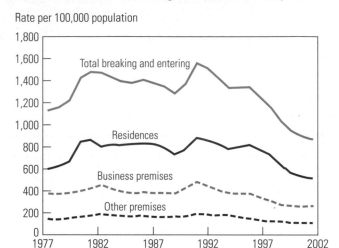

Figure 8.2

Breaking-and-entering Incidents, by Type, Canada, 1977–2002

Source: Fedorowycz, O. 2004. "Breaking and Entering in Canada 2002." *Juristat* 24(5): 3. Used by permission of Statistics Canada.

Recidivism

Repetition or recurrence of delinquent or criminal behaviour or behaviour disorder, especially following punishment or rehabilitation.

Engagement in household theft, as well as movement out of this type of crime with advancing age, can be understood in terms of control theory. Household theft easily resists detection (Maguire and Bennett, 1982). Offenders learn from their own and others' experiences that their chances of getting caught committing a particular crime are very slim (Bennett and Wright, 1984). But they also recognize that if they become known to the police as thieves and fail to vary their methods of crime commission, their chances of getting caught will increase over time; this reduces the attractiveness of this form of crime (Cromwell, Olson, and Avary, 1991). The professional thief can be said to have a lengthy criminal career; in contrast, many juvenile offenders commit crimes only rarely, and do so with even less frequency as they get older (Shover, 1983). The number of repeat offenders, as measured by the **recidivism** rate for burglary, is higher for break and enter than for many other crimes, but many juvenile offenders do not repeat the crime at all (Maguire and Bennett, 1982).

As events, crimes against households can be relatively uncomplicated. Quite often, an opportunistic thief passes a house and notices some item of value lying unguarded on the front lawn or in the driveway (Lynch and Cantor, 1992). Seeing no one around, the thief grabs the item and continues on his or her way. Similarly, under cover of darkness in the early hours of the morning, the thief may happen on an unlocked car and steal either its contents or the car itself.

Break and enters vary in terms of how much planning they require. In many break and enters, a young offender targets a house not far from his or her own residence (Brantingham and Brantingham, 1984; Cohen and Cantor, 1981; Hough, 1985). The proximity of the target reflects two distinct considerations: the offender's relatively limited mobility (e.g., he or she may be too young to drive) and his or her direct knowledge of the contents and routine activities of the household (that is, he or she may have been in it before, in the course of routine activities). In cases like this, entry may be "child's play" (Maguire and Bennett, 1982). The offender tests the door and, if it is open, enters the house. The thief moves through the house quickly, more interested in getting in and out with something of value than with the wanton destruction of property (Maguire and Bennett, 1982; Waller and Okihiro, 1978). UCR data suggest that the items stolen often include audio/video equipment, jewellery, and money (Fedorowycz, 2004).

The more professional burglar often selects a target more carefully. This selection process may have several stages: the offender decides which neighbourhood will be victimized, and which block in the neighbourhood, and which house on the block (Taylor and Gottfredson, 1986). The offender may cultivate relationships with "tipsters" who can provide information about vacant homes and potentially large "scores" (Shover, 1973). Some tipsters may be "fences" attempting to boost their inventory; others may be thieves who for some reason cannot undertake the crime themselves. Also, in the course of their regular travels through the neighbourhood, thieves may watch out for homes that look empty or that promise easy entry. Waiting at a traffic light may provide potential burglars with the opportunity to view potential targets without attracting attention (Cromwell, Olson, and Avary, 1991).

Risk, Ease of Entry, and Reward

Irrespective of the level of professionalism, burglars who are intent on break and enter must consider three questions: Can they get away with the crime (risk)? Can they commit the crime without great difficulty (ease)? Can they get anything out of it (reward)? (Bennett, 1989). Of these three factors, the first (degree of risk) is probably the most important. Homes that are difficult to

---

BOX 8.4

Occupancy Probes

In their interviews with burglars, Cromwell, Olson, and Avary (1991) discovered that these offenders use several imaginative methods to determine whether anyone is home.

1. If working as part of a team, the most "presentable" burglar knocks on the door or rings the doorbell. If someone answers, the burglar asks for directions or for a nonexistent person.
2. The burglar rings the doorbell and, if someone answers, claims that his or her car broke down and that he or she needs to use the phone. If the resident refuses, the burglar leaves without attracting suspicion. If the resident consents, the burglar can check out the merchandise in the home as well as whatever security measures exist.
3. The burglar telephones the residence to be broken into from a nearby phone and then returns to the residence. If he or she can hear the telephone ringing, it is unlikely that anyone is at home.
4. The burglar targets a house next to a residence that has a "for sale" sign on the front lawn. Posing as a buyer, the burglar can then examine the target household from the vantage of the sale property.

One informant in the Cromwell et al. study would dress in a track suit, jog to the front door of the target household, remove a piece of mail from the potential victim's mailbox, and ring the doorbell. If anyone answered, he would say that he found the letter and was returning it. The track suit suggested a reason why a stranger might be ringing a doorbell in the neighbourhood; the apparently neighbourly gesture suggested that he was a good citizen and therefore above suspicion.

---

observe from other homes present the offender with fewer risks. The mere presence of passersby may not influence the decision to offend, since thieves are concerned not about being seen, but rather about being seen *and* reported (Cromwell, Olson, and Avary, 1991).

Probably the most important aspect of risk is whether the home is occupied or not. The presence of a car in the driveway or signs of movement or activity in the house may encourage the potential offender to look elsewhere (Bennett, 1989). Some offenders engage in sophisticated **occupancy probes** (see Box 8.4) to establish whether the household is vacant.

An occupied home is to be avoided not only because of the risk of detection but also because of a concern on the part of the offender that if someone is home, the crime of break and enter could escalate into a more serious offence. Some researchers (Kennedy and Silverman, 1990; Maxfield, 1990) have observed that, although a rare occurrence, there is a higher-than-expected number of homicides involving elderly victims in their homes. This

Occupancy probes
Imaginative methods that the offender uses to determine whether anyone is home.

may be because the elderly occupy households that seem uninhabited during the day. The burglar, surprised by an unexpected encounter, may strike out against the elderly person, with fatal consequences. All of this suggests that offenders may not be quite as adept at assessing occupancy as is sometimes thought (Hough, 1985).

The second factor (ease of entry) concerns how hard it would be to enter the residence. Usually this factor cannot be assessed until the offence is under way (Bennett and Wright, 1984). Often it is a simple matter to break a door or a window; even the presence of special locks and security hardware may not serve as a strong deterrent (Lynch and Cantor, 1992; Maguire and Bennett, 1982). Many professional burglars report that they can, if they have to, deal effectively with alarms or watchdogs; but they also report that the large number of households that are unprotected by such measures makes attempted burglary of protected homes unnecessary (Maguire and Bennett, 1982).

The final factor (the potential reward) is probably the least important consideration. Offenders who engage in break and enter may be unable to determine before committing the crime whether anything of value is to be gained (Lynch and Cantor, 1992; Miethe and Meier, 1994). As noted earlier, information from a tipster may decrease uncertainty, and higher-status households may hold the promise of greater rewards. However, usually the thief can be fairly certain that something of value will be collected in the course of the crime (Cromwell, Olson, and Avary, 1991).

The Aftermath

According to the 2004 GSS, the economic loss in two-thirds of the household victimization incidents was less than $500. In 10 percent of the incidents, there was no loss at all. This is explained in part by the fact that 28 percent of the break and enters and 43 percent of the thefts of automobiles and parts were attempts. Of course, financial loss can be mitigated by the payments made by insurance companies and other sources.

All of this provides only a partial picture of the impact of household crime. Illegal entries that escalate into assaults, robberies, sexual assaults, or homicides have very direct and immediate physical consequences (Warr, 1988). Because incidents of this type are relatively rare, and because household crimes generally involve rather small net losses, these crimes are sometimes assumed to have little psychological impact on victims. That is not the case, especially with respect to break and enter (Budd, 1999). In the 2004 GSS, victims of break and enter were four times more likely to report being afraid than victims of other kinds of property crime (Gannon and Mihorean, 2005). Many victims—especially women—may be badly shaken by the event (Maguire and Bennett, 1982). Victims may experience feelings of vulnerability, concern that the offender will return, and fear of being alone—even in situations that are not directly related to household crime. They may also experience long-term sleeping disorders or require tranquillizers for an extended period.

Many crimes against households are not reported to the police. Data from the 2004 GSS indicated that about four in ten incidents of all household crimes were reported (54 percent of attempted or successful break and enters, 49 percent of thefts of motor vehicles or motor vehicle parts, 29 percent of thefts of household property, and 31 percent of acts of vandalism) (Gannon and Mihorean, 2005). With property crime, as with personal crimes, when victims fail to report, it is because they define the incidents as not worth reporting or because they do not believe there is much the police can do. Victimization data suggest that property crimes are more likely to be reported than personal crimes, in part because insurance policies require that they be reported before insurance money can be collected. The 2004 GSS found that the likelihood of reporting household crime was related to the total loss associated with the incident. Thus, unreported household crimes—at least in the legal context— are generally less serious than those that come to the attention of the police.

There is research to suggest that the decision to report property crimes to the police involves three different social processes (Greenberg and Beach, 2004). The first is termed the cognitively driven cost-benefit process of reporting. The suggestion in this respect is that victims report crimes to the police out of utilitarian motives. In other words, it is the desire to collect insurance compensation or the belief that the items taken are worth getting back that prompts the call to authorities. A second process involves affect-driven reporting. This means that victims might report their property crimes as a result of some kind of emotional arousal. The victim who is angry or afraid may be more like to telephone the police than the victim who is not. A third process involved in reporting is socially driven. Victims may report their property crimes to the police because friends and family members with whom they consult in the aftermath of the crime encourage them to do so.

Reported household crimes carry with them a small likelihood of arrest. In 2002, only about 16 percent of break and enters were cleared either by the laying of a charge or "otherwise" (Fedorowycz, 2004). These crimes have low clearance rates because by the time they are reported to the police, the perpetrator is long gone. Also, there is no immediate suspect, as there typically is for crimes against persons (Maguire and Bennett, 1982).

In the aftermath of the crime, offenders are probably less concerned with arrest than with the uses to which they can put the stolen merchandise. Cash or alcohol can be used for "partying." Although the offender may keep and use some stolen merchandise, there is a limit to how much loot one person can use this way. Also, retaining too many stolen goods can increase the risk of arrest.

Much of what is stolen may be converted into cash through sale. A substantial market exists for stolen goods (Schneider, 2005)—especially for lightweight electronic goods—but typically, offenders recoup a relatively small amount from each item. Some stolen goods are sold directly to private buyers for their own use. These people may see this exchange not as a criminal activity but as "good business." Their reasoning may be, "It was already stolen, and if I don't buy it, someone else will" (Cromwell, Olson, and Avary, 1991). Merchandise can also be sold to "fences," who purchase the items for resale. Some fences are businesspeople who do not have a criminal record; others are ex-thieves (Maguire and Bennett, 1982).

One popular public response to the increase in property crime has been to attempt to make homes less vulnerable to attack. "**Target hardening**" activities include installing deadbolt locks on doors and bars on windows, purchasing alarms and watchdogs, and developing programs (such as Neighbourhood Watch) that increase the surveillance of property.

Target hardening
Increasing protection of premises to deter a criminal through fear of detection or because the target has been made inaccessible.

SUMMARY

Violent events within families can be attributed in part to the value our society places on family privacy. Feminist researchers see family violence as reflecting the power differentials within families—in other words, men use violence against women and children as a form of control over their actions (Simpson, 1989: 611).

To understand family violence, we must consider the stresses placed on families, the reluctance of victims to report the violence, how parents manage conflict and anger (and why they manage these the way they do), the breakdown of social control mechanisms that restrain interpersonal violence, and the paucity of deterrence strategies. The uncovering in recent years of the extent of family violence, coupled with changes in societal values, has done much to redefine violent events within families as criminal events. Changes in the law and in how the police enforce it are reinforcing this new definition.

Property crime is a booming business. The target of most of this crime is the household, which is filled with portable appliances that can easily be transported and resold. Much property crime is opportunistic in nature, involving the presence of a thief at a place where and time when property is unguarded and easy to steal. A lot of the property crime committed by youthful offenders falls into this category. The more complicated crime of break and enter, which often requires considerable planning and technical expertise, tends to be committed by professional burglars, who not only take the time to plan the event but also ensure that the merchandise can be disposed of after the fact. Sometimes, owing to a miscalculation by the offender, residents may be unexpectedly encountered during the household burglary. The consequences—especially for elderly victims—can be fatal.

Many property crimes are not reported to the police. People who do not report may feel that there is little the police can do to solve the crime or that the crime is not serious enough to warrant reporting. Increasingly, homeowners are engaging in target-hardening activities intended to discourage both opportunistic and professional burglars.

There is growing interest in confronting crimes that occur in or are directed toward the household. Intrafamily violence is attracting a great deal of public attention, and demands have been growing that more action (in the form of education and changes in the law) be taken to reduce the likelihood that this kind of violence will occur. Attempts have been made to give victims of family violence greater protection under the law and to provide them with safe havens, as well as to treat offenders (see Chapter 11). As our review of family violence has shown, it is important to consider different theoretical approaches to the problem. New perspectives that draw attention to such things as power differentials in families are providing us with explanations of family violence and with possible ways to respond to it.

There are many different views regarding why people commit property crimes. Obviously, not everyone who is given the opportunity to steal does so. Depending on our perception of human behaviour, we might assume that people will steal if they know they won't get caught (social control), if they see others doing the same thing (cultural influence), or if they feel pressured by social circumstances (strain). All of these explanations rely on the idea that the offender has the opportunity (and some skills) to commit the crime and little fear of apprehension. Probably, the most effective means of combatting property crime is to limit the opportunities for it.

QUESTIONS FOR REVIEW AND DISCUSSION

1. Why has there been so much resistance to the claim that family violence is a serious problem?

2. How can we use strain theory to explain wife assault?

3. Many people argue that sibling violence is normal and that this kind of violence is very different from the kinds of violence we label "wife assault" and "child abuse." Do you agree? Explain.

4. Many notorious court cases have revolved around family violence issues (perhaps the OJ Simpson case is the best example). Is the high level of media attention devoted to these cases a good thing or a bad thing?

5. Marcus Felson has argued that in the past few decades, the decrease in levels of household occupancy and the proliferation of "lightweight durable consumer goods" have resulted in a "deskilling of crime." How valid is this proposition with respect to crimes against the household?

6. With respect to your own residence, how might a potential thief or burglar make decisions about "risk," "ease," and "reward"?

RECOMMENDED READINGS

AuCoin, K. 2005. *Family Violence: A Statistical Profile*. Ottawa: Centre for Justice Statistics, Statistics Canada.

Corbett, C. 2003. *Car Crime*. Cullompton, Devon: Willan Publishing.

Johnson, H. 1996. *Dangerous Domains*. Scarborough: Nelson Canada.

Loseke, D., R.J. Gelles, and M.M. Cavanaugh. 2005. *Current Controversies on Family Violence*. Thousand Oaks, CA: Sage.

Wright, R., and S.H. Decker. 1994. *Burglars on the Job: Streetlife and Residential Break-Ins*. Boston: Northeastern University Press.

INFOTRAC® COLLEGE EDITION

Explore InfoTrac® College Edition, your online university library, which includes hundreds of popular and scholarly journals in which you can find articles related to the topics in this chapter. Visit InfoTrac® through your web browser (**www.infotrac-college.com**) or through this book's website (**www.criminalevent-4e.nelson.com**).

WHAT'S ON THE WEB?

For chapter links and quizzes, check out the accompanying website at **www.criminalevent-4e.nelson.com**.

Chapter 9 Crime and Leisure

INTRODUCTION

In this chapter, we discuss a second social domain that is significant to the study of criminal events—the leisure domain. The relationship between leisure and crime has several interesting dimensions. People who are "at leisure" seem to be especially at risk for many different types of criminal victimization. Furthermore, many types of offending—especially juvenile offending—are themselves forms of leisure. Our language reflects this fact, for instance, when we describe illegal drug use as "recreational drug use" and when we describe stealing a car for fun as "joyriding." The leisure preferences of young people are often seen as a cause of crime. This is evident in periodic scares in our society about the criminogenic effects of violent television, popular music, fantasy role-playing games, and video games.

We will also see that certain leisure settings, such as bars and sports complexes, are often scenes of crime and victimization. The street is also a likely location for crime victimization, as people adopt lifestyles that take them away from their homes and into public areas in pursuit of leisure activities. We begin our review of the relationship between leisure and criminal activities with a discussion of the concept of leisure.

WHAT IS LEISURE?

Leisure can be defined in a variety of ways (Wilson, 1980). We often use the term in an objective way to describe the "spare time" or "free time" that is left over after paid work and other obligations (such as child care) have been taken care of (Iso-Ahola, 1980). However, leisure has a subjective as well as an objective character. In other words, leisure is not just free time, but free time that is used in a particular way—usually for play or recreation. Leisure activity can be regarded as intrinsically satisfying in that it provides its own rewards (Roberts, 1983). Also, we usually assume that leisure activities are freely chosen and that leisure interaction occurs among peers. In contrast, family or work-related activities tend to be less voluntary and are characterized by authority relations enforced by law or custom.

Leisure
Free time (after work, familial, and other obligations are met) that can be used for play or recreation.

Like other scarce resources, leisure time is unequally distributed (Jones, 1994). Teenagers and the elderly tend to have more leisure time than young parents and the middle-aged. And because household tasks and child care responsibilities reduce free time, men generally have more leisure time than women. People also differ with respect to their leisure preferences and the resources they have to pursue them. Those in higher-income groups are more likely to frequent restaurants. Young people are more likely to go to bars, movies, or video arcades. The elderly are less likely to go out in the evening for leisure of any kind (Golant, 1984). Elderly people who do engage in leisure outside the home tend to visit friends or family.

The amount of leisure time that people have available to them and the uses to which they put it are important elements of what we refer to as *lifestyle* (see Chapter 6). Moreover, the leisure content of people's lifestyles has important implications for the kinds of criminal events in which they are involved, as offenders or as victims. Opportunity theories are especially attentive to the linkage between lifestyle and crime.

Precursors

What does leisure have to do with the timing, location, and relative involvement of particular types of people in particular types of criminal events? There are two answers to this question. The first stresses how specific types of leisure activities motivate offenders toward offending or free them from constraints against offending. The second suggests that leisure activities and settings facilitate encounters between offenders and potential victims. These perspectives are not contradictory, but they do differ in their fundamental emphases. The former is offender-centred; the latter is opportunity-centred.

BOX 9.1

Patterns of Television Viewing

Television can affect behaviour, including criminal behaviour, in two important ways. First, it is a purveyor of content. Second, it is an activity which structures our time—especially the time we have available for leisure.

The average number of hours Canadians spend viewing television has not changed very much over the last several years, hovering around 22 hours a week. In part, this is because young people are spending less time watching television, which balances out the greater amount of time which their grandparents are spending in front of the tube.

Television Viewing by Age and Sex, Average Number of Hours per Week				
Total Population 2 Years or Older	Children 2 to 11 Years	Teens 12 to 17 Years	18 Years or Older	
			Males	Females
21.7	14.0	14.8	20.7	26.3

Source: Statistics Canada. http://www40.statcan.ca/l01/cst01/arts23.htm

Leisure as a Corrupter

Arguments about the corrupting influences of leisure have typically been made with respect to youthful offenders. Since the emergence of modern mass culture, every major form of youth leisure activity has been characterized by interest groups as a corrupter of young people. Feature films, rock 'n' roll, rap music, heavy metal music, video games, comic books, Saturday morning cartoons, and television commercials have all, at one time or another, been accused of weakening youthful inhibitions, providing negative role models, destroying childhoods, and disrupting the bonds between adolescents and adult authority figures (Best, 1990; Gray, 1989; Maguire, Sandage, and Weatherby, 2000; Tanner, 2001).

Literally hundreds of studies have investigated the potentially negative effects of television violence. This issue has been the focus of attention from the public, as well as Royal Commissions in Canada and Presidential Panels in the United States (Tate, 1998). The argument that television violence has some causal relationship with real-life violence seems to be supported by much anecdotal evidence (in the form of so-called copycat crimes, for example) and by common sense. We know that television is a powerful persuader; otherwise, advertisers would not spend so much money buying commercial time to convince consumers to purchase their products. We also know that television is a violent medium and that young people—who are most likely to behave violently—have high levels of exposure to such content.

However, despite anecdotal evidence and common sense notions, it is not at all clear what effects television violence has on viewers or how strong those effects are. The effects of television violence on criminal motivation are probably limited by several factors. *First,* according to UCR data, violent crimes account for only a small proportion of total crime. So, unless we want to argue that television violence affects nonviolent crime in some as yet undetermined fashion, the amount of crime that could be causally linked to violent content is limited, even if the effects on violence are substantial. In fact, some researchers *have* suggested that the real effects of television may be on property crimes rather than violent crimes (Hennigen et al., 1982). The basis for this argument is that the emphasis in the media on consumerism raises people's expectations regarding the amounts of material goods to which they think they are entitled (Surette, 1992). However, the link between television and property crime has not received sufficient research attention to warrant firm conclusions.

Second, given that criminal motivation is a complex issue, any effects produced by media exposure must be understood in the context of many other factors that encourage or restrain offending. The amount of variation attributable to media exposure is likely to be smaller than many observers would argue. Some researchers claim that 5 to 10 percent of violent and nonviolent criminal behaviour is attributable to exposure to media (Surette, 1992). Whether this means that television violence is a relatively important or unimportant factor in real-life violence remains unresolved.

Third, many research experiments have shown that exposure to violent content in laboratory settings triggers violent arousal, but the same effects are not necessarily produced by media exposure in the real world (Howitt, 1998). In lab experiments, subjects may be encouraged to behave violently (or at least not discouraged from doing so); in contrast, violent behaviour in most social contexts is discouraged. Also, how violence is measured in the lab (e.g., the willingness of children to play with violent toys, or of subjects to administer a harmless electrical shock to another person) may not have much to do with the willingness of people to beat, assault, rob, or kill others. Studies that try to link television violence to aggressive behaviour in real-life settings have often been less successful than those that try to find these effects in the laboratory.

All of this suggests that the relationship between television violence and criminal violence is more complicated, and perhaps less substantial, than we sometimes think. Much of the research supports the view that television violence may influence the behaviour of a pool of at-risk individuals who may be especially susceptible to its effects. In other words, television violence may be most likely to affect the behaviour of individuals already predisposed to behave aggressively. Unfortunately, we lack detailed knowledge of the size of this at-risk pool or of the factors that put these people at risk. Media violence may not cause interpersonal aggression in any direct way, but it may reinforce pre-existing tendencies or shape them in particular ways. In the case of copycat crimes, for instance, media violence may not motivate someone to commit a crime, but it may affect *how* that person commits a crime.

The effects of television (or movie) violence may often be short-term. Anyone who has ever left a movie theatre feeling excited or energized may intuitively understand the nature of this temporary arousal. We know that such effects tend to dissipate rather quickly as we return to the family, work, or school responsibilities that structure our lives. Thus, whether people behave violently after this arousal may have as much to do with the situations and circumstances in which they find themselves as with their level of arousal. That being said, it is important to note that we know relatively less about the long-term effects of high levels of media violence on cultural beliefs and social practices.

Regarding adults (as opposed to juveniles), public alarm about the effects of pornography on sex crimes reflects concerns similar to those voiced by critics of television violence. Again, people who try to draw direct causal links between violent pornography (e.g., "slasher" movies that combine sexual scenes with violent ones) and sex crimes are ignoring the complexity of the issue. A large body of experimental literature suggests that exposure to this kind of pornography promotes negative attitudes toward women, a greater acceptance of rape myths (e.g., that rape victims are to blame for what happens to them), and a decreased sensitivity toward female victims of violence (Malamuth, 1983; Malamuth and Donnerstein, 1984). Yet, as in the case of television violence, the effects of violent pornography on perpetrators of sex crimes may be most evident in men who are already predisposed to behave violently toward women.

To a considerable extent, the traditional concern about television violence and pornography has been eclipsed by more recently developing anxieties which relate to newer forms of technology and cultural expression. Probably the kinds of technology that excite the greatest concern now are those relating to computers and video gaming.

In a way that parallels the earlier concern about television violence, several critics have raised questions about the criminogenic character of violent video games such as *Grand Theft Auto, Soldier of Fortune,* and *Mortal Kombat* (Healy, 2005). It is argued that the role-playing nature of these games, and in particular the ways in which the games let the player assume the guise of a killer, can desensitize players to violence and teach aggression (Funk et al., 2004). As the graphics become increasingly real and as the plot lines of these games become increasingly violent, it is suggested that these games may be capable of far greater harm than traditional television viewing ever was.

While the effects of violent video games have not been extensively studied, a research literature has begun to accumulate which suggests that they may indeed encourage aggression (Anderson and Dill, 2000; Funk et al., 2004). One such study by Douglas A. Gentile and his colleagues examined video game habits among a sample of 600 8th and 9th grade students (Gentile et al., 2004). The study revealed that the playing of such games was common, while parental monitoring of such gaming was not. Moreover, the correlational study revealed that individuals who had greater exposure to video games were more hostile, more likely to get into arguments with teachers, more likely to get involved in physical fights, and less likely to do well at school. At the same time, some observers suggest that the worry over violent video games, like the worry over all types of media, is exaggerated (Sternheimer, 2003).

However, the concern with video games is only one aspect of the anxiety over the corrupting character of computer technology. Other writers have argued that the Internet has emerged as the principal site for the sale and distribution of child pornography (Jenkins, 2001). Several organizations (quite ironically) maintain websites which warn computer users of the dangers of "Internet addiction." One such website (Center for Internet Addiction Recovery, http://www.netaddiction.com/faq.htm) defines this addiction as:

> any online-related, compulsive behavior which interferes with normal living and causes severe stress on family, friends, loved ones, and one's work environment. Internet addiction has been called Internet dependency and Internet compulsivity. By any name, it is a compulsive behavior that completely dominates the addict's life. Internet addicts make the Internet a priority more important than family, friends, and work. The Internet becomes the organizing principle of addicts' lives. They are willing to sacrifice what they cherish most in order to preserve and continue their unhealthy behavior.

Another significant concern in this respect relates to the problem of "cyber-stalking" (Bocij and McFarlane, 2003). In very large numbers, it is suggested that sexual predators use the Internet to meet, seduce, and otherwise exploit young children. Young users of the Internet and their parents are warned about the dangers of online predation by a wide variety of policing and social service agencies. One relevant website (Child & Family Canada, http://www.cfc-efc.ca/docs/mnet/00001239.htm) advises parents about actions they might take if they suspect their child has been communicating with a predator and provides "easy tips" that parents can use to find out where their child has been on the Internet. Even what appear to be relatively benign Internet activities, such as the widespread use of MySpace and similar websites where teenagers can post their ideas, have attracted attention from offenders, who use the posted information to make contact with victims. The site providers have issued warnings about providing personal information, but the easy access to corroborating information about persons posting on these sites has created worry among law enforcement agencies, who monitor these sites in search of sexual predators in particular. The sites remain popular, however, despite these concerns.

Among the newer forms of cultural expression, the one that probably excites the greatest amount of alarm among parents, educators, police, and others is rap music and associated forms of hip hop culture (Rome, 2004). In public opinion polls, respondents often cite the glamorization of gang culture in rap videos and lyrics as an important cause of what they see as a rapid escalation of gang violence (Kohler, 2005). In 2005, one concerned activist brought a lawsuit against HMV record stores for distributing rap music that she argued was a form of hate speech directed against women (Laucius, 2005). Indeed, the misogynistic character of many (but not all) forms of rap has been documented by a number of researchers (Armstrong, 2001). More generally, the content and themes of much rap music and their association with street violence has meant that many claims-makers have sought to argue strongly that rap music—like rock and roll, heavy metal, and jazz before it—is a corrupter of youth. As with other forms of music, the research record would seem at least partially to support the case (Miranda and Claes, 2004). On the other side, some researchers argue that there is evidence to suggest that claims about the effects of rap are vastly overstated. Instead, youthful listeners often have a critical and subtle understanding of lyrics and do not respond to the messages in music in any simple way (Mahiri and Connor, 2003).

The irony with respect to this situation is that rap music (and other aspects of hip hop culture) arose in part at least in response to the violence and depredations of inner-city life in the devastated South Bronx area of New York City in the 1980s. Its association with drugs and violence at that point were largely tangential. It was only with the emergence of so-called "gangsta rap" that crime, misogyny, and violent hypermasculinity became focal concerns.

Leisure and Freedom from Social Control

In the case of juveniles, it is sometimes argued that patterns of leisure activity increase the likelihood that crimes will occur by freeing youth from the social controls that might otherwise check or restrain delinquent conduct. This position builds on the theories presented in Chapter 5.

Typically, juvenile leisure is pursued out of the sight of parents and teachers and in the presence of peers (Agnew and Peterson, 1989; Osgood et al., 1996). The modern video arcade, like the pool hall of an earlier era, is off-limits to adults. "Hanging out" at the video arcade, at the mall, or on the street corner may provide the behavioural freedom that makes group delinquency possible. A study by Riley (1987) of juvenile crime in England and Wales found that offenders and non-offenders engaged in different types of leisure activities. Non-offenders generally spent more time with parents and around the home; offenders were more likely to spend their time in peer activities away from home. Also, offenders were more often out in the evening, were expected home later, and were more likely to spend their money on youth-oriented amusements. These leisure activities removed some of the obstacles to delinquency by lessening the chances of apprehension and by providing exposure to behavioural contexts that facilitated delinquent action (Hartmann, 2001).

In contrast, leisure activities organized by adults and leisure time spent with parents can be expected to decrease the likelihood of delinquency by strengthening social bonds and thereby rendering delinquency less attractive (Agnew, 1985a; Messner and Blau, 1987). Athletic programs, in particular, have long been used to discourage youthful offending.

One study found that "hanging out" and social activities such as dating and partying were associated with higher levels of delinquent involvement, whereas organized leisure was associated with lower levels of delinquent involvement (Agnew and Peterson, 1989). However, the researchers also reported that it is not enough for youths to be engaged in "positive" leisure for a decrease in delinquency to occur—they must also enjoy the activity. In other words, coercive leisure cannot be expected to bring about a decrease in offending behaviour.

When it comes to the development or freeing of delinquent motivation, leisure may affect males more than females (Riley, 1987). In part, as power–control theory has argued, this is because female adolescents have traditionally been subject to higher levels of control, which restricts their leisure options (Hagan, Gillis, and Simpson, 1985; Singer and Levine, 1988). These gender differences may be rooted in patterns of family socialization. Risk-taking behaviour is encouraged in male children; female children are generally subjected to significantly greater parental control (see Chapter 5). Gender differences in delinquent leisure may reflect these patterned gender differences in risk-taking and control.

However, Tanner (2001) notes that the behaviour of boys also has a significant effect on the routine leisure activities of female adolescents. Girls are often missing from deviant youth cultures because males exclude them. Male delinquents do not always welcome female participants except as ancillaries or as objects of sexual goals. As Tanner points out, there is really no reason to think that delinquent males are any less sexist than non-delinquent males.

Leisure Activities and Opportunities

Leisure activities are important occasions for criminal events of various types, as evidenced by the times when and places where crimes occur. A large number of personal victimizations occur in the evenings and on weekends, when most people are "at rest," when they have dropped their more serious work roles, and when the formal social controls of the school and the workplace are not operative (Luckenbill, 1977; Melbin, 1987). Also, personal victimizations occur disproportionately in leisure settings—that is, in informal contexts that host a wide range of activities such as drinking, gambling, dancing, and playing games. In a study of high school youth in Tucson, Arizona, Jensen and Brownfield (1986) found partying, cruising, and visiting bars—in general, the social pursuit of fun—to be significantly related to victimization risk.

Permissive environs
Social settings, such as bars and parties, where individuals feel free of many of the constraints that operate in other settings, such as the school and the workplace.

Bars are good examples of **permissive environs**. Bars are the site of many criminal events, and so are the blocks where they are located (Roncek and Maier, 1991; Roncek and Pravatiner, 1989). There are many reasons. Bars do most of their business in the evening, when people are released from many of the social controls that structure their working days. Bars also deal in cash and liquor, which are easily stolen and easily used by the offender. Furthermore, bars tend to place no real restrictions on who can enter, and they are especially popular among young people. Finally, alcohol consumption increases the probability of interpersonal conflicts; it also impairs judgments regarding the scale of these conflicts (Engs and Hanson, 1994).

Generally, activities that bring people out of their homes in the evening increase the likelihood of personal and household crime (Kennedy and Forde, 1990). Messner and Blau (1987) found that the volume of leisure activity *in* the home (indexed by levels of reported television viewing) is related to lower rates of victimization, while the volume of leisure activity *outside* the home (indexed by the number of sports and theatrical facilities available) is related to higher rates of victimization.

A similar and consistent pattern has been revealed by victimization surveys. Violent and household victimizations increase as evening activities outside the home increase. This relationship is independent of marital status, employment status, and age (Kennedy and Sacco, 1998; Gottfredson, 1984). Going out on weekends increases these risks more than going out during the week. Engaging in leisure pursuits increases risk more than going to work or to school (Lasley and Rosenbaum, 1988; Sacco, Johnson, and Arnold, 1993).

Leisure can be part of a **risky lifestyle** that has dangerous consequences (Kennedy and Forde, 1999). Clearly, some types of leisure are riskier than others. Young single males are more likely than others to go to bars where—as we have seen—the risks are higher. In contrast, elderly people are less likely to leave their homes for leisure in the evening; when they do, they are less likely to come into contact with potential offenders.

Risky lifestyle
A regular pattern of activities that exposes individuals to higher levels of risk of criminal victimization.

Several studies suggest that forms of leisure that are themselves criminal may pose especially high victimization risks (Gottfredson, 1984; Jensen and Brownfield, 1986; Lauritsen, Sampson, and Laub, 1991; Sampson and Lauritsen, 1990). In part, this is because offenders make good victims: they are unlikely to call the police, and if they do, they will likely have difficulty establishing their credibility (Fishman et al., 2002).

Transactions

The content of criminal events varies across leisure settings and activities. Criminologists have paid particular attention to the street, bars, dating, and tourism.

The Street

For many youths, the street is itself a leisure setting (Kennedy and Sacco, 1998). For others, it is the route they take from one setting to another or from these settings to their homes (Felson, 2002). Criminal events in the street seem to support the argument of opportunity theorists that people are victims of routines that leave them vulnerable to offenders. Actually, research indicates that despite the horror stories from inner-city areas suggesting that people of all ages are vulnerable to crime, young males are more likely than any other group to be involved in "risky" routines on the street (Stevenson et al., 1998). Their behaviour tends to be more public than that of most other groups, and they frequent the street to a greater degree than others.

Young Males

As stated previously, the groups most vulnerable to assaults in public places are young, unmarried males who frequent bars, go to movies, go out to work, or spend time out of the house walking or driving around (Felson, 2002). This lifestyle exposes them to risk. Victimization data support the conclusion that much violent crime involving youths takes place in public places.

For example, data from the 2003 Canadian UCR 2 indicate that while children under the age of 11 were more likely to be physically assaulted in a private dwelling, male youth victims, aged 11 years and older, experienced a larger proportion of physical assaults on streets and roads and in parking lots and open areas (32 percent of 11-to-13-year-olds and 35 percent of 14-to-17-year-olds). For these victims, the second most common location of a physical assault was a school (28 percent for male victims aged 11-to-13 and 22 percent for males aged 14-to-17). In contrast, female victims of physical assault aged 11 years and older, similar to younger female victims, experienced a higher proportion of assaults, relative to male victims of the same age, in a private dwelling (38 percent of female victims aged 11-to-13 and 42 percent of female victims aged 14-to-17) (AuCoin, 2005). In the case of sexual assault, a similar locational pattern can be observed. With respect to the largely female victims of this crime, those who are younger tend to experience their victimization in a private home, but the street and other public settings emerge as important victimization settings for older victims.

Violent crime is often spontaneous; that being said, its targets tend to be people who are in places that are conducive to violent conflict. This observation does not account for the motivation behind violent crime, but it does explain the high levels of victimization among particular groups based on their exposure to certain settings and activities. Kennedy and Forde (1990) report a similar pattern for robberies: young, unmarried males who frequent bars and who are out walking or driving around are more likely to be victims of this crime.

The behaviour of young males who just hang around on the street is often seen as criminogenic. According to Skogan and Maxfield (1981), urban residents are most afraid of rundown urban areas where teenagers are hanging around on street corners. Even if the loitering is harmless and the individuals who are engaging in it never become involved in crime, the street is seen as a dangerous place.

When these youths are loosely attached to one another, those whom they encounter in street situations are likely to be acquaintances, and the chances of violence are likely to be low. When individuals are more closely affiliated, as in a gang, the chances of violence increase, although—as Kennedy and Baron (1993) report—violence may not be a routine outcome of activity by gangs on the street. Much of the crime engaged in by gangs actually occurs as a result of contact with other gangs. Minor theft and robbery certainly occur, but not to the extent the public believes. Also, the view that gangs pursue violence for the sake of violence, as would be predicted by the subculture-of-violence theory, is not substantiated by the research.

Individuals on the street who are potential offenders can also be victims. Young men in risky areas can easily become targets of assaults and robberies. When alcohol or drugs are involved, spontaneous conflicts may arise between individuals who are complete strangers to each other. Motivation to behave violently among young males, whether in gangs or not, may simply be based on "tests of character" (Luckenbill, 1977); that is, males engage in violence in order to prove their courage or manliness.

Any women who are present in street environments are less likely to become involved in conflicts directly; however, they may act as third parties in escalating or defusing the conflict. Women alone tend to avoid areas they perceive as risky (especially the street) and situations that could lead to violence or loss of property. Of course, women can be targets of theft just as easily as men—purse snatching is all too common. That being said, street crime seems to be predominantly the domain of young men, both as offenders and as victims.

According to Hocker and Wilmot (1985: 38), important precursors of assaults and robberies are conflict styles, which vary with individual personality and with the social situations individuals confront. These researchers assume that people develop patterned responses to conflict. These response styles are based on past experience and on learning (that is, on observing others' behaviour and trying out different responses).

Third parties play an important role in conflict escalation and de-escalation. Young boys often jokingly exhort their friends to physically restrain them when they are confronting a foe. The opponent is advised, "You're lucky he's holding me back," or "You'd be sorry!" This type of posturing, which is facilitated by third parties, can work to dissipate conflict, but it can also have the opposite effect. The joking may become serious, and third parties may promote the conflict instead of acting to reduce it. However, even when one participant lands a blow that in legal terms could be considered criminal assault, it is probably not viewed as such by the parties involved. There is likely too much confusion as to the identities of the instigator and the victim (Van Brunschot, 2000). Only when serious physical harm is inflicted do these situations lead to the involvement of a formal third party (that is, the police).

Vandalism

People's attitudes toward city streets are affected not only by the presence of gangs but also by graffiti and other signs of vandalism and decay (see Chapter 7). When people see these signs, and the patterns of movement around them, their fears are often awakened. Though **vandalism** is not a criminal event in the conventional sense (that is, an event in which at least two parties are involved in a criminal action), we can still approach it in event terms. Vandalism differs from other criminal events in that there is a time delay between the offence and the victimization.

Criminologists have paid more attention to the consequences of vandalism than to its causes. Some criminologists (Skogan, 1990b; Kelling and Coles, 1996; Wilson and Kelling, 1982) identify vandalism as a major contributor to the public's declining sense of security in a given neighbourhood. Wilson and Kelling contend that disorder and crime are inextricably linked in a kind of developmental sequence. Wilson (1983: 78) notes that social psychologists and police officers tend to agree that if a building window is broken and left unrepaired, the remaining windows will soon be damaged. Vandalism occurs more often in areas where surveillance is low. However, once vandalism has occurred, it tends to further lower surveillance and thus increase "untended" behaviour. This leads to further vandalism and even crime. That is, vandalism makes people afraid and discourages people from routinely using the streets. This reduces the informal surveillance which constrains disorderly behaviour. As vandalism increases and the neighbourhood continues to decline, residents may even move to safer, more congenial environments.

These **broken window theories** are interesting and have been influential in policy circles. However, they are certainly not without criticism. The major problem, according to some writers, is that explanations which focus on the role played by vandalism and other disorders in the spiral of crime, lack empirical support (Harcourt, 2001; Taylor, 2001). In their complex examination of the relationships involving crime and disorder, Robert Sampson and Stephen

Vandalism
The deliberate damaging or destruction of public or private property.

Broken window theories
Theories that disorder, such as broken windows, leads to more serious crime in a particular neighbourhood.

Raudenbush (1999) found that it was not possible to argue that disorder leads to crime in the kind of developmental sequence just described. Instead, disorder and crime occur together because they have common causes—most notably, high levels of neighbourhood poverty and a lack of community efficacy.

Other critics suggest that the "broken windows" argument proceeds from some dubious assumptions. Bernard Harcourt (2001) states that the theory asks us to assume that it is possible to distinguish between "orderly" and "disorderly" people. As well, we are asked to assume that orderly and disorderly people react to their environments in much different ways; orderly people are cowed but disorderly people are emboldened by signs of environmental deterioration. As well, Harcourt asks, is it only the lives of those who live in graffiti-strewn neighbourhoods who are affected by disorder? What about those situations in which middle-class people cheat on income tax or pay service people cash to avoid sales tax? Aren't these forms of broken windows as well?

What motivates most vandalism? Thrill-seeking and the fact that it doesn't seem to harm anyone are probably significant causative factors. At another level, it can be argued that what some see as vandalism others see as a legitimate art form by which urban artists express their identities and their discontent with an otherwise drab and depressing urban landscape (Austin, 2001). Seen in this way, the graffiti which make up so much of what the law refers to as the willful destruction of property is part of a struggle over who it is who owns and therefore has a right to decorate public space. For the graffiti artist, the grassroots expressions of the disenfranchised, who lack other artistic outlets, should not be barred from the urban public sphere only to make room for corporate logos and fast-food billboards. Such a view is, of course, consistent with theories of crime which emphasize the conflictual nature of law. Notwithstanding the efforts made to curtail it in many cities, vandalism is almost impossible to detect and deter.

Bars

People go to bars (taverns, lounges, and so on) to relax, meet friends, listen to music, and drink. Most bars escape the frenzied aggressiveness that may lead to crime; some attract it (Kennedy and Sacco, 1998). In these locations, where alcohol and drugs mix with loud music and bravado, violence often erupts. Bar owners are growing more and more concerned about this violence but often don't know how to reduce it. They hire bouncers to remove the most raucous clients, but sometimes these bouncers incite more violence. When one asks college or university criminology students where they would go to find a fight on any given night, they can easily list two or three notorious bars in town

BOX 9.2

Broken Windows to Broken Bottles

The "broken windows" theory asks how one broken window in an abandoned building becomes many broken windows in an abandoned building. The answer relates to the ways in which less serious infractions of the law create an environment in which people who wish to do so feel few restraints to the breaking of more serious laws. Thus, untended people and untended situations seem to suggest that no one really cares and that anyone who wishes to break the law will not meet much resistance. Less serious offences against the public order such as vandalism, loitering, and playing loud music in public can encourage greater amounts of even more serious rule-breaking. Can such an argument be used to explain behaviour in riots?

Over the last several decades, university and college campuses in North America have been the site of increasingly large numbers of what sociologists call "celebratory riots." Such riots are not motivated, in general, by deprivation or injustice but usually seem to suggest ritualistic ceremonies which have gone awry. Such events might follow a sporting event or other kind of celebration. They typically begin late in the evening and involve excessive alcohol consumption and very large numbers of people congregating in some public setting, such as the street. Most of those in attendance are not actively involved in wrongdoing (other than perhaps drinking in public or drinking underage), but some become belligerent with police, throw beer bottles, start fires, or upend cars.

Exactly such an event occurred at Queen's University in Kingston, Ontario during homecoming celebrations in September 2005. Because of some problems with homecoming during previous years, the university attempted to arrange for evening activities which would keep large numbers of students from congregating on a particular neighbourhood street near the campus. These efforts were largely fruitless. Beginning on Friday morning of homecoming weekend, large number of students (from Queen's and elsewhere) began to party—first on the lawns of private student rental homes and then on the public street. Over the course of the day, and especially in the evening, the crowd grew in size, reaching, by some estimates, 7,000. According to witnesses, large numbers of people began to hurl beer bottles at emergency personnel and at random targets. Several members of the crowd turned a car over and were encouraged by many of those in attendance to set it on fire. While the police tried to maintain order, there were too many celebrants present to control. Early Sunday morning, after several arrests and amid mounds of broken glass, the crowd dissipated.

Some crowd experts argue that riot situations deteriorate in the same ways that neighbourhoods do (Useem, 1998). In other words, a failure to effectively police even minor violations of the law creates an environment in which people who wish to hurl a beer bottle or overturn a car feel that both the crowd and the lax enforcement of minor laws give them permission to do so. Thus, just as one broken window becomes many broken windows, one broken beer bottle becomes many broken beer bottles. The social processes are the same, although the time frame is much shorter.

Source: *Kingston Whig-Standard*

http://www.thewhig.com/webapp/sitepages/content.asp?contentID=127094& catname=Local+News where violence regularly occurs. Apparently these places attract a clientele that tends to be more aggressive than average—a conclusion that supports the subculture-of-violence perspective.

Most of the criminal events that occur in bars are minor assaults, especially between young males. This is consistent with the finding that many victimization incidents occur when people are drinking. Commonly, victimization surveys find that a large proportion of crime and victimization is related to the use of alcohol or drugs by the accused or the victim or both (Desjardins and Hotton, 2004). These events may also involve vandalism (breaking windows, chairs, and tables). Events involving interpersonal conflict may conclude without violence, with the protagonists either walking away or being pulled away from each other. When there is escalation, violence may erupt. All of this suggests that such events are spontaneous; however, the idea that certain bars attract this type of problem implies that some individuals go to those bars in search of trouble. Luckenbill's (1977) characterization of the "character contest" seems to apply to such situations (see Chapter 6). The jostling and shoving that precede a fight may be combined with insults and threats. When the fight breaks out, those around the combatants may add fuel to it by offering encouragement or by joining in.

Kathryn Graham and Samantha Wells (2003) investigated the causes and contexts of male-to-male violence in barroom settings by interviewing a small sample of 20-to-24-year-olds in a medium sized Canadian city. Their research revealed that alcohol contributed to violent encounters because it made participants less aware of and more willing to take risks. Alcohol also reportedly made participants more emotional in their responses to others and more aggressive. In explaining their combative behaviour, the participants suggested that fighting was often necessary to defend personal or group honour and that sometimes it was simply a fun thing to do. Graham and Wells report, however, that the dominant factor which explains such fighting is the prevalence of a cultural setting which defines barroom violence as permissible or even appropriate. In a larger survey of Ontario residents, Graham, Wells, and Jennifer Jelley (2002) reported that in bars and nightclubs, as opposed to other settings, violent incidents tended to occur between strangers, to involve only men, and to involve more than two people. The proportions of respondents and opponents who had been drinking were higher in this setting than in other contexts.

Dating Violence

According to popular thinking, adolescent dating is a context for innocent exploration, whereas violence is a feature of conflict-ridden and constricting

BOX 9.3

Making Bars Safer

Do bars have to be dangerous places? According to the Center for Problem Oriented Policing (Scott, 2006), several steps can be taken to increase the level of safety in public bars and taverns. These steps include the following:

1. Train bar staff to handle intoxicated patrons in a nonviolent manner   This reduces the level of aggression and encourages the staff to intervene before assaults occur.
2. Establish adequate transportation   This reduces the number of people on the street after bars close and reduces conflict over available taxicabs or other means of transportation.
3. Relax or stagger bar closing times   By implication, this reduces the number of people on the street at any one time at the end of the evening.
4. Control bar entrances, exits, and immediate surroundings   This step can reduce underage drinking and minimize conflict at high-demand venues.
5. Maintain an attractive, entertaining, and comfortable setting   This will help reduce the frustration and boredom that often leads to aggression.
6. Establish and enforce clear rules of conduct   This reduces conflict among patrons and promotes a calmer atmosphere.
7. Reduce the occurrence of weapons   This reduces the likelihood of injury.
8. Ban known troublemakers   This step removes high-risk offenders from high-conflict situations.

marital relationships (Sugarman and Hotaling, 1989). However, in recent years, violence has been recognized as existing in some unknown proportion of dating relationships.

How common is the problem of dating violence? This question is not easily answered since estimates are affected by a number of factors, including the manner in which abuse is defined and the reference period about which respondents are asked. In addition, for a variety of reasons, relatively few studies which have investigated dating violence have included youth as young as 12 or 13, which is the period during which dating—and hence dating violence—can begin (Department of Justice Canada, 2006). It is also true that many young women who are victims of dating violence do not define what happens to them as criminal—or even as violent in any traditional sense. Instead, they may blame themselves or otherwise excuse the behaviour of their abusers (Harned, 2005; Mahlstedt and Welsh, 2005).

Most of the contemporary discussion about dating violence has focused on the subject of date rape (Karmen, 2001; Gabor, 1994a). Because these assaults occur in a social context where consensual sex is a possibility, until recently the tendency has been to view date rape as something other than "real rape" (Bechhofer and Parrot, 1991). This has led to a victim-blaming strategy, as well as to a widespread willingness to dismiss the injury or trauma experienced by victims. A more realistic appraisal links date rape to culturally supported dating rituals that reflect patriarchal assumptions about male power and privilege (DeKeseredy and Kelly, 1993). Research suggests that male sexual aggression is more likely when males exert greater control over the dating process—that is, when they control the initiation of dating, assume responsibility for expenses and transportation, and choose the dating activity (Harney and Muehlenhard, 1991).

BOX 9.4

Risk Factors for Courtship Violence

With respect to courtship violence, who is at risk of offending and victimization? The Centers for Disease Control in Atlanta, Georgia, have drawn on a large body of empirical research to provide the following profiles:

Characteristics of Victims

- Women aged 12 to 18 who are victims of violence are more likely than older women to report that their offenders were acquaintances, friends, or intimate partners.
- The likelihood of becoming a victim of dating violence is associated with having female peers who have been sexually victimized, lower church attendance, a greater number of past dating partners, acceptance of dating violence, and personally having experienced a previous sexual assault.

Characteristics of Perpetrators

- Studies have found the following to be associated with sexual assault perpetration: the male having sexually aggressive peers; heavy alcohol or drug use; the male's acceptance of dating violence; the male's assumption of key roles in dating such as initiating the date, being the driver, and paying dating expenses; miscommunication about sex; previous sexual intimacy between the offender and the victim; a history of interpersonal violence; a belief in traditional sex roles; adversarial attitudes about relationships; and rape myths.
- Men who have a family history of observing or experiencing abuse are more likely to practise abuse, violence, and sexual aggression.
- As the consumption of alcohol by either the victim or the perpetrator increases, the rate of serious injuries associated with dating violence also increases.

Source: Centers for Disease Control and Prevention. 2006. *Intimate Partner Violence Fact Sheet.*
http://www.cdc.gov/ncipc/factsheets/ipvfacts.htm

Male control may translate into sexual aggression in two distinct ways. *First,* many men interpret a woman's willingness to allow the male to make decisions about where they will go on a date, what they will do, and who will pay for it, as a sign of interest in sexual activity (Johnson, Palileo, and Gray, 1992). These men may be reasoning that if women don't object to coming back to their room or accompanying them to a secluded spot, they must be interested in sex, even if they say otherwise. Also, because dating is a leisure activity in late adolescence or early adulthood, it often involves the use of alcohol (or other drugs). This means that courtship sexual violence often occurs in contexts that involve alcohol consumption (Meadows, 1998). A woman's heavy consumption of alcohol may be interpreted by the male as a sign of sexual interest (Benson, Charlton, and Goodhart, 1992; Vogel and Himlein, 1995).

Second, to the extent that the male controls the circumstances of dating, he controls the opportunities for offending. For instance, when he controls transportation, he can effectively impede the female's ability to escape a situation in which sexual assault is likely. A woman who is in an isolated spot with a sexually aggressive male may be reluctant to leave the car because she has been warned that even greater dangers confront women who are not protected by male companions. Not surprisingly, date rapes typically occur in the home of the offender, inside an automobile, or in some other isolated location (Harney and Muehlenhard, 1991). The Violence Against Women Survey (VAWS) found that 20 percent of date-related sexual assaults took place in the home of the male, and another 25 percent in a car; a further 24 percent occurred in the victim's home, 21 percent in a public place, and 10 percent in someone else's home (Johnson, 1996). The consequences of male control—misinterpretation of sexual interest and the creation of opportunity—often work in concert. For example, "parking" combines privacy, which provides the opportunity for sexual aggression, with the likelihood that the male will overestimate the female's willingness to engage in sexual relations (Muehlenhard and Linton, 1987). The common use of alcohol and drugs by both the victims and the offenders engaged in various forms of courtship violence suggests that this kind of violence, like other forms of violence, may be associated with a "risky lifestyle" (Gover, 2004; Schwartz et al., 2001).

According to police data, the rates of sexual violence by a dating partner are highest for girls under the age of 16, while women between the ages of 18 and 20 have the highest rates of physical assaults by dates. On the other hand, males reported relatively few cases of sexual violence by dating partners and lower rates of physical assault (Kong et al., 2003).

In courtship violence, like marital violence, violence is supported by the patriarchal belief that the use of force by men against women is legitimate (Maxwell et al., 2003; Schwartz et al., 2001). Studies of youth sexual offenders tend to find that between 25 and 50 percent blame the victim for their sexual assaults, usually by identifying styles of dress or behaviours by the victim believed to provoke sexual violence. However, even if great force is used, the offenders are unlikely to label the act as rape if the couple had previously dated. In some settings, such as the male peer group on the university or college campus, these attitudes can be mutually reinforcing. This creates an environment in which some kinds of sexual violence are understood as normal (Schwartz et al., 2001). On the other side, women who are assaulted by boyfriends frequently cite jealousy or attempts to terminate the relationship as the precipitating factors. Quite ironically, such dating violence may be viewed as a sign of love by either or both parties.

"Stalking," as defined by academics and criminal justice practitioners, suggests a related problem (Lowney and Best, 1995). Typically, stalking involves various forms of criminal harassment in which an offender follows, telephones, or otherwise physically and emotionally intimidates a victim. The available data clearly indicate that in the overwhelming majority of cases of stalking, the offender is male and the victim is female. In terms of their relationships, the 2004 GSS data suggest that the most common relationship between a stalker and victim is "friend" or "current or ex-intimate partner" (AuCoin, 2005c). For stalking victims pursued by a current or an ex-intimate partner, the 2004 GSS data suggest that females are more often (19 percent of victims) stalked by a former intimate partner (either an ex-spouse or an ex-boyfriend)). For both females and males, the greatest threat is posed by an ex-boyfriend/ex-girlfriend (11 percent of female stalking victims and 6 percent of male stalking victims), followed by an ex-spouse (8 percent of female stalking victims and 4 percent of male stalking victims).

Tourism

It is impossible to ignore the growing importance of tourism in our society. Large amounts of money are spent on tourist attractions, and people are allocating more and more of their disposable income to travel. Despite the growing awareness that tourists are not immune to crime, hotels and travel agencies have been slow to warn tourists about potentially dangerous areas. For a variety of reasons, tourists tend to be easy targets for pickpockets, robbers, sexual offenders, and other lawbreakers (Glensor and Peak, 2005). First, tourists are often lucrative targets because they carry large sums of money—often in cash. Second, tourists are likely to be relaxed and off guard while on vacation. Finally, tourists are often unlikely to report crimes because they wish to avoid the need to return to the scene of the crime at some future date.

A tourist is more likely to be a victim of theft or robbery than of personal attack. Most commonly, luggage is stolen or pockets are picked. As thieves develop sophisticated techniques for picking or jimmying locks, they are preying more and more on cars as well. In one scam, the thief drives along a beach road that is not too crowded and checks out the parked cars. If there are signs of an attractive target (e.g., a foreign licence plate or a rental car), and if the owner is nowhere to be seen (and thus presumably down at the beach), the thief parks behind the car, approaches it, and breaks through its lock (with special tools, this can be accomplished easily). Then the thief quickly searches the car and exits with whatever loot he has found. Slashing a tire prevents the victim from attempting pursuit. Some countries are responding to crime against tourists by developing programs to enhance security in resort areas and to educate travellers about the hazards they may encounter in certain areas. Tourist-directed crime seems to be best explained by opportunity theorists, who view tourists as vulnerable targets in areas where surveillance may be low and precautions more difficult to take.

Victimization of travellers is hardly a recent phenomenon. In the Middle Ages, castles were built in the south of France to protect pilgrims travelling through areas inhabited by thieves and robbers. And although modern tourism has left the impression that tourists are not likely to be victims, they *are,* and they need to take precautions to protect themselves. Tourists are becoming increasingly aware of their vulnerability; as a result, many are staying away from once-popular tourist destinations.

Destinations which are known for high crime rates or inadequate policing can suffer declines in tourist-related business (Hanson et al., 2004). A major example of this, of course, was the very substantial drop in tourist business that followed the terrorist attacks on September 11, 2001. Indeed, terrorism, or at least the threat of terrorism, has come to exert a rather significant effect on travel and tourism in recent years (Cousins and Brunt, 2002; Eisinger, 2004). Also, travel agencies and tour groups now steer clients away from areas they consider dangerous. The governments of many countries issue warnings to their nationals to avoid certain areas—in particular, areas characterized by political instability or violence against tourists. In circumstances like this, travellers may become a target of local anger and frustration.

Major outbreaks of violence against tourists receive widespread media attention; often this attention comes with advice to tourists about how they can protect themselves. Attacks on foreign tourists in parts of East Africa and Egypt have led to a worldwide alert to avoid these areas. It is sometimes the case, however, that these threats are greatly exaggerated. For instance, a major panic ensued in the middle of the 1990s when 10 tourists were killed in a single year in Florida (Greek, 1993). The Florida Department of Law Enforcement, however, was quick to advise visitors to its website that in 1994, for instance, 40 million tourists visited the state, only seven-hundredths of one percent of these visitors were victims of crime, and only six-thousandths of one percent suffered any physical injury (McKay, B., 1996).

Victimization data can help us understand how tourism and other forms of travel affect our chances of becoming crime victims. Using survey data, Wellford (1997) estimated the victimization rates of domestic travellers in the United States. His findings were not what we might expect. He found that for all types of crime, victimization rates for domestic travellers were substantially lower than those for the general population. Also, gender differences with respect to victimization were the same for travellers as for the general population.

How do we reconcile these results with our assumptions about the dangers of travel? Wellford suggests that routine activities theory offers one way of understanding the results. Perhaps crime rates are lower for travellers in large part because they tend to take more concrete steps to control target suitability and guardianship. For example, tourists are generally more likely to go out in groups and to spend their time in well-travelled "tourist areas." This interpretation is consistent with the observation that those notorious cases of tourist victimization that we read or hear about typically seem to involve people who wandered off the beaten path into high-crime areas or who took the "wrong" exit ramp off the highway. Clearly, the topic of tourism and victimization deserves more focused attention.

The Aftermath

Victimizations that occur in leisure settings often go unreported. For example, the tourist victim may not speak the local language or know how to find the police. If the loss or the injury is not great, the tourist victim may decide that reporting the incident to the police is not worth it. Victimizations may also go unreported when the leisure activity is itself regarded as a form of disreputable behaviour. Victims who have been drinking or who encounter offenders in a known "deviant context" (e.g., in a bar with a notorious reputation) may be reluctant to bring the incident to the attention of the police. Given the generally negative attitude toward many forms of youthful leisure activities, it is not surprising when crimes in these settings go undiscovered or unrecorded by police.

Victims respond in various ways to crimes committed against them in leisure settings. One common response is to avoid encounters or circumstances of the type during which the victimization occurred. Leisure activity is by definition discretionary activity, so it is easier to avoid than home or work-related activities. Thus, the victim of courtship violence may refrain from dating, and the jogger who has been mugged may stop jogging and take up "mall walking," perceiving it to be safer than running on city streets or park paths.

A participant in a street fight or barroom brawl may prefer to seek revenge rather than report the crime to police. Of course, the status of these individuals as "victims" may itself be questionable, as they themselves may have struck the first blow or picked the fight. Also, many criminal events involving young males are of little interest to police, who are being encouraged more and more to manage their workloads by assigning a higher priority to the victimization of women and children than to that of young males.

The long-term consequences of leisure-related victimizations are not yet evident. The effects may be short-lived (except when it comes to sexual assaults). The punks that Baron (1989) talked with simply shrugged off their own victimization, regarding it as a routine hazard of life on the street. The degree to which individuals are deterred from becoming involved in leisure-related crimes may have more to do with the risk of being hurt than with the risk of being arrested. This is not to suggest that the police do not deter; their presence on the street and in bars plays an important role in keeping potentially dangerous behaviour under control. The evidence seems to indicate that the behaviour of young males on the street and in other settings can change from passive to violent fairly easily, especially given the fact that victims and offenders are often hard to distinguish and that public guardians (police and citizens) are not always available to stop a brewing conflict from becoming serious.

The need for guardianship has long driven the policy whereby police attempt to maintain a high profile on the street. This high profile has been achieved through the use of random patrols (that is, cars cruising neighbourhoods looking for problems). However, patrol tactics seem to have little influence on the amount of neighbourhood crime (see Chapter 3). As a result, some police departments have established neighbourhood mini-stations, increased foot patrols, and established neighbourhood consultations—tactics they believe can prevent and deter crime more effectively than a highly visible police presence in the form of random patrols. The most effective guardians against crime are not the police, but rather other people who frequent leisure settings and who call the police when needed.

There have been attempts to control crime by influencing how leisure is used. Especially conspicuous have been efforts to develop **positive leisure** alternatives for young people who are actually or potentially delinquent (Agnew and Peterson, 1989). This approach reflects the maxim, made explicit in social control theory, that "idle hands are the devil's workshop." Youths get themselves into trouble—through various forms of "hanging out"—because they lack positive options. The reasoning behind the positive leisure approach is that summer camps, organized clubs, and other so-called forms of healthy recreation will expose youths to an environment that discourages involvement in crime and delinquency.

A similar approach focuses on the need to control "negative" and "corrupting" forms of youth leisure. This approach reflects the view that if they are left to make their own leisure choices, youths will almost always make the wrong ones. The past several decades have witnessed many crusades intended to impose legal and social restrictions on the ability of young people to make their own choices. These campaigns were directed against feature films in the 1930s; comic books and rock 'n' roll in the 1950s; "drug-influenced" protest music in the 1960s; and rap and heavy metal music and video games in the late twentieth and early twenty-first centuries. Television violence has been subject to recurrent crusades every five or ten years since the 1960s (Best, 1990; Gray, 1989). However, there is an ironic character to crusades like these. According to Tanner (2001), they reflect a perennial tendency on the part of adults to rediscover, to stigmatize, and to attempt to control the culture and behaviour of the generations that follow them. The Elvis Presley and Beatles fans and the hippies and student radicals of earlier eras now express bewilderment and concern about the corruptive nature of the cultural worlds in which they believe their own children to be immersed. Contemporary charges that rap music inspires gang formation and random violence might tell us more about how anxieties about youth are reproduced across generations than about the uniquely deviant characteristics of contemporary youth.

Positive leisure
Forms of leisure activity that link adolescents to conformist others and that are thought to insulate against delinquency.

SUMMARY

When people are "at leisure," they are also at risk of involvement in criminal events, as offenders or as victims. The links between leisure activity and criminal activity are highly complex. It has been argued that some forms of leisure

can cause crime—for example, that the content of youth-oriented media may provide the motives for crime. It has also been suggested that peer activities may provide freedom from the social controls that might be expected to inhibit offending.

Much leisure activity takes place in public spaces. Street crime involves people who are passing through an area from one place to another or who are simply "hanging out." In these contexts, crime itself can be a form of leisure, as seems to be the case with vandalism and graffiti writing. In leisure settings such as streets and bars, it is often difficult to distinguish offender from victim when a conflict escalates into assault or some other form of violence. This form of opportunity crime tends to be based on the risky lifestyles of the individuals involved, and is more likely to be deterred by retribution than by reporting the crime to the police.

In date rape, the routine activity of courtship takes on a criminal character when aggressive behaviour translates into sexual assault against an unwilling participant. Much of this behaviour goes unreported.

Tourism crime targets people who are at leisure in unfamiliar places; their lack of understanding of which areas are safe and which are unsafe may put them at risk. It is often difficult for tourists who have been victimized to find someone to whom to report the crime. They may decide they simply don't want the hassle of getting involved with the police in a foreign country. Increasingly, travel agencies and governments are briefing tourists on how to travel safely and advising them of areas to avoid altogether. A tourist's most effective deterrent against crime is to not travel in unsafe areas at all; this removes the opportunity for crime.

Some leisure pursuits place people at particular risk of victimization. The risky lifestyles in which people engage may make the search for a "good time" result in a "bad time." It must be emphasized that in the leisure domain, as in other domains, the processes we are describing are not deterministic. In other words, exposure to criminogenic influences or to threats of victimization does not necessarily result in a criminal event; these things only make a criminal event more probable by bringing together opportunities for crime with motivations to offend.

QUESTIONS FOR REVIEW AND DISCUSSION

1. Why are bars the site of so much crime? Can you name some bars in your area that are associated with high rates of crime?
2. Is dating violence a serious problem on your campus? What measures (if any) have been taken by school officials to deal with the problem?

3. How do you account for the recurrent tendency on the part of adults to view the cultural trappings of adolescents as troublesome?

4. In what ways can vandalism be understood as a juvenile form of leisure activity?

5. How do patterns of leisure activity change over the life cycle? What implications do these changes have for victimization risk?

6. Why are many of the crimes committed against tourists never reported to the police?

RECOMMENED READINGS

Austin, J. 2001. *Taking the Train: How Graffiti Art became an Urban Crisis in New York City.* New York: Columbia University Press.

Davis, K.E., I.H. Hanson, and R.D. Maiuri. 2002. *Stalking: Perspectives on Victims and Perpetrators.* New York: Springer.

Howitt, D. 1998. *Crime, the Media and the Law.* New York: Wiley.

Jenkins, P. 2001. *Beyond Tolerance: Child Pornography on the Internet.* New York: New York University Press.

Pizam, A., and Y. Mansfeld. 1996. *Tourism, Crime and International Security Issues.* New York: Wilcy.

INFOTRAC® COLLEGE EDITION

Explore InfoTrac® College Edition, your online university library, which includes hundreds of popular and scholarly journals in which you can find articles related to the topics in this chapter. Visit InfoTrac® through your web browser (**www.infotrac-college.com**) or through this book's website (**www.criminalevent-4e.nelson.com**).

WHAT'S ON THE WEB?

For chapter links and quizzes, check out the accompanying website at **www.criminalevent-4e.nelson.com**.

Chapter 10   Crime and Work

LEARNING OBJECTIVES:

- investigate how criminal events are contextualized by the third social domain in which we are interested—the work domain
- discuss how particular kinds of employment experiences affect victimization risks
- examine how the conventional work roles which people play give them access to criminal opportunities
- discuss how crime takes on the character of work in the context of ongoing criminal enterprises

INTRODUCTION

In this chapter, we consider crime in the social domain of the workplace. This social domain was largely neglected by criminologists until recently (Gill, 1994). Our discussion is organized around two broad topics.

The *first* is the relationship between participation in the legitimate labour force and the occurrence of criminal events. Two major issues concern us here. In what ways are patterns of victimization associated with patterns of employment? That is, how do our jobs affect the victimization risks we face? And in what ways does seemingly honest work make available opportunities for criminal behaviour, involving either employers (or employees) or members of the public?

The *second* major theme of this chapter is crime as an occupational activity. Here we examine "enterprise crime," which involves exploiting opportunities for the development of criminal businesses.

EMPLOYMENT AND VICTIMIZATION

The Canadian labour force has undergone several important changes in the past few decades. Female labour force participation has increased greatly in recent years, especially among married women. The types of jobs available have also changed in the past two decades. Employment in the manufacturing sector has fallen since 1979, but the availability of jobs in the service sector has increased. However, compared with goods-producing jobs, service jobs tend to pay less and to more often involve part-time work. Unemployment remains especially prevalent among young people and members of minority groups, who as we already know are at high risk for involvement in criminal events as both victims and offenders. At the end of 2005, the overall unemployment rate in Canada was 6.8 percent, while the unemployment rate for youth was 12.2 percent (Statistics Canada, 2005).

The nature of work itself has also undergone important changes. Many of these changes are attributable to technological innovations, especially in computer technology. These changes, which are intended to make the workplace more efficient—and from the employer's viewpoint, more profitable—have affected the pacing and timing of jobs. Many employees have computer hookups in their homes that allow them to reduce the amount of time required at their formal places of work. Fax machines, e-mail, instant messaging, and cellphones quicken the pace at which information can be transmitted and blur, for many, the distinction between private time and work time.

How do patterns of employment and experiences in the labour force relate to patterns of involvement in criminal events? Public awareness of workplace stress has been increasing in recent years. Work-related stressors include job demands, hours of work, the threat of layoff, poor interpersonal relations, the risk of accident or injury, harassment, discrimination, and even fear for one's life.

Individual and Occupational Characteristics

Although it is not generally recognized, the threat of criminal victimization may be an important source of job stress for many people. Victimization surveys tell us that the chances of being a victim of crime are not randomly distributed across occupational groups. This is not surprising, given that occupations differ with respect to the work they require of people and with respect to where, when, and under what conditions that work is done. As we will see, the characteristics of some jobs increase risk, and the characteristics of other jobs decrease risk.

Yet when we compare the victimization risks associated with different occupations, it can be difficult to determine whether it is the job itself or the characteristics of the people who hold that job that affects the risk of victimization. For instance, if we were to discover that part-time employees of fast-food restaurants face especially high risks of victimization, we would not necessarily be justified in concluding that there is something about cooking or serving hamburgers that makes one more vulnerable to criminal danger (although there may be!). Fast-food employees tend to be teenagers, and, in view of the relationship between age and victimization, the higher risks may be due to age-related rather than work-related factors. In fact, we might not even be surprised to discover that though these employees report higher rates of crime, the experiences they tell us about typically occur outside of work rather than on the job. In sum, a cursory review of victimization risks and occupations can easily mislead us.

Information about how victimization risks vary across occupations is hard to come by. This is because the statistical rarity of victimization incidents often prevents survey researchers from computing separate victimization rates for a detailed inventory of occupations. Some research indicates that risks are higher for members of the military (Harlow, 1991), probation officers (Lindner and Bonn, 1996), police officers, welfare workers, those who work in bars (Mayhew, Elliott, and Dowds, 1989), and other occupations that involve regular and frequent contact with high-risk populations.

Even more problematic is any attempt to calculate victimization risks for people engaged in illegal or semi-legal occupations. As we have seen, people who work at the margins of the law can be seen as ideal victimization targets from the point of view of the offender. These people might be unwilling to report crimes to the police, and even if they do, the police might be less likely to take the reports seriously. As discussed in Chapter 6, the risks associated with illegal occupations are vividly illustrated by data which describe differential homicide risks. In 2004, national police data indicated that 18 prostitutes had been killed. This was the third year in a row in which the murders of prostitutes had been linked to a single murder investigation in the city of Port Coquitlam, British Columbia. As well, there were another hundred homicides against people working in other illegal occupations such as drug dealers and members of other organized crime groups (Dauvergne, 2005). According to Statistics Canada, between 1992 and 2002, 11 percent of homicide incidents were thought to be drug-related. The most common reason for these homicides was what Statistics Canada and policing agencies call a "settling of accounts." This reason ranked well ahead of financial gain, the protection of assets, or simple arguments as an explanation (Desjardins and Hotten, 2004).

As well, those who control the working environment might be very interested in doing whatever is possible to prevent detection of **workplace crime**. One reason for this approach relates to the fact that a store or business which develops a reputation as a place where crimes occur could be

Workplace crime
Criminal events that emerge out of relations formed by labour force participation in the context of legitimate or illegitimate economies.

hurt financially, although this is not always the case. For instance, some restaurants where famous gangland hits have occurred have become even more popular as a result.

In some cases, business owners or workplace managers might discourage crime reporting because they themselves are the victimizers. Certainly, with respect to the problem of sexual harassment on the job or with respect to the more general problem of workplace bullying, those with more power in the workplace victimize those with less power in both criminal and non-criminal ways. Indeed, the intimidation which bullying and harassment imply is itself a strong deterrent against speaking informally about or reporting formally one's victimization experiences.

An early large-scale study of occupational differences in victimization risk was undertaken by Block, Felson, and Block (1984), who calculated the victimization rates for 426 occupations using data on 108,000 crime incidents reported to U.S. National Crime Survey (NCS) interviewers between 1973 and 1981. For the five offences these researchers examined—robbery, assault, burglary, larceny, and automobile theft—victimization risk was inversely related to "occupational status," which they defined as the average income for each occupation. In other words, as the average income of an occupation increased, the risks of being victimized decreased. The study also showed wide variations in levels of victimization risk. For instance, for all offences, recreation workers (e.g., workers at amusement parks) and hospitality workers (e.g., busboys, dishwashers, and servers) were among the top five for risk of victimization. Sheriffs and police officers had the highest assault rates; taxi drivers and newspaper vendors were among the most often robbed. The lowest rates of victimization were found among certain farm workers, and among telephone and electrical workers, opticians, stenographers, and radio operators.

The authors readily acknowledged that data of this sort are difficult to interpret:

On the one hand, better jobs tend to provide more good things in life, presumably including safety and security from crime. More income and credit allow people to purchase security devices, safer locations to live in, better parking spots, and the like. Better jobs may also help people avoid public transit and unfavourable hours for trips to work and elsewhere. Better credit allows avoidance of cash. In general, more resources, including money, credit, and control over time, should help people to obtain security from crime.

On the other hand, better jobs may bring with them more luxury goods to attract offenders. Higher strata individuals may also go out more at night, enjoying sport and cultural events or visiting restaurants or other night spots. Good jobs are often found within a metropolis rather than in rural areas with lower risk. One suspects that modern offenders have little trouble finding the higher occupational strata in order to victimize them, security efforts notwithstanding (Block, Felson, and Block, 1984: 442).

So, analyses of the victimization rates of different occupational groups are interesting and informative, but they do not necessarily tell us very much about crimes that occur in the workplace. This requires a more focused investigation of the crimes that happen while people are at work.

BOX 10.1

Victimization Risks across Occupations

A comprehensive examination of the way in which victimization risk is distributed across occupations was undertaken by the U.S. Bureau of Justice Statistics. The research examined 1.7 million victimization incidents which occurred between 1993 and 1999. Workplace violence accounted for about 18 percent of all victimizations during the seven-year period. Rates for the 1993–1999 period for selected occupations were as follows:

Occupation	Average Annual Rate per 1,000 Workers
Law enforcement officers	260.8
Corrections officers	155.7
Taxicab drivers	128.3
Bartenders	81.6
Mental health custodians	69.0
Special education teachers	68.4
Gas station attendants	68.3
Mental health professionals	68.2
Junior high school teachers	54.2
Convenience store workers	53.9
Bus drivers	38.2
High school teachers	38.1
Nurses	21.9
Physicians	16.2
All workers	12.6
College teachers	1.6

Source: Duhart, D.T. 2001. *Violence in the Workplace: 1993–1999.* Washington, DC: U.S. Department of Justice.

A recent analysis of American NCS data from 1992 to 1996 provided a helpful discussion of the relationship between work and victimization risk (Warchol, 1998). The analysis revealed that the most common violent crime experienced by victims working or "on duty" at the time of their victimization was simple assault. Also, as Box 10.1 shows, the rate per 1,000 workers of violent workplace victimization varies quite dramatically across occupations. These data suggest that for the occupational categories listed, the highest rates of violent workplace victimization are experienced by those involved in law enforcement, and the lowest rates are experienced by teachers. Data from the British Crime Survey (Upson, 2004) revealed that people who worked in protective service occupations, such as police officers, were most at risk of violence at work, while science and technology professionals, such as mechanics, faced the lowest risks. The category of "health and social welfare associate professionals," which included nurses and medical and dental practitioners, were also at relatively high risk.

Precursors

In very general terms, workplace settings have characteristics that both encourage and inhibit victimization. On the one hand, full-time employees spend many hours "at risk" of whatever threats the workplace presents. On the other hand, workplace settings tend to be much more highly structured than, for instance, leisure settings and thus more subject to a variety of social controls that discourage victimization. Some degree of order and control is usually deemed necessary if the organizational goals of the workplace are to be achieved efficiently.

How much crime happens in the workplace? As stated, answers to this question are not easy to derive from most kinds of existing data sets, which are usually intended to answer more general types of questions. Data from an analysis of 20 years of NCS data in the U.S. provide some clarification (Zawitz et al., 1993). This analysis revealed that with respect to violent crime, about 14 percent of incidents occurred while the victim was working or "on duty." In contrast, 16 percent of incidents occurred while the victim was participating in an activity at home (that is, some activity other than sleeping), and 29 percent occurred while the victim was engaged in a leisure activity away from home. Data from the 2004 Canadian General Social Survey indicate that violent incidents were most likely to occur in a commercial establishment or public institution Overall, 38 percent of the incidents took place in these settings. In 43 percent of these commercial or public setting incidents, however, the location was also the site of the victim's workplace (Gannon and Mihorean, 2005).

One type of worksite for which detailed information about victimization risk is readily available is schools. In recent years, much attention has been paid to schools as settings that pose serious criminal dangers to both students and teachers (Devoe et al., 2005; Duwe, 2005; Rountree, 2000; Sheley and Wright, 1998).

Viewed from one perspective, the problem of school crime can be understood as a logical by-product of the demographic structure of educational institutions. Schools, after all, provide services to groups in the population at greatest risk of offending and victimization. As we have discussed, all of the kinds of data sources on which criminologists routinely depend indicate that the relationship between crime and youthfulness is rather robust, and that this holds for a range of societies and a range of historical periods for which relevant information is available (Tittle and Grasmick, 1998).

Schools, then, concentrate on a daily basis the age groups at greatest risk of offending and victimization. Toby (1995) contends that the risks associated with school populations are compounded by the requirement of compulsory attendance. Disruptive or troublesome students who do not wish to attend school are required to do so. For this reason, he suggests, junior high schools have more serious rates of victimization than senior high schools.

Also, until recently, schools have been relatively open settings, easily accessible to potential offenders who do not attend them. These "intruders" may include not only the stereotypical predator but also the angry parent or the student who is upset at having been expelled. Although schools are capable of exercising some degree of guardianship against victimization, a school of above-average size that allows students considerable freedom of movement may provide many settings that facilitate criminal activity. In school buildings, more victimizations typically take place in less supervised areas, such as hallways and restrooms, than in more controlled places, such as classrooms and libraries (Garofalo, Siegel, and Laub, 1987).

Several investigations have addressed the problem of school crime in the Canadian context. A study by Tanner and Wortley (2002) of victimization among high school students and street youth in Toronto revealed relatively high rates of victimization among both groups. For example, two-fifths of high school students reported that they had been physically assaulted in the years before the survey was done, and one-third reported that they had been the victims of a minor theft. With respect to the worst victimization experienced by respondents, the most commonly cited locations were the school (21 percent), the street (19 percent), and the respondent's own home (17 percent). An investigation of school crime in Calgary, undertaken by Paetsch and Bertrand (1999), reported high levels of victimization both within and beyond the school. Overall, 81.5 percent of the students reported that they had been victimized at least once within the past year. The most prevalent type of victimization was having something stolen (55.6 percent of the total sample), followed by having something damaged on purpose (43.6 percent) and being threatened (42.3 percent). The least prevalent type of victimization was being attacked by a group or gang (6.0 percent), followed by being threatened with a weapon (8.2 percent) and someone exposing himself or herself (14.2 percent).

Studies which focus on bullying as a distinct kind of school problem also tend to describe an ominous picture of schoolyard victimization. Craig and her colleagues (1998) have argued that a significant proportion of school-aged children are either bullies (14 percent) or victims of bullying (5 percent). Moreover, they suggest that there is little overlap in these categories, to the point that bullies and their victims tend to represent two quite distinct social groups. Such estimates, it is argued, are consistent with those derived from studies in other countries. Another survey, of over 4,000 children in grades 1 to 8, found that 6 percent of children admitted bullying others "more than once or twice" in the past six weeks, and 15 percent of children reported that they had been victimized at the same rate. Very few children (2 percent) reported being both bullies and victims (Pepler et al., 1997).

In contrast, Doob and Cesaroni (2004) suggest that there might be a considerable gap between the rhetoric and the reality of school crime and violence—especially lethal violence. Their review of the available evidence leads them to conclude that the case for a worsening social problem of school crime is made only with great difficulty. Indeed, Doob and Cesaroni point to the irony of increasing anxiety about school crime during a period in which actual levels of such behaviour might be falling. In the American context, Joel Best (2002) states that not only schoolyard deaths but also many non-lethal forms of violence were in decline during the period when high visibility events such as the Columbine shooting exacerbated public concern about unsafe schools. Such a conclusion is, of course, consistent with the more general decline in crime rates that was evident during the 1990s. According to Best, for every million children who attend school, there is less than one violent school-related death per year. Moreover, only about 1 percent of children killed by violence are hurt at school, even though they spend such a large amount of time there.

While the available data seem to support a variety of views regarding the prevalence of school crime, they also support the conclusion that crimes committed at school—like all other forms of victimization—are non-random occurrences. A variety of social factors, including gender, grade level, minority status, attending school outside of one's neighbourhood, and having delinquent friends, have all been linked to victimization risk in the research literature (Brown and Benedict, 2004; Craig et al., 1998; DeVoe et al., 2005; Paestech and Bertrand, 1999; Schreck et al., 2003).

Notwithstanding the statistics indicating that schools generally are safe, there is increased anxiety that they might be targets of attacks. This fear increased substantially as a result of the attacks on the school in Breslan, Russia in 2003. In response to such fear, many authorities are addressing issues related to the preparedness of school employees to deal with crisis situations. Security audits to determine vulnerabilities are an important first step. These are usually followed by the development of readiness plans that identify the roles that all individuals in a school would play in an emergency. These plans, developed in conjunction with local law enforcement agencies, are increasingly seen to be as important for school safety as are routine fire drills.

How do workplace characteristics relate to variations in the levels of workplace danger? Data from victimization surveys have been used to describe the types of workplace conditions that seem to facilitate employee victimization (Collins, Cox, and Langan, 1987; Lynch, 1987). These studies suggest that the risks of becoming a crime victim on the job are greater in the following circumstances:

- When the job involves face-to-face contact with a large number of people on a routine basis. (That is, if the workplace restricts access to authorized persons, the risks of crime are lower.)
- When the job involves handling money.
- When the job involves overnight travel or travel between worksites.
- When the job involves the delivery of passengers or goods.

The importance of these factors becomes apparent when we assess them in reference to routine activities theory and associated concepts such as exposure and guardianship. People who work in settings that leave them unprotected and at the same time exposed to a large number of people (some of whom may be "motivated offenders") are more likely to be victimized in the workplace. Victimization studies also indicate that it is not the characteristics of the victims (such as sex and age) but rather the nature of the work that affects an individual's likelihood of becoming a crime victim in the workplace.

The routine activities associated with some work locations tend to make them less vulnerable to crime. Desroches (1995) notes that department stores and supermarkets are known to carry large amounts of cash yet are generally not perceived as desirable targets by robbers. Supermarkets are likely to have security equipment, and there are often many people in the store at any given time. The high shelves in most grocery stores do not allow the potential thief an unobstructed view of the setting, and because there are usually two exits, it is difficult to control movement in and out of the store. Furthermore, the separation of the cash registers by relatively wide aisles makes the collection of the stolen money a time-consuming activity. In short, targets such as this offer too many risks for too little money.

Transactions

Much of the violent victimization that occurs in the workplace results from conflicts between employees and customers or clients. A bartender tells an inebriated customer he is "cut off," a teacher tries to enforce classroom discipline, a sales clerk refuses to permit a return of merchandise, a police officer tries to intervene in an argument, and so on.

Data from the British Crime Survey (Upson, 2004) on the transactional character of workplace crime revealed that:

- Incidents of workplace violence were more likely to take place during the week and were less likely to occur in the evening or at night than non-work-related violent incidents.
- Male offenders carried out most of the incidents of violence at work—approximately four-fifths of incidents involved male offenders only.
- Forty-one percent of physical assaults at work involved offenders aged 25 to 39, and 30 percent involved offenders aged 16 to 24.
- Victims of actual or threatened violence at work said that the offender was under the influence of alcohol in a third of incidents, and that the offender was under the influence of drugs in a fifth of the incidents.
- The majority of violent incidents that occurred while the victim was working involved offenders whom the victim did not know before the incident.

The situational context of much workplace victimization is revealed in a study by Salinger and colleagues (1993) of assaults on flight attendants. This study found that flight attendants have rates of assault as much as 10 times higher than the average. Most assaults involved a conflict between a passenger and an attendant over some mandatory flight regulation, relating, for example, to baggage arrangements or food or drink service. The researchers found that first-class passengers, who are only 10 percent of the travelling public, accounted for 20 percent of assaults—a finding that may be explained by the higher expectations of service, passengers' perception of their status relative to that of the attendant, and the consumption of alcohol. The study also found that assaults were most likely to occur during takeoffs and landings, which are the most distressing times for passengers who are afraid of flying. Also, at takeoff, the authority role of the attendant may not yet be clearly understood.

Violent school crimes, except perhaps those involving intruders, are probably more likely than other workplace crimes to include as participants offenders and victims who are known to each other (Whitaker and Bastian, 1991). According to Garofalo, Siegel, and Laub (1987), many of these events result from frictions between peers which arise from normal daily activities. Schoolgrounds and trips to and from school provide ample opportunities for interactions that can escalate into relatively minor victimizations. "Weapons" often consist of available items grabbed on the spur of the moment. Items stolen from victims often seem to be the targets of mischievous and even malicious motivations (Garofalo, Siegel, and Laub, 1987: 333).

The Aftermath

Victimizations in the workplace do not seem to differ much from other types of victimizations in terms of levels of property loss and injury (Whitaker and Bastian, 1991). Data from the 1997 Canadian UCR suggest that few physical injuries result from incidents in schools (Stevenson et al., 1998); fewer than 5 percent of victims reported serious physical injuries. This probably reflects the fact that violent incidents that occur in schools are unlikely to involve the use of a weapon.

As with other social domains, much of the crime that occurs in the workplace is not reported to the police (Warchol, 1998). As noted earlier, school crime is an exception since mandatory reporting rules often apply. At least two characteristics of the work domain may discourage reporting. *First*, many work environments have alternative means for dealing with crime. The handling of an incident often proceeds no further than bringing it to the attention of a supervisor or private security officer (Warchol, 1998). Businesses, restaurants, and even schools may choose to avoid the publicity associated with the visit of a police patrol car by dealing with less serious incidents themselves.

BOX 10.2

School Massacres

In the late 1990s and early 2000s, several high-profile incidents in Canada and the United States led to a widespread concern about the threat of mass murder in schools. Though these incidents are statistically rare, the horrific violence associated with them has had profound consequences for how politicians, security experts, and parents think about school safety.

Criminologists John Alan Fox and Jack Levin note that for the public, "lethal violence inside the school struck a nerve" (2001: 94). To some degree, these incidents were made all the more shocking by their contexts. Because they did not occur in minority communities in urban centres, where drugs and street violence are seen as pervasive, they shocked the consciousness of those who tended to believe they were safe from violence.

Fox and Levin observe that the search for explanations of these incidents quickly settled on the family. Popular wisdom suggests that bad kids come from bad homes. Though parenting is an important factor, these researchers also direct our attention to the social dynamics of schools. With respect to perhaps the most notorious incident of school violence —the mass murder at Columbine High School in April 1999— the schoolyard snipers were seen by others as "geeks" or "nerds." Largely excluded from student cliques and from the mainstream of school life, they banded together with fellow outcasts in what they called the "Trench Coat Mafia." The image of themselves they attempted to construct emphasized power, invincibility, and incivility. Fox and Levin conclude:

> Birds of a feather may kill together. Harris, the leader, would likely have enjoyed the respect and admiration from Klebold, who in turn would have felt uplifted by the praise he received from his revered buddy. In their relationship, the two boys got from one another what was otherwise missing from their lives—they felt special, they gained a sense of belonging, they were united against the world. As Harris remarked, as he and his friend made last-minute preparations to commit mass murder: "This is just a two-man war against everything else" (Fox and Levin, 2001: 94).

Second, employees who are victimized as a result of their dealings with the public may be persuaded by their employers that these incidents only occur when they are not doing their work properly. In other words, they may come to believe that "cooling off" belligerent customers or clients is one of their job responsibilities. Even in severe cases, the victim may fear being blamed for having started the incident by behaving rudely toward the customer (Salinger et al., 1993).

Jobs can become hazardous when they expose employees to clients and situations that provide opportunities for crime. One step that can be taken to

BOX 10.3

Feeling Safe at Work

Crime in the workplace has become a public issue, and many people are feeling less secure at work than they used to. But we know relatively little about the character of workplace fear of crime. Esther Madriz (1996) used data from the American NCS to investigate the factors that affect fear at work. She found that people are more likely to judge the workplace as unsafe when

- they live in bigger cities
- they have contact with potential offenders
- they handle money in their jobs
- they work in places that employ fewer security measures
- they work evenings
- they use public transportation
- they have been victims of crime in the past

Madriz notes that many of these factors are related not only to fear of crime but also to the actual risks of victimization.

deter these crimes is to provide employees with the resources they need to deal with client-related problems. Also, employers must be ready to react strongly to crimes that occur on their premises; this will ensure that their employees can do their jobs with a greater sense of security.

CRIME AND LEGITIMATE WORK

Many people—including many criminologists—tend to think about criminal offending and legitimate work as mutually exclusive. But as Fagan and Freeman (1999) note, the relationship between crime and legitimate work is hardly that simple. Many individuals are simultaneously involved in legitimate labour *and* the world of crime. Crime, after all, need not take all that much time and energy; and legitimate jobs do not necessarily remove criminal motivation, especially if they pay badly. Even more importantly, legitimate jobs often provide workers with criminal opportunities to which they would otherwise not have access. In this section, we explore some of the ways that work makes offending possible.

What Is Occupational Crime?

The scope of work-related crime is potentially as broad as the types of jobs that exist in an economic system (Croall, 1987). An employee with unsupervised access to his employer's inventory may find that his job provides a unique opportunity for theft. A physician or a lawyer may charge for services she hasn't performed (Arnold and Hagan, 1992). Stores may use illegal sales practices to defraud the public. Large corporations may engage in the sale and manufacture of dangerous products, pollute the environment, and maintain unsafe working conditions. Work-related crime ranges from pilfering by a disgruntled employee to the gargantuan thefts associated with the savings and loan scandal in the United States (Sherrill, 1997).

Modern interest in the concept of work-related crime is usually traced back to the writings of the famous American criminologist Edwin Sutherland (see Chapter 4). Sutherland (1940) used the term **white-collar crime** to refer to crimes committed in the context of work by people of high status and respectability. He saw a need to correct the imbalance in criminological thinking that associated crime almost exclusively with the actions of the poor and the powerless. Through a study of major American corporations, he sought to prove that individuals who are fully and gainfully employed, and whose jobs accord them considerable power and economic security, are often responsible for serious breaches of the law.

Since Sutherland's time, the concept of white-collar crime has undergone adjustments that reflect changes in the meaning of white-collar work. For Sutherland, the term *white-collar crime* denoted the criminal conspiracies of major corporations. Today many forms of work—for example, sales and computer programming—do not involve manual labour, yet even so cannot be considered positions in some sort of economic or corporate elite. This is why criminologists have introduced such terms as *professional crime, elite deviance, corporate crime, organizational crime, respectable crime,* and *business crime.* Our interest in social domains as the context of criminal events requires us to pay close attention not only to the crimes of powerful jobholders but also to the crimes of those whose jobs denote lower-ranked positions. Encompassing both types of crime is the term **occupational crime**, which Akers (1985: 228) defines as the "violation of legal norms governing lawful occupational endeavours."

There are different varieties of occupational crime. Some kinds are intended to provide only the jobholder with direct benefits. The person who pilfers from an employer does so for personal benefit; the same with the bank teller who embezzles or the systems analyst who steals computer time. In these situations, the agency or organization is the victim, and the employee is the offender.

White-collar crime
A crime committed by a person of respectability and high status in the course of his or her occupation.

Occupational crime
Violation of legal norms governing lawful occupational endeavours.

But other times the organization is not the victim but rather a weapon being used against those outside the organization or at the bottom of the organizational hierarchy. In these situations, the crime may profit the job-holder *indirectly*, in that direct benefits accrue to the organization itself. In these circumstances, the victims may be other business organizations (e.g., a corporation hires industrial saboteurs to steal competitors' secrets), clients or customers (e.g., a corporation engages in deceptive advertising or sells untested pharmaceutical or food products), or low-level organizational members (e.g., an employer maintains unsafe working conditions or violates laws relating to labour relations). Furthermore, in some situations, the victim is society at large. Political bribery, tax fraud, and polluting the environment fall into this category, in the sense that society in general suffers for these crimes.

Occupational crimes also vary by setting. Some types involve an offender acting alone or with a handful of offenders. Medical fraud and dishonest household repair schemes typically involve the actions of a single offender, who is dealing directly with victims and whose activities are not dependent on institutional support from co-workers. At the other extreme, **corporate crime** can involve "large vertical slices" of complex organizations (Snider, 1993: 321). In these situations, it can be difficult to say who did and who did not behave criminally, since each individual's actions contributed in small ways to the criminal event.

The scope of corporate crime can be vast indeed. This was well illustrated by what Canadians have come to know as the "sponsorship scandal" or "Adscam." In short, the issue here concerned a number of quasi-legal or illegal transactions between the Liberal administration of Prime Minister Jean Chrétien and private companies which were identified as supporters of the Liberal party in Quebec. In 1995, in the aftermath of an unsuccessful attempt on the part of separatist forces in Quebec to secede from Canada, the federal government developed the sponsorship program. The purpose of the program was to promote the idea of federal unity though the sponsorship of cultural and athletic events in Quebec. The subsequent scandal involved the misuse and misdirection of funds which were intended to support these activities. An investigation by the Auditor General revealed that as much as 100 million of the 250 million dollars directed towards the sponsorship program had been misused (2003). In 2005, the report of a Federal Commission chaired by Mr. Justice Gomery concluded, among other things, that there had been direct political involvement in the administration of the program, gross overcharging by communications companies, inflated commission and production costs, and deliberate attempts to avoid compliance

Corporate crime
Acts committed by businesses in the interests of generating profit and avoiding losses and prosecution.

with federal legislation. The report was explicit about the scope of the offending behaviours, in that it concluded that there existed:

> A complex web of financial transactions among Public Works and Government Services Canada (PWGSC), Crown Corporations and communication agencies involving kickbacks and illegal contributions to a political party in the context of the Sponsorship Program (Gomery Commission, 2005: 6).

The sponsorship scandal followed closely on the heels of a large number of corporate scandals to which the media in North American had paid rather close attention. In fact, the uncommon term, "corporate crime wave," became somewhat of a media catchphrase during the period. While the most notorious incident involved the Enron corporation, the most famous offender was the domestic celebrity Martha Stewart. In addition to Martha Stewart and executives at Enron, however, high-ranking personnel from a large number of companies, including WorldCom, Global Crossing, Adelphia, and Tyco, were accused of various forms of corporate wrongdoing. An analysis of these cases suggests they appeared to lack the somewhat subtle character that we sometimes associate with corporate crime (as opposed to more "garden variety" forms of offending). In the case of Enron, for instance, it was claimed that company executives deliberately hid the extent of company losses from investors and that despite their awareness of the shaky future of the company, encouraged employees to buy Enron stock.

Criminologist David Friedrichs (2004) argues that these "Enron et al." crimes had three major characteristics in common. First, all of these cases involved efforts either by the corporation or its top executives to misrepresent the financial status of the organization. Second, in a very large number of cases, top executives received extremely generous compensation despite the failure of the company. Third, these incidents involved the cooperative involvement of a broad network of other parties, including accounting firms, stock analysts, and investment banking firms.

We now examine the social organization of work routines in order to understand how and why occupational crimes occur.

Precursors

The relationship between work routines and criminal offending can be understood with reference to the concepts of opportunity and motivation

BOX 10.4

Corporate Opinion and Corporate Offending

In the aftermath of lengthy prison sentences given to some American corporate offenders, Compas Inc. Public Opinion and Customer Research sought the opinions of Canadian corporate officials regarding the most appropriate way to deal with these types of offenders.

Contrary to what we might expect, the Canadian CEOs and business leaders rather unanimously expressed the belief that the American legal system was dealing with corporate crime in an effective and fair way. Indeed, some expressed the view that the American authorities were not going far enough. The overwhelming majority believed that it was important for Canadian regulatory authorities to learn from the American experience.

Many of the panelists expressed the view that despite some of the severe sentences handed down in the aftermath of the corporate crime wave of the early 2000s, American authorities are missing a large part of the picture. They believed that American authorities have only been dealing with the "tip of the iceberg."

On the surface at least, it appears that corporate opinion and public opinion may be less divergent than we might think. What remains unaddressed, however, is the extent to which these corporate views represent corporate public relations rather than genuine opinion.

Source: Compas Inc. 2005. *Crime, Punishment, Compensation and CEOs.*
http://www.compas.ca/data/050627-CrimePunishment-PB.pdf

(Coleman, 1987, 1991). In other words, the social organization of work may give people the means with which to violate the law, and their feelings about their work or employers may supply them with reasons for doing so.

In terms of opportunity, some work routines give employers or employees access to people and things to victimize. Doctors have access to patients, lawyers have access to clients, corporations have access to markets, and bank tellers have access to "other people's money" (Calavita and Pontell, 1991). While this access does not necessarily result in criminal action, it does make such action possible.

According to Coleman (1987, 1991), at least four factors influence the evaluation of opportunities to commit white-collar crime. The *first* factor is the perception of how large a gain can be expected from using the opportunity. The *second* is the perception of potential risks associated with the opportunity. The exploration of criminal opportunities is more likely when effective control is lacking. For example, many professional groups claim to be self-regulating and discourage the efforts of government agencies to investigate them except in the most extreme cases. Also, many crimes that are associated with large corporations are so complex that they are policed only with great difficulty. Some observers have argued that the power of professional groups and large corporations discourages effective enforcement by state agencies (Hagan, 1992). The *third* factor is the degree of compatibility between the use of the opportunity and the potential offender's beliefs, attitudes, and ethical view of the situation. *Fourth* and finally, the evaluation of the opportunity is based on the potential offender's perception of the benefits of one opportunity relative to other opportunities to which that person has access.

The motivations for occupational crime are a matter of considerable debate. Some observers claim that these motivations reside in the nature of work itself or in the wider socio-economic setting of the workplace. Insofar as capitalism promotes a "culture of competition" that encourages the pursuit of economic profit, the profit motive can be said to be the criminal motive (Calavita and Pontell, 1991). In a related way, political critiques of the role played by a wide variety of individual and corporate actors in the sponsorship scandal often spoke of a "culture of corruption."

The role of culture has also been highlighted by Friedrichs (2004) in his discussion of the "Enron et al." crime wave. He argues that while this kind of crime can be traced back many centuries, it is also true that these more recent examples have many elements that seem to reflect "postmodern" elements of culture. Unlike earlier examples of companies involved in corporate crime, the Enron-type offenders mainly produced services rather than products. In addition, like other elements of postmodern culture, the Enron-style companies actively blurred the line between reality and illusions so that investors took as real a company image and economic future which was largely fictional.

But the ways in which particular businesses and industries are organized can also serve as important motivating factors. Industries that experience severe competition, that are engaged in the sale or distribution of potentially dangerous—and therefore highly regulated—goods, or that operate in an uncertain economic environment may feel pressure to operate unlawfully in order to achieve organizational goals (Keane, 2000; Snider, 1993).

In very large corporations or businesses, pressures to behave criminally may be accentuated by the pressure placed on underlings to achieve organizational goals. Simon and Eitzen (1993) suggest members of senior management may act as "corporate Frankensteins" by establishing goals or quotas that everyone knows cannot be achieved within the limits imposed by current regulations. At the same time, management may be able to insulate itself from any covert criminal actions that result from these corporate objectives (Hagan, 1992). Those who, pursuing the goals of senior management, make the decisions to engage in actual criminal wrongdoing may be actively or passively discouraged from reporting their activities to senior management (Coleman, 1987). If the acts are discovered by enforcement agencies or the public, management can then disavow any knowledge of wrongdoing. If the acts are not discovered, management can claim credit for the high profit yields (Snider, 1993).

The role of market forces in criminal events is illustrated clearly by the case of the Ford Pinto. This car was placed on the market in 1970, largely in response to fears of competition from Japanese car manufacturers. Lee Iacocca, who was president of Ford at the time, told his engineers they had to produce a car that weighed less than 2,000 pounds and that cost less than $2,000. The Pinto met these specifications, but it also contained serious design flaws. Most critical was the placement of the gas tank, which increased the likelihood that the car would explode in a rear-end collision. It was later discovered that the corporate officers had known about this design flaw and about the actions that could be taken to correct it. But instead of acting on this knowledge, they calculated the cost of these modifications and compared them with the costs likely to be incurred in lawsuits resulting from injuries to or deaths of Pinto drivers. The costs of the improvements were estimated to be greater than the costs associated with death and injury, so Ford decided not to repair the defect.

Some criminologists have emphasized the significant role played by "definitions of the situation"—definitions that favour criminal offending (Keane, 2000). Coleman (1987) proposes the following six such definitions:

1. Defining acts of theft as "borrowing."
2. Denying that white-collar crimes result in any real harm.
3. Claiming that the laws prohibiting the behaviour are unfair or unjust.
4. Claiming that certain types of criminal behaviour are necessary if organizational goals are to be achieved.
5. Claiming that the behaviour is normal and "everybody does it."
6. Claiming that employee theft is not really stealing since the money was owed (e.g., for uncharged overtime).

Thus, acts that might be seen as criminal by others are often seen as excusable behaviours by the embezzler who defines theft as "borrowing" and by the corporate executive who defines the violation of fair labour laws as "just good business."

Much of the debate about the motivations to commit occupational crime has centred on questions about the distinctiveness of occupational offenders. Many criminologists have long contended that white-collar offenders differ from street criminals in important ways. Many white-collar offenders are neither poor nor powerless. Their crimes are not impulsive, irrational, or the product of inadequate planning. Thus, many of the factors that are usually associated with crime and criminals have little to do with the behaviour of white-collar offenders, especially those at the top of corporate hierarchies. It follows that the causes of these types of crime must lie elsewhere.

In contrast, the architects of the "general theory of crime," Gottfredson and Hirschi (1990), argue that the similarities between street criminals and occupational criminals are more important than the differences. For Gottfredson and Hirschi, the key explanatory mechanism for both groups is "self-control." Special theories are no more necessary to explain the criminal in a legitimate business than they are to explain the criminal in the university, the military, or the church. People who have low self-control are likely to engage in a variety of types of crime and deviance as the opportunities to do so present themselves.

Gottfredson and Hirschi argue that because occupations that present significant criminal opportunities tend to be occupations that require a considerable degree of self-control, the rates of occupational crime are lower than is popularly believed. Moreover, they suggest that when differences in opportunity are taken into account, demographic correlates of street and occupational crime are similar. They conclude that there is no need to presume special motivational circumstances in the case of the occupational offender, such as "the culture of competition" and other types of factors described here. Instead, they assert that "the distinction between crime in the street and crime in the suite is an *offence* rather than an *offender* distinction [and] that offenders in both cases are likely to share similar characteristics" (Gottfredson and Hirschi, 1990: 200).

Benson and Moore (1992) used data on the sentencing patterns for a large number of white-collar crimes (bank embezzlement, bribery, income tax evasion, false claims, and mail fraud) and common crimes (narcotics offences, postal forgery, and bank robbery) to test some of the implications of Gottfredson and Hirschi's theory. Specifically, they attempted to determine whether white-collar offenders were as "criminally versatile" as common offenders, and whether they were prone to as wide a range of deviant activities. They found that a minority of white-collar offenders behaved as the theory predicted; most did not. According to Benson and Moore, low self-control is not the only path to occupational crime. Offenders with high self-control may employ it to pursue ego gratification in an aggressive and calculating manner. The culture of competition rewards these individuals by giving them positions of trust and opportunities for committing serious (and often undetected) crimes. In between those with high self-control and those with low self-control are individuals who may or may not take advantage of occupational opportunities depending on their personal situations. For these individuals, fear of economic or occupational failure can create a circumstance in which a once adequate level of self-control is now inadequate; when this happens, the individual's ability to resist occupational opportunities for crime can be weakened.

Recent history might be seen as calling into question the relevance of the general theory of crime to an understanding of offending among high-ranking members of organizations. After all, if we are to describe the corporate actors in the Enron-style incidents or in the sponsorship scandal as having done what they did as a result of low self-control, it is not clear who it is in society who does not have low self-control. A study by Lisa L. Spahr and Laurence J. Alison (2004) directly addresses the relevance of Gottfredson and Hirschi's theory to savings and loan frauds. Using data relating to 481 fraud offenders, the researchers hypothesized that if Gottfredson and Hircshi are correct, individuals higher in their respective occupational hierarchies would be less likely to commit fraud since the greater degree of self-control necessary to achieve their higher positions would discourage such behaviour. Instead, in a manner inconsistent with the general theory of crime, they found that individuals higher in the occupational hierarchy were more likely to commit fraud.

In a general way, rational choice theories are useful in an attempt to understand the processes of occupational crime (Simpson and Piquero, 2002). Typically, such crimes do not reflect "passion" or any other kind of emotion but seem to be motivated by an attempt to maximize gains and minimize losses. This would seem to hold true both at the level of the individual and at the level of the organization itself.

Transactions

It is difficult to determine how much crime is committed in the course of legitimate work. There are many reasons, the main one being that this kind of crime is often almost impossible to detect. Corporate crimes that victimize consumers, clients, or members of the public are very often "invisible" (Coleman, 1987). For example, people who are ill do not necessarily know that their illness is the result of inadequately tested drugs. Workers who are injured by hazardous working conditions may be inclined to blame themselves rather than their employers for their injuries (Croall, 1987). Our terminology encourages this tendency: we routinely call such occurrences "accidents" rather than "assaults."

Unlike more garden variety forms of offending, occupational crimes are largely hidden from public view. The employee who has access to opportunities for offending often escapes public scrutiny. The offender who uses a computer to embezzle can often do so in such a way that the crime goes undetected by the employer, co-workers, and enforcement agencies. Corporate conspiracies are even less visible. Evidence about corporate decisions regarding offending is not accessible to those outside the corporation. Moreover, because a corporate crime may involve actions by members at all levels of the organization, many of those participating in the event may not even be aware of the true character of their actions.

As with other categories of crime, occupational crimes do not usually come to the attention of policing or regulatory agencies as a result of vigorous enforcement practices. At the same time, victims may be poorly positioned to know about (so that they can respond to) the occupational crimes that victimize them. The regulatory agencies that are supposed to police and scrutinize corporate behaviour face many obstacles. According to Snider (1992), these obstacles include the following:

- The massive economic and political power of corporations, which favours non-enforcement.
- Lack of staff and funds.
- Frequent lack of support from the governments that appoint them.
- The high cost of investigating complaints.
- Support only from weak consumer or labour groups.
- Minimal accountability to the public or the media.

A consequence of these obstacles is that many occupational crimes that are discovered are not reported. A business that learns its employees have been embezzling funds may not wish the matter to be widely known because it could reduce public trust in the company. In other words, the long-range negative consequences of reporting may be seen to outweigh any immediate benefits.

Police data on occupational offences are of only limited use. These offences are underreported, and often (e.g., in the case of fraud) it can't be determined whether they occurred in the context of work. This is partly because occupational crime is a conceptual rather than a legal category. Victimization surveys can supplement official record-keeping systems, but these, too, are limited, given the absence so often of a "direct victim" and the inability of the victim to recognize occupational and corporate offending.

The Aftermath

Our best estimates suggest that the crimes committed by people in the course of legitimate occupational activities result in considerable levels of financial and physical harm and loss of life (Simon, 1996). Snider (1993) contends that "corporate crime is a major killer, causing more deaths in a month than all the mass murderers combined do in a decade." According to one estimate, Canadians are 10 times more likely to die as a result of unsafe or unhealthy workplace conditions than they are to be murdered (Reasons, Ross, and Paterson, 1981). It is estimated that the economic costs of corporate crime also exceed the costs of "street" crimes such as burglary and larceny. In the United States, one particularly notorious case of corporate offending, the savings and loans scandal, will end up costing American taxpayers as much as $500 billion (Gabor, 1994a).

Controlling crimes that occur in the context of legitimate work roles is no easy task. It is sometimes assumed that the public is less concerned about occupational crimes than about more direct forms of predatory crime; however, this does not seem to be the case (Hans and Ermann, 1989). Even so, the fact remains that the low level of visibility associated with occupational crimes makes effective deterrence difficult (Coleman, 1987). Some studies suggest that threats of legal sanction have less impact on corporate crime than does the market environment in which companies operate (Keane, 2000; Simpson and Koper, 1992).

It is worth noting that several of the corporate offenders associated with the most serious and most visible Enron-style crimes have been dealt with rather harshly by the courts—at least in comparison to the ways in which these crimes have been dealt with in the past (*Vancouver Sun*, 2005). However, the pattern is far from consistent. Martha Stewart emerged from prison with new cachet. Her company was soon on the way to record profits, making her a billionaire once more. Moreover, shortly after her release from prison, she was involved in two television programs, a fourth furniture line was to be unveiled, and she was involved in a lucrative new deal with K-Mart (Naughton, 2005).

ENTERPRISE VERSUS ORGANIZED CRIME

Enterprise crime
Sale of illegal goods and services to customers who know that the goods and services are illegal.

Sometimes crime can be thought of as an occupation or business. We can define **enterprise crime** as the "sale of illegal goods and services to customers who know that the goods or services are illegal" (Haller, 1990: 207). What constitutes an illegal good or service ultimately depends on what the law disallows.

The sale of illegal drugs or pornography, the operation of illegal gambling houses, loan sharking, and "contract killing" are all examples of enterprise crime, as are arms smuggling, identity theft, and trafficking in human beings.

Enterprise crime is usually referred to by criminologists and others as "organized crime" (Lyman and Potter, 2004). This concept conjures up a number of familiar images gleaned from movies such as *The Godfather,* television shows such as *The Sopranos,* and newspaper coverage of "mob trials" (e.g., the trial of John Gotti) (Dubois, 2002). However, for reasons that will become clear, the concept of organized crime obscures rather than enhances our understanding of the types of events in which we are interested.

What Is Organized Crime?

The study of enterprise crime has been compromised by what some writers have referred to as the "official myth of organized crime" (Kappeler and Potter, 2004). Typically, the term *organized crime* has been used to refer to long-term, highly organized criminal syndicates that are involved in a number of criminal businesses (Naylor, 2002). These syndicates are said to be organized along ethnic lines, to have well-established patterns of recruitment and authority, and to function in much the same way as legitimate business corporations (Cressey, 1969). According to this view, organized crime functions largely as an "alien parasitic conspiracy" (Smith, 1975).

The most widely discussed group of organized criminals in the criminological and popular literature on the subject is the Mafia, also known as La Cosa Nostra. This particular form of criminal conspiracy is said to have dominated organized crime in North America for most of the twentieth century, although its significance is generally thought to have declined in recent years (Jacobs, 1999; Reuter, 1995).

How useful is it to think of organized crime as the exclusive domain of alien ethnic conspirators? Critics contend that the tendency to equate organized crime with particular types of criminal organizations discourages our understanding of the many and various other parties involved in organized crime. In other words, there is more to organized crime than organized criminals: there are also victims, customers, regulators, suppliers, competitors, and innocent bystanders. The criminal association is only one part of a much larger web of social relationships. Sociologist Margaret Beare (1996) has argued that the most useful way to think of organized crime is to view it as a "process" rather than as a structure or a group. In other words, organized crime is not a type of crime, but rather a way of committing crimes.

La Cosa Nostra
Literally, "our thing." This term is understood as the formal designation of the Italian-American crime syndicate which dominated enterprise crime during the twentieth century.

This tendency to "other" those involved in organized crime results in what Michael Woodiwiss (2001) has termed a "dumbing of the discourse." This phrase implies that the complexity of various kinds of criminal enterprises and their solutions is sacrificed for the sake of melodramatic narratives which see the world in terms of heroes and villains. An example of how the dumbing of the discourse plays itself out has been provided by Margaret Beare (2002) in her examination of the problem of tobacco smuggling between Canada and the United States during the 1990s. Beare describes the situation in which very high tobacco taxes in Canada, as compared to the United States, created the conditions for a lucrative cross-border business. Not only were American cigarettes smuggled in and sold illegally in Canada, but much more interestingly, Canadian cigarettes which had been legally exported to the United Sates were smuggled back into the country. As Beare notes, the tobacco companies were complicit in the entire enterprise. Their executives knew that the increase in exports was directly related to the smuggling problem, and, in fact, they built these increases into their business plan. Despite this, the media and policymakers continued to construct the issue as one relating principally to the lone figure on the snowmobile rather than the guilty corporation. The rhetoric of control and traditional law enforcement marginalized a consideration of other policy options such as those relating to

---

BOX 10.5

How Prevalent Is Organized Crime?

Most of our traditional data systems provide us with little information about the prevalence of "organized crime." What we know about prevalence derives from a relatively small number of focused studies. For example, a 1998 survey of 16 police agencies which dealt with criminal organizations found that such groups were most frequently involved in drug trafficking (88 percent), extortion (71 percent), and illegal trafficking in firearms (71 percent).

A study by Wallace of the involvement of organized crime groups in motor vehicle theft used the rate of stolen vehicles not recovered as a proxy measure of organizational involvement. Using 2002 data from 22 police forces, he found that 20 percent of the cars were never recovered, compared with about 2 percent in the early 1970s.

It is also possible to access statistical information relating to "gang" or "organized crime" homicides. These data indicate that such homicides have increased steadily from 4 percent of all homicides in 1994 to 15 percent in 2003.

Given the need for organized crime data, plans were put into place to use the UCR system to collect organized crime information beginning in 2005.

Source: Kong, R. (ed.). 2005. *Criminal Justice Indicators*. Ottawa: Centre for Justice Statistics, Statistics Canada.

tax reductions in Canada or an effort to hold the tobacco companies account-able for their increase in exports.

Precursors

As already noted, enterprise crime involves selling and distributing illegal goods and services. What kinds of social conditions make enterprise crime likely? The *first* condition, of course, is the existence of laws prohibiting the goods and services in question. In other words, enterprise crime is made pos-sible when the law creates market opportunities. Prohibition, which was in force in the United States between 1920 and 1933, directly created an oppor-tunity for financial gain that was soon exploited by criminal entrepreneurs (Packer, 1969; Schelling, 1967). Similarly, attempts to use the law to control the availability of illicit drugs—such as marijuana and cocaine—or to use high rates of taxation to control the availability of legal drugs such as tobacco, make enterprise crime possible. The gap between what people want and what the law allows them to legitimately have suggests an important way in which our society creates the conditions for enterprise crime.

This point is obscured when we think of such crime as merely the product of a parasitic conspiracy. Too often, the tendency is to take the law as a given and to focus only on the lawbreaking activities. To do so, however, is to miss an important part of the story since it is the zealous agitation for new laws and the over-reach of the law which can create the markets which enterprise crim-inals easily exploit. Some authors have suggested that the moral climate of the 1990s ushered in a new Puritanism in which energized moral entrepreneurs sought to ban a wide range of goods and services (Wagner, 1997).

A *second* factor is systematic corruption. To the extent that enterprise criminals have access to police or political officials who are interested in coop-erating with them, the agencies of legal control may be neutralized. Bribery and corruption offer some enterprise criminals protection from the law and make other enterprise criminals the objects of much more aggressive enforce-ment. Just as in the more legitimate sectors of the economy, the establishment of cozy relationships between those who do the policing and those who are supposed to be policed may help the latter strengthen their control of the market. Where bribery and corruption don't exist, criminal enterprise markets are more unstable.

A *third* factor is the existence of partnerships. These arrangements play the same role in illegal businesses as they do in legal ones: they allow entrepreneurs to share risks—especially the risk of business failure—and they allow people with different types of resources to pool those resources. This means that individuals who have capital, political influence, or managerial skills can combine their talents in ways that increase the potential for profit.

A study of the role of organized crime groups in motor vehicle theft illustrates the complexity of these networks and associations (Wallace, 2004). While cars are often stolen by opportunistic offenders for the purposes of joyriding, it is also the case that many are taken for purposes of resale, often in other countries. With respect to the latter type of offence, the automobile is much less likely to be recovered. To be a profitable enterprise, the theft and resale of cars involves a large number of actors with rather diverse skills. Typically, brokers make arrangements with middlemen to hire thieves. Other experts engage in chopping (dismantling a vehicle for parts) or re-Vinning (altering the vehicle identification number to disguise the vehicle). Still others need to know how to forge the appropriate documents and arrange for the safe shipment of the cars to an appropriate foreign locale. At the point of importation arrival, someone needs to arrange to receive the cars and to finalize the sale. The organization can be described as multi-layered in that middlemen deal with thieves and brokers but are unlikely to interact with choppers or exporters.

In many cases, this emphasis on partnerships suggests that instead of being hierarchically or bureaucratically organized, enterprise crime is much more likely to involve informal styles of association (Ianni and Reuss-Ianni, 1972; Haller, 1992). Partnerships may arise when they are deemed necessary or desirable for business purposes, and they may be dissolved when they have served their purpose or when they cease to be profitable. Moreover, as Haller (1990) notes, within these partnerships not everyone need be thought of as equal. Some entrepreneurs may exercise much more power than others because they have the political or economic resources that enable them to participate in several enterprises simultaneously. Haller (1990, 1992) suggests that, like the Chamber of Commerce or the Rotary Club, La Cosa Nostra should be viewed not as an organization that operates illegal (or legal) businesses, but rather as an association that businesspeople join partly to further their business careers.

Canadian policing agencies have identified a large number of groups who are said to be involved in various kinds of enterprise crime activities (Criminal Intelligence Service of Canada, 2005). These include:

- Asian-based organized crime (AOC) in the Lower Mainland of British Columbia and the Greater Toronto Area. It is suggested that Vietnamese-based groups are extensively involved in multiple residential marijuana grow operations for distribution within Canada and to the U.S.

- Eastern European-based organized crime (EEOC) networks operate across the country but are concentrated in Ontario, British Columbia, Alberta, and Quebec.

- Outlaw motorcycle gangs include most notably the Hells Angels, with the Outlaws and Bandidos currently maintaining a low profile.

- Traditional (Italian-based) organized crime (TOC) is centred in Montreal, the Greater Toronto Area, Hamilton, and the Niagara region. These groups are also present in Vancouver and Calgary and appear to have influence in other regions across the country.

- Aboriginal-based crime groups, which take advantage of some Aboriginal reserves on or near the Canada/U.S. border to facilitate or conduct criminal activities.

Finally, Haller notes, many economic factors shape illegal enterprises, and these factors both enhance and reduce cooperation. Enterprises that involve importing drugs such as cocaine and heroin may require a high degree of cooperation among many groups in both the exporting and the receiving country, including drug networks at local levels. As well, large drug deals require a large initial investment. Factors such as these encourage monopolies since few groups have the contacts or the economic resources to bring off large transactions. The market for marijuana is structured quite differently. This illicit commodity does not have to be imported and can be distributed on a small scale by independent entrepreneurs catering to the needs of a small, local clientele. Markets of this type are much more resistant to monopolization. In general, as noted in a report by the Auditor General of Canada (2002), criminal groups of this type profit from any sort of development which assists legitimate economic organizations. Such developments include, for instance, the growth of a relatively unrestricted cross-border movement of goods, capital and people and the growth of the borderless world of high-speed communications technology.

Transactions

If we think about enterprise crime as a type of business, the questions to which we seek answers are not unlike the ones we might ask regarding more legitimate businesses. What is the nature of the market? How are goods and services produced and distributed? What are the sources of capital that underwrite the costs of doing business? How do the various groups involved in these businesses cope with changing markets? What types of people are attracted to this particular line of work, and why?

BOX 10.6

Criminal Business Organizations in Vancouver

Robert M. Gordon (2000) investigated various criminal organizations around Vancouver. Specifically, he collected information about 128 known gang members. Of the forms of criminal organization—street gangs, wanna-be groups, and criminal business organizations—it is the last that relates most directly to the study of what has traditionally been called organized crime.

Gordon found that criminal business organizations are carefully structured and highly sophisticated. Most of their members are adults engaging in crime mainly for economic reasons. Unlike street gangs, these groups try to maintain a low public profile. Gordon focused on 24 members of six criminal organizations. His research revealed the following:

- Members tended to be older, better educated males. They were less likely to be economically disadvantaged (in large part because their illegal enterprises were so successful).
- Typically, these enterprises engaged primarily (but not exclusively) in the supply of illegal goods and services (such as illegal drugs). Other business activities included robbery and extortion.
- The lucrative character of the business associations made it difficult for some members to leave. Most had minimal work skills and could not expect to command comparable incomes in the legitimate economy.
- Members were more likely to have immigrated to Canada than, for example, street gang members; they were also more likely to be members of a visible ethnic group. Sixteen of the 24 were of Vietnamese or Chinese ethnic origin.
- Data gathered from the offenders themselves—and from their probation officers—indicated that membership in these organizations may have provided members with a cultural bond and helped them cope with what they experienced as a sense of ethnic marginality.

Criminologists are especially interested in the fact that the business is illegal (Haller, 1990). As economist Thomas Schelling (1967) notes, when a business is made illegal, entry into the marketplace is restricted to those who are willing and able to behave criminally. In other words, illegal business is perhaps most attractive to those who have no strong reservations about acting in ways that are prohibited by law.

As we pointed out earlier, much has been made of the ethnic character of organized crime. Apart from La Cosa Nostra, commonly cited groups include the Chinese Triads, the Jamaican Posse, and associations loosely referred to in the popular press as the Colombian, Irish, and Vietnamese "mafias." This emphasis on ethnicity has often reinforced the popular view that criminal enterprise is an "alien" problem.

Over five decades ago, Daniel Bell (1953) rejected this view, arguing that organized crime serves as a "queer ladder of social mobility" in societies that emphasize material success but fail to provide all racial and economic groups with equal opportunities for achieving it. Like Robert Merton (1938), Bell maintained that groups that find the legitimate channels of upward mobility blocked may turn to illegal alternatives. A key implication of this argument is that enterprise crime, seen as a form of economic activity, is most attractive to those who are at or near the bottom of the social hierarchy.

O'Kane (1992), like Bell, has argued that involvement in enterprise crime is characterized by ethnic succession rather than by any enduring criminal conspiracy. Particular ethnic groups may dominate organized crime until legitimate channels of upward mobility become generally accessible. At that point, the influence of a particular group may decline, as other groups move in to fill the void created by the outward movement. Thus, the Italian presence in organized crime, which peaked just before Prohibition, was preceded by an Irish and Jewish presence and succeeded by a Cuban and African-American presence. The emergence in Canada of Vietnamese, Chinese, and Aboriginal gangs suggests a similar process of ethnic succession.

This is not to say that the domination of enterprise crime by any particular group is irrelevant to how markets are structured or exploited (Light, 1977). Members of ethnic groups may be able to draw on their cultural capital in ways that enable them to be especially effective in particular types of enterprise crime. They may also share particular cultural traditions that facilitate criminal organization. According to Ianni (1971), the significance of the family as a central organizing theme in Italian culture has contributed to the creation of remarkably durable criminal enterprises structured along kinship lines.

A second important implication that flows from the illegal nature of criminal enterprises relates to the role of regulation. Obviously, when a market is declared illegal, it cannot be controlled by government agencies responsible for mediating disputes or resolving conflicts in other sectors (Reuter, 1984b). Criminal entrepreneurs cannot seek recourse for the harm done against them by going to the police or initiating lawsuits. One mobster cannot sue another because a promised shipment of heroin was not delivered or because a promise to influence the vote of a labour union was not kept. This is why violence, or the threat of violence, looms so large in the business affairs of criminal entrepreneurs. Violence is one of the few means by which contracts can be enforced and compliance with agreements can be assured (Black, 1983).

The criminal events that are central to enterprise crime are complicated, but much popular thinking on the subject glosses over these complexities. We are used to thinking about enterprise crime as nothing more than the acts of vicious gangsters whose ways of thinking and acting are foreign to the societies in which we find them. This makes for good pulp fiction, but it is not very illuminating. Organized crime events are shaped by the societal context and are in no fundamental way alien to it. The gap between popular demand and efforts to legally control supply makes illegal markets possible in the first place. By declaring these markets off limits to legal regulation, society creates circumstances in which the potential for violence is considerable. Similarly, society is stratified, and it imposes restrictions on upward mobility. As a result, some of those who are adversely affected come to see enterprise crime as a viable means of achieving socially accepted goals.

The Aftermath

In 1998, the Solicitor General commissioned a study of the impact of organized crime on Canadian society (Solicitor General of Canada, 1998). Here are some of the report's findings:

- The Canadian illegal drug market is between $7 and $10 billion dollars per year.
- Economic crimes such as securities and telemarketing fraud cost Canadians $5 billion per year.
- Between $5 and $17 billion are laundered in Canada each year.
- As many as 16,000 people are smuggled into Canada each year.
- Counterfeit products (that is, their production and sale) cost Canadians as much as $1 billion each year.
- The illegal smuggling of tobacco, alcohol, and jewellery costs the government as much as $1.5 billion a year in taxes.

Of course, these economic costs fail to capture the numerous other ways in which enterprise crime produces consequences for society. These include the undermining of the tax base through the sale of illegal goods and services, the generation of disrespect for law, and the increased level of violence associated with such enterprises. Increasingly, since the events of September 11, 2001, it has been argued that the revenues derived from "organized crime" are used to fund terrorist activities (Helfand, 2003).

One activity which has attracted considerable attention is the laundering of money by those involved in enterprise crime. Quite obviously, if enterprise crime groups are to continue to operate without attracting the attention of policing agencies, it is essential that they be able to hide the large amounts of money (frequently in cash) which their activities generate. Money laundering refers to the various means by which the money made illegally is hidden or made to appear as legal income. In global terms, according to the International Monetary Fund, annual money laundering amounts to between US$590 billion and $1.5 trillion.

A study of 371 money laundering cases drawn from the files of the RCMP was undertaken by Schneider (2004). The research found that there are several activities which generate large amounts of income. However, drug trafficking emerged as the largest single source of income. The two most popular destinations for drug money were deposits (in institutions) and real estate. Laundering techniques were highly varied and might involve having a large number of individuals (known as "smurfs") make many small deposits. Alternatively, the attempt might be made to create the perception that the money was legally earned. Other attempts to money launder might involve the use of "nominees," or third parties, who prevent the appearance of a direct link between the money and the person who acquired the money.

Schneider concludes that, in and of itself, there is little evidence that money laundering has negative ramifications for the Canadian economy. However, it can be argued that it is the ability to hide the source of funds which allows criminal enterprises to prosper and persist. As well, it might be suggested that it is through the laundering of money that some criminal enterprises are able to infiltrate the legitimate economy.

Public reactions to enterprise crime often fail to take account of the wider context. As we have argued, this is necessary if we are to understand this type of crime. When we read about a gangland killing in an urban ethnic restaurant or a police seizure of drug assets off the B.C. coast, we rarely consider the social character of these crimes. We are encouraged to think about organized crime as a force at war with "decent society"—as something that preys on citizens and threatens to corrupt our public officials and undermine our basic social institutions. Rarely are we encouraged to think about criminal enterprise as a logical product of social conditions. As McIntosh (1975) argued, criminal entrepreneurs are part of a larger configuration that includes not only the criminal but also victims, police, politicians, customers, and others. The activities of the criminal entrepreneur cannot be understood by focusing on the entrepreneur alone. As these larger configurations change, so do the types of events in which criminal entrepreneurs are likely to be involved. In the absence of this more complex and detailed understanding, enterprise crime will be seen as alien and parasitic. As the recent evidence of a large-scale sports betting ring in New Jersey continues to pour out, it is evident that criminal enterprise is often entangled with non-criminal activity. Sports betting is legal in Canada when done through Crown agencies but not when done through individual entrepreneurs. Even more confusing, as the case of the former NHL players accused of being involved in this case indicates, it is illegal to run a betting ring in New Jersey but not to place bets. Further, the connections of this betting ring to a larger network of criminals has made this case even more complex. This betting ring provides a good example of how social conditions (e.g., the interest in and acceptability of betting on sports, access to highly motivated participants, and large amounts of money) can contribute to this type of crime.

How is enterprise crime to be controlled? The idea that enterprise crime is an alien, parasitic conspiracy rather than a social product supports the position that this type of crime is a law enforcement problem. From this perspective, enterprise crime is best controlled by aggressively prosecuting criminal entrepreneurs. But when we conceptualize the problem in terms of criminal enterprise rather than in terms of organized crime, we recognize that this "gangbuster mentality" has serious limitations. If enterprise crime really does function like other economic markets, the removal of criminal entrepreneurs through arrest and imprisonment cannot significantly affect market operations, since these actions will have no effect on the demand for illegal goods. We recognize this fact quite explicitly when it comes to legal markets. When an entrepreneur who sells legal goods—for instance, shoes—is removed from the market as a result of death, illness, or retirement, shoes remain available (Van den Haag, 1975). This is because the demand for shoes will prompt others to enter the market to fill the void. It can be argued that an aggressive policy of prosecution may actually increase the prices for illegal goods and services, and the profits to be made from them, by increasing the risks of involvement in these businesses.

SUMMARY

The roles we play in the workplace structure the kinds of involvements we are likely to have in various types of criminal events. Some jobs increase employees' risks of criminal victimization; others provide employees with opportunities to victimize others, be they subordinates, co-workers, clients, customers, or society at large. Also, various types of enterprise crime constitute a form of work.

Criminology has long focused on how exclusion from the world of legitimate work motivates criminality. Though this remains an important (if unresolved) issue, it is equally important to understand how the organization of work fosters or hinders criminality. Theories that emphasize the role of social inequality in the generation of crime quite naturally suggest that not having a job may encourage the development of criminal motivations. Victimization risks differ between those who are employed and those who are not. But crime does not involve only the unemployed. It is also important to understand that particular forms of labour force participation make crime possible. Relevant here are two factors: the relationship between the jobs people have and the victimization risks they face, and the ways that jobs provide people with opportunities to behave criminally.

Victimization risk at work is inversely related to occupational status, measured by income; those in lower-income occupations are more vulnerable. However, occupation alone is not enough to establish victimization risk. The workplace setting can strongly influence opportunities for crime. Risk may be heightened by the fact that money is available to be stolen. Sometimes the nature of the job can have a provoking effect on customers, who may vent their anger and frustration toward the employee. Crimes that occur in these circumstances are not easy to deter and are underreported. In the aftermath of violent encounters, employees may accept the blame or assume that the employer will blame them for handling the situation poorly. Often these incidents are handled informally to avoid the complexities associated with police involvement.

Work-related crime ranges all the way from pilfering by a disgruntled employee to the gargantuan thefts associated with the savings and loan scandal in the United States. Sutherland (1940) used the term *white-collar crime* to refer to crimes committed by people of respectability and high status in the course of their occupations. He saw a need to correct the imbalance in criminological thinking that associated crime almost exclusively with the actions of the poor and the powerless.

Occupational crimes can be distinguished in two important ways. *First*, they differ with respect to the nature of the offender–victim relationship. Some kinds of crimes are intended to provide direct benefits only for the jobholder, as in the case of the employee who steals. In these instances, the agency or organization is the victim, and the employee is the offender. Other times, the organization itself may be used to attack those outside the business or at the bottom of the organizational hierarchy. With respect to these criminal events, the crime may profit the jobholder indirectly, in that more direct benefits accrue to the organization itself. Finally, more general patterns of victimization result from crimes that inflict harm on very broad segments of society. These crimes include political bribery, tax fraud, and industrial pollution.

Second, occupational crimes differ according to the nature of the organizational settings in which they occur. Some types of occupational crime involve either a lone offender or a small number of offenders (e.g., medical frauds and dishonest household repair services). At the other extreme, corporate crime can sometimes involve "large vertical slices" of complex organizations. In these situations, it may be difficult to say who did and who did not behave criminally, since each individual's actions constitute only a small portion of the criminal event.

We can also view crime as operating in a marketplace in which illicit substances and services are sold to customers who know they are illegal. Instead of viewing these activities in terms of ethnically based organized crime, we instead use the term *enterprise crime*. Enterprise crime occurs as a result of laws that prohibit certain goods and services. In other words, enterprise crime is made possible when the law creates market opportunities. Enterprise crime needs the presence of systematic corruption, partnership arrangements between illegal and legal businesses, and favourable market conditions such as a monopoly on the illegal goods.

When we conceptualize the problem of "organized crime" in terms of criminal enterprise rather than in terms of organized crime, it becomes apparent that law enforcement responses to crime have serious limitations. If enterprise crime functions like other economic markets, removing criminal entrepreneurs through arrest and imprisonment cannot significantly affect market operation or reduce the demand for illegal goods.

QUESTIONS FOR REVIEW AND DISCUSSION

1. What criminological factors would help to explain why taxi drivers tend to experience high rates of robbery?
2. What measures could be taken to reduce the problems of crime and victimization in high schools? Would these solutions interfere with the basic mission of schools to provide education?
3. Do you agree that corporate crime is a more serious problem than street crime? How do corporations discourage us from adopting this view?
4. In reference to a job you currently hold (or perhaps a previous summer job), what opportunities for crime did your employment make available to you?

5. How do television and movie portrayals of organized crime distort public understanding of the problem? Can you think of some specific examples?

6. "Despite their differences, most offender-based theories lead us to expect a higher rate of crime among people who are unemployed than among people who are employed." Discuss this statement.

RECOMMENDED READINGS

Beare, M. 1996. *Criminal Conspiracies.* Scarborough: Nelson Canada.

Craig, W.M., R.DeV. Peters, and R. Konarski. 1998. *Bullying and Victimization among Canadian School Children.* Hull, PQ: Human Resources Development Canada.

Desroches, F. 2005. *Crime that Pays.* Toronto: Canadian Scholars Press.

Pearce, F., and L. Snider. 1995. *Corporate Crime: Contemporary Debates.* Toronto: University of Toronto Press.

Woodiwiss, M. 2001. *Organized Crime and American Power.* Toronto: University of Toronto Press.

INFOTRAC® COLLEGE EDITION

Explore InfoTrac® College Edition, your online university library, which includes hundreds of popular and scholarly journals in which you can find articles related to the topics in this chapter. Visit InfoTrac® through your web browser (**www.infotrac-college.com**) or through this book's website (**www.criminalevent-4e.nelson.com**).

WHAT'S ON THE WEB?

For chapter links and quizzes, check out the accompanying website at **www.criminalevent-4e.nelson.com**.

Part 4

Responses to Crime

Chapter 11 | Summary and Review of Public Policy Responses to Crime

LEARNING OBJECTIVES:

- review what we have learned about criminal events
- discuss in detail some public policy responses to crime
- provide a critical perspective on public policy
- discuss the major components of contemporary crime prevention, specifically situation prevention, social development, and community policing

INTRODUCTION

The objectives of this chapter are *first,* to summarize what we have learned in previous chapters about the nature, causes, and consequences of criminal events, and *second,* to sketch some of the major policy responses available to us. These objectives are interrelated in that what we can do about criminal events should follow logically from a detailed understanding of their causes and content.

SUMMARY OF FINDINGS ON THE CRIMINAL EVENT

We began in Chapter 1 by discussing some important concepts guiding the study of criminal events. Most notably, we emphasized that there are no simple answers to the questions, "What is crime?" and "How is crime to be studied?" It is too glib to say that crime is simply behaviour that violates the law. Such a definition obscures our view of the complex social realities that underlie crime. We emphasized a need to recognize that there is more to crime than the behaviour of a lawbreaker. As social events, crimes involve not only offenders but also other participants, including victims, the police, witnesses, and bystanders, all of whom act and react within particular social and physical circumstances. We discussed as well how the mass media and day-to-day conversations influence public views of crime. Unfortunately, media images of crime tend to exaggerate the frequency of serious violent crime and to emphasize the sensationalist character of both crime and its solutions.

In Chapter 2, we introduced the criminal event framework. Most fundamentally, we observed that criminal events are social events in the sense that they involve interaction between human beings. The dynamics of this interaction shape the content of the event and thus the consequences for those involved. We discussed the roles played by the principal protagonists in criminal events: offenders, victims, bystanders, and the police. In examining the social and demographic characteristics of victims and offenders, we noted that for many categories of crime, offenders and victims have much in common (a finding contrary to what media reporting usually leads us to believe). Both victims and offenders tend to be young, socially disadvantaged, and—for many categories of crime—males. There are, of course, important exceptions to this pattern. For obvious reasons, corporate crimes are not typically perpetrated by disadvantaged young males, and many forms of violence (such as rape and domestic assault) uniquely victimize women. We also pointed out that criminal events do not occur with equal frequency in all types of communities, in all types of neighbourhoods within communities, or at all types of locations.

In Chapter 3, we saw that the data on crime are derived mainly from two types of investigative strategies: observations and reports. Some researchers attempt to gather information about crime through their observations of crime in naturalistic settings and/or in experimental and quasi-experimental settings. But most contemporary research focuses on reports of crime from police, victims, and offenders. Though there is much debate about the innate superiority of one type of report over another, we suggested that each type must be approached in terms of its own particular strengths and weaknesses. Different types of reports provide us with different perspectives on and different data about criminal events. Their variable nature does not make them unusable; however, we should be critical and judicious when employing their data.

Chapters 4 to 7 described the major theoretical orientations that have dominated criminology in recent decades. We defined criminological theories as generalized explanations of criminal phenomena. We look to theories to make sense of our observations of the empirical world. Conversely, we look to the empirical world for confirmation or refutation of our theoretical views.

Theoretical interest in crime has generally meant theoretical interest in offenders. For this reason, we devoted two chapters to describing alternative conceptualizations of the offender. Chapter 4 focused on theories that derive from "positivist" views of the offender. Chapter 5 presented explanations based on "classical" thought. The distinction between positivist and classical views has to do with the degree to which human will is thought to dominate social action. Broadly stated, positivist theories seek to understand why offenders do what they do, whereas classical theories emphasize the significance of rational choice in influencing the behaviour of the criminal offender.

Chapter 4 discussed many of the causal theories that have been offered to explain criminal behaviour. Some of these theories emphasize biological, constitutional, or genetic causes of criminal conduct, but most emphasize social factors. We examined two main types of social explanations. The *first* considers how socially induced frustration can contribute to the development of criminal motivations. Robert Merton argued that the gap between people's aspirations and what is actually available to them can lead to a form of frustration, which in turn leads to criminal conduct.

The *second* social explanation of criminal motivation stresses the role of culture. Subcultural theories suggest that people learn motivations to behave criminally the same way they learn motivations to do anything else. The emphasis here is on the immediate environments that offenders operate in and on how these environments can foster the learning of cultural lessons supporting criminal conduct. The most important early proponent of this view was Edwin Sutherland, whose theory of differential association emphasized that crime should be viewed as a learned behaviour. The subcultural theorists who have followed Sutherland encourage us to think about the relationship between criminal behaviour and exposure to criminal cultures. Theorists such as David Matza and Gresham Sykes contend that we need to appreciate how lessons that might motivate offending can be learned from mainstream culture.

In Chapter 5, we focused on offenders' decision-making processes rather than on their motivations. According to theorists of the classical school, there is little to be gained from searching for unique factors that motivate offending behaviour. They suggest instead that such behaviour is better understood in relation to the formal and informal social controls that might be expected to restrain offending behaviour. When these controls are ineffective or when individuals are insensitive to them, potential offenders are primed to become actual offenders. In these circumstances, people are free to act in ways that, criminal though they may be, reflect rational self-interest. Social controls that discourage individuals from engaging in the criminal pursuit of self-interest include their social bonds to conformist others, their relationships with their communities, and the sanctions promised by the legal system. It was also argued that too much control, like too little control, can be a serious problem. For instance, labelling theorists maintain that society's reaction to minor or petty acts of nonconformity may result in stigmatization, which frustrates the labelled person and thereby contributes indirectly to more serious violations of the law.

The theoretical explanations discussed in Chapter 6 differ fundamentally from those presented in previous chapters. Specifically, they do not focus on the behaviour of offenders, but rather on the opportunities to which offenders have access and on the situations in which they find themselves. According to these theories, an individual who is ready, willing, and able to break the law will not necessarily do so. Other elements must come into play, and depending on how these elements come together, the offender may end up committing one type of crime rather than another.

Opportunity theories suggest that the ways in which people "distribute their lives" over time and across space either increase or decrease the number of criminal opportunities to which offenders have access. Lifestyle exposure theory contends that individuals who pursue lifestyles that bring them into contact with likely offenders or that put them in dangerous places face higher victimization risks. Similarly, routine activities theory suggests that crimes result when motivated offenders, suitable targets, and an absence of capable guardianship converge in time and space. Other theories reviewed in Chapter 6 focus on how the interactions between offenders and their victims influence criminal outcomes. Relatively simple theories that speak of "victim precipitation" have been replaced in recent years by theories about crime as a situated transaction that is the product not only of an offender's will or motivation but also of social interaction.

In Chapter 7, we discussed theories and research relating to the aftermath of criminal events. We examined the variety of ways— obvious and not so obvious—that involvement in these events may affect victims and offenders. We also discussed how the effects of crime extend beyond the immediate victim. For example, the fear of crime can have important implications for the well-being of individuals and their communities. In extreme cases, the public response in the aftermath of criminal events may amount to a panic.

Our theoretical elaboration of criminal events led us to conclude that it is worth investigating these events in the context of particular social domains. Social domains can be defined as the major spheres of life in which we spend most of our time and energy. Three of these domains—the family and the household, recreation and leisure, and the workplace—provided the organizing themes for the substantive analysis of criminal events presented in Chapters 8 to 10. We argued that a comprehensive examination of criminal events in these domains requires us to focus on three important components: precursors, the transaction, and the aftermath. This approach helps us understand *first*, how social arrangements affect the distribution and timing of criminal events, *second*, why some groups in society are more likely than others to be involved in criminal events, whether as offenders or victims, *third*, why particular types of criminal events have the content they have, and *fourth*, how victims and others are affected by these events.

Our discussion of criminal events in specific social domains in Chapters 8 to 10 enabled us to apply the theoretical and research lessons that emerged from earlier chapters. In Chapter 8, we took up the issue of criminal events in the home. Two general categories of events were discussed. The *first* was interpersonal violence in the context of familial relationships. This sort of violence emerges from and reflects the social organization of family life. The very factors that lead us to idealize family life—intimacy and privacy—increase the risks to more vulnerable family members. The data clearly indicate that women and children suffer most from violence in the home.

The *second* major type of criminal event in the family and household domain is property crime. Break and enter and the theft of household goods are very common crimes and result in substantial financial loss. We suggested that much of this crime is opportunistic in nature and involves rational offenders who encounter opportunities for theft. Our discussion of family life and family organization revealed how routine activities create such opportunities.

In Chapter 9, we took up several issues relating to criminal events in the leisure domain. We saw that, especially in the case of juveniles, leisure is often understood as a "cause" of crime. It has been argued that many leisure pursuits that youths engage in promote criminal conduct directly or indirectly. We also saw how leisure pursuits may free youths from social controls and at the same time provide them with opportunities for offending. Finally, we investigated how particular leisure contexts—the street, bars and taverns, dating, and tourism—provide settings for criminal events.

A final social domain, the workplace, was discussed in Chapter 10. The nature and degree of people's involvement in the work domain have important implications for the kinds of criminal events they engage in. Two major issues emerged from our discussion of the work domain. The *first* was the relationship between involvement in the legitimate world of work and involvement in criminal events. Particular kinds of work expose employees to particular kinds of victimization risks. Jobs that involve handling money, travel between remote worksites, or regular exposure to high-risk populations increase the risks people face at work. Highly publicized homicides in the workplace have brought this issue into sharp relief. The jobs people have may also provide them with unique opportunities to break the law. For instance, corporate criminals have access to highly profitable offending opportunities and very often remain insulated from controls that are supposed to deter their behaviour.

The *second* major issue discussed in Chapter 10 was crime as a form of work. Like legitimate business enterprises, criminal enterprises are sensitive to market conditions, endeavour to forge stable partnership arrangements, and attempt to manage their relationships with state agencies that try to control their activities.

In the course of this book, we have emphasized an appreciation for the variety and the complexity of criminal events. Though these events occur in diverse social domains and involve different categories of actors, this does not mean they are not amenable to criminological analysis. Throughout our analysis of criminal events, the same fundamental questions kept recurring: Why do offenders and victims come together when they do, as they do, and where they do? Why does the event evolve as it does? What are the consequences of the event for its participants? Instead of seeking highly specific answers to these questions, we have attempted to link specific concerns to theoretical ones. We have also been attentive to the pictures of criminal events that are revealed to us by the main criminological data sources. We conclude here with a brief consideration of how understanding these events in criminological terms helps us make sense of public attempts to deal with the problem of crime.

RESPONDING TO CRIME

Getting Tough on Crime

Too often our thinking about crime is less imaginative than it could be. Fed by sensationalist media reporting and political rhetoric, we tend to think of "getting tough" as the most appropriate response to crime: hire more police, hand down longer sentences, and build more prisons.

To a considerable degree, public anxiety about crime can promote what James Finckenauer (1982) referred to as a philosophy of "doism." This means that we often believe that we are better off doing something than nothing. The problem with doism is that it encourages the adoption of policy approaches which are not thought out or which lack any kind of empirical basis

(Welsh and Farrington, 2005). Such policies can waste scarce resources and lead to widespread cynicism regarding all innovative approaches—including those which actually could work.

The so-called "scared straight" approach is a good example of doism. For a period of time in the 1970s and 1980s, it became fashionable in many circles to argue that an effective approach to the problem of youth crime was to establish programs in which young people encountered in a frank and verbally brutal way, incarcerated offenders. Advocates of the programs argued that the emotional character of these sessions was so intense that the youth who participated were discouraged from future offending. There really was no research evidence to support this conclusion, and the energy and the credibility of the agencies who sponsored such programs was needlessly squandered (McCord, 2003).

For many critics, doism was also an operative principle behind the passage of the 1995 Firearms Act. The Act required Canadian gun owners to apply for a licence by January 1, 2001 from the Canadian Firearms Centre (a branch of the Justice Department) and to register their guns with the Royal Canadian Mounted Police (RCMP) by the beginning of 2003. Many observers saw this legislation, which created a national firearms registry, as poorly conceived and as a political response to the problem of violence in Canada. It is argued that the impetus for the law could be found in high-visibility acts of violence such as the "Montreal massacre" in which Marc Lepine murdered 14 women at Montreal's L'École Polytechnique. As well, Canadian public opinion has always reflected a real concern about gun violence (Kohler, 2005). For the critics, the attempt to register all of the guns in Canada was both a logistical and financial nightmare. In 2002, the Auditor General of Canada reviewed the registration policy and stated that the original estimates of $119 million to implement the legislation (offset by $117 million in fees) were dramatic underestimates. Instead, the Auditor General argued that the legislation would, within a few years, end up costing about $1 billion (Auditor General of Canada, 2002). As well, it has been argued by some criminologists that the legislation poses some real threats to civil liberties while it does little to achieve the objective of keeping guns out of the hands of people who are willing to use them illegally (Gabor, 2003; Stenning, 2003). Of course, other criminologists, such as Neil Boyd (2003), argued that the legislation is indeed effective and worth the costs associated with its implementation.

Despite their sometimes doist nature, many observers have argued that get-tough responses to the problem of crime are inherently limited (Donzinger, 1996; Standing Committee on Justice and the Solicitor General,

1993). As they see it, the problem is twofold. *First,* there is little convincing evidence that we are controlling crime effectively when we simply invest more resources in the criminal justice system (Graham, 1990). *Second,* when we view the criminal justice system as the principal social mechanism for responding to crime, we approach the problem in a reactive rather than a proactive manner and thus never really address the underlying factors associated with crime and criminality.

As with other social problems, it is perhaps more sensible to think about strategies of prevention. **Crime prevention** has been defined as "the anticipation, recognition and appraisal of a crime risk and the initiation of some action to reduce or remove it" (National Crime Prevention Institute, 1986: 2). Clearly, the criminal justice system is itself part of an overall crime prevention strategy, for two reasons: the threat of legal penalty is meant to deter potential offenders; and prison terms, in their capacity to either punish or rehabilitate, are intended to prevent reoffending.

Crime prevention
The anticipation, recognition, and appraisal of a crime risk and the initiation of some action to reduce or remove it.

Get-tough approaches to crime tend to involve options that are associated specifically with the criminal justice system. As used by criminologists, the term *crime prevention* is more broadly based, referring to strategies or tactics that might involve the police (or other criminal justice functionaries) but are rooted in the physical and social character of the local community. From this perspective, crime prevention involves a range of strategies, including installing lights on city streets, initiating citizen police patrols, developing Neighbourhood Watch programs, mounting public information campaigns, locking doors, carrying weapons or alarms, and introducing programs aimed at reducing unemployment and poverty. As Lawrence Sherman and his associates (1998) have stated, crime prevention is not defined by its intentions but by its consequences. These consequences can be understood in at least two ways: One is with reference to a reduction in the number of criminal events; the other is with respect to a reduction in the number of criminal offenders. Others might argue that it could also be defined with reference to the amount of harm prevented or to a reduction in the number of victims harmed or harmed repeatedly.

Politicians often like to portray themselves as prisoners of a punitive public which demands that punishment trump all other policy options. Of course, get-tough policies

WHAT DOES IT MEAN?

Crime Prevention

Crime prevention refers to the anticipation, recognition, and appraisal of a crime risk and the initiation of some action to reduce or remove it. The action usually consists of strategies or tactics that, though they may involve the police (or other criminal justice functionaries), are rooted in the physical and social character of the local community.

BOX 11.1

Are Boot Camps a Viable Solution to Juvenile Crime?

One solution to the crime problem that is popular with conservative policymakers is the boot camp. These military-style correctional facilities reflect the widespread view that misbehaviour among juveniles emerges out of a basic lack of discipline. The quick fix that boot camps promise is especially popular among politicians who wish to demonstrate that they are "cracking down" on delinquents. Tabloid talk shows find it easy to exploit for ratings purposes the pain and suffering caused by both crime and boot camp solutions to crime. It is often assumed that boot camps produce the desired outcomes; the available research suggests otherwise. Specifically, recent studies indicate the following:

- Boot camps do not have a significant impact on recidivism.
- Compared to prisons, boot camps are not more cost-effective and are sometimes less cost-effective.
- Boot camps result in needless incarceration, because judges who support them may use them simply because they are available, when offenders might otherwise have been put on probation.

Sources: Doob, A.N., and C. Cesaroni. 2004. *Responding to Youth Crime in Canada*. Toronto: University of Toronto Press. Saleno, A.W. 1994. "Boot Camps: A Critique and Proposed Alternative." *Journal of Offender Rehabilitation* 20: 147–58. Shamsie, J., S. Nicholl, and K.C. Madsen. 1999. *Antisocial and Violent Youth*. Toronto: Lugus.

are the crime-fighting techniques with which the general public is most familiar, and they seem to many the most logical solution to the problem. However, as crime prevention expert Ross Hastings (2005) and many others (Cullen et al., 1998; Tufts, 2000) have argued, there is also considerable evidence to suggest that public support for effective non-punitive approaches to crime is also rather strong. In particular, the public seems willing to support programs of early intervention directed at helping young children avoid a life of crime, as well as less coercive sanctions for youthful and first-time offenders.

Public Health and Public Safety

Public policy in the area of health care suggests interesting parallels to the issue of crime prevention (Anderson, Grandison, and Dyson, 1996). One way society can deal with medical problems is to wait until people get sick and then make health care services available to them. Similarly, we can wait until people commit crimes and then take action by using criminal justice resources to catch and then confine or treat them. The use of the word *rehabilitation* in reference to prison programs suggests a quite literal application of the medical model to our thinking about crime and punishment.

In the field of public health, most policy planners recognize the value of applying limited resources in a preventive rather than a reactive manner. If we can prevent illness, we won't need to treat it after the fact. This is why people are advised to get regular medical checkups, exercise, and watch their diets. We could view the problem of crime in a similar way. It is more sensible to take action *before* crimes occur than after harm has been done. Public health-style approaches to violence emphasize four basic elements (Anderson, Grandison, and Dyson, 1996; Durant, 1999; Potter and Saltzman, 2000):

1. Identifying patterns and epidemics of violence.
2. Conducting epidemiological research on the causes of violence.
3. Designing and evaluating prevention interventions.
4. Implementing prevention programs.

Borrowing from the language of public health, we can think of crime prevention as having primary, secondary, and tertiary dimensions (Brantingham and Faust, 1976; Lab, 1992; van Dijk and de Waard, 1991). *Primary* prevention includes programs aimed at either the entire community or the population at risk. Good examples of primary prevention are crime prevention programs that teach risk-reducing skills to large audiences (Davis and Smith, 1994; Sacco and Silverman, 1982). Pamphlets, brochures, and posters providing information on family violence are examples of (mass media) primary prevention. *Secondary* prevention refers to programs aimed at those segments of the population that are at especially high risk (or, in public health language, that show early symptoms of the problem). Examples of secondary prevention include targeting high-crime areas for special treatment (such as neighbourhood redevelopment or Neighbourhood Watch programs) and installing security equipment in schools that have experienced problems with intruders. *Tertiary* prevention refers to strategies that are intended to prevent the recurrence of crime. Examples of tertiary prevention include victim–offender mediation, training courses for drunk drivers, treatment programs for wife assaulters, and various forms of diversion and community service.

In the rest of this section and in the two sections that follow, we examine three major approaches to crime prevention that extend well beyond traditional get-tough approaches. Each picks up an important theme in the study of criminal events; in combination, they form the basis for what many would argue is a comprehensive approach to crime prevention. **Opportunity reduction** focuses on how social and environmental factors could be brought to bear on the reduction of crime opportunities. **Social development approaches** look to create social conditions that discourage long-term serious offending

Opportunity reduction
Focuses on how social and environmental factors can be brought to bear on the reduction of crime opportunities.

Social development approach
An approach to crime prevention which attempts to create social conditions that discourage long-term serious offending and that empower potential victims while at the same time contributing to the rebuilding of communities.

BOX 11.2

Co-offending and Crime Prevention

It is well known that juvenile offenders tend to commit crimes in the company of others (Warr, 2002). However, this aspect of criminal events is rarely taken into account when crime rates are calculated or when efforts are taken to deal with crime. With respect to crime measurement, we have tended to assume for computational purposes that each crime has one offender. However, the large number of crimes committed by co-offending juveniles can result in an overestimate of the criminal involvement of young people. Moreover the criminal justice system assumption that a crime is "solved" when an individual is apprehended may misdirect many of our prevention efforts.

A study by criminologists Joan McCord and Kevin Conway was intended to clarify the role of co-offending in crime causation and crime policy. Their investigation of criminal offending among a large sample of Philadelphia youth found that:

- offenders under the age of 13 were more likely to engage in co-offending than were older offenders.
- co-offenders were more likely to be recidivists.
- co-offending is related to the probability of committing violent crimes.

These findings have some important implications for crime prevention. One such implication relates to the need for crime information systems to provide information relevant to co-offending. Second, and perhaps more important, is the need to target youthful co-offenders for policy interventions. Such action is necessary to break the cycle by which youths learn crime by doing crime with friends and acquaintances.

Source: McCord, J., and K.P. Conway. 2005. *Co-Offending and Patterns of Juvenile Crime.* Washington DC: U.S. Department of Justice, Office of Justice Services.

Community-based policing
Expansion of the policing role beyond the traditional narrow reactive role.

and that empower potential victims while at the same time contributing to the rebuilding of communities. **Community-based policing**—or problem-oriented policing—considers how the policing role could be expanded beyond the narrow reactive role that brings the police into criminal events only when the events are either already under way or finished.

Crime Prevention through Opportunity Reduction

As we have seen, the event conceptualization of crime emphasizes the importance of opportunity in determining where and when crimes occur. Only when people who are ready, willing, and able to offend encounter conditions favourable to offending are criminal events likely to develop. So, from a policy standpoint, actions that control the appearance or accessibility of opportunities to engage in crime may help prevent much crime. The important implication of this approach is that we can manage the risks of crime without changing the character of offenders. Because the emphasis in opportunity reduction is on modifying the situations in which crimes occur, crime prevention through opportunity reduction is sometimes referred to as **situational crime prevention** (Brantingham et al., 2005).

Situational prevention is based on two important assumptions. *First,* crimes are prevented most effectively when we are attentive to their particular characteristics (Brantingham et al., 2005; Gottfredson and Hirschi, 1995). So, the first step in opportunity reduction is careful crime analysis: Who commits these crimes? When are they committed? Where do they most often occur? What do offenders hope to achieve by committing them? How might certain characteristics of the physical environment contribute to them? Are there natural forces of guardianship that could be activated in the situations in which crimes typically occur? The answers to questions such as these help crime prevention planners tailor specific solutions to specific crime problems.

Second, crimes can be prevented when we are attentive to the thinking behind offenders' actions. Offenders' decisions are based on their assessment of the various costs and benefits associated with a particular course of action (Cornish and Clarke, 1986). They ask themselves questions such as: How easily can a crime be committed? Is anyone who might take action to prevent the crime standing guard? Are there less risky ways of obtaining the rewards that the commission of the crime promises? Offenders seek answers to these questions and then behave in ways that reflect their best interests. If the opportunities conducive to crime can be made less attractive or less plentiful, many types of crimes—especially those that are largely opportunistic in nature—may occur much less often. According to Clarke (1992), situational prevention involves increasing the risks and decreasing the rewards associated with crime. As offending situations become riskier, more difficult, and less rewarding, rational offenders will be discouraged from offending.

One obvious way that people make crimes more difficult to carry out is through target hardening. This refers to measures that decrease the vulnerability of personal or household property. Entry into a house with locked doors and windows is more difficult than entry into a house without them. Various forms of access control, such as locked gates and entry phones, also increase the degree of effort needed to commit certain crimes.

The risks involved in the commission of crime can be increased by measures that make it more likely—or at least make it *seem* more likely—that the offender will be discovered and apprehended. A high level of surveillance by security guards or citizen patrols clearly is intended to serve this purpose.

Situational crime prevention
Efforts to prevent crime that focus on the suppression of criminal opportunities (rather than, for instance, the reform of offenders).

BOX 11.3

The National Strategy

The National Crime Prevention Strategy is the Government of Canada's action plan to reduce crime through social development principles. The approach is predicated on the assumption that the most effective way to prevent crime is to address those "root causes" which increase risk, such as family violence, school problems, and drug abuse.

The National Crime Prevention Strategy intends to provide communities with the tools, knowledge, and support necessary for effective crime prevention.

Phase I started in 1994. It provided a framework for coordinating a range of federal initiatives that emphasized a proactive, social development model for crime prevention. Phase II, launched in 1998, supports Canadian communities in undertaking crime prevention activities, primarily through the distribution of grants and contributions but also through the dissemination of "lessons learned." In other words, it enabled the Government of Canada to broaden its partnerships and help communities design and implement innovative and sustainable ways to prevent crime.

The objectives of the strategy can be summarized as follows:

- To promote partnerships between governments, businesses, community groups, and individuals to reduce crime and victimization
- To assist communities in developing and implementing community-based solutions to local problems that contribute to crime and victimization
- To increase public awareness of, and support for, crime prevention
- To conduct research on crime prevention and establish best practices

Source: Public Safety and Emergency Preparedness Canada. http://www.psepc-sppcc.gc.ca/prg/cp/ncps-en.asp#1

Perhaps less obvious is the role played by other types of crime prevention measures, such as locks. As Felson (1992: 32) notes:

> The strategic role of a lock is not to prevent entry! Rather, its strategic role is to force the offender to make a lot of noise, in hope that others will hear that noise. Ideally, the potential offender will take a look at the lock, note the noise it will force him to make, fear the consequences of that noise, and decide against committing the crime.

As discussed in Chapter 5, in recent years, especially since the terrorist attacks of September 11, 2001, closed-circuit television systems have become extremely popular measures directed toward the reduction of criminal opportunities.

Prevention involves more than establishing defensible space. According to Merry (1981), a neighbourhood may be architecturally designed to discourage crime but still not be adequately defended, because it has little or no social cohesion. Krupat and Kubzansky (1987: 61) note:

> Even when buildings are low and the entrances and public spaces focus around a small set of families, people will not react to crime when they believe that they are on someone else's turf, when they do not consider the police effective or when they fear retribution.

Finally, crime can be made less attractive by reducing the rewards associated with it. For example, requiring bus riders to have exact change decreases the amount of money that must be handled by any particular bus driver; this makes robbing drivers a less attractive proposition. Similarly, markings that identify individual ownership of property may discourage the conspicuous use of stolen merchandise and seriously hurt the chances for resale.

BOX 11.4

Situational Prevention and Gang Violence

As crime prevention specialists have become more skilled at implementing principles of situational prevention, it has become clear that the approach has broad applicability. Common uses of the approach suggest that it is best suited for controlling minor nuisance crimes such as trespassing and vandalism. However, it has also been used to control much more serious offences.

The Los Angeles Police Department employed situational prevention principles in an attempt to reduce levels of assault and homicide. This program, known as Operation Cul de Sac (OCDS), involved efforts to control and reroute traffic so as to "design out" crime by reducing the opportunities to commit it.

Traffic barriers were placed in neighbourhoods where gangs and gang violence had become especially serious problems. Police data indicated that most drive-by shootings and violent gang encounters occurred in clusters on the periphery of neighbourhoods linked to major thoroughfares. To control the problem, the police closed all of the major roads leading to and from these identified "hot spots" by placing cement barriers at the ends of the streets that led to these roads. This redesign in effect created cul-de-sacs.

This approach assumes that though gang violence may have deep-seated structural causes, it also has significant opportunity dimensions. So instead of focusing on the "root causes" of gang violence, it focuses on "proximate causes."

An evaluation of the program showed that the number of homicides and assaults in the OCDS area fell significantly after two years, and rose again after it ended. (In a comparison area, it remained constant.) Importantly, the evaluation also showed that crime was not displaced to other areas.

Source: Lasley, J. 1998. "'Designing Out' Gang Homicides and Street Assaults." National Institute of Justice: Research in Brief. Washington, DC: U.S. Department of Justice. Used by permission.

The most sophisticated forms of situational prevention employ knowledge about all elements of the criminal event. Paul and Patricia Brantingham (2001), the foremost authorities on this approach, identify several such elements:

1. **The offender**   All crimes require an offender. Traditional approaches to crime prevention focus on changing the offender's motivation; in contrast, situational approaches direct our attention to the routine activities of offenders and to their patterns of decision making.

2. **Target**   All predatory crimes have targets or victims. Situational approaches are sensitive to the role played by victim precipitation and carelessness.

3. **Site**   Every criminal event has a site—a discrete location in space and time—at which the criminal action by the offender against the target takes place. These sites can be analyzed to reveal patterns that will help prevention planners understand the spatial (and temporal) regularities in crime occurrence (Rossmo, 2000).

4. **Situations**   Crimes require specific behavioural settings and situations. Just because a potential offender and victim find themselves in each other's presence does not mean that a crime will happen. It is also essential that the offender define the situation as appropriate. This could involve, for instance, the absence of official protectors—such as property managers, landlords, or security guards.

5. **Mechanics of the crime**   The criminal event model of crime prevention also directs our attention to the sequence of actions the offender must take to accomplish the crime once the offender, target, site, and situation have combined to create a criminal opportunity. Most criminal action sequences are short and technically simple, but they are sometimes quite complex. Knowledge of the mechanics of this process makes possible the development of strategies intended to disrupt this sequence.

The Brantinghams contend that situational prevention strategies must not only account for each of these factors but also be informed by an awareness of their various combinations. The many ways in which each combines and intersects with the others suggest to careful planners a wide range of prevention opportunities. It is also important that situational crime prevention approaches be embedded if their greatest potential is to be achieved. This means, according to Patricia Brantingham and her colleagues, that the strategy be "moved to an established basis with ongoing funding" (Brantingham et al., 2005: 282). Embedding the strategy would assign it a priority within government decision-making processes and ensure that appropriate evaluation data are collected and used to refine and monitor the success of the strategy.

Unquestionably, opportunity reduction has been effective in a variety of specific settings and with respect to a variety of offences (Clarke, 1993, 1994). But this approach has its critics. Some suggest that removing opportunity is more likely to displace crime than to prevent it. In other words, if we make it difficult for a motivated offender to offend in one situation, he or she may simply find another situation more conducive to offending. If one store takes precautions to prevent theft, can we really be sure the would-be thief will not simply seek out targets where these precautions have not been taken? The evidence suggests that displacement may be a problem with some types of crime and some types of offenders (Gabor, 1990). That being said, many forms of opportunity reduction do in fact prevent crimes—they don't simply displace them (Brantingham and Brantingham, 1990).

More specific forms of opportunity reduction invite more specific criticisms. Various target-hardening methods, such as installing locks on doors and bars on windows, may be faulted for encouraging a "fortress mentality" that enhances fear of crime in society (Graham, 1990). Some critics see the use of electronic surveillance as part of a gradual shift toward a "surveillance society" (Lyon, 1994).

Perhaps the most common and general criticism of opportunity reduction approaches is that by placing so much emphasis on reducing opportunities for crime, they ignore the underlying causes of crime (Waller and Weiler, 1984). It has been argued that because these strategies do not address the root causes of crime, they achieve short-term benefits at best. If we wish to consider these root causes, we must turn to another important approach: crime prevention through social development.

Crime Prevention Through Social Development

Any number of social problems, from family victimization to poverty and racism, provide fertile breeding grounds for crime. Advocates of the social development approach see community building as a comprehensive strategy that reduces crime by discouraging potential offenders and strengthening potential victims. Crime prevention through social development aims to correct the criminogenic social conditions that are assumed to be the root causes of crime (National Crime Prevention Centre, 2000). This approach focuses on long-range prevention; it seeks to eliminate the underclass, from which serious repeat offenders typically emerge (Standing Committee on Justice and the Solicitor General, 1993).

Advocates of this approach contend that investing early in children, schools, and families pays long-term financial dividends (Cohen, 1998; Canadian Council on Social Development, no date). Though the prevention of crime is not reducible to money issues, it does have financial dimensions. It is less costly to prevent a child from going down a criminal path than it is to deal with an adult offender (Parks, 2000). These savings can be of several types:

- savings in welfare assistance
- savings in special education
- savings to the criminal justice system
- savings to crime victims
- increased tax revenue from higher earnings

BOX 11.5

Some Social Development Principles

As the body of research relating to crime prevention through social development accumulates, it is becoming clear that there are some important principles that should guide such interventions.

1. Intervene early   The risks of becoming delinquent almost certainly develop early in childhood. For youths at greatest risk, waiting until adolescence may be too late.
2. Intervene in multiple settings   Interventions that simultaneously occur in schools, in the home, in the peer group, and in the neighbourhood are preferable to interventions in only one setting. For one thing, children are more responsive to lessons that are reinforced across settings.
3. Move beyond the individual child   The larger context should be taken into account. Children do not function in a vacuum; family, peer, and classroom contexts are integrally related to a child's functioning.
4. Motivate children, teachers, and parents   Despite their good intentions, programs often fail because parents and teachers do not reinforce desired behaviours by exhibiting them.
5. Set and enforce appropriate limits   It is essential that programs be prepared to sanction negative behaviour as well as reward positive behaviour.
6. Use modelling as a positive influence   It is essential that children have adequate access to pro-social behaviours that can be modelled.
7. Involve the community   The level of violence in schools and in homes is related to the character and viability of the broader community. So it is important that prevention efforts take the community into account.
8. Provide adequate alternatives   Effective programming is about providing positive alternatives to aggression and violence.

Source: Prinz, R. 2000. "Research-Based Prevention of School Violence and Youth Antisocial Behavior: A Developmental and Education Perspective." In *Preventing School Violence: Plenary Papers of the 1999 Conference on Criminal Justice Research and Evaluation—Enhancing Policy and Practice Through Research*. Vol. 2. Washington, DC: U.S. Department of Justice. Used by permission.

Some data to illustrate this have been provided by the National Crime Prevention Centre (no date). Basing its results on a fictional but typical case, this study found that the costs of a delinquent career generated by a repeat offender before the age of 18 were roughly $511,500.

The notion that crime can be prevented by eliminating the social ills that breed crime (especially teenage crime) is not new. There is a long history of social reformism that argues we can best fight crime by fighting poverty, racism, unemployment, and other forms of social disadvantage (Graham, 1990; Rosenbaum, 1988). The social development approach differs from these older approaches in its more systematic efforts to identify and attack the root causes of crime.

Because predatory crime is part of the "tangle of pathologies" (Wilson, 1987) that characterizes the lives of the socially disadvantaged, our policy approaches to crime prevention must extend beyond the criminal justice system into the areas of family, education, housing, and health policy (Canadian Criminal Justice Association, 1989; Graham, 1990).

Advocates of the social development approach do not see crime prevention as the exclusive domain of any one social or governmental agency. Rather, they strongly emphasize the need to establish partnerships and crime prevention councils at the federal and municipal levels (Kellam, 2000). These councils would bring together groups with a stake in a broad range of social welfare issues: voluntary agencies; the police; those with responsibility for health, family, employment, and housing policy; and so on. The idea behind all this is that once ownership of the crime problem is shared, more comprehensive solutions will be developed.

The social development approach has been more popular in some European countries than in North America, but it is clearly gaining momentum in Canada and the United States (Donzinger, 1996; Waller, 1989). Some advocates of opportunity reduction maintain that social development strategies fail to recognize that crime is not a homogeneous event and that different crimes require different intervention strategies (Brantingham, 1989).

Other critics question whether we in this society have the political will to launch social development programs, and whether—in this time of fiscal restraint—we are ready to make the financial commitments that such comprehensive programs would require. It has also been questioned whether the links between crime and factors such as family upbringing, employment, and school experience are as obvious and as straightforward as proponents of social development programs make them out to be. The social development approach draws our attention to a long and unwieldy list of causative factors, and as we have seen, there is honest debate among criminologists about the relative importance of these factors (Graham, 1990). There is a tendency to group together all "positive" interventions as likely to reduce crime; the empirical record suggests that not all of them do. For example, preschool and weekly home visits by teachers, and parent training about risk factors for delinquency, may reduce youthful engagement in crime, whereas subsidized work programs for at-risk youth may not (Sherman et al., 1998). All of these social development initiatives may have some merit and therefore be worthy of public support, but it does not follow that they are all equally likely to reduce crime.

For the purposes of presentation, we have drawn a distinction between opportunity reduction and social development, but there is not really an inherent conflict between these two approaches. In the same way that we have borrowed from different theories to explain criminal events, we can borrow from these different perspectives to create an integrated approach to crime prevention. Many policymakers have advocated that these strategies be combined with community policing to form an integrated approach to crime prevention (Canadian Criminal Justice Association, 1989; Standing Committee on Justice and the Solicitor General, 1993).

Community-Based Policing

Gottfredson and Hirschi (1995) argue that the natural limits of law enforcement are set by the spontaneous nature of crime: the offender sees that he or she can get something for nothing and seizes the opportunity. No increases in law enforcement, they suggest, can truly deter this type of behaviour. Research in Canada (Koenig, 1991) and elsewhere (Bayley, 1985; Jackson, 1989) has provided strong evidence that there is no relationship between the level of crime in a society and the number of police available to control this crime (Felson, 2002; Koenig, 1991). Gottfredson and Hirschi (1990: 270) maintain that in the overwhelming majority of robberies, burglaries, assaults, homicides, thefts, and drug deals, "the offender does not know or care about the probability of being observed by the police." The primary role of the police, they suggest, is to respond to criminal activity and to maintain social control; there is no evidence that increasing police tactical resources reduces crime rates.

Unfortunately, police resources have become scarcer, and what the police do primarily is respond to complaints (not crime), maintain visibility in neighbourhoods, and control traffic. In a study of police activity, Lawson (1982) found that the police spend only 10 to 15 percent of their time engaged in actual law enforcement. Bayley (1994) reports that patrol officers, who are responsible for most contacts with the general population, rarely make an arrest. In the United States, there is less than one arrest per officer per fifteen working days. According to Ericson and Shearing (1986), Canadian police officers make on average one criminal arrest per month, and encounter a recordable criminal offence only once a week. The police spend the rest of their time on order maintenance.

The pressures of order maintenance and restricted resources have forced police agencies to rethink their law enforcement strategies (Schneider et al., 2003; Van Brunschot, 2003). The police role has expanded partly because the police are the only 24-hour social agency that is easy to reach and that will make house calls. As we discussed earlier, the 911 line leaves police overwhelmed with calls that require them to serve not a law enforcement function but rather a regulatory or order maintenance function (Kennedy and Veitch, 1997). As Bayley (1994) points out, most of the time, the police do not use the criminal law to restore calm and order:

> The police "sort out" situations by listening patiently to endless stories about fancied slights, old grievances, new insults, mismatched expectations, indifference, infidelity, dishonesty, and abuse. They hear about all the petty, mundane, tedious, hapless, sordid details of individual lives. None of it is earthshaking, or worthy of a line in a newspaper— not the stuff that government policy can address, not even especially spicy: just the begrimed reality of the lives of people who have no one else to take their problems to (20).

The police are being urged to become more actively involved in crime prevention. This is partly a response to the increased levels of unease that people are feeling in urban areas. Given the assumption of routine activities theory that crime is made possible by the availability of offenders and victims and *also* by the absence of visible guardians (such as the police), it is hard to believe that the police have *no* deterrent effect on crime. But for many reasons, hiring more police does not necessarily reduce crime. In earlier chapters, we examined the role of the police in defining criminal events. The criteria that the police use to determine whether to make an arrest are shaped by a number of factors: the nature of the police organization and its strategies of policing, differing interpretations of criminal events, differing assessments of the characteristics and motivations of participants in those events, variations in the interpretations of the law, variations in the level of

---

BOX 11.6

Crime Concentration and Police Problem Solving

How should police do "problem-oriented policing"? One answer to this question suggests that the police need to collect better crime data and need to think imaginatively about how to use that data. A good example of problem-solving logic is provided by John Eck (2001). Eck contends that traditionally, police managers have not been attentive enough to how crimes are clustered. We know, Eck says, that 10 percent of the places with the most crime account for about 60 percent of crime, that 10 percent of offenders are involved in about 50 percent of the offences, and that 10 percent of victimized people are involved in about 40 percent of victimizations. The implications of this are profound. It is possible that a community has a high crime rate because a small number of offenders are committing a lot of crime (career criminals), or because a small number of victims are repeatedly being victimized (hot dots), or because a small number of places are hosting a large number of events (hot spots). Eck nicknames these problems "ravenous wolves," "sitting ducks," and "dens of iniquity" respectively. Clearly, these represent quite different types of crime problems. Merely knowing that the crime rate is high or that it has increased doesn't tell us whether we have a wolf problem, a duck problem, or a den problem, or some combination. For instance, if a housing project has a high rate of break and enters, we need to know whether this rate reflects a small number of offenders victimizing a lot of residences, or a small number of victims being repeatedly victimized, or a certain group of residences getting victimized repeatedly no matter who lives there. Perhaps it is even more complicated: perhaps the problem is 80 percent wolf, 10 percent duck, and 10 percent den, or some other such combination. These differences matter because wolf, duck, and den problems require different types of police interventions.

Wolves   The primary response to a pure wolf problem is, of course, to remove the wolves through incapacitation or rehabilitation. This is the traditional approach of the criminal justice system. Because many offenders use tools, another wolf solution is to make those tools less effective. For instance, metal detectors in schools can be used to systematically disarm potential wolves.

Ducks   Duck problems require different solutions than do wolf problems. Since victims and offenders must persistently come together at the same place for a crime problem to occur, one approach to preventing repeat victimization is to keep victims away from offenders or places where offenders tend to gather. Also, potential victims can be encouraged to improve their use of tools—to install locks, increase lighting, and do other things to help them detect and avoid offenders. Police crime prevention programs can be important sources of relevant information and hardware.

Dens   Den problems require still other types of tactics. Dens can be made less accessible to victims or offenders, or they can be removed permanently. For example, the open hours of ATM machines can be limited. The typical den solution involves changing the physical environment. Again, the police can be expected to play an active consultative and facilitative role with respect to implementing crime prevention through environmental design.

Eck's analysis shows that a careful and judicious analysis of crime data by policing agencies can point out a range of options that are not obvious in the context of traditional models of policing.

---

cooperation from the public, and so on. We will soon consider how each of these factors influences the new problem-oriented strategies—referred to as community-based policing—that are intended to help the police deal with crime. But first we consider the changes that have taken place over the years in how the police function.

In the nineteenth century, the mandate of the police was order maintenance (Wilson, 1983). The order maintenance or compliance role of the police was coterminous with "community relations." The police were to protect the community from disorderly behaviour and to control conflict where they found it (Monkkonen, 1983). This role required them to act as "watchmen," keeping track of comings and goings in the community and looking out for behaviour that might constitute a threat to public order. The compliance role is associated with the "proactive" policing we discussed in earlier chapters. As Klockars (1985: 106–7) has stated, the police are not law enforcement agencies, but rather regulatory institutions; their job is not to enforce laws but to regulate relationships between people.

The main objective of compliance law enforcement is to secure conformity with the law through means that induce that conformity (Reiss, 1984). Compliance systems return to the original mandate of the police, whereby one seeks to create law-abidingness through preventive or remedial actions. With these systems, the main focus of policing shifts from detecting and penalizing violators to providing incentives to individuals to comply with the law. Compliance-based policing recognizes the need to include the public in controlling social disorder beyond merely reporting crime to the police. The public is encouraged to include the police as intermediaries in situations of community conflict (Normandeau and Leighton, 1993).

The public has been demanding more social order since at least the 1850s (Monkkonen, 1983). In comparison with crime control, order control, as practised by the police, has had a long and successful record. As Monkkonen notes, Victorian morality has triumphed on most of North America's city streets. We expect, and get, quiet and predictable behaviour from almost everyone. Vice is no longer highly visible. Yet the dramatic rise in crime rates, and the apparent ineffectiveness of the police in dealing with crime and its consequences, has again raised concerns about social order. Monkkonen attributes increases in crime rates to a number of factors, including urbanization and demographic change. Early in the twentieth century, changes such as these narrowed the focus of police agencies to crime control alone; problems of general order maintenance were left to other agencies.

The main objective of crime control or deterrence law enforcement is to detect violations of the law, identify the offenders responsible for those violations, and penalize the perpetrators. The goal is to diminish the likelihood of future offences both by the offender (specific deterrence) and by others who may contemplate the same criminal act (general deterrence) (Reiss, 1984: 91). Until recently, contemporary policing had as its stated objective the apprehension of offenders through arrest; this led to "reactive" policing, which still dominates the work of police agencies (Reiss, 1984: 84).

Police are now beginning to realize that crime control requires broadening their mandate to once again include order maintenance or compliance law enforcement (Greene, 1998). But this notion is being resisted by police agencies, which still regard law enforcement as their principal mandate. The internal workings of police organizations are such that peacekeeping and order maintenance functions are perceived as residual matters (Bayley, 1994: 34). Real policing, some argue, involves making arrests. As Kelling (1999) notes, many people—including many police—view community policing as "soft" policing, "comparable to community relations, or worse yet, social work" (Kelling, 1999: 10). However, Kelling notes, the styles of police work that are associated with crime fighting are inherently more conservative than community policing, which is inherently proactive. Traditional policing requires police to respond to citizen requests for assistance; in contrast, community policing requires officers to scan for problems, diagnose the problems, try to limit the damage, and restore victim–offender and community relations. According to Kelling, the equation of community policing with soft policing is troublesome because it supports the view that "real" crime problems require "real" solutions and thus fails to appreciate how community policing styles can be effective even when crime problems are serious.

The philosophy of community-based policing challenges this view. The problem is that many compliance-based actions are still without legitimation in police organizations. Also, little training is provided for compliance-based operations. As Mastrofski (1983: 34) notes, the crime fighting and the non-crime public service functions coexist uneasily in the police profession. The former dominates training curricula, career incentives, and organization evaluations; the latter dominates the workload.

Notwithstanding all this, community-based policing has replaced professional crime control policing as the dominant ideological and organizational model of progressive policing in Canada (Murphy, 1993). Bayley (1988: 226) identifies four main features of community-based policing: community-based crime prevention; proactive service as opposed to emergency response; public participation in the planning and supervision of police operations; and the shifting of command responsibility to lower-level ranks. Accompanying these organizational and procedural changes is an emphasis on identifying and solving problems, which are defined in terms of breaches of both law and social order. Furthermore, the solutions to these problems do not reside merely in the rules and regulations of the police service; they also acknowledge the concerns and desires of the community in which the problems occur.

According to Goldstein (1990), community-based policing requires at least five major adjustments in current thinking.

- *First,* police officers must be encouraged to search for alternatives to law enforcement. This encouragement must be reflected in a consistent, agency-wide commitment to improving the quality of police service.
- *Second,* the police must not restrict their attention to actions that have the potential to reduce crime. Sometimes crime is only the final consequence of unresolved, non-crime-related problems.
- *Third,* consistent with the view that policing encompasses all of a community's problems, those that do not fit strict law enforcement criteria must also be addressed.
- *Fourth,* some effort must be made to understand the nature of the problems encountered in a given area before any alternatives are set out. Too often, alternatives are prescribed that simply do not work because they are not suited to the area being policed. Like other large organizations, police services have difficulty resisting internal pressures to follow established but rigid objectives and procedures.
- *Fifth,* police must be open to the idea of allowing other agencies to fulfil the job in conjunction with or in place of the police. According to Goldstein (1990: 104), this strategy "is intended to dissuade the police from applying a generic response to a generic problem, or to applying a single response haphazardly to a wide range of different types of problems."

Bayley (1988: 226) suggests that if it is done correctly, community-based policing will constitute the most fundamental change in policing since the rise in police professionalism early in this century. Therefore, it is important that community policing initiatives be rigorously evaluated (Kennedy, 1991; Chicago Community Policing Evaluation Consortium, 2000) so that we can understand how and why they actually work. In the absence of good evaluation data, there is the risk that the police may simply end up doing the same thing as before but labelling it as something else, or doing something differently but not as well as before.

At the heart of the community-based policing concept is neighbourhood team policing, which involves the long-term assignment of officers to a particular area. (For a discussion of the experience in Halifax with this strategy, see Clairmont, 1990.) This strategy allows officers to make a commitment to an area and to assume a broader level of authority in providing policing that is more sensitive to community needs. Neighbourhood team programs have not been embraced by many police managers, who see the decentralization associated with this approach as limiting their control over their officers (Scheingold, 1984: 134). Also, the aggressive patrol tactics used in crime control may diminish police rapport with the public and thereby undermine the effectiveness of community-based policing (Scheingold, 1984: 135). Finally, their fear of being seen as indecisive may cause many officers to play the role of enforcer rather than that of peacemaker (Palenski, 1984: 35).

Police must look to community members to support them in their efforts to bring about order in the community (Scott and Goldstein, 2005). This support can take the form of self-help, as discussed earlier, or it can involve a kind of co-production, whereby the police use community members as supporters of police activity (Krahn and Kennedy, 1985). Co-production can range from passive responses, such as locking doors, to more active responses, such as participating in crime prevention programs and acting as informants (Skolnick, 1966). As Black (1980) points out, since the typical criminal act occurs at an unpredictable time and place, the police must rely on citizens—most often the victims of a crime—to involve them.

Resources for community-based policing (outside of community support) have been hard to come by. Police budgets are still based on the number of calls for service and on crime rates. Community-based policing, directed as it is at problem solving and at making referrals to outside programs, may create an impression of reduced activity; in turn, this may suggest that budgets can be cut. The use of alternative programs also brings the police into conflict with other agencies; this makes it more difficult for them to define their role in the community and to obtain the resources they need to meet their objectives (Kennedy and Veitch, 1997). Despite these problems, the solutions that have been offered for handling demands from the public—including initiatives such as building community police stations—have been quite successful. Walker and Walker (1993) document Victoria's positive experiences with mini-stations, which have worked in that city to reduce strain on centralized police functions and have increased the police department's ability to solve problems at the community level.

It is very difficult for some police agencies to remain apolitical when they are fighting for budget allocations and arguing for certain policing strategies. The lobbying by communities and by volunteers in community-based policing programs may make the police seem more politically active than local politicians want them to be, and may make their requests for more funds even more tenuous. Police chiefs are confronted with a plethora of community constraints, which they must overcome before they can show they are fulfilling the objectives of compliance-based policing. Improving police–community relations is a crucial first step (Sacco, 1998; Shaffer, 1980). The members of the community must get to know the police as concerned and sympathetic individuals as well as controlling and disciplining law officers. Without communication and cooperation between the police and the public, effective and fair policing is impossible.

SUMMARY

One response to crime is to see it as a public health problem that is best addressed by removing some of the major instruments that bring about injury (e.g., guns). A second view advocates that social institutions and resources be mobilized as a means for empowering victims to defend themselves against criminal attack. Because public health institutions already face tough challenges in dealing with problems unrelated to crime, our heavy reliance on the police to confront the crime problem is unlikely to change, at least in the near future.

We can look at prevention from the perspective of either opportunity reduction or social development. Prevention can involve a number of things, from target hardening to increased surveillance. It can also set as a priority the targeting of violence and offer ways for averting violence. Situational prevention is based on two important assumptions: that crime is most effectively prevented when we attend to the particular characteristics of the type of crime in question; and that we are usually dealing with a rational offender who considers risks, benefits, and ease of accomplishment before committing a crime. It follows from this that raising the costs associated with crimes (which are largely opportunistic in nature) may reduce the frequency with which they occur. Neighbourhood Watch and Block Watch programs assume that crime can be prevented by increasing surveillance and thus the risk of detection and apprehension as it is perceived by the potential offender.

In contrast to the other prevention strategies, social development approaches focus on the serious, repeat offender. A relatively small number of offenders may be responsible for a disproportionately large number of crimes. These individuals tend to have in common many social and demographic characteristics. The aim of crime prevention through social development is to correct the criminogenic social conditions that are assumed to be important causes of crime. The focus of social development is on long-range outcomes that enhance social security and reduce crime incidence.

Community-based policing is a new approach that combines opportunity reduction with social development. The police are shifting their attention away from crime fighting (that is, deterrence-based policing) toward compliance policing, which is more directly integrated with the community. The main objective of compliance law enforcement is to secure conformity with the law through systems that encourage community participation in defining and solving problems. The former emphasis on detecting and punishing violators has given way to an emphasis on providing incentives to individuals to encourage them to comply with the law.

Compliance-based policing recognizes the need to include the public in controlling social disorder beyond merely reporting crime to the police. Bringing together a number of services within the community, as well as community members, can help form a multipronged attack on crime, involving re-education, mediation, opportunity removal, resource mobilization, the targeting of the roots of crime, and problem solving. Our success in controlling crime and diminishing the incidence of criminal events depends on our ability to understand where crime comes from, and also on our commitment to expend resources in broadening our responses to it.

QUESTIONS FOR REVIEW AND DISCUSSION

1. Why is there a popular tendency to think about "more police and more prisons" as the *obvious* solution to the crime problem?
2. What similarities are there in the ways in which Canadian society approaches the problem of crime and the problem of disease?
3. With reference to the community where you live, to what extent are local crime problems wolf, duck, or den problems?
4. How do policies of situational prevention emerge logically from theoretical ideas that emphasize "rational offenders" and "social control"?

5. What does it mean to say that "there is much more to community-based policing than law enforcement"?

6. According to critics, what are some of the more important limitations of traditional responses that assign the central responsibility for crime control to the criminal justice system?

RECOMMENDED READINGS

Brodeur, J-P. 1998. *How to Recognize Good Policing.* Beverly Hills: Sage.

Clarke, R. 1995. "Situational Crime Prevention." In M. Tonry and D. Farrington (eds.), *Building a Safer Society.* Chicago: University of Chicago Press.

Donziger, S.R. (ed.). 1996. *The Real War on Crime: The Report of the National Criminal Justice Commission.* New York: Harper Perennial.

Federation of Canadian Municipalities. 1994. *Youth Violence and Youth Gangs: Responding to Community Concerns.* http://ww2.psepc-sppcc.gc.ca/publications/policing/199456_e.asp

Sherman, L., D.C. Gottfredson, D.L. MacKenzie, J. Eck, P. Reuter, and S.D. Bushway. 1998. *Preventing Crime: What Works, What Doesn't, What's Promising.* National Institute of Justice Research in Brief. Washington, DC: Office of Justice Programs, U.S. Department of Justice. http://www.ncjrs.org/works/

INFOTRAC® COLLEGE EDITION

Explore InfoTrac® College Edition, your online university library, which includes hundreds of popular and scholarly journals in which you can find articles related to the topics in this chapter. Visit InfoTrac® through your web browser (**www.infotrac-college.com**) or through this book's website (**www.criminalevent-4e.nelson.com**).

WHAT'S ON THE WEB?

For chapter links and quizzes, check out the accompanying website at **www.criminalevent-4e.nelson.com**.

GLOSSARY

Numbers in parentheses refer to the chapter containing the main discussion of the term.

Actus reus
The mere physical criminal act. (1)

Adoption studies
The behavioural comparison of near-birth adoptees to their genetic and their adoptive parents. (4)

Aftermath
Events that occur after the committed crime. (2)

Age-specific crime rate
The crime risk for a certain age group. (3)

Aggregate UCR survey
Records the total number of crime incidents reported to the police. (3)

Anomie theory
Theory that says anomie occurs when there is a lack of integration between the cultural goals which people are encouraged to pursue and the legitimate means available for achieving those goals. (4)

Atavism
The theory that offenders are less likely to conform to the demands of contemporary social life because they reflect a more primitive evolutionary condition. (4)

Attachment
The degree to which children are sensitive to the expectations of parents or teachers. (5)

Attachment costs
The costs associated with the weakening of ties to loved ones that may make an arrest a fearsome prospect. (5)

Avoidance behaviour
Behaviour by which victims seek to distance themselves from the kinds of people or situations they perceive as dangerous. (7)

Battered woman syndrome
The sense of helplessness felt by women who come to believe that they can neither leave an abusive relationship nor effectively act to reduce the violence. (1)

Belief
The degree to which youths believe that the conformist values of parents and teachers are worthy of respect. (5)

Body type
In order to determine the relationship between physique and criminality, Sheldon categorized ("somatotyped") three basic types of body build—endomorphic, ectomorphic, and mesomorphic—that are associated with a particular type of temperament. (4)

Broken Windows Theory
Theories that disorder, such as broken windows, leads to more serious crime in a particular neighbourhood. (9)

Bystanders
Criminal event participants whose presence may affect the course of action even though they are not centrally involved in the event as offenders or victims. (2)

Canadian General Social Survey (GSS)
A large Canadian national survey that periodically has as a focus criminal victimization, crime prevention behaviour, and perceptions of crime. (2)

Celerity
With reference to deterrence, the swiftness (perceived or objectively measurable) with which an offender is apprehended and punished. (5)

Certainty
With reference to deterrence, the likelihood (perceived or objectively measurable) that an offender will be apprehended or punished. (5)

Claims-making
The making of assertions about the existence of some problem that requires a policy solution. (7)

Classical school
A set of theories that views the offender as a "rational person" who would be deterred only by the threat of sanction. (4)

Clearance status
A judgment made by the police based on identification of at least one of the offenders involved in an offence. (3)

Commitment
The size of the investment of time and energy that a youth has made to a conventional activity, such as getting good grades. (5)

Commitment costs
The possibility that arrest may jeopardize people's investments in some legitimate activity. (5)

Community-based policing
Expansion of the policing role beyond the traditional narrow reactive role. (11)

Conflict pattern
A pattern of delinquency that occurs in socially disorganized neighbourhoods, where youth often experience the disparity between legitimate goals and legitimate opportunities, and this leads to aggressive behaviour. (4)

Conflict theory
Theory that argues that in a complex society, social groups may pursue different interests and the achievement of success depends on how powerful they are. Responses to crime are interpreted as part of a larger struggle among groups that attempt to use law, or legal control, in pursuit of their own interests. (1)

Consensus theory
Theory proposing that laws and punishment are enforced in order to maintain the collective interests shared by members of society. (1)

Constitutional structure
Predispositions toward crime are claimed to be expressed by biological factors, such as phenotypes (body types) and psychological propensities. (4)

Containment theory
Theory, based on control theory, that youth are insulated from delinquency by inner and outer containments that constrain nonconformist behaviour. (5)

Control theory
A group of theories which proceed from the assumption that criminal behaviour emerges in the absence of controls (internal or external) that might check or contain it. (5)

Corporate crime
Acts committed by businesses in the interests of generating profit and avoiding losses and prosecution. (10)

Costs of victimization
Losses of a physical, financial, emotional, and social nature that can be attributed to the victimization experience. (7)

Crime
A behaviour that breaks the criminal law and is liable to public prosecution and punishment. (1)

Crime funnel
A "volume-reducing system," meaning that there is a high level of attrition as cases travel through various stages of the criminal justice system. (3)

Crime gene
The sociobiological perspective that certain genes may be linked to criminality. (4)

Crime myths
Distorted and misleading pieces of information that nevertheless are accepted as fact. (1)

Crime prevention
The anticipation, recognition, and appraisal of a crime risk and the initiation of some action to reduce or remove it. (11)

Crime rate
A measure that calculates the amount of crime relative to the occurrence of some count of events, conditions, or people. (3)

Criminal event
Comprises its precursors, including the locational and situational factors that bring people together in time and space; the event itself, including how the interactions among participants define the outcomes of their actions; and the aftermath of the event, including the reporting to the police, their response, the harm done, the redress required, and the long-term consequences of the event in terms of public reactions and the changing of laws. (2)

Criminal pattern
A rational delinquency oriented toward the pursuit of monetary objectives, exemplified by organized theft and the sale of illicit goods or services. (4)

Criminological theories
Generalized explanations of why, how, and with what consequences crimes occur. (4)

Crude crime rate
A crime rate measure which employs as a denominator the total population in some jurisdiction and thus which takes no account of the demographic structure of the population. (3)

Cultural goals
Legitimate objectives held by all or by diversely located members of society. (4)

Culture of competition
A cultural atmosphere in which crime is promoted by competition that defines wealth and success as central goals of human activity. (4)

Defensible space
The physical design of a place that may deter an offender. (2)

Deterrence
Theory of prevention in which the threat of punishment or retribution is expected to forestall some act from occurring. (5)

Diet
The concept that the behaviour of certain individuals can be affected by their diet. (4)

Differential adjudication hypothesis
The theory that delinquents with learning disabilities who are arrested and charged are more likely to be convicted of crimes due to their inability to cope with the process of criminal justice adjudication. (4)

Differential arrest hypothesis
The theory that learning disabled children are more likely to be apprehended by the police since they are less likely to conceal their activities. (4)

Differential association
The theory that criminal behaviour is learned in the process of interaction with intimate groups. (4)

Differential disposition hypothesis
The theory that learning disabled delinquents have a higher chance of receiving harsher sentences than other delinquents. (4)

Direct observation
A technique in which an investigator attempts to develop a theory through exploration, or confirm hypotheses through direct participation in and observation of the community or other social grouping being studied. (3)

Duress defence
Some unlawful constraint or influence used to force an individual to commit an act that he or she otherwise would not have committed. (1)

Ecological position
Incorporates geographic and economic relationships within a community into the analyses of crime rates. (3)

Elite-engineered model
Argues that moral panics represent the deliberate attempt on the part of the economic or political elite to promote public concern about some issue that does not involve the elite's interests. (7)

Enterprise crime
Sale of illegal goods and services to customers who know that the goods and services are illegal. (10)

Ethnographic research
Studies in which the researcher attempts to directly observe and interact with the people being studied in a naturally occurring context. (3)

Excuse
Denial of responsibility for an acknowledged wrongful act. (2)

Experimental observation
An experimental method, often used in laboratories, in which the experimenter creates the conditions necessary for observation rather than searching for naturally occurring situations. (3)

Family
Any enduring pattern of social relationships through which domestic life is organized. (8)

Family violence
Child abuse, wife assault, elder abuse, and other forms of physical coercion that are contextualized by domestic living arrangements. (8)

Fear of crime
A concern or anxiety relating to the possibility of criminal victimization and usually assessed in social research through the measurement of attitudes or reported behaviours. (7)

Feminist
A theoretical orientation that critically assesses power relationships in society particularly as those relationships relate to gender inequality. (1)

Focal concerns
Concerns around which life in the lower class is organized: trouble, toughness, smartness, excitement, fate, and autonomy. (4)

Folk hero syndrome
A residual belief that the criminal should be admired for expressing some degree of resistance to convention. (5)

Formal social controls
Conventional methods of technology and physical coercion, such as the police force, used to maintain social order. (5)

General deterrence
The ways in which individuals, on seeing offenders receiving punishment, will be deterred from breaking the law themselves. (5)

General pedigree studies
A non-experimental approach to the study of intergenerational transmission of genetically predisposed behaviour between related individuals. (4)

General strain theory
A focus on negative relationships between people that promote anger, fear, and frustration, which may lead to delinquency. (4)

General theory of crime
The theory that criminal activity appeals to people who are impulsive, short-sighted, physical, risk-taking, nonverbal, and, most importantly, low in self-control. (5)

Genetics
In criminology, a field of study that attempts to determine how certain presocial factors such as family ties and blood relations influence criminal outcomes (often in conjunction with environmental factors). (4)

Grassroots model
Views moral panics as originating in the mood of the public. (7)

Hedonism
The principle that the seeking of pleasure and the avoidance of pain are

the ultimate aims and motivating forces of human action. (4)

Hot spots
High-crime locations. (6)

Household
The social and physical setting within which family life is organized. (8)

Illegitimate means
Two aspects of the delinquent opportunity structure: opportunity to learn and to play the delinquent role. (4)

Improvised news
Similar to rumour; expresses anxieties and uncertainties about some aspect of social life. (1)

Incivility
Physical conditions such as abandoned buildings and strewn trash, as well as social conditions such as public drinking or drug use. (7)

Informal social control
Casual methods of coercion employed by community members to maintain conformity. (5)

Inner containments
The products of effective socialization and the successful internalization of rules regarding acceptable behaviour. (5)

Interactional theory of delinquency
The theory that weak ties to conventional others increase the likelihood of delinquent behaviour, but that these ties can be strengthened over time in response to changing circumstances. (5)

Interest-group model
Argues that moral panics can be set in motion by the actions of small groups, such as politicians, crusading journalists, or professional associations. (7)

Involvement
Participation in the world of conformity so that little time is left for delinquency. (5)

IQ
A measure of intelligence derived from standardized testing procedures that compare individuals' mental and chronological ages. (4)

Justification
Accepting responsibility for the act while denying the immorality of the act. (2)

Karyotype studies
These claim that an individual's chromosomes—that is, their size, shape, and number—are a causal factor in criminality. (4)

La Cosa Nostra
Literally, "our thing." This term is understood as the formal designation of the Italian-American crime syndicate which dominated enterprise crime during the twentieth century. (10)

Labelling theory
The theory that frustration created by particular social arrangements, such as identifying a person as a criminal, may motivate criminal behaviour. (5)

Learning disabilities
Difficulties faced by children and youths such as dyslexia, dysgraphia, aphasia, perceptual and motor deficits, poor intersensory

integration, and minimal brain dysfunction. (4)

Legitimate means
Widely accepted routes of achieving cultural goals through institutions (4).

Leisure
Free time (after work, familial, and other obligations are met) that can be used for play or recreation. (9)

Life course perspective
Adult criminality is strongly influenced by patterns of childhood behaviour, and changes in people's lives affect the likelihood of involvement in crime. (5)

Lifestyle exposure theory
Focuses on patterned ways in which people with certain demographic characteristics distribute their time and energies across a range of activities, and the relationship of these patterned ways to the risk of victimization by motivated offenders. (6)

Mala in se
Crimes that are perceived historically and cross-culturally as wrong. (1)

Mala prohibita
Crimes that are condemned through prohibition. (1)

Mandatory charge rule
Legal or procedural regulation that requires the police, in domestic violence cases, to make an arrest when they have physical evidence that an assault has taken place. (2)

Mens rea
The willful quality of a criminal act. (1)

Middle-class measuring rod
The middle-class ethic, which people use to compare and determine their status, that prescribes an obligation to strive, by dint of rational, ascetic, self-disciplined, and independent activity, to achieve worldly success. (4)

Moral panic
The behaviour of some members of society is seen as so problematic, evil, or harmful to the society that it becomes a social imperative to control the behaviour, punish the offenders, and repair the damage (e.g., the Great European witch hunts). (7)

Neighbourhood Watch
A community crime prevention program in which residents monitor neighbourhood life and exert guardianship over each other's property. (7)

Neuropsychological theory
The theory that people with identical IQ scores can have very different patterns of mental strengths and weaknesses (e.g., verbal skill, spatial perception) that can influence behaviour. (4)

Neutralization theory
The view that delinquents often use linguistic constructions (that is, excuses or rationalizations) to reduce the guilt resulting from their delinquent behaviour. (4)

Norms
Rules that govern social activities and define social roles, role relations, and standards of appropriate conduct. (1)

Occasional offenders
Commit crimes when opportunities

or situational inducements present themselves. (8)

Occupancy probes
Imaginative methods that the offender uses to determine whether anyone is home. (8)

Occupational crime
Violation of legal norms governing lawful occupational endeavours. (10)

Offender reports
Data gathered from a sample of known offenders, such as prison inmates. (3)

Opportunity reduction
Focuses on how social and environmental factors can be brought to bear on the reduction of crime opportunities. (11)

Outer containments
Aspects of the individual's social environment (e.g., primary groups) that help ensure that delinquent behaviour does not occur. (5)

Permissive environs
Social settings, such as bars and parties, where individuals feel free of many of the constraints that operate in other settings, such as the school and the workplace. (9)

Positive leisure
Forms of leisure activity that link adolescents to conformist others and that are thought to insulate against delinquency. (9)

Positivist school
The philosophical position, developed by Auguste Comte, that scientific knowledge can come only from direct observation, experimentation, and provision of quantitative data. (4)

Power–control theory
The theory that due to differential control (that is, girls are subject to greater control than boys) within the patriarchal family, males have a higher propensity to engage in risk taking and delinquent behaviour. (5)

Precursors
Situational factors that bring people together in time and space. (2)

Proactive policing
Police involvement in incidents as a result of their own investigative or patrol activities, which bring to their attention events that may be designated as crimes. (2)

Professional offenders
Burglars with considerable technical competence who are connected to a network of thieves, tipsters, and fences. (8)

Psychopathology
Study of abnormal behaviour. (4)

Psychopathy
A sociopathic disorder characterized by lack of moral development and the inability to show loyalty to others. (4)

Punishment
Confinement, restriction of activities, infliction of pain, and other measures taken to exact retribution, to enforce compliance, or to bring about behavioural changes. (5)

Rational choice theories
These focus on the offenders' actions and decisions as they are based on

perceived benefits rather than on precipitating or psychological factors. (5)

Rational reconstruction
Occurs when individuals recall their crimes and suggest there was more planning than actually took place. (8)

Reactive policing
Police involvement in criminal events at the request of a member of the public. (2)

Recidivism
Repetition or recurrence of delinquent or criminal behaviour or behaviour disorder, especially following punishment or rehabilitation. (8)

Retreatist pattern
Pattern exhibited by people who are unable to succeed through either legitimate or illegitimate means (double-failures), and who resort to delinquency organized around the consumption of drugs. (4)

Risky lifestyle
A regular pattern of activities that exposes individuals to higher levels of risk of criminal victimization. (9)

Routine activities theory
A theory which proposes that the presence of a motivated offender, the presence of a suitable target, and the absence of capable guardianship are vital to the completion of a crime. (6)

School failure hypothesis
The theory that self-perpetuating academic failure resulting from learning disabilities causes frustration and aggressive behaviour. (4)

Secondary deviance
The idea that feedback that consistently sends the message that one is a disreputable person may eventually lead to the acceptance of the definition. (5)

Self-defence
Actions taken to protect oneself or one's property, involving reasonable force, in the face of a threat. (1)

Self-fulfilling prophecy
The theory that people who are perceived as beyond redemption will come to act as if they are. (5)

Self-report studies
Respondents' reports about their involvement as offenders. (3)

Severity
With reference to deterrence, the perceived or actual seriousness of the penalty for a legal infraction. (5)

Situated transaction
Process of interaction involving two or more individuals that lasts as long as they find themselves in one another's presence. (6)

Situational crime prevention
Efforts to prevent crime that focus on the suppression of criminal opportunities (rather than, for instance, the reform of offenders). (11)

Situational deterrence
The ways in which the offender's fear of apprehension is related to the specific circumstances of the criminal event. (5)

Social bond
In social control theory, the strength and quality of the relationships that

link potential offenders to conformist others and that serve to insulate them from criminal influences. (5)

Social control
The regulatory institutions of society—especially the law enforcement and judicial systems—and how they operate, encompassing rule enforcement at all levels. (1)

Social development approach
An approach to crime prevention which attempts to create social conditions that discourage long-term serious offending and that empower potential victims while at the same time contributing to the rebuilding of communities. (11)

Social disorganization
Long-term, widespread deterioration of social order and control in a population. (5)

Social domains
Major spheres of life in which we spend most of our time and energy. (2)

Social organization
Coherence and continuity in the social environment, and rational co-operation among individuals and social institutions. (8)

Sociopathy
Antisocial personality disorder involving a marked lack of ethical or moral development. (4)

Specific/special deterrence
The ways in which individuals are deterred from offending or reoffending by receiving punishment. (5)

Stigma of arrest
The belief that apprehension by the police may harm one's reputation. (5)

Strain theory
The theory that the constant emphasis on success in society and its possible attainment consistently contradicts the actual opportunity facing people—especially at the bottom of society, where the greatest amount of crime occurs. (4)

Subculture
A group of people in a dominant culture with different values, evident in their expression of deviant behaviour. (4)

Subculture of violence
A subculture in which disproportionate rates of criminal violence are the product of a group's commitment to subcultural values and norms that condone violence as an acceptable means of resolving interpersonal conflict. (4)

Subterranean values
Values that are held by many in society, although they may conflict with other cherished values. (4)

Susceptibility hypothesis
The theory that learning disabled students have unique characteristics, such as impulsiveness and irritability, and thus are more likely to become delinquent. (4)

Symbolic interactionism
The role of linguistic interaction in developing a social identity and functioning according to shared norms and values. (6)

Target hardening
Increasing protection of premises to deter a criminal through fear of detection or because the target has been made inaccessible. (8)

Telescoping
Reporting a crime as occurring during the reference period when it actually occurred at an earlier time. (3)

Theory of the bond
Theory that strong social bonds insulate youths against the delinquent environment. (5)

Trace elements
Mineral content in the subject's body which determines episodic violence or antisocial behaviour. (4)

Trajectories
In the life course perspective, these describe the directions in which lives seem to be moving. (5)

Transactions
The interactions between individuals that have led to the outcome of a crime being committed. (2)

Transitions
In the life course perspective, specific events that may or may not alter trajectories. (5)

Twin studies
A non-experimental study designed to research and compare criminal predispositions between dizygotic and monozygotic twins. (4)

Twinkie defence
When a defendant experiences diminished mental capacity and is therefore not guilty of criminal behaviour due to an over-consumption of junk food. (4)

Uniform Crime Reporting system (UCR)
The UCR is a survey collated by Statistics Canada based on crime reports from police departments nationwide. The information is available to the government, criminologists, politicians, and the mass media. (3)

Urban legend
Captivating and plausible fictional oral narratives that are widely regarded as true stories. (1)

Valence issues
Issues that do not have an adversarial quality. (7)

Vandalism
The deliberate damaging or destruction of public or private property. (9)

Victim precipitation
Occurs when the opportunity for crime is created by some action of the victim. (6)

Victim reports/surveys
Large-scale studies that ask individuals about their experience with crime. (3)

Victimless crimes
Criminal events in which a victim does not exist in any direct and immediate way. Examples: gambling or abusing drugs by personal choice. (2)

Vulnerability conversion
Especially for victims of violence, development of a sudden understanding by victims that they are more susceptible to the dangers of life than they thought. (7)

White-collar crime
A crime committed by a person of respectability and high status in the course of his or her occupation. (10)

Workplace crime
Criminal events that emerge out of relations formed by labour force participation in the context of legitimate or illegitimate economies. (10)

YCJA
The *Youth Criminal Justice Act* was passed by the Parliament of Canada in 2002, and became effective in 2003. The Act details the principles, rules, and procedures regarding youthful offenders. (1)

REFERENCES

Addington, L.A. 2003. "Students Fear after Columbine: Findings from a Randomized Experiment." *Journal of Quantitative Criminology* 19(4): 367–87.

Agnew, R. 1985a. "A Revised Strain Theory of Delinquency." *Social Forces* 64(1): 151–67.

——— 1985b. "Neutralizing the Impact of Crime." *Criminal Justice and Behavior* 12: 221–39.

——— 1990. "The Origins of Delinquent Events: An Examination of Offender Accounts." *Journal of Research in Crime and Delinquency* 27(3): 267–94.

——— 1992. "Foundation for a General Strain Theory of Crime and Delinquency." *Criminology* 30: 47–87.

——— 1993. "Why Do They Do It? An Examination of the Intervening Mechanisms between 'Social Control' Variables and Delinquency." *Journal of Research in Crime and Delinquency* 30(3): 245–66.

Agnew, R., and L. Broidy. 1997. "Gender and Crime: a General Strain Theory Perspective." *Journal of Research in Crime and Delinquency* 34(3): 275–306.

Agnew, R., and A.R. Peters. 1986. "The Techniques of Neutralization: An Analysis of Predisposing and Situational Factors." *Criminal Justice and Behavior* 13: 81–97.

Agnew, R., and D.M. Peterson. 1989. "Leisure and Delinquency." *Social Problems* 36(4): 332–50.

Agnew, R., and H.R. White. 1992. "An Empirical Test of General Strain Theory." *Criminology* 30: 475–99.

Akers, R.L. 1985. *Deviant Behavior: A Social Learning Approach.* Belmont: Wadsworth.

——— 1994. *Criminological Theories.* Los Angeles: Roxbury Publishing.

Alarid, L.F., V.S. Burton, Jr., and F.T. Cullen. 2000. "Gender and Crime among Felony Offenders: Assessing the Generality of Social Control and Differential Association Theories." *Journal of Research in Crime and Delinquency* 37(2): 171–99.

Alexander, A.D., and T.J. Bernard. 2002. "A Critique of Mark Colvin's, Crime and Coercion: An Integrated Theory of Chronic Criminality." *Crime, Law and Social Change* 38(4): 389–98.

Almey, M. 2000. "Family Status." *Women in Canada 2000.* Ottawa: Minister of Industry.

Amir, M. 1971. *Patterns of Forcible Rape.* Chicago: University of Chicago Press.

Andersen, M.A., G.W. Jenion, and M.L. Jenion. 2003. "Conventional Calculations of Homicide Rates Lead to an Inaccurate Reflection of Canadian Trends." *Canadian*

Journal of Criminology and Criminal Justice 45(1): 1.

Anderson, A.L., and R.F. Meier. 2004. "Interactions and the Criminal Event Perspective." *Journal of Contemporary Criminal Justice* 20(4): 416–40.

Anderson, C.A., and K.E. Dill. 2000. "Video Games and Aggressive Thoughts, Feelings, and Behavior in the Laboratory and Life." *Journal of Personality and Social Psychology* 78(4): 772–90.

Anderson, E. 1999. *Code of the Street: Decency, Violence and the Moral Life of the Inner City.* New York: W.W. Norton.

Anderson, J.F., T. Grandison, and L. Dyson. 1996. "Victims of Random Violence and the Public Health Implication: A Health Care or Criminal Justice Issue." *Journal of Criminal Justice* 24(5): 379–91.

Armstrong, E.G. 2001. "Gangsta Misogyny: A Content Analysis of the Portrayals of Violence against Women in Rap Music 1987–1993." *Journal of Criminal Justice and Popular Culture* 8(2): 96–126.

Arneklev, B.J., H.G. Grasmick, and R.J. Bursik, Jr. 1999. "Evaluating the Dimensionality and Invariance of 'Low Self-Control.'" *Journal of Quantitative Criminology* 15(3): 307–31.

Arnold, B.L., and J. Hagan. 1992. "Careers of Misconduct: Prosecuted Professional Deviance among Lawyers." *American Sociological Review* 57(6): 771–80.

Asbridge, M., R.E. Mann, R. Flam-Zalcman, and G. Stoduto. 2004. "The Criminalization of Impaired Driving in Canada: Assessing the Deterrent Impact of Canada's First Per Se Law." *Journal of Studies on Alcohol* 65(4): 450–59.

AuCoin, K. 2003. "Violence and Abuse against Children and Youth by Family Members." In H. Johnson and K. AuCoin (eds.) *Family Violence in Canada: A Statistical Profile, 2003.* Ottawa: Minister of Industry.

———— 2005a. "Children and Youth as Victims of Violent Crime." *Juristat* 25(1).

———— 2005b. *Family Violence in Canada: A Statistical Profile.* Ottawa: Centre for Justice Statistics, Statistics Canada.

———— 2005c. "Stalking—Criminal Harassment." In K. AuCoin (ed.), *Family Violence in Canada: A Statistical Profile.* Ottawa: Centre for Justice Statistics, Statistics Canada.

Auditor General of Canada. 2002a. *Department of Justice—Costs of Implementing the Canadian Firearms Program.* Ottawa: Office of the Auditor General. http://www.oag-bvg.gc.ca/domino/reports.nsf/html/20021210ce.html#ch10hd3a

———— 2002b. *The Criminal Justice System: Significant Challenges.* Ottawa: Office of the Auditor General. http://www.oag-bvg.gc.ca/domino/media.nsf/html/02pr04_e.html

——— 2003. *Government-Wide Audit of Sponsorship, Advertising, and Public Opinion Research.* Office of the Auditor General. http://www.oag-bvg.gc.ca/domino/media.nsf/html/20031103pr_e.html

Austin, D.M., L.A. Furr, and M. Spine. 2002. "The Effects of Neighborhood Conditions on Perceptions of Safety." *Journal of Criminal Justice* 30(5): 417–27.

Austin, J. 2001. *Taking the Train: How Graffiti Art became an Urban Crisis in New York City.* New York: Columbia University Press.

Bagdikian, B. 2004. *The New Media Monopoly.* Boston: Beacon Press.

Baldassare, M. 1986. "The Elderly and Fear of Crime." *Sociology and Social Research* 70: 218–21.

Balkin, S. 1979. "Victimization Rates, Safety and Fear of Crime." *Social Problems* 26(3): 343–58.

Baron, S.W. 1989. "The Canadian West Coast Punk Subculture: A Field Study." *Canadian Journal of Sociology* 14(3): 289–316.

——— 1997. "Risky Lifestyles and the Link between Offending and Victimization." *Studies on Crime and Crime Prevention* 6(1): 53–71.

——— 2002. "Street Youth and Labor Market Strain." *Journal of Criminal Justice* 30(6): 519–33.

——— 2003. "Self-control, Social Consequences and Criminal Behavior: Street Youth and the General Theory of Crime." *Journal of Research in Crime and Delinquency* 40(4): 403–25.

——— 2004. "General Strain, Street Youth and Crime: A Test of Agnew's Revised Theory." *Criminology* 42(2): 457–83.

Baron, S.W., and T.F Hartnagel. 1996. "'Lock em up': Attitudes towards Punishing Juvenile Offenders." *Canadian Journal of Criminology* 38: 191–212.

Baron, S.W., L.W. Kennedy, and D. Forde. 2001. "Conflict Styles among Street Youth and the General Theory of Crime." *Justice Quarterly* 18(4): 759–90.

Bartol, Curt R. 1991. *Criminal Behaviour: A Psychosocial Approach.* 3rd ed. Englewood Cliffs, NJ: Prentice-Hall.

Bartusch, D.R., D.R. Lynam, T.E. Moffitt, and P.A. Silva. 1997. "Is Age Important? Testing a General versus a Developmental Theory of Antisocial Behavior." *Criminology* 35(1): 13–47.

Baumer, T.L. 1978. "Research on Fear of Crime in the United States." *Victimology* 3: 254–64.

Baunach, P.J. 1990. "State Prisons and Inmates: The Census and Survey." In D.L. Mackenzie, P.J. Baunach, and R.R. Robert (eds.), *Measuring Crime: Large-Scale, Long-Range Efforts.* Albany: State University of New York.

Bayley, D.H. 1985. *Patterns of Policing: A Comparative International Analysis.* New Brunswick, NJ: Rutgers University Press.

——— 1988. "Community Policing: A Report from the Devil's

Advocate." In J.R. Greene and D. Mastrofski (eds.), *Community Policing: Rhetoric or Reality.* New York: Praeger.

———— 1994. *Police for the Future.* New York: Oxford University Press.

Beare, M. 2002. "Organized Corporate Criminality: Tobacco smuggling between Canada and The United States." *Crime, Law and Social Change* 37(3): 225–343.

Beare, M.E. 1996. *Criminal Conspiracies.* Scarborough: Nelson Canada.

Beattie, K. 2005. "Family Homicides." In K. AuCoin (ed.), *Family Violence in Canada: A Statistical Profile.* Ottawa: Minister of Industry.

Bechhofer, L., and A. Parrot. 1991. "What Is Acquaintance Rape?" In A. Parrot and L. Bechhofer (eds.), *Acquaintance Rape: The Hidden Crime.* New York: John Wiley.

Becker, H.S. 1963. *Outsiders: Studies in the Sociology of Deviance.* New York: Free Press.

Beckett, K., and T. Sasson. 2000. *The Politics of Injustice.* Thousand Oaks: Pine Forge Press.

Bell, D. 1953. "Crime as an American Way of Life." *The Antioch Review* 13 (June): 131–54.

Bell, D.J. 1987. "The Victim–Offender Relationship: A Determinant Factor in Police Domestic Dispute Dispositions." *Marriage and Family Review* 12(1/2): 87–102.

Bellair, P.E. 2000. "Informal Surveillance and Street Crime: A Complex Relationship." *Criminology* 38(1): 137–70.

Bennett, T. 1989. "Burglars' Choice of Targets." In D.J. Evans and D.T. Herbert (eds.), *The Geography of Crime.* London: Routledge.

Bennett, T., and R. Wright. 1984. *Burglars on Burglary.* Brookfield: Gower.

Benson, D., C. Charlton, and F. Goodhart. 1992. "Acquaintance Rape on Campus: A Literature Review." *College Health* 40 (January): 157–65.

Benson, M.L. 1985. "Denying the Guilty Mind: Accounting for Involvement in a White-Collar Crime." *Criminology* 23(4): 583–607.

Benson, M.L., and E. Moore. 1992. "Are White Collar and Common Offenders the Same? An Empirical and Theoretical Critique of a Recently Proposed General Theory of Crime." *Journal of Research in Crime and Delinquency* 29(3): 251–72.

Bernard, T.J. 1981. "The Distinction between Conflict and Radical Criminology." *Journal of Criminal Law and Criminology* 72(1): 362–79.

Bernstein, L. 2002. *The Greatest Menace.* Amherst MA: University of Massachusetts Press.

Besserer, S., and C. Trainor. 2000. "Criminal Victimization in Canada, 1999." *Juristat* 20(10).

Best, J. 1988. "Missing Children: Misleading Statistics." *The Public Interest* 92 (Summer): 84–92.

——— 1990. *Threatened Children.* Chicago: University of Chicago Press.

——— 1995. *Images of Issues.* New York: Aldine de Gruyter.

——— 1999. *Random Violence: How We Talk about New Crimes and New Victims.* Berkeley: University of California Press.

——— 2001. *Damned Lies and Statistics: Untangling Numbers from the Media, Politicians and Activists.* Berkeley: University of California Press.

——— 2002. "Monster Hype." *Education Next* (Summer): 51–55.

Best, J., and D.F. Luckenbill. 1994. *Organizing Deviance.* 2nd ed. Englewood Cliffs: Prentice Hall.

Biderman, A.D., and J.P. Lynch. 1991. *Understanding Crime Incidence Statistics.* New York: Springer-Verlag.

Birkbeck, C., and G. LaFree. 1993. "The Situational Analysis of Crime and Deviance." *Annual Review of Sociology* 19: 113–37.

Black, D. 1970. "Production of Crime Rates." *American Sociological Review* 35: 733–47.

——— 1971. "The Social Organization of Arrest." *Stanford Law Review* 23: 1087–1111.

——— 1976. *The Behavior of Law.* New York: Academic Press.

——— 1980. *The Manners and Customs of the Police.* New York: Academic Press.

——— 1983. "Crime as Social Control." *American Sociological Review* 48 (February): 34–45.

Black, W. 2003. "Getting away with Murder." *Belleville Pioneer* (online edition), October 25, 2003. http://www.thepioneer.com/oct25_editorial.htm

Blackstock, C., N. Troome, and M. Bennet. 2004. "Child Maltreatment Investigation Among Aboriginal and Non-Aboriginal Families in Canada." *Violence Against Women* 10(8): 901–16.

Blackwell, B.S., and A.R. Piquero. 2005. "On the Relationships Between Gender, Power Control, Self-Control, and Crime" *Journal of Criminal Justice* 33(1): 1–17.

Blau, J.R., and P.M. Blau. 1982. "The Cost of Inequality: Metropolitan Structure and Violent Crime." *American Sociological Review* 4 (February): 114–29.

Block, C.R., and R.L. Block. 1984. "Crime Definition, Crime Measurement, and Victim Surveys." *Journal of Social Issues* 40(1): 137–60.

Block, R. 1974. "Why Notify the Police? The Victim's Decision to Notify the Police of an Assault." *Criminology* 11(4): 555–69.

Block, R., M. Felson, and C.R. Block. 1984. "Crime Victimization Rates for Incumbents of

246 Occupations." *Sociology and Social Research* 69(3): 442–51.

Blumstein, A., J. Cohen, and R. Rosenfeld. 1992. "The UCR–NCS Relationship Revisited: A Reply to Menard." *Criminology* 30(1): 115–24.

Bocij, P., and L. McFarlane. 2003. "The Internet: A Discussion of Some New and Emerging Threats to Young People." *Police Journal* 76(1): 3–13.

Bockman, L.S. 1991. "Interest, Ideology and Claims-Making Activity." *Sociological Inquiry* 61(4): 452–70.

Bograd, M. 1988. "How Battered Women and Abusive Men Account for Domestic Violence: Excuses, Justifications or Explanations." In G.T. Hotaling, D. Finkelhor, J.T. Kirkpatrick, and M.A. Straus (eds.), *Coping with Family Violence.* Newbury Park: Sage.

Bohm, R.M. 1997. *A Primer on Crime and Delinquency.* Belmont: Wadsworth.

Boritch, H. 1992. "Gender and Criminal Court Outcomes: An Historical Analysis." *Criminology* 30(3): 293–325.

————— 1997. *Fallen Women: Female Crime and Criminal Justice in Canada.* Scarborough: Nelson Canada.

Bottomley, A.K., and K. Pease. 1986. *Crime and Punishment— Interpreting the Data.* Philadelphia: Open University Press.

Box, S. 1981. *Deviance, Reality, and Society.* London: Holt, Rinehart & Winston.

Boyd, N. 2000. "Canadian Criminal Law." In R.A. Silverman, J.J. Teevan, and V.F. Sacco (eds.), *Crime in Canadian Society,* 6th ed., pp. 20–31. Toronto: Harcourt Brace.

————— 2002. *Canadian Law: An Introduction.* 3rd ed. Toronto: Nelson Thomson.

————— 2003. "Gun Control: Placing Costs in Context." *Canadian Journal of Criminology and Criminal Justice* 45(4): 473–78.

Braithwaite, J. 1989. *Crime, Shame and Reintegration.* Cambridge: Cambridge University Press.

Brannigan, A., W. Gemmell and D. Pevalin. 2002. "Self-Control and Social Control in Childhood Misconduct and Aggression: The Role of Family Structure, Hyperactivity and Hostile Parenting." *Canadian Journal of Criminology* 44(2): 119–42.

Brantingham, P.J., and P.L. Brantingham. 1984. *Patterns in Crime.* New York: Macmillan.

Brantingham, P.J., and F.L. Faust. 1976. "A Conceptual Model of Crime Prevention." *Crime and Delinquency* 22: 284–96.

Brantingham, P.J., S. Mu, and A. Verma. 1995. "Patterns in Canadian Crime." In M.A. Jackson and C.T. Griffiths (eds.), *Canadian Criminology,* pp. 187–245. Toronto: Harcourt Brace.

Brantingham, P.L. 1989. "Crime Prevention: The North American Experience." In D.J. Evans and D.T. Herbert (eds.), *The Geography of Crime*. London: Routledge.

Brantingham, P.L., and P.J. Brantingham. 1990. "Situational Crime Prevention in Practice." *Canadian Journal of Criminology* 32(1): 17–40.

———. 1993. "Situational Crime Prevention in Practice." In R.V. Clarke and M. Felson (eds.), *Routine Activity and Rational Choice*. New Brunswick, NJ: Transaction.

———. 2001. "The Implications of the Criminal Event Model for Crime Prevention." In R.F. Meier, L.W. Kennedy, and V.F. Sacco (eds.), *The Process and Structure of Crime*. Vol. 9, Advances in Criminological Theory. Piscataway: Transaction Press.

Brantingham, P.L., P.J. Brantingham, and W. Taylor. 2005. "Situational Crime Prevention as a Key Component in Embedded Crime Prevention." *Canadian Journal of Criminology and Criminal Justice* 47(2): 271–92.

Brennan, P.A., S.A. Mednick, and J. Volavka. 1995. "Biomedical Factors in Crime." In J.Q. Wilson and J. Petersilia (eds.), *Crime*, pp. 65–90. San Francisco: Institute for Contemporary Studies Press.

Brezina, T. 1996. "Adapting to Strain: An Examination of Delinquent Coping Responses." *Criminology* 34(1): 39–60.

———. 1999. "Teenage Violence Towards Parents as an Adaptation to Family Strain: Evidence from a National Survey of Male Adolescents." *Youth and Society* 30(4): 416–44.

———. 2000. "Delinquent Problem Solving." *Journal of Research in Crime and Delinquency* 37(1): 3–30.

Brezina, T., R. Agnew, and F.T. Cullen. 2004. "The Code of the Street: A Quantitative Assessment of Elijah Anderson's Subculture of Violence Thesis and Its Contribution to Youth Violence Research." *Youth Violence and Juvenile Justice* 2(4): 303–28.

Brillon, Y. 1985. "Public Opinion about the Penal System: A Cynical View of Criminal Justice." In D. Gibson and J.K. Baldwin (eds.), *Law in a Cynical Society? Opinion and Law in the 1980s*. Calgary: Carswell.

Brodeur, J-P. 1998. *How to Recognize Good Policing*. Beverly Hills: Sage.

Brown, B., and W.R. Benedict. 2004. "Bullets, Blades, and Being Afraid in Hispanic High Schools: An Exploratory Study of the Presence of Weapons and Fear of Weapon-Associated Victimization Among High School Students in a Border Town". *Crime & Delinquency* 50(3): 372–94.

Browning, C.R. 2002. "The Span of Collective Efficacy: Extending Social Disorganization Theory to

Partner Violence." *Journal of Marriage and Family* 64(4): 833–50.

Brownridge, D.A. 2003. "Male Partner Violence Against Aboriginal Women in Canada." *Journal of Interpersonal Violence* 18(1): 65–83.

Brownridge, D.A. and S.S. Halli. 2002. "Double Jeopardy? Violence against Immigrant Women in Canada." *Violence and Victims* 17(4): 455–71.

Brunvand, J.H. 1981. *The Vanishing Hitchhiker: American Urban Legends and Their Meaning.* New York: Norton.

———— 1984. *The Choking Doberman and Other "New" Urban Legends.* New York: Norton.

———— 1986. *The Mexican Pet.* New York: Norton.

———— 1989. *Curses! Broiled Again!* New York: Norton.

Budd, T. 1999. *Burglary of Domestic Dwellings: Findings from the British Crime Survey.* London: Home Office Statistical Bulletin.

Bunge, V.P., H. Johnson, and T.A. Baldé. 2005. *Exploring Crime Patterns in Canada.* Ottawa: Canadian Centre for Justice Statistics, Statistics Canada.

Burgess, A.W., L.L. Holmstrom, and M.P. McCausland. 1977. "Child Sexual Assault by a Family Member: Decisions Following Disclosure." *Victimology: An International Journal* 2(2): 236–50.

Bursik R.J. 1999. "The Informal Control of Crime through Neighborhood Networks." *Sociological Focus* 32(1): 85–97.

Bursik, Jr., R.J., and H.G. Grasmick. 1993. *Neighborhoods and Crime: The Dimensions of Effective Community Control.* New York: Lexington Books.

Burt, M.R., and B.L. Katz. 1985. "Rape, Robbery and Burglary: Responses to Actual and Feared Criminal Victimization with Special Focus on Women and the Elderly." *Victimology* 10: 325–58.

Burton, Jr., V.S., F.T. Cullen, T.D. Evans, L.F. Alarid, and R.G. Dunaway. 1998. "Gender, Self-Control." *Journal of Research in Crime and Delinquency* 35(2): 123–47.

Calavita, K., and H.N. Pontell. 1991. "'Other People's Money' Revisited: Collective Embezzlement in the Savings and Loan Insurance Industries." *Social Problems* 38(1): 94–112.

Calhoun, T.C., and G. Weaver. 1996. "Rational Decision-Making among Male Street Prostitutes." *Deviant Behavior* 17: 209–27.

Canada. 1982. *The Criminal Law in Canadian Society.* Ottawa: Government of Canada.

Canadian Centre for Justice Statistics. 1990. *The Development of Data Quality Assessment Procedures for the Uniform Crime Reporting Survey: A Case Study of Calgary–Edmonton.* Ottawa: Statistics Canada.

———— 2004. *Canadian Crime Statistics 2003.* Ottawa: Statistics Canada.

Canadian Council on Social Development. No date. *Crime Prevention through Social Development.* http://www.ccsd.ca/cpsd/ccsd/sd.htm

Canadian Criminal Justice Association. 1989. "Safer Communities: A Social Strategy for Crime Prevention in Canada." *Canadian Journal of Criminology* 31(4): 359–63.

Canadian General Social Survey. 2005. Statistics Canada, Family, Household and Social Statistics Division.

Carnochan, T. 2005. "Safe Streets and Dangerous Rhetoric: Press Constructions of Squeegeeing and Panhandling." MA Thesis. Kingston, ON: Department of Sociology, Queen's University.

Carrington, P.J. 2001. "Population Aging and Crime in Canada, 2000–2041." *Canadian Journal of Criminology* 43(3): 331–57.

Carrington, P.J., and J.L. Schulenburg. 2004. "The Youth Criminal Justice Act." *Canadian Journal of Criminology and Criminal Justice* 46(3): 219–389.

Carter, D.L. 1985. "Hispanic Perceptions of Police Performance: An Empirical Assessment." *Journal of Criminal Justice* 13: 487–500.

Cavender, G. 1998. "In the 'Shadow of Shadows': Television Reality Crime Programming." In M. Fishman and G. Cavender (eds.), *Entertaining Crime: Television Reality Programs.* New York: Aldine de Gruyter.

Center for Internet Addiction Recovery. No date. http://www.netaddiction.com/faq.htm

Center for Problem Oriented Policing. 2003. "Situational Crime Prevention." http://www.popcenter.org/about-situational.htm

Centers for Disease Control and Prevention. 2006. *Intimate Partner Fact Sheet.* http://www.cdc.gov/ncipc/factsheets/ipvfacts.htm

Cernkovitch, S.A., P.C. Giordano, and J.L. Ruddolph. 2000. "Race, Crime, and the American Dream." *Journal of Research in Crime and Delinquency* 37(2): 131–70.

Chambliss, W. 1975. "On the Paucity of Original Research on Organized Crime: A Footnote to Galliher and Cain." *The American Sociologist* 10: 36–39.

Chambliss, W.J. 1986. "On Lawmaking." In S. Brickey and E. Comack (eds.), *The Social Basis of Law.* Toronto: Garamond Press.

Chapple, C.L. 2005. "Self-control, Peer Relations, and Delinquency." *Justice Quarterly* 22(1): 89–105.

Chen, J.J., and D.E. Giles. 2004. "Gender Convergence in Crime: Evidence from Canadian Adult Offense Charge Data." *Journal of Criminal Justice* 32(6): 593–606.

Chermak, S. 1998. "Predicting Crime Story Salience: The Effects of Crime, Victim, and Defendant Characteristics." *Journal of Criminal Justice* 26(1): 61–70.

Chibnall, S. 1977. *Law-and-Order News.* London: Tavistock.

Chicago Community Policing Evaluation Consortium. 2000. *Community Policing in Chicago, Year Seven: An Interim Report.* Chicago: Illinois Criminal Justice Information Authority.

Child & Family Canada. http://www. cfc-efc.ca/docs/mnet/ 00001239.htm

Chilton, R. 1991. "Images of Crime: Crime Statistics and Their Impact." In J.F. Sheley (ed.), *Criminology: A Contemporary Handbook*: pp. 45–65. Belmont: Wadsworth.

Clairmont, D. 1990. *To the Forefront: Community-Based Zone Policing in Halifax.* Ottawa: Canadian Police College.

Clark, R.D. 1988. "Celerity and Specific Deterrence: A Look at the Evidence." *Canadian Journal of Criminology* 30(2): 109–20.

Clarke, R.V. 1995. "Situational Crime Prevention." In M. Tonry and D. Farrington (eds.), *Building a Safer Society.* Chicago: University of Chicago Press.

Clarke, R.V. 1992. "Introduction." In R.V. Clarke (ed.), *Situational Crime Prevention.* Albany: Harrow & Heston.

—— 1993. *Crime Prevention Studies*, Vol. 1. Monsey: Criminal Justice Press.

—— 1994. *Crime Prevention Studies*, Vol. 2. Monsey: Criminal Justice Press.

Clarke, R.V., P. Ekblom, M. Hough, and P. Mayhew. 1985. "Elderly Victims of Crime and Exposure to Risk." *Journal of Criminal Justice* 23: 1–9.

Clarke, R.V., and M. Felson. 1993. "Introduction: Criminology, Routine Activity, and Rational Choice." In R.V. Clarke and M. Felson (eds.), *Routine Activity and Rational Choice.* New Brunswick, NJ: Transaction Publishers.

Clermont, Y. 1996. "Robbery." In L.W. Kennedy and V.F. Sacco (eds.), *Crime Counts: A Criminal Event Analysis.* Toronto: Nelson.

Cloward, R.A. 1959. "Illegitimate Means, Anomie, and Deviant Behavior." The Bobbs-Merrill Reprint Series in the Social Sciences. Reprinted by permission of *American Sociological Review* 24 (April): 164–76.

Cloward, R.A., and L.E. Ohlin. 1960. *Delinquency and Opportunity.* New York: Free Press.

Cohen, A.K. 1955. *Delinquent Boys: The Culture of the Gang.* New York: Free Press.

Cohen, L.E., and D. Cantor. 1981. "Residential Burglary in the United States: Lifestyle and Demographic Factors Associated with the Probability of

Victimization." *Journal of Research in Crime and Delinquency* 18(1): 113–27.

Cohen, L.E., and M. Felson. 1979. "Social Change and Crime Rate Trends: A Routine Activity Approach." *American Sociological Review* 44 (August): 588–608.

Cohen, L.E., J.R. Kluegel, and K.C. Land. 1981. "Social Inequality and Predatory Criminal Victimization: An Exposition and Test of a Formal Theory." *American Sociological Review* 46 (October): 505–24.

Cohen, M. 2005. *The Costs of Crime and Justice*. London: Routledge.

Cohen, M.A. 1998. "The Monetary Value of Saving a High-Risk Youth." *Journal of Quantitative Criminology* 14(1): 5–33.

Cohen, S. 1972. *Folk Devils and Moral Panics*. London: MacGibbon & Kee.

Coleman, C., and C. Norris. 2000. *Introducing Criminology*. Portland: Willan Publishing.

Coleman, J.W. 1987. "Toward an Integrated Theory of White-Collar Crime." *American Journal of Sociology* 93(2): 406–39.

——— 1991. "Respectable Crime." In J.F. Sheley (ed.), *Criminology: A Contemporary Handbook*. Belmont: Wadsworth.

Collins, J.J., B.G. Cox, and P.A. Langan. 1987. "Job Activities and Personal Crime Victimization: Implications for Theory." *Social Science Research* 16: 345–60.

Colvin, M. 2000. *Crime and Coercion: An Integrated Theory of Criminality*. New York: St Martin's Press.

Colvin, M., F.T. Cullen, and V.V. Thomas. 2002. "Coercion, Social Support and Crime: An Emerging Theoretical Consensus." *Criminology* 40(1): 19–42.

Comack, E. 1986. "'We Will Get Some Good out of this Riot Yet': The Canadian State, Drug Legislation and Class Conflict." In S. Brickey and E. Comack (eds.), *The Social Basis of Law*. Toronto: Garamond.

Comack, E., V. Chopyk, and L. Wood. 2000. *Mean Streets: The Social Location, Gender Dynamic and Patterns of Violent Crime in Winnipeg*. Ottawa: Canadian Center for Policy Alternatives.

Compas Inc. 2005. *Crime, Punishment, Compensation and CEOs*. http://www.compas.ca/data/050627-CrimePunishment-PB.pdf

Conklin, J.E. 1975. *The Impact of Crime*. New York: Macmillan.

Cook, F.L., and W.G. Skogan. 1990. "Agenda Setting and the Rise and Fall of Policy Issues: The Case of Criminal Victimization of the Elderly." *Environment and Planning C: Government and Policy* 8: 395–415.

Cook, P.J. 1977. "Punishment and Crime: A Critique of Current Findings Concerning the Preventive Effects of Punishment." *Law and Contemporary Problems* 41(1): 164–204.

Cook, S. 1969. "Canadian Narcotics Legislation 1908–1923: A Conflict Model Interpretation." *Canadian Review of Sociology and Anthropology* 6: 36–46.

Cooney, M., 1998. *Warriors and Peacemakers: How Third Parties Shape Violence.* New York: New York University Press.

Corbett, C. 2003. *Car Crime.* Cullompton, Devon: Willan Publishing.

Cornish, D.B., and R.V. Clarke (eds.). 1986. *The Reasoning Criminal.* New York: Springer-Verlag.

Cornwall, A., and H.N. Bawden. 1992. "Reading Disabilities and Aggression: A Critical Review." *Journal of Learning Disabilities* 25(5): 281–8.

Costello, B.J. 2000. "Techniques of Neutralization and Self-Esteem: A Critical Test of Social Control and Neutralization Theory." *Deviant Behavior* 21: 307–29.

Coston, C.T.M. 2004. *Victimizing Vulnerable Groups.* Westport, CT: Praeger.

Courtwright, D.T. 1998. *Violent Land: Single Men and Social Disorder from the Frontier to the Inner City.* Cambridge MA: Harvard University Press.

Cousins, K., and P. Brunt. 2002. "Terrorism, Tourism and the Media." *Security Journal* 15(1): 19–32.

Craig, W.M., R. DeV. Peters, and R. Konarski. 1998. *Bullying and Victimization among Canadian School Children.* Hull, QC: Human Resources Development Canada. http://www.hrsdc.gc.ca/en/cs/sp/sdc/pkrf/publications/research/1998-000130/page00.shtml

Cressey, D.R. 1969. *Theft of the Nation.* New York: Harper & Row.

Criminal Intelligence Service of Canada. 2005. *2004 Annual Report on Organized Crime in Canada.* http://www.cisc.gc.ca/annual_reports/annual_report2004/frontpage_2004_e.htm

Critcher, C. 2003. *Moral Panics and the Media.* Buckingham: Open University Press.

Croall, H. 1987. "Who Is the White Collar Criminal?" *British Journal of Criminology* 29(2): 157–74.

Cromwell, P.F., J.N. Olson, and D.W. Avary. 1991. *Breaking and Entering: An Ethnographic Analysis of Burglary.* Newbury Park: Sage.

Cullen, F.T., and R. Agnew. 1999. *Criminological Theory: Past to Present.* Los Angeles: Roxbury.

Cullen, F.T., J.P. Wright, S. Brown, M.M. Moon, M.B. Blankenship, and B.K. Applegate. 1998. "Public Support for Early Intervention Programs: Implications for a Progressive Policy Agenda." *Crime & Delinquency* 44(2): 187–204.

Culliver, C., and R. Sigler. 1991. "The Relationship between Learning Disabilities and Juvenile Delinquency." *International*

Journal of Adolescence and Youth 3(1–2): 117–28.

Curran, D.J., and C.M. Renzetti. 2001. *Theories of Crime*. 2nd ed. Boston: Allyn and Bacon.

Currie, E. 1985. *Confronting Crime: An American Challenge*. New York: Pantheon.

Cusson, M. 1993. "Situational Deterrence: Fear During the Criminal Event." In R.V. Clarke (ed.), *Crime Prevention Studies*, Vol. 1. Monsey: Criminal Justice Press.

Daly, K., and L. Maher. 1998. *Criminology at the Crossroads*. New York: Oxford University Press.

Daly, M., and M. Wilson. 1988. *Homicide*. Chicago: Aldine de Gruyter.

Daly, M., M. Wilson, and S. Vasdev. 2001. "Income and Homicide Rates in Canada and the United States." *Canadian Journal of Criminology* 43(2): 219–37.

Dauvergne, M. 2005. "Homicide in Canada." *Juristat* 25(6).

Davis, C.R., and B. Smith. 1994. "Teaching Victims Crime Prevention Skills: Can Individuals Lower Their Costs of Crime?" *Criminal Justice Review* 19(1): 56–68.

Davis, K.E., I.H. Hanson, and R.D. Maiuri. 2002. *Stalking: Perspectives on Victims and Perpetrators*. New York: Springer.

Davis, P.W. 1991. "Stranger Intervention into Child Punishment in Public Places." *Social Problems* 38(2): 227–46.

———— 1994. "The Changing Meaning of Spanking." In J. Best (ed.), *Troubling Children*. New York: Aldine de Gruyter

Dawson, M. 2004. "Rethinking the Boundaries of Intimacy at the end of the Century: The Role of Victim-defendant Relationship in Criminal Justice Decisionmaking Over Time." *Law and Society Review* 38(1): 105–38.

Decker, S.H. 1995. "Reconstructing Homicide Events: The Role of Witnesses in Fatal Encounters." *Journal of Criminal Justice* 23(5): 439–50.

Deisman, W. 2003. *CCTV: Literature Review and Bibliography*. Ottawa: Research and Evaluation Branch, Community, Contract and Aboriginal Policing Directorate, RCMP.

DeKeseredy, W., and R. Hinch. 1991. *Woman Abuse: Sociological Perspectives*. Ottawa: Thomson Educational Publishing.

DeKeseredy, W., and K. Kelly. 1993. "The Incidence and Prevalence of Woman Abuse in Canadian University and College Dating Relationships." *Canadian Journal of Sociology* 18(2): 137–59.

de Léséleuc, S., and R. Kong. 2004. *Victim Services in Canada: National, Provincial and Territorial Fact Sheets*. Ottawa: Canadian Centre for Justice Statistics, Statistics Canada.

DeLisi, M., and A. Hochstetler. 2002. "An Exploratory Assessment of Tittle's Control Balance Theory. Results from the National Youth Study." *Justice Professional* 15(3): 261–72.

Department of Justice Canada. 2006. "Dating Violence: A Fact Sheet." http://canada.justice.gc.ca/en/ps/ fm/datingfs.html

Desjardins, N., and T. Hotton. 2004. "Trends in Drug Offences and the Role of Alcohol and Drugs in Crime." *Juristat* 24(1).

Desroches, F.J. 1991. "Tearoom Trade: A Law Enforcement Problem." *Canadian Journal of Criminology* 33(1): 1–21.

———— 1995. *Force and Fear: Robbery in Canada*. Toronto: Nelson Canada.

———— 2005. *Crime that Pays*. Toronto: Canadian Scholars' Press.

Devereaux, M.S. 1990. "Decline in the Number of Children." *Canadian Social Trends* 18 (Autumn): 32–34.

Devoe, J.F., K. Peters, M. Noonan, T.D. Snyder, and K. Baum. 2005. *Indicators of School Crime and Safety*. Washington D.C.: U.S. Department of Education and Bureau of Justice Statistics.

DiIulio, J.J. 1989. "The Impact of Inner-City Crime." *Public Interest* 96: 28–46.

Dobrin, A. 2001. "The Risk of Offending on Homicide Victimization: A Case Control Study." *Journal of Research in Crime and Delinquency* 38(2): 154–73.

Donovan, P. 2004. *No Way of Knowing: Crime, Urban Legends and the Internet*. New York: Routledge.

Donzinger, S.R. (ed.). 1996. *The Real War on Crime: The Report of the National Criminal Justice Commission*. New York: Harper Perennial.

Doob, A.N. 1982. "The Role of Mass Media in Creating Exaggerated Levels of Fear of Being the Victim of a Violent Crime." In P. Stringer (ed.), *Confronting Social Issues: Applications of Social Psychology*. Toronto: Academic Press.

Doob, A.N., and C. Cesaroni. 2004. *Responding to Youth Crime in Canada*. Toronto: University of Toronto Press.

Doob, A.N., and G.E. MacDonald. 1976. "Television Viewing and Fear of Victimization: Is the Relationship Causal?" *Journal of Personality and Social Psychology* 37: 170–9.

Dorfman, A. 1984. "The Criminal Mind." *Science Digest* 92(10): 44–47, 98.

Dower, K. 2004. "Comparing American and Canadian Local Television Crime Stories: A Content Analysis." *Canadian Journal of Criminology and Criminal Justice* 46: 573–97

Dozier, R.W. 1999. *Fear Itself*. New York: St Martin's Griffin.

Dubois, J. 2002. *Media Coverage of Organized Crime—Police*

Managers Survey. Ottawa: Research and Evaluation Branch, Community, Contract, and Aboriginal Policing Directorate, Royal Canadian Mounted Police.

DuBow, F., E. McCabe, and G. Kaplan. 1979. *Reactions to Crime: A Critical Review of the Literature.* Washington: U.S. Department of Justice.

Dugan, L. 1999. "The Effect of Criminal Victimization on a Household's Moving Decision." *Criminology* 37(4): 903–30.

Duhart, D.T. 2001. *Violence in the Workplace: 1993–1999.* Washington, DC: U.S. Department of Justice.

Du Mont, J., K. Miller, and T.L. Myhr. 2003. "The Role of 'Real Rape' and 'Real Victim' Stereotypes in the Police Reporting Practices of Sexually Assaulted Women." *Violence Against Women* 9(4): 466–86.

Durant, T.J. 1999. "Violence as a Public Health Problem: Toward an Integrated Paradigm." *Sociological Spectrum* 19: 267–80.

Durkheim, E. 1897. *Le Suicide.* Paris: Alcan.

———— 1933. *The Division of Labor in Society.* Trans. G. Simpson. Glencoe: Free Press.

Dutton, D., S. Hart, L.W. Kennedy, and K. Williams. 1992. "Arrest and the Reduction of Repeat Wife Assault." In E. Buzawa and C. Buzawa (eds.), *Domestic Violence: The Changing Criminal Justice Response.* Westport: Greenwood Press.

Dutton, D.G. 1987. "The Criminal Justice Response to Wife Assault." *Law and Human Behavior* 11(3): 189–206.

Duwe, G. 2005. "A Circle of Distortion: The Social Construction of Mass Murder in the United States." *Western Criminology Review* 6(1): 59–78.

Dyson, E. 2005. Is Bill Cosby Right? Or Has the Black Middle Class Lost Its Mind? New York: Basic Civitas Books.

Eck, J.E. 1997. "Preventing Crime at Places." in L.W. Sherman, D. Gottfredson, D. MacKenzie, J. Eck, P. Reuter, and S. Bushway (eds.), *Preventing Crime: What Works, What Doesn't, What's Promising—A Report to the Attorney General of the United States.* Washington, DC: United States Department of Justice, Office of Justice Programs.

———— 2001. "Problem-Oriented Policing and Crime Event Concentration." In R.F. Meier, L.W. Kennedy, and V.F. Sacco (eds.), *The Process and Structure of Crime.* Vol. 9, Advances in Criminological Theory. Piscataway: Transaction Press.

The Economist. 2006. "The Omega Point." Jan. 19. http://www.economist.com/scienc eEisinger, P. 2004. "The American City in the Age of Terror: A Preliminary Assessment of the

Effects of September 11th."
Urban Affairs Review 40(1):
115–30.

Eisler, L., and B. Schissel. 2004.
"Privation and Vulnerability to
Victimization for Canadian
Youth: The Contexts of Gender,
Race, and Geography." *Youth
Violence and Juvenile Justice* 2(4):
359–73.

Eitle, D., and R.J. Turner. 2002.
"Exposure To Community
Violence and Young Adult Crime:
The Effects." *Journal of Research
In Crime and Delinquency* 39(2):
214–37.

Eitle, D.J. 1998. "Exploring a Source
of Deviance-producing Strain
for Females: Perceived
Discrimination and General
Strain Theory." *Journal of
Criminal Justice* 30(5): 429–442.

Ellis, L. 1982. "Genetics and Criminal
Behavior." *Criminology* 20(1):
43–66.

Engs, R.C., and D.J. Hanson. 1994.
"Boozing and Brawling on
Campus: A National Study of
Violent Problems Associated with
Drinking over the Past Decade."
Journal of Criminal Justice 22(2):
171–80.

Ericson, R.V. 1982. *Reproducing Order:
A Study of Police Patrol Work.*
Toronto: University of Toronto
Press.

——— 1991. "Mass Media, Crime,
Law, and Justice: An Institutional
Approach." *The British Journal of
Criminology* 31(3): 219–49.

Ericson, R.V., P.M. Baranek, and J.B.L.
Chan. 1987. *Visualizing Deviance.*
Toronto: University of Toronto
Press.

Ericson, R.V., and C. Shearing. 1986.
"The Scientification of Police
Work." In G. Boehme and
N. Stehr (eds.), *The Knowledge
Society*, pp. 129–59. Dordrecht: D.
Reidel.

Eschholz, S., M. Mallard, and S. Flynn.
2004. "Images of Prime Time
Justice: A Content Analysis of
'NYPD Blue' and 'Law and
Order.'" *Journal of Criminal Justice
and Popular Culture* 10(3):
161–80.

Evans, D.J. 1989. "Geographical
Analyses of Residential Burglary."
In D.J. Evans and D.T. Herbert
(eds.), *The Geography of Crime.*
London: Routledge.

Fagan, A. 2003. "The Short and Long-
Term Effects of Adolescent
Victimization Experienced within
the Family and the Community."
Violence and Victims 18(4):
445–59.

Fagan, J., and R.B. Freeman. 1999.
"Crime and Work." *Crime and
Justice: A Review of Research* 25:
113–78.

Fagan, J., and S. Wexler. 1987. "Family
Origins of Violent Delinquents."
Criminology 25: 643–69.

Farrell, G., and K. Pease. 2001. *Repeat
Victimization.* Monsey, NY:
Criminal Justice Press.

Farrington, D.P. 2003. "Developmental
and Life-course Criminology: Key

Theoretical and Empirical Issues. The 2002 Sutherland Award Address." *Criminology* 41(2): 221–55.

Farrington, D.P., S. Bowen, A. Buckle, T. Burns-Howell, and J. Burrows. 1993. "An Experiment on the Prevention of Shoplifting." In R.V. Clarke (ed.), *Crime Prevention Studies*. Monsey: Criminal Justice Press.

Farrington, D.P., and B. Welsh. 2002. *Effects of Improved Street Lighting on Crime: A Systematic Review*. London: Home Office.

Fattah, E.A. 1976. "The Use of Victim as an Agent of Self-Legitimation: Toward a Dynamic Explanation for Criminal Behavior." *Victimology* 1(1): 162–9.

———— 1991. *Understanding Criminal Victimization*. Scarborough: Prentice-Hall.

———— 1993. "The Rational Choice/ Opportunity Perspectives as a Vehicle for Integrating Criminological and Victimological Theories." In R.V. Clarke and M. Felson (eds.), *Routine Activity and Rational Choice*. New Brunswick, NJ: Transaction.

Fattah, E.A., and V.F. Sacco. 1989. *Crime and Victimization of the Elderly*. New York: Springer-Verlag.

Federal/Provincial, Territorial Ministers Responsible for the Status of Women. 2002. *Assessing Violence against Women: A Statistical Profile*. Ottawa: Status of Women Canada.

Federation of Canadian Municipalities. 1994. *Youth Violence and Youth Gangs: Responding to Community Concerns*. http://ww2.psepc-sppcc.gc.ca/publications/policing/199456_e.asp

Fedorowycz, O. 2004. "Breaking and Entering in Canada 2002." *Juristat* 24(5).

Fekete, J. 1994. *Moral Panic: Biopolitics Rising*. Montreal: Robert Davies Publishing.

Felson, M. 1987. "Routine Activities and Crime Prevention in the Developing Metropolis." *Criminology* 25(4): 911–31.

———— 1992. "Routine Activities and Crime Prevention." *Studies in Crime and Crime Prevention Annual Review* 1(1): 30–34.

———— 2002. *Crime and Everyday Life*. 3rd ed. Thousand Oaks, CA: Sage Publications.

Felson, M., and R. V. Clarke. 1998. *Opportunity Makes the Thief*. London: Home Office.

Felson, R.B., W.F. Baccaglini, and S.A. Ribner. 1985. "Accounting for Criminal Violence: A Comparison of Official and Offender Versions of the Crime." *Sociology and Social Research* 70(1): 93–101.

Felson, R.B., A.E. Liska, S.J. South, and T.L. McNulty. 1994. "The Subculture of Violence and Delinquency: Individual vs. School Context Effects." *Social Forces* 73(1): 155–73.

Felson, R.B., and S. Messner. 1996. "To Kill or Not to Kill: Lethal Outcomes in Injurious Attacks." *Criminology* 34(4): 519–45.

Ferracuti, S. 1996. "Cesare Lombroso (1835–1907)." *Journal of Forensic Psychiatry* 7(1): 130–149.

Ferraro, K.J. 1989. "Policing Woman Battering." *Social Problems* 36(1): 61–74.

Ferraro, K.J., and J.M. Johnson. 1983. "How Women Experience Battering: The Process of Victimization." *Social Problems* 30: 325–35.

Finckenauer, J.O. 1982. *Scared Straight! And the Panacea Phenomenon.* Englewood Cliffs, NJ: Prentice-Hall.

Fischer, B., K. Ala-Leppilampi, E. Single, and A. Robins. 2003. "Cannabis Law Reform in Canada: Is the 'Saga of Promise, Hesitation and Retreat' Coming to an End?" *Canadian Journal of Criminology and Criminal Justice* 45(3): 265–98.

Fisher, B., and J.L. Nasar. 1995. "Fear Spots in Relation to Microlevel Physical Cues: Exploring the Overlooked." *Journal of Research in Crime and Delinquency* 32(2): 214–39.

Fischer, C.S. 1975. "The Effect of Urban Life on Traditional Values." *Social Forces* 53: 420–32.

——— 1981. "The Public and Private Worlds of City Life." *American Sociological Review* 46 (June): 306–16.

——— 1995. "The Subcultural Theory of Urbanism: A Twentieth-Year Assessment." *American Journal of Sociology* 101(3): 543–77.

Fishman, G., G.S. Mesch, and Z. Eisikovits. 2002. "Variables Affecting Adolescent Victimization: Findings from a Nation Youth Survey." *Western Criminology Review* 3(2). http://wcr.sonoma.edu/v3n2/v3n2.html

Fishman, M. 1978. "Crime Waves as Ideology." *Social Problems* 25(5): 531–43.

——— 1981. "Police News: Constructing an Image of Crime." *Urban Life* 9(4): 371–94.

Fishman, M., and G. Cavender. 1998. *Entertaining Crime: Television Reality Programs.* New York: Aldine de Gruyter.

Fitzgerald, R., M. Wisener, and J. Savoie. 2004. *Neighbourhood Characteristics and the Distribution of Crime in Winnipeg.* Ottawa: Canadian Centre for Justice Statistics, Statistics Canada.

Fleisher, M.S. 1995. *Beggars and Thieves: Lives of Urban Street Criminals.* Madison: University of Wisconsin Press.

Fleisher, M.S., and J.L. Krienert. 2004. "Life-course Events, Social Networks, and the Emergence of Violence among Female Gang members." *Journal of Community Psychology* 32(5): 607–22.

Fleury, R.E., C.M. Sullivan, D.I. Bybee, and W.S. Davidson. 1998. "What Happened Depends on Whom You Ask: A Comparison of Police Records and Victim Reports Regarding Arrests for Women Battering." *Journal of Criminal Justice* 26(1): 53–59.

Flowers, R.B. 1989. *Demographics and Criminality: The Characteristics of Crime in America.* New York: Greenwood Press.

Fox, J.A., and J. Levin. 2001. *The Will to Kill: Making Sense of Senseless Murder.* Boston: Allyn and Bacon.

Friedrichs, D. 2004. "Enron Et Al: Paradigmatic White Collar Crime Cases for the New Century." *Critical Criminology* 12: 113–32.

Frieze, I.H., and A. Browne. 1989. "Violence in Marriage." In L. Ohlin and M. Tonry (eds.), *Family Violence.* Chicago: University of Chicago Press.

Frinell, D.E., E. Dahlstrom III, and D.A. Johnson. 1980. "A Public Education Program Designed to Increase the Accuracy and Incidence of Citizens' Reports of Suspicious and Criminal Activities." *Journal of Police Science and Administration* 8(2): 160–5.

Funk, J.B., H.B. Baldacci, T. Pasold, and L. Baumgardner. 2004. "Violence Exposure in Real-life, Video Games, Television, Movies and the Internet: Is There Desensitization?" *Journal of Adolescence* 27: 23–39.

Furstenberg, F. 1971. "Public Reactions to Crime in the Streets." *The American Scholar* 40: 601–10.

Gabler, N. 1998. *Life the Movie.* New York: Alfred A. Knopf.

Gabor, T. 1990. "Crime Displacement and Situational Prevention: Toward the Development of Some Principles." *Canadian Journal of Criminology* 32(1): 41–73.

——— 1994a. *Everybody Does It: Crime by the Public.* Toronto: University of Toronto Press.

——— 1994b. "The Suppression of Crime Statistics on Race and Ethnicity: The Price of Political Correctness." *Canadian Journal of Criminology* 36(2): 153.

——— 2003. "The Federal Gun Registry: An Urgent Need for Independent, Non-partisan Research." *Criminology and Criminal Justice* 45(4): 489–98.

——— 2004. "Inflammatory Rhetoric on Racial Profiling Can Undermine Police Services." *Canadian Journal of Criminology and Criminal Justice* 46(4): 457–66.

Gabriel, U., and W. Greve. 2003. "The Psychology of Fear of Crime: Conceptual and Methodological Perspectives." *British Journal of Criminology.* 43: 594–608.

Gambetta, D.1993. *The Sicilian Mafia.* Cambridge MA: Harvard University Press.

Gannon, M., and K. Mihorean. 2005. "Criminal Victimization in Canada 2004." *Juristat* 25(7).

Gans, H. 1962. *The Urban Villagers.* New York: Free Press.

Garofalo, J. 1981a. "Crime and the Mass Media: A Selective Review of Research." *Journal of Research in Crime and Delinquency* (July): 319–50.

———— 1981b. "The Fear of Crime: Causes and Consequences." *The Journal of Criminal Law and Criminology* 72: 839–57.

Garofalo, J., L. Siegel, and J. Laub. 1987. "School-Related Victimizations among Adolescents: An Analysis of National Crime Survey (NCS) Narratives." *Journal of Quantitative Criminology* 3(4): 321–38.

Garofalo, R. 1914. *Criminology.* Boston: Little, Brown.

Gartner, G., and B. McCarthy 1996. "The Social Distribution of Femicide in Urban Canada: 1921–1988." In R.A. Silverman, J.J. Teevan, and V.F. Sacco (eds.), *Crime in Canadian Society,* 5th ed., pp. 177–85. Toronto: Harcourt Brace.

Gartner, R. 2000. "The Centre for Criminology at the University of Toronto." *The Criminologist* 25(4): 1, 3–4.

Gartner, R., and A. Doob. 1994. "Trends in Criminal Victimization: 1988–1993." *Juristat* 14(13).

Gartner, R., and R. Macmillan. 2000. "Victim–Offender Relationship and Reporting Crimes of Violence against Women." In R.A. Silverman, J.T. Teevan, and V.F. Sacco (eds.), *Crime in Canadian Society,* 6th ed. Toronto: Harcourt Brace.

Gaskell, G.D., D.B. Wright, and C.A. O'Muircheartaigh. 2000. "Telescoping of Landmark Events: Implications for Survey Research." *Public Opinion Quarterly* 64: 77–89.

Gatez, S. 2004. "Safe Streets for Whom? Social Exclusion and Criminal Victimization." *Canadian Journal of Criminology and Criminal Justice* 46(4): 423–56.

Gelles, R.J., and M.A. Straus. 1988. *Intimate Violence.* New York: Simon & Schuster.

Gentile, D.A., P.J. Lynch, J.R. Linder, and D.A. Walsh. 2004. "The Effects of Violent Video Game Habits on Adolescent Hostility, Aggressive Behaviors and School Performance." *Journal of Adolescence* 27(1): 5–22.

Gibbs, J.P. 1966. "Conceptions of Deviant Behavior: The Old and the New." *Pacific Sociological Review* 9: 9–14.

Gibbs, J.P., and M.L. Erikson. 1976. "Crime Rates of American Cities in an Ecological Context." *American Journal of Sociology* 82(3): 605–20.

Gilbert, N. 1997. "Advocacy Research and Social Policy." In M. Tonry (ed.), *Crime and Justice: A Review of Research,* Vol. 22, pp. 101–48.

Chicago: University of Chicago Press.

Gill, Martin. 1994. *Crime at Work: Studies in Security & Crime Prevention.* Leicester: Perpetuity Press.

Gillespie, C. 1989. *Justifiable Homicide: Battered Women, Self Defense, and the Law.* Columbus: Ohio State University Press.

Gillespie, D.L., and A. Leffler. 1987. "The Politics of Research Methodology in Claims-Making Activities: Social Science and Sexual Harassment." *Social Problems* 34(5): 490–501.

Gilsinan, J.F. 1989. "They is Clowning Tough: 911 and the Social Construction of Reality." *Criminology* 27(2): 329–44.

Glensor, R.W., and K.J. Peak. 2005. "The Problem of Crimes against Tourists." *Center for Problem-Oriented Policing.* http://www.popcenter.org/Problems/problem-crimes_tourists.htm

Goff, C., and N. Nason-Clark. 1989. "The Seriousness of Crime in Fredericton, New Brunswick: Perceptions Toward White-Collar Crime." *Canadian Journal of Criminology* 31(1): 19–34.

Goffman, E. 1959. *The Presentation of Self in Everyday Life.* Garden City: Doubleday.

———— 1963. *Stigma: Notes on the Management of Spoiled Identity.* Englewood Cliffs: Prentice-Hall.

Golant, S.M. 1984. "Factors Influencing the Nighttime Activity of Old Persons in Their Community." *Journal of Gerontology* 39: 485–91.

Gold, A.D. 2003. "Media Hype, Racial Profiling and Good Science." *Canadian Journal of Criminology and Criminal Justice* 45(3): 391–99.

Gold, M. 1970. *Delinquent Behavior in an American City.* Belmont: Brooks/Cole.

Goldstein, H. 1990. *Problem-Oriented Policing.* Philadelphia: Temple University Press.

Gomery Commission. 2005. *Volume 1: Who is Responsible?* Ottawa: Minister of Public Works and Government Services.

Gondolf, E.W., and J.R. McFerron. 1989. "Handling Battering Men and Police Action in Wife Abuse Cases." *Criminal Justice and Behavior* 16: 429–39.

Goode, E., and N. Ben-Yehuda. 1994. *Moral Panics: The Social Construction of Deviance.* Oxford: Blackwell.

Goodstein, L., and R.L. Shotland. 1982. "The Crime Causes Crime Model: A Critical Review of the Relationship between Fear of Crime, Bystander Surveillance, and Changes in the Crime Rate." *Victimology* 5(2–4): 133–51.

Gordon, M.T., and L. Heath. 1981. "The News Business, Crime and Fear." In D.A. Lewis (ed.), *Reactions to Crime.* Beverly Hills: Sage.

Gordon, M.T., and S. Riger. 1989. *The Female Fear*. New York: Free Press.

Gordon, R.M. 2000. "Criminal Business Organizations, Street Gangs and 'Wanna-be' Groups: A Vancouver Perspective." *Canadian Journal of Criminology* 42(1): 39–60.

Gorelick, S.M. 1989. "'Join Our War': The Construction of Ideology in a Newspaper Crimefighting Campaign." *Crime and Delinquency* 35(3): 421–36.

Gottfredson, M.R. 1984. *Victims of Crime: The Dimensions of Risk*. A Home Office Research and Planning Unit Report. London: HMSO Books.

Gottfredson, M.R., and D. Gottfredson. 1988. *Decisionmaking in Criminal Justice*. 2nd ed. New York: Plenum.

Gottfredson, M.R., and T. Hirschi. 1990. *A General Theory of Crime*. Stanford, CA: Stanford University Press.

———. 1995. "National Crime Prevention Policies." *Society* 32(2): 30–36.

Gould, L.C. 1989. "Crime, Criminality, and Criminal Events." Paper presented at the Annual Meetings of the American Society of Criminology, Reno, Nevada.

Gove, W.R. 1975. *The Labelling of Deviance: Evaluating a Perspective*. New York: Sage.

Gove, W.R., M. Hughes, and M. Geerken. 1985. "Are Uniform Crime Reports a Valid Indicator of the Index Crimes? An Affirmative Answer with Minor Modifications." *Criminology* 23(3): 451–501.

Gover, A.R. 2004. "Risky Lifestyles and Dating Violence: A Theoretical Test of Violent Victimization." *Journal of Criminal Justice* 32(2): 171–80.

Graham, J. 1990. *Crime Prevention Strategies in Europe and North America*. Helsinki: Helsinki Institute for Crime Prevention and Control.

Graham, K., and S. Wells. 2003. "Somebody's Gonna Get Their Head Kicked in Tonight: Aggression Among Young Males in Bars—A Question of Values?" *British Journal of Criminology* 43(3): 546–66.

Graham, K., S. Wells, and J. Jennifer. 2002. "The Social Context of Physical Aggression Among Adults." *Journal of Interpersonal Violence* 17(1): 64–83.

Grattet, R., V. Jenness, and T.R. Curry. 1998. "The Homogenization and Differentiation of Hate Crime Law in the United States, 1978 to 1995: Innovation and Diffusion in the Criminalization of Bigotry." *American Sociological Review* 63: 286–307.

Gray, H. 1989. "Popular Music as a Social Problem: A Social History of the Claims against Popular Music." In J. Best (ed.), *Images of Issues*. New York: Aldine de Gruyter.

Greek, C. 1993. "Attacks on Florida Tourists." Florida State University. http://www.fsu.edu/~crimdo/tourists.html

Greenberg, M.S., R.B. Ruback, and D.R. Westcott. 1984. "Social Influence and Crime-Victim Decision Making." *Journal of Social Issues* 40(1): 51–76.

Greenburg, M.S., and S.R. Beach. 2004. "Property Crime Victims' Decision to Notify the Police: Social, Cognitive and Affective Determinants." *Law and Human Behavior* 28(2): 177–86.

Greene, J. 1998. "Evaluating Planned Change Strategies in Modern Law Enforcement: Implementing Community-Based Policing." In J-P. Brodeur (ed.), *How to Recognize Good Policing: Problems and Issues.* Thousand Oaks, CA: Sage.

Gusfield, J. 1963. *Symbolic Crusade: Status Politics and the American Temperance Movement.* Urbana: University of Illinois Press.

——— J. 1989. "Constructing the Ownership of Social Problems: Fun and Profit in the Welfare State." *Social Problems* 36(5): 431–41.

Haen Marshall, I. 2004. "Introduction." *Journal of Contemporary Criminal Justice.* 20: 344–47.

Hagan, J. 1980. "The Legislation of Crime and Delinquency: A Review of Theory, Method and Research." *Law and Society Review* 14(3): 603–28.

——— 1985. *Modern Criminology.* New York: McGraw-Hill.

——— 1989. *Structural Criminology.* New Brunswick, NJ: Rutgers University Press.

——— 1992. "White Collar and Corporate Crime." In R. Linden (ed.), *Criminology: A Canadian Perspective.* Toronto: Harcourt Brace Jovanovich.

Hagan, J., A.R. Gillis, and J.H. Simpson. 1979. "The Sexual Stratification of Social Control: A Gender-Based Perspective on Crime and Delinquency." *British Journal of Sociology* 30(1): 25–38.

——— 1985. "The Class Structure of Gender and Delinquency: Toward a Power–Control Theory of Common Delinquent Behavior." *American Journal of Sociology* 90(6): 1151–78.

Hagan, J., G. Hefler, G. Classen, K. Boehnke, and H. Merkens. 1998. "Subterranean Sources of Subcultural Delinquency Beyond the American Dream." *Criminology* 36(2): 309–42.

Hagan, J., J. Simpson, and A.R. Gillis. 1987. "Class in the Household: Deprivation, Liberation and a Power–Control Theory of Gender and Delinquency." *American Journal of Sociology* 92(4): 788–816.

——— 1988. "Feminist Scholarship, Relational and Instrumental Control, and a Power–Control Theory of Gender and Delinquency." *The British Journal of Sociology* 39(3): 301–36.

Haggerty, K.D. 2001. *Making Crime Count.* Toronto: University of Toronto Press.

Hall, S., C. Critcher, C. Jefferson, T. Jefferson, J. Clarke and

B. Roberts. 1978. *Policing the Crisis: Mugging, the State and Law and Order.* London: Macmillan

Haller, M.H. 1990. "Illegal Enterprise: A Theoretical and Historical Interpretation." *Criminology* 28(2): 207–35.

———— 1992. "Bureaucracy and the Mafia: An Alternative View." *Journal of Contemporary Criminal Justice* 8: 1–10.

Halpern, D. 2005. *Social Capital.* Cambridge: Polity.

Hamilton, C.E., L. Falshaw, and K.D. Browne. 2002. "The Link Between Recurrent Maltreatment and Offending Behavior." *International Journal of Offender Therapy and Comparative Criminology* 46(1): 75–94.

Hamlin, J.E. 1988. "The Misplaced Role of Rational Choice in Neutralization Theory." *Criminology* 26: 425–38.

Hans, V.P. 1990. "Law and the Media: An Overview and Introduction." *Law and Human Behavior* 14(5): 399–407.

Hans, V.P., and D. Ermann. 1989. "Responses to Corporate versus Individual Wrongdoing." *Law and Human Behavior* 13(2): 151–66.

Hanson, R., G. Warchol, and L. Zupan. 2004. "Policing Paradise: Law and Disorder in Belize." *Police Practice and Research* 5(3): 241–57.

Hanson, R.K., O. Cadsky, A. Harris, and C. Lalonde. 1997. "Correlates of Battering Among 997 Men:

Family History, Adjustment, and Attitudinal Differences." *Violence and Victims* 12(3): 191–208.

Harcourt, B. 2001. *Illusions of Order: The False Promise of Broken Windows Policing.* Cambridge Mass.: Harvard University Press.

Harding, D.J., C. Fox, and J.D. Mehta. 2002. "Studying Rare Events through Qualitative Case Studies: Lessons from a Study of Rampage School Shootings." *Sociological Methods and Research* 31(2): 174–217.

Harlow, C.W. 1991. *Female Victims of Violent Crime.* Washington: U.S. Department of Justice.

Harned, M.S. 2005. "Understanding Women's Labeling of Unwanted Sexual Experiences with Dating Partners: A Qualitative Analysis." *Violence Against Women* 11(3): 374–413.

Harney, P.A., and C.L. Muehlenhard. 1991. "Factors that Increase the Likelihood of Victimization." In A. Parrot and L. Bechhofer (eds.), *Acquaintance Rape: The Hidden Crime.* New York: John Wiley.

Harris, M.K. 1991. "Moving into the New Millennium: Toward a Feminist Vision of Peace." In H.E. Pepinsky and R. Quinney (eds.), *Criminology as Peacemaking.* Bloomington: Indiana University Press.

Harrison, D. 2002. *The First Casualty: Violence against Women in Canadian Military Communities.* Toronto: Lorimer.

Hartman, D.P., D.M. Gelfand, B. Page, and P. Walder. 1972. "Rates of Bystander Observation and Reporting of Contrived Shoplifting Incidents." *Criminology* (November): 247–67.

Hartmann, D. 2001. "Notes on Midnight Basketball and the Cultural Politics of Recreation, Race and At-risk Urban Youth." *Journal of Sport and Social Issues* 25(4): 339–71.

Hartnagel, T.F. 2000. "Correlates of Criminal Behaviour." In R. Linden (ed.), *Criminology: A Canadian Perspective,* 4th ed. Toronto: Harcourt Brace.

Hastings, R. 2005. "Perspectives on Crime Prevention: Issues and Challenges." *Canadian Journal of Criminology and Criminal Justice* 27(2): 209–15.

Hatt, Ken. 1994. "Reservations About Race and Crime Statistics." *Canadian Journal of Criminology* 36(2): 164.

Healy, M. "Battling over Videogame Violence: American Politicians Take Aim at Gory Titles." *The Ottawa Citizen,* Oct 20, 2005: F7.

Heath, L., and K. Gilbert. 1996. "Mass Media and Fear of Crime." *American Behavioral Scientist* 39(4): 379–86.

Helfand, N.S. 2003. *Asian Organized Crime and Terrorist Activity in Canada, 1999–2002.* Washington, D.C: Federal Research Division, Library of Congress.

Hennigen, K.M., L. Heath, J.D. Wharton, M.L. Del Resario, T.D. Cook, and B.J. Calder. 1982. "Impact of the Introduction of Television on Crime in the United States: Empirical Findings and Theoretical Implications." *Journal of Personality and Social Psychology* 42(3): 461–77.

Henshel, R.L., and R.A. Silverman. 1975. *Perception in Criminology.* Toronto: Methuen.

Herrera, V.M., and L.A. McCloskey. 2003. "Sexual Abuse, Family Violence and Female Delinquency: Findings from a Longitudinal Study." *Violence and Victims* 18(3): 319–34.

Herrnstein, R.J. 1995. "Criminogenic Traits." In J.Q. Wilson and J. Petersilia (eds.), *Crime,* pp. 39–64. San Francisco: Institute for Contemporary Studies Press.

Hickey, E. 1991. *Serial Murderers and Their Victims.* Belmont: Wadsworth.

Hickman, M., and A. Piquero. 2001. "Exploring the Relationships Between Gender, Control Balance, and Deviance" *Deviant Behavior* 22(4): 323–51.

Higgins, G.E. 2002. "General Theory of Crime and Deviance: A Structural Equation Model Approach." *Journal of Crime & Justice* 25(2): 71–95.

——— 2004. "Gender and Self-Control Theory: Are there Differences in the Measures and the Theory's Causal Model?" *Criminal Justice Studies* 17(1): 33–55.

——— 2005. "Can Low Self Control Help with the Understanding of the Software Piracy Problem?" *Deviant Behavior.* 26(1): 1–24.

Higgins, G.E., and C. Lauterbach, 2004. "Control Balance Theory and Exploitation: An Examination of Contingencies." *Criminal Justice Studies.* 17(3): 291–310.

Hindelang, M.J., M.R. Gottfredson, and J. Garofalo. 1978. *Victims of Personal Crime: An Empirical Foundation for a Theory of Personal Victimization.* Cambridge: Ballinger.

Hirschi, T. 1969. *Causes of Delinquency.* Berkeley: University of California Press.

Hirschi, T., and M.J. Hindelang. 1977. "Intelligence and Delinquency: A Revisionist View." *American Sociological Review* 42: 571–87.

Hocker, J.L., and W.W. Wilmot. 1985. *Interpersonal Conflict.* 2nd ed. Dubuque: William C. Brown.

Hodgins, S. 2000. "Biological Factors in Criminal Behavior." In R. Linden, *Criminology: A Canadian Perspective,* 4th ed. Toronto: Harcourt Brace.

Hoffman, J.P., and S.S. Su. 1997. "The Conditional Effects of Stress on Delinquency and Drug Use: A Strain Theory Assessment of Sex Differences." *Journal of Research in Crime and Delinquency* 34(1): 46–78.

Hoffman, K., K.J. Kiecolt, and J.N. Edwards. 2005. "Physical Violence between Siblings: A Theoretical and Empirical Analysis." *Journal of Family Issues* 26(8): 1103–30.

Hollinger, R.C., and L. Lanza-Kaduce. 1988. "The Process of Criminalization: The Case of Computer Crime Laws." *Criminology* 26(1): 101–13.

Home Office. 2005. *DNA Expansion Programme 2000–2005: Reporting Achievement.* London.

Hotaling, G.T., and D. Finkelhor. 1990. "Estimating the Number of Stranger-Abduction Homicides of Children: A Review of Available Evidence." *Journal of Criminal Justice* 18: 385–99.

Hotaling, G.T., and M.A. Straus (with A.J. Lincoln). 1990. "Intrafamily Violence and Crime and Violence Outside the Family." In M.A. Straus and R.J. Gelles (eds.), *Physical Violence in American Families: Risk Factors and Adaptations to Violence in 8,145 Families.* New Brunswick, NJ: Transaction.

Hough, M. 1985. "The Impact of Victimisation: Findings from the British Crime Survey." *Victimology* 10: 488–97.

Howarth, G., and P. Rock. 2000. "Aftermath and the Construction of Victimisation: 'The Other Victims of Crime.'" *The Howard Journal* 39(1): 58–78.

Howitt, D. 1998. *Crime, the Media and the Law.* New York: Wiley.

Humphries, D. 1981. "Serious Crime, News Coverage and Ideology: A Content Analysis of Crime Coverage in a Metropolitan Paper." *Crime and Delinquency* 27(2): 191–205.

Hunt, J. 1985. "Police Accounts of Normal Force." *Urban Life* 13(4): 315–41.

Ianni, F.A.J. 1971. "The Mafia and the Web of Kinship." *The Public Interest* 16: 78–100.

Ianni, F.A.J., and E. Reuss-Ianni. 1972. *A Family Business: Kinship and Social Control in Organized Crime.* New York: Russell Sage Foundation.

Innes, C.A., and L.A. Greenfeld. 1990. "Violent State Prisoners and Their Victims." *Bureau of Justice Statistics Special Report.* Washington: U.S. Department of Justice.

Iso-Ahola, S. 1980. *The Social Psychology of Leisure and Recreation.* Dubuque: William C. Brown.

Jackson, P.G. 1990. "Sources of Data." In K.L. Kempf (ed.), *Measurement Issues in Criminology.* New York: Springer-Verlag.

Jackson, P.I. 1989. *Minority Group Threat, Crime, and Policing.* New York: Praeger.

Jacobs, J.B. 1999. *Gotham Unbound: How New York was Liberated from the Grip of Organized Crime.* New York: New York University Press.

Jacobs, N. 1965. "The Phantom Slasher of Taipei: Mass Hysteria in a Non-Western Society." *Social Problems* 12: 318–28.

Janhevich, D., M. Gannon, and N. Morisset. 2003. "Impaired Driving and Other Traffic Offences—2002." *Juristat* 23(9): 3.

Janoff-Bulman, R., and I.H. Frieze. 1983. "A Theoretical Perspective for Understanding Reactions to Victimization." *Journal of Social Issues* 39(2): 1–17.

Jeffery, C.R. 1990. *Criminology: An Interdisciplinary Approach.* Englewood Cliffs: Prentice-Hall.

Jenkins, P. 1994. *Using Murder: The Social Construction of Serial Homicide.* New York: Walter de Gruyter.

Jenkins, P. 2001. *Beyond Tolerance: Child Pornography on the Internet.* New York: New York University Press.

———— 2003. *Images of Terror: What We Can and Can't Know about Terrorism.* Hawthorne, NY: Aldine de Gruyter.

Jensen, G. 2002. "Typologizing Violence: a Blackian Perspective." *International Journal of Sociology and Social Policy* 22(7): 75–108.

Jensen, G.F., and D. Brownfield. 1986. "Gender, Lifestyles, and Victimization: Beyond Routine Activity." *Violence and Victims* 1(2): 85–99.

Johnson, D.M. 1945. "The 'Phantom Anesthetist' of Mattoon: A Field Study of Mass Hysteria." *Journal of Abnormal and Social Psychology* 40: 175–86.

Johnson, G.D., G.J. Palileo, and N.B. Gray. 1992. "Date Rape on a Southern Campus." *Sociology and Social Research* 76(2): 37–41.

Johnson, H. 1996. *Dangerous Domains.* Scarborough: Nelson Canada.

——— 2001. "Contrasting Views of the Role of Alcohol in Cases of Wife Assault." *Journal of Interpersonal Violence* 16(1): 54–72.

Johnson, H., and V.P. Bunge. 2001. "Prevalence and Consequence of Spousal Assault in Canada." *Canadian Journal of Criminology* 43(1): 27–35.

Johnson, H., and T. Hotten. 2003. "Losing Control: Homicide Risk in Estranged and Intact Intimate Relationships" *Homicide Studies* 7(1) 58–84.

Johnson, H., and V. Sacco. 1995. "Researching Violence against Women: Statistics Canada National Survey." *Canadian Journal of Criminology* 37(3): 281–304.

——— 2000. "Violence against Women: A Special Topic Survey." In R.A. Silverman, J.J. Teevan, and V.F. Sacco (eds.), *Crime in Canadian Society,* 6th ed. Toronto: Harcourt Brace.

Johnson, I.M., and R.T. Sigler. 2000. "Public Perceptions: The Stability of the Public's Endorsements of the Definition and Criminalization of the Abuse of Women." *Journal of Criminal Justice* 28: 165–79.

Johnson, K.J., and M.P. Ferraro. 2000. "Research on Domestic Violence in the 1990s: Making Distinctions." *Journal of Marriage and the Family* 62: 948–63.

Johnson, S. 2004. "Adult Correctional Services in Canada, 2002/2003." *Juristat* 24 (10).

Johnston, J.P. 1994. "Academic Approaches to Race-crime Statistics Do Not Justify Their Collection." *Canadian Journal of Criminology* 36(2): 166.

Jones, M. 1994. "Time Use of the Elderly." In *Canadian Social Trends: A Canadian Studies Reader,* pp. 349–51. Toronto: Thompson Educational Publishing.

Jones, S., and N. Quisenberry. 2004. "The General Theory of Crime: How General is it?" *Deviant Behavior* 25(5): 401–26.

Junger, M. 1987. "Women's Experiences of Sexual Harassment: Some Implications for Their Fear of Crime." *British Journal of Criminology* 27(4): 358–83.

Junger-Tas, J., and I.H. Marshall. 1999. "The Self-Report Methodology in Crime Research." In M. Tonry (ed.), *Crime and Justice: A Review of Research,* Vol. 25, pp. 291–367. Chicago: University of Chicago Press.

Jupp, V. 1989. *Methods of Criminological Research.* London: Unwin Hyman.

Kantor, G.K., and M.A. Straus. 1987. "The Drunken Bum Theory of Wife Beating." *Social Problems* 34(2): 213–30.

Kapferer, J.N. 1989. "A Mass Poisoning Rumor in Europe." *Public Opinion Quarterly* 53: 467–81.

Kappeler, V.E., and G.W. Potter. 2004. *The Mythology of Crime and Criminal Justice.* 4th ed. Long Grove, IL: Waveland Press.

Karmen, A. 2001. *Crime Victims: An Introduction to Victimology.* 4th ed. Belmont: Wadsworth.

Katz, J. 1987. "What Makes Crime 'News.'" *Media, Culture and Society* 9: 47–75.

Katz, J., and W.J. Chambliss. 1995. "Biology and Crime." In J.F. Sheley (ed.), *Criminology,* 2nd ed, pp. 275–304. Belmont: Wadsworth.

Kaukinen, C. 2002a. "The Help-Seeking Decisions of Violent Crime Victims: An Examination of Direct and Conditional Effects of Gender and The Victim-Offender Relationship" *Journal of Interpersonal Violence* 17(4): 432–56.

——— 2002b. "The Help-Seeking of Women Violent Crime Victims: Findings from the Canadian Violence Against Women Survey." *International Journal of Sociology and Social Policy* 22(7): 5–44.

Kazemian, L., and M. LeBlanc. 2004. "Exploring Patterns of Perception of Crime Across the Life Course: Offense and Offender-based Viewpoints." *Journal of Contemporary Criminal Justice* 20(4): 393–415.

Keane, C. 1995. "Victimization and Fear: Assessing the Role of Offender and Offence." *Canadian Journal of Criminology* 37(3): 431–55.

——— 2000. "Corporate Crime." In R.A. Silverman, J.J. Teevan, and V.F. Sacco (eds.), *Crime in Canadian Society,* 6th ed. Toronto: Harcourt Brace.

Keane, C., P.S. Maxim, and J.J. Teevan. 1996. "Testing a General Theory of Crime." In R.A. Silverman, J.J. Teevan, and V.F. Sacco (eds.), *Crime in Canadian Society.* 5th ed. Toronto: Harcourt Brace.

Kellam, S.G. 2000. "Community and Institutional Partnerships for School Violence Prevention." In *Preventing School Violence: Plenary Papers of the 1999 Conference on Criminal Justice Research and Evaluation— Enhancing Policy and Practice through Research,* Volume 2. Washington: Office of Justice Programs, National Institute of Justice.

Kelling, G.L. 1999. "'Broken Windows' and Police Discretion." *National Institute of Justice Research Report.* Washington: Office of Justice Programs, National Institute of Justice.

Kelling, G.L., and C.M. Coles. 1996. *Fixing Broken Windows.* New York: The Free Press.

Kennedy, L.W. 1988. "Going It Alone: Unreported Crime and Individual Self-Help." *Journal of Criminal Justice* 16(5): 403–12.

——— 1991. "Evaluating Community Policing." *Canadian Police College Journal* 15(4): 275–90.

Kennedy, L.W., and S. Baron. 1993. "Routine Activities and a Subculture of Violence: A Study of Violence on the Street." *Journal of Research in Crime and Delinquency* 30(1): 88–112.

Kennedy, L.W., and D.R. Forde. 1990. "Routine Activities and Crime: An Analysis of Victimization in Canada." *Criminology* 28(1): 101–15.

——— 1999. *When Push Comes to Shove: A Routine Conflict Approach to Violence.* Albany: State University of New York Press.

Kennedy, L.W., and V.F. Sacco. 1996. *Crime Counts: A Criminal Event Analysis.* Toronto: Nelson.

——— 1998. *Crime Victims in Context.* Los Angeles: Roxbury.

Kennedy, L.W., and R.A. Silverman. 1990. "The Elderly Victim of Homicide: An Application of the Routine Activities Approach." *Sociological Quarterly* 31(2): 307–19.

——— 1985. "Significant Others and Fear of Crime among the Elderly." *International Journal of Aging and Human Development* 20(4): 241–56.

Kennedy, L.W., and D. Veitch. 1997. "Why Are the Crime Rates Going Down? A Case Study in Edmonton." *Canadian Journal of Criminology* 39(1): 51–69.

Kierkus, C.A., and D. Baer. 2002. "A Social Control Explanation of the Relationship Between Family Structure and Delinquent Behavior." *Canadian Journal of Criminology and Criminal Justice* 44(4): 425–58.

Kinderlehrer, J. 1983. "Delinquent Diets: Partners in Crime." *Prevention* (October): 141–4. *Kingston Whig-Standard* http://www.thewhig.com/webapp/ sitepages/content.asp?contentID= 127094&catname=Local+News

Kitsuse, K.I. 1962. "Societal Reaction to Deviant Behavior: Problems of Theory and Method." *Social Problems* 9: 247–56.

Klaus, P.A., and M.R. Rand. 1984. *Family Violence.* Washington: Bureau of Justice Statistics.

Kleck, G., and S. Sayles. 1990. "Rape and Resistance." *Social Problems* 37(2): 149–62.

Klockars, C.B. 1985. *The Idea of Police.* Beverly Hills: Sage.

Koenig, D.J. 1991. *Do Police Cause Crime? Police Activity, Police Strength, and Crime Rates.* Ottawa: Canadian Police College.

Kohler, N. 2005. "Gun Crime Biggest Fear." *National Post,* Oct 25, 2005: p A.1.

Kong, R. (ed.). 2005. *Criminal Justice Indicators.* Ottawa: Centre for Justice Statistics, Statistics Canada.

Kong, R., and K. Beattie. 2005. "Collecting Data on Aboriginal People in the Criminal Justice

System: Methods and Challenges." Statistics Canada (May).

Kong, R., H. Johnson, S. Beattie, and A. Cardillo. 2003. "Sexual Offences in Canada." *Juristat.* 23(6).

Kooistra, P.G., and J.S. Mahoney, Jr. 1999. "The Historical Roots of Tabloid TV Crime." In J. Ferrell and N. Websdale, *Making Trouble: Cultural Constructions of Crime, Deviance and Control.* New York: Aldine de Gruyter.

Kornhauser, R. 1978. *Social Sources of Delinquency.* Chicago: University of Chicago Press.

Krahn, H., and L.W. Kennedy. 1985. "Producing Personal Safety: The Effects of Crime Rates, Police Force Size, and Fear of Crime." *Criminology* 23(4): 697–710.

Krajicik, D.J. 1998. *Scooped: How Media Miss Real Story While Chasing Sex, Sleaze and Celebrity.* New York: Columbia University Press.

Krupat, E., and P. Kubzansky. 1987. "Designing to Deter Crime." *Psychology Today* (October): 58–61.

Kruttschnitt, C. 2002. "Women's Involvement in Serious Interpersonal Violence." *Aggression and Violent Behavior* 7: 529–65.

Kubrin, C.E., and R. Weitzer. 2003. "New Directions in Social Disorganization Theory." *Journal of Research in Crime and Delinquency* 40(4): 374–402.

Kueneman, R. 2000. "The Origins and Role of Law in Society." In R. Linden (ed.), *Criminology:*

A Canadian Perspective, 4th ed. Toronto: Harcourt Brace.

Kurz, D. 1987. "Emergency Department Responses to Battered Women: Resistance to Medicalization." *Social Problems* 34(1): 69–81.

Lab, S.P. 1992. *Crime Prevention: Approaches, Practices and Evaluations.* 2nd ed. Cincinnati: Anderson.

LaGrange, R.L., and K.F. Ferraro. 1987. "The Elderly's Fear of Crime: A Critical Examination of the Research." *Research on Aging* 9: 372–91.

——— 1989. "Assessing Age and Gender Differences in Perceived Risk and Fear of Crime." *Criminology* 27: 697–719.

LaGrange, R.L., K.F. Ferraro, and M. Supancic. 1992. "Perceived Risk and Fear of Crime: Role of Social and Physical Incivilities." *Journal of Research in Crime and Delinquency* 29: 311–34.

LaGrange, T.C., and R.A. Silverman. 1999. "Low Self-Control and Opportunity: Testing the General Theory of Crime as an Explanation for Gender Differences in Delinquency." *Criminology* 37(1): 41–72.

Lamb, S. 1996. *The Trouble with Blame: Victims, Perpetrators and Responsibility.* Cambridge, MA: Harvard University Press.

Lane, J. 2002. "Fear of Gang Crime: A Qualitative Examination of the Four Perspectives." *Journal of*

Research In Crime and Delinquency 29(4): 437–71.

La Prairie, C. 2002. "Aboriginal Over-Representation in the Criminal Justice System: A Tale of Nine Cities." *Canadian Journal of Criminology* 44(2): 181–208.

Lasley, J. 1998. "'Designing Out' Gang Homicides and Street Assaults." National Institute of Justice Research in Brief. Washington, DC: U.S. Department of Justice.

Lasley, J.R., and J.L. Rosenbaum. 1988. "Routine Activities and Multiple Personal Victimization." *Sociology and Social Research* 73(1): 47–50.

Laub, J.H. 1990. "Patterns of Criminal Victimization in the United States." In A.J. Lurigio, W.G. Skogan, and R.C. Davis (eds.), *Victims of Crime: Problems, Policies and Programs.* Newbury Park: Sage.

Laub, J.H. 2004. "The Life Course of Criminology in the United States: The American Society of Criminology 2003 Presidential Address." *Criminology* 42(1): 1–26.

Laub, J.H., and R.J. Sampson. 1993. "Turning Points in the Life Course: Why Change Matters to the Study of Crime." *Criminology* 31(3): 301–25.

Laucius, J. "Rights Crusader Fights 'Hate Rap.'" *The Ottawa Citizen,* Oct. 10, 2005: A3.

Lauritsen, J.L., R.J. Sampson, and J.H. Laub. 1991. "The Link between Offending and Victimization among Adolescents." *Criminology* 29(2): 265–92.

Lawson, P.E. 1982. *Solving Somebody Else's Blues.* Latham: University Press of America.

Lawson, W. 2003 "Fighting Crime One Bite at a Time: Diet Supplements Cut Violence in Prisons—Nutrition" *Psychology Today* (March-April): 22.

Lea, S.J., U. Lanvers, and S. Shaw. 2003. "Attrition in Rape Cases: Developing a Profile and Identifying Relevant Factors." *British Journal of Criminology.* 43: 583–99.

Le Bourdais, C., G. Neill, and P. Turcotte. 2000. "The Changing Face of Conjugal Relationships." *Canadian Social Trends* Spring: 14–17.

Lee, M.R. 2000. "The Social Dimensions of Interpersonal Dispute Resolution: A Test of a General Theoretical Framework with Survey Data." *Sociological Inquiry* 70(2): 137–56.

Lejeune, R., and N. Alex. 1973. "On Being Mugged." *Urban Life and Culture* 2(3): 259–83.

Lemert, E.M. 1951. *Social Pathology.* New York: McGraw-Hill.

Leroux, T.G., and M. Petrunik. 1990. "The Construction of Elder Abuse as a Social Problem: A Canadian Perspective." *International Journal of Health Services* 20(4): 651–63.

Levi, K. 1981. "Becoming a Hit Man: Neutralization in a Very Deviant Career." *Urban Life* 10: 47–63.

Lichter, R.S., L.S. Lichter, and S. Rothman. 1994. *Prime Time: How TV Portrays American Culture.* Washington: Regnery Publishers.

Light, I. 1977. "The Ethnic Vice Industry, 1880–1944." *American Sociological Review* 42 (June): 464–79.

Lindner, C., and R.L. Bonn. 1996. "Probation Officer Victimization and Fieldwork Practices: Results of a National Study." *Federal Probation* 60(2): 16–23.

Lindquist, J.H., and J.M. Duke. 1982. "The Elderly Victim at Risk." *Criminology* 20(1): 115–26.

Liska, A.E., and W. Baccaglini. 1990. "Feeling Safe by Comparison: Crime in the Newspapers." *Social Problems* 37(3): 360–74.

Liska, A.E., and B.D. Warner. 1991. "Functions of Crime: A Paradoxical Process." *American Journal of Sociology* 6: 1441–63.

Lizotte, A.J. 1985. "The Uniqueness of Rape: Reporting Assaultive Violence to the Police." *Crime and Delinquency* 31(2): 169–90.

Locher, D.A. 2002. *Collective Behavior.* Upper Saddle River NJ: Prentice-Hall.

Loeber, R., D.P. Farrington, and D.A. Waschbusch. 1998. "Serious and Violent Juvenile Offenders." In R. Loeber and D.P. Farrington (eds.), *Serious & Violent Juvenile Offenders: Risk Factors and Successful Interventions.* Thousand Oaks, CA: Sage.

Longshore, D. 1998. "Self-Control and Criminal Opportunity: A Prospective Test of the General Theory of Crime." *Social Problems* 45(1): 102–13.

Longshore, D., and S. Turner. 1998. "Self-Control and Criminal Opportunity: Cross-Sectional Test of the General Theory of Crime." *Criminal Justice and Behavior* 25(1): 81–98.

Loseke, D.R. 1989. "'Violence' Is 'Violence' . . . or Is It? The Social Construction of 'Wife Abuse' and Public Policy." In J. Best (ed.), *Images of Issues: Typifying Contemporary Social Problems.* New York: Aldine de Gruyter.

——— 2000. *Thinking about Social Problems: An Introduction to Constructionist Perspectives.* Hawthorne: Aldine de Gruyter.

Loseke, D., R.J. Gelles, and M.M. Cavanaugh. 2005. *Current Controversies on Family Violence.* Thousand Oaks, CA: Sage.

Lowenkamp, C.T., F.T. Cullen, and T.C. Pratt. 2003. "Replicating Sampson and Groves's Test of Social Disorganization Theory: Revisiting a Criminological Classic" *Journal of Research in Crime and Delinquency* 40(4): 351–73.

Lowney, K.S., and J. Best. 1995. "Stalking Strangers and Lovers: Changing Media Typifications of a New Crime Problem." In J. Best (ed.), *Images of Issues,* 2nd ed. New York: Aldine de Gruyter.

Luckenbill, D.F. 1977. "Criminal Homicide as a Situated Transaction." *Social Problems* 25(2): 176–86.

——— 1984. "Murder and Assault." In R.F. Meier (ed.), *Major Forms of Crime.* Beverly Hills: Sage.

Lurigio, A.J. 1987. "Are All Victims Alike? The Adverse, Generalized and Differential Impact of Crime." *Crime and Delinquency* 33: 452–67.

Luxton, M. 1988. "Thinking About the Future." *Family Matters: Sociology and Contemporary Canadian Families.* Toronto: Methuen.

Lyman, M.D., and G.W. Potter, 2004. *Organized Crime.* Upper Saddle Creek, NJ: Prentice-Hall.

Lynch, J.P. 1987. "Routine Activity and Victimization at Work." *Journal of Quantitative Criminology* 3(4): 283–300.

Lynch, J.P., and D. Cantor. 1992. "Ecological and Behavioral Influences on Property Victimization at Home: Implications for Opportunity Theory." *Journal of Research in Crime and Delinquency* 29(3): 335–62.

Lyon, D. 1994. *Electronic Eye: The Rise of Surveillance.* Cambridge: Polity Press.

McCarthy, B., and J. Hagan. 1991. "Homelessness: A Criminogenic Situation?" *British Journal of Criminology* 31(4): 393–410.

McCarthy, B., J. Hagan, and J. Monica. 2002. "In and Out of Harm's Way: Violent Victimization and the Social Capital in Fictive Street Families." *Criminology* 40(4): 831–66.

McCarthy, B., J. Hagan, and T.S. Woodward. 1999. "In the Company of Women: Structure and Agency in a Revised Power–Control Theory of Gender and Delinquency." *Criminology* 37(4): 761–88.

McClearly, R.M., B.C. Nienstedt, and J.M. Erven. 1982. "Uniform Crime Reports as Organizational Outcomes: Three Time Series Experiments." *Social Problems* 29(4): 361–72.

McCord, J. 1991. "Family Relationships, Juvenile Delinquency, and Adult Criminality." *Criminology* 29(3): 397–417.

——— 2003. "Cures That Harm: Unanticipated Outcomes of Crime Prevention Programs." *The Annals of the American Academy of Political and Social Science* 587: 17–30.

McCord, J., and K.P. Conway. 2005. *Co-Offending and Patterns of Juvenile Crime.* Washington DC: U.S. Department of Justice, Office of Justice Services.

McCorkle, R.C., and T. Miethe. 2002. *Panic: The Social Construction of the Street Gang Problem.* Upper Saddle River, NJ: Prentice-Hall.

McIntosh, M. 1975. *The Organization of Crime.* London: Macmillan.

McKay, B. 1996. *Visitor Crime in Florida: The Perception Vs the Reality.* Florida Department of Law Enforcement. http://www.fdle.state.fl.us/fsac/archives/visitor_crime.pdf.

McMahon, J.M., and J. Clay-Warner. 2002. "Child Abuse and Future Criminality: The Role of Codial Service Placement, Family Disorganization and Gender." *Journal of Interpersonal Violence* 17(9): 1002–19.

McMahon, T. "Race Study Results Under Fire: Criminologist Takes Aim at 'Inconclusive' Findings" *Kingston Whig-Standard,* June 7, 2005, p. 1.

Macmillan, R. 1995. "Changes in the Structure of Life Courses and the Decline of Social Capital in Canadian Society: A Time Series Analysis of Property Crime Rates." *Canadian Journal of Sociology* 20(1): 51–79.

———— 2000. "Adolescent Victimization and Income Deficits in Adulthood: Rethinking the Costs of Criminal Violence from a Life-Course Perspective." *Criminology* 38(2): 553–88.

———— 2001. "Violence and the Life Course: Assessing the Consequences of Violent Victimization for Personal and Social Development." *Annual Review of Sociology,* 27: 1–22.

McMullan, J.L., and D.C. Perrier. 2003. "Technologies of Crime: The Cyber Attacks on Electronic Gambling Machines." *Canadian Journal of Criminology and Criminal Justice* 45(2): 159–186.

Madriz, E. 1996. "The Perception of Risk in the Workplace: A Test of Routine Activity Theory." *Journal of Criminal Justice* 24(5): 407–18.

———— 1997. *Nothing Bad Happens to Good Girls.* Berkeley: University of California Press.

Maguire, B., D. Sandage, and G.A. Weatherby. 2000. "Violence, Morality, and Television Commercials." *Sociological Spectrum* 20: 121–43.

Maguire, M., with T. Bennett. 1982. *Burglary in a Dwelling: The Offence, the Offender and the Victim.* London: Heinemann.

Mahiri, J., and E. Connor. 2003. "Black Youth Violence has a Bad Rap." *Journal of Social Issues.* 59(1): 121–40.

Mahlstedt, D.L., and L.A. Welsh. 2005. "Perceived Causes of Physical Assault in Heterosexual Dating Relationships" *Violence Against Women* 11(4): 447–72.

Malamuth, N.M. 1983. "Factors Associated with Rape as Predictors of Laboratory Aggression against Women." *Journal of Personality and Social Psychology* 45: 432–42.

Malamuth, N.M., and E. Donnerstein. 1984. *Pornography and Sexual Aggression.* Orlando: Academic Press.

Mann, R.M. 1999. *Who Owns Domestic Abuse? The Local Politics of a Social Problem.* Toronto: University of Toronto Press.

Marcus, B. 2004. "Self-control in the General Theory of Crime: Theoretical Implications of a Measurement Problem." *Theoretical Criminology* 8(1): 33–55.

Martin, R., R.J. Mutchnick, and W.T. Austin. 1990. *Criminological Thought: Pioneers Past and Present.* New York: Macmillan.

Massey, J.L., M.D. Krohn, and L.M. Bonati. 1989. "Property Crime and the Routine Activities of Individuals." *Journal of Research in Crime and Delinquency* 26(4): 378–400.

Mastrofski, S. 1983. "The Police and Noncrime Services." In G. Whitaker and C.D. Phillips (eds.), *Evaluating Performance of Criminal Justice Agencies.* Beverly Hills: Sage.

Mastrofski, S.D., J.B. Snipes, R.B. Parks, and C.D. Maxwell. 2000. "The Helping Hand of the Law: Police Control of Citizens on Request." *Criminology* 38(2): 307–42.

Matza, D., and G.M. Sykes. 1957. "Techniques of Neutralization: A Theory of Delinquency." *American Sociological Review* 5: 1–12.

——— 1961. "Juvenile Delinquency and Subterranean Values." *American Sociological Review* 26: 712–19.

Maxfield, M.G. 1987. "Household Composition, Routine Activity, and Victimization: A Comparative Analysis." *Journal of Quantitative Criminology* 3(4): 301–20.

——— 1990. "Homicide Circumstances, 1976–1985: A Taxonomy Based on Supplementary Homicide Reports." *Criminology* 28: 671–95.

Maxfield, M.G., B.L. Weiler, and C.S. Widom. 2000. "Comparing Self-Reports and Official Records of Arrests." *Journal of Quantitative Criminology* 16(1): 87–110.

Maxwell, C.D., A.L. Robinson, and L.A. Post. 2003. "The Nature of Predictors of Sexual Victimization and Offending Among Adolescents." *Journal of Youth and Adolescence* 32(6): 465–77.

Maxwell, S.R., and M.K. Gray. 2000. "Deterrence: Testing the Effects of Perceived Sanction Certainty on Probation Violations." *Sociological Inquiry* 70(2): 117–36.

May, D.C., and R.G. Dunaway. 2000. "Predictors of Fear of Criminal Victimization at School among Adolescents." *Sociological Spectrum* 20: 149–68.

May, H. 1999. "Who Killed Whom? Victimization and Culpability in the Social Construction of Murder." *British Journal of Sociology* 50(3): 489–506.

Mayhew, P., D. Elliott, and L. Dowds. 1989. *The 1988 British Crime Survey: A Home Office Research and Planning Unit Report.* London: HMSO Books.

Mazerolle, L., D. Hurley, and M.B. Chamlin. 2002. "Social

Behavior in a Public Space: An Analysis of Behavioral Adaptation to CCTV." *Security Journal* 15(3): 59–75.

Mazerolle, P. 1998. "Gender, Strain and Delinquency: An Empirical Examination." *Justice Quarterly.* 15(1): 65–91.

Mazerolle, P., R. Brame, R. Paternoster, A. Piquero, and C. Dean. 2000. "Onset Age, Persistence, and Offending Versatility: Comparisons Across Gender." *Criminology* 38(4): 1143–72.

Meadows, R.J. 1998. *Understanding Violence and Victimization.* Upper Saddle River, NJ: Prentice Hall.

Mednick, S., T. Moffitt, and S. Stack. 1987. *The Causes of Crime: New Biological Approaches.* New York: Cambridge University Press.

Meehan, A.J. 2000. "The Organizational Career of Gang Statistics: The Politics of Policing." *Sociology Quarterly* 41(3): 337–70.

Meier, R., and G. Geis. 1997. *Victimless Crimes?: Prostitution, Drugs, and Abortion.* Los Angeles: Roxbury.

Meier, R.F., L.W. Kennedy, and V.F. Sacco (eds.). 2001. *The Process and Structure of Crime: Criminal Events and Crime Analysis.* Vol. 9, Advances in Criminological Theory. Piscataway, NJ: Transaction Publishers.

Melbin, M. 1987. *Night as Frontier.* New York: The Free Press.

Melchers, R. 2003. "Do Toronto Police Engage in Racial Profiling?" *Canadian Journal of Criminology*

and Criminal Justice 45(3): 347–66.

Menard, S. 1995. "A Developmental Test of Mertonian Anomie Theory." *Journal of Research in Crime and Delinquency* 32(2): 136–74.

Menard, S. 2002. "Short- and Long-Term Consequences of Adolescent Victimization." *OJJDP Youth Violence Research Bulletin.* Washington, DC: U.S. Department of Justice, Office of Juvenile Justice and Delinquency Prevention; Centers for Disease Control and Prevention.

Menard, S., and H.C. Covey. 1988. "UCR and NCS: Comparisons over Space and Time." *Journal of Criminal Justice* 16: 371–84.

Merry, S.E. 1981. *Urban Danger.* Philadelphia: Temple University Press.

Merton, R.K. 1938. "Social Structure and Anomie." *American Sociological Review* 3: 672–82.

Messner, S., and R. Rosenfeld. 1997. *Crime and the American Dream.* 2nd ed. Belmont: Wadsworth.

Messner, S.F., and J.R. Blau. 1987. "Routine Leisure Activities and Rates of Crime: A Macro-Level Analysis." *Social Forces* 65: 1035–51.

Michalowski, R.J., and E.W. Bohlander. 1976. "Repression and Criminal Justice in Capitalist America." *Sociological Inquiry* 46(2): 95–106.

Miethe, T.D. 1995. "Fear and Withdrawal from Urban Life."

Annals of the American Academy of Political and Social Science 539: 14–27.

Miethe, T.D., and K.A. Drass. 1999. "Exploring the Social Context of Instrumental and Expressive Homicides: An Application of Qualitative Comparative Analysis." *Journal of Quantitative Criminology* 15(1): 1–21.

Miethe, T.D., and G.R. Lee. 1984. "Fear of Crime among Older People: A Reassessment of the Predictive Power of Crime-Related Factors." *The Sociological Quarterly* 25: 397–415.

Miethe, T.D., and R. McCorkle. 1998. *Crime Profiles: The Anatomy of Dangerous Persons, Places, and Situations.* Los Angeles: Roxbury.

Miethe, T.D., and R.F. Meier. 1994. *Crime and Its Social Context.* Albany: State University of New York Press.

Miethe, T.D. and W. Regoeczi. 2004. *Rethinking Homicide: Exploring the Structure and Process Underlying Deadly Situations.* Cambridge: Cambridge University Press.

Mihorean, K. 2005. "Trends in Self-Reported Spousal Violence." In K. AuCoin (ed.), *Family Violence in Canada: A Statistical Profile 2005.* Ottawa: Canadian Centre for Justice Statistics, Statistics Canada.

Milan, A. 2000. "One Hundred Years of Families." *Canadian Social Trends* Spring: 2–12.

Miller, J.L., and A.B. Anderson. 1986. "Updating the Deterrence Doctrine." *Journal of Criminal Law and Criminology* 77(2): 418–38.

Miller, L.J. 1990. "Violent Families and the Rhetoric of Harmony." *British Journal of Sociology* 41(2): 263–88.

Miller, S.L. 2005. *Victims as Offenders.* New Brunswick, NJ: Rutgers University Press.

Miller, S.L., and C. Burack. 1993. "A Critique of Gottfredson and Hirschi's General Theory of Crime: Selective (In)attention to Gender and Power Positions." *Women and Criminal Justice.* 4(2): 115–34.

Miller, T.R., M.A. Cohen, and B. Wiersema. 1996. *Victim Costs and Consequences: A New Look.* Washington: National Institute of Justice.

Miller, W. 1958. "Lower Class Culture as a Generating Milieu of Gang Delinquency." *Journal of Social Issues* 14: 5–19.

Minor, W.W. 1981. "Techniques of Neutralization: A Reconceptualization and Empirical Examination." *Journal of Research in Crime and Delinquency* 18: 295–318.

Miranda, D., and M. Claes. 2004. "Rap Music Genres and Deviant Behaviors in French-Canadian Adolescents." *Journal of Youth and Adolescence* 33(2): 113–22.

Mirrlees-Black, C., T. Budd, S. Partridge, and P. Mayhew. 1998.

"The 1998 British Crime Survey." *Home Office Statistical Bulletin* 21.

Mirrlees-Black, C.P. Mayhew, and A. Percy. 1996. *The 1996 British Crime Survey.* London: Home Office.

Moeller, G.L. 1989. "Fear of Criminal Victimization: The Effects of Neighborhood Racial Composition." *Sociological Inquiry* 59: 208–21.

Moffitt, T.E., D.R. Lynam, and P.A. Silva. 1994. "Neuropsychological Tests Predicting Persistent Male Delinquency." *Criminology* 32(2): 277–300.

Monkkonen, E.H. 1983. "The Organized Response to Crime in Nineteenth- and Twentieth-Century America." *Journal of Interdisciplinary History* 14(1): 113–28.

Morin, E. 1971. *Rumor in Orléans.* New York: Pantheon.

Mosher, C.J., T.D. Miethe, and D.M. Phillips. 2002. *The Mismeasure of Crime.* Thousand Oaks, CA: Sage Publications.

Muehlenhard, C.L., and M.A. Linton. 1987. "Date Rape and Sexual Aggression in Dating Situations: Incidence and Risk Factors." *Journal of Counseling Psychology* 34(2): 186–96.

Murphy, C. 1993. "The Development, Impact, and Implications of Community Policing in Canada." In J. Chacko and S.E. Nancoo (eds.), *Community Policing in Canada*, pp. 13–26. Toronto: Canadian Scholars' Press.

Murray, C., and R. Herrnstein. 1994. *The Bell Curve.* New York: The Free Press.

Nagin, D.S., and R. Paternoster. 1993. "Enduring Individual Differences and Rational Choices of Crime." *Law and Society Review* 27(3): 467–96.

Nakhaie, M.R., R.A. Silverman, and T.C. LaGrange. 2000. "Self Control and Social Control." *Canadian Journal of Sociology* 25(1): 35–59.

National Crime Prevention Centre. 2000. *Policy Framework for Addressing Crime Prevention and Youth Ages 12 to 18.* Ottawa: National Crime Prevention Centre.

National Crime Prevention Centre. No date. *Jack's Troubled Career.* Ottawa: National Crime Prevention Centre.

National Crime Prevention Institute. 1986. *Understanding Crime Prevention.* Boston: Butterworths.

Naughton, K. 2005. "Martha Breaks Out." *Newsweek.* (March 7): 36

Naylor, R.T. 2002. *Wages of Crime: Black Markets, Illegal Finance and the Underworld Economy.* Ithaca, NY: Cornell University Press.

Ness, C.D. 2004. "Why Girls Fight: Female Youth Violence in the Inner City." *Annals of the American Academy of Political and Social Science* 595: 32–48

Nettler, G. 1984. *Explaining Crime.* New York: McGraw-Hill.

Newman, G.R. 1990. "Popular Culture and Criminal Justice: A Preliminary Analysis." *Journal of Criminal Justice* 18: 261–74.

Newman, O. 1972. *Defensible Space: Crime Prevention through Urban Design.* New York: Macmillan.

Nicholas, S., D. Povey, A. Walker, and C. Kershaw. 2005. *Crime in England and Wales 2004/2005.* London: Home Office Statistical Bulletin. http://www.homeoffice. gov.uk/rds/

Normandeau, A. 1987. "Crime on the Montreal Metro." *Sociology and Social Research* 71(4): 289–92.

Normandeau, A., and B. Leighton. 1993. "A Growing Canadian Consensus: Community Policing." In J. Chacko and S.E. Nancoo (eds.), *Community Policing in Canada.* Toronto: Canadian Scholars' Press.

Nye, F.I. 1958. *Family Relationships and Delinquent Behavior.* New York: John Wiley.

Obeidallah, D., and F.J. Earls. 1999. *Adolescent Girls: The Role of Depression in the Development of Delinquency.* Washington: Office of Justice Programs, U.S. Department of Justice.

Oberwittler, D. 2004. "A Multilevel Analysis of Neighborhood Contextual Effects on Serious Juvenile Offending: The Role of Subcultural Values and Social Disorganization." *European Journal of Criminology* 1(3): 201–35.

O'Brien, R.M. 1985. *Crime and Victimization Data.* Vol. 4, Law and Criminal Justice Series. Beverly Hills: Sage.

——— 1986. "Rare Events, Sample Sizes and Statistical Problems in the Analysis of the NCS City Surveys." *Journal of Criminal Justice* 14: 441–48.

O'Grady, B. 1989. "Crime Violence and Victimization: A Newfoundland Case." *Canadian Criminology Forum* 10: 1–16.

O'Kane, J.M. 1992. *Crooked Ladder: Gangsters, Ethnicity and the American Dream.* New Brunswick, NJ: Transaction Books.

O'Keefe, G.J. 1984. "Public Views on Crime: Television Exposure and Media Credibility." In R.N. Bostrom (ed.), *Communication Yearbook* 8. Beverly Hills: Sage.

Osgood, D.W., and J.M. Chambers. 2000. "Social Disorganization Outside the Metropolis: An Analysis of Rural Youth Violence." *Criminology* 38(1): 81–115.

Osgood, D.W., J.K. Wilson, P.M. O'Malley, J.G. Bachman, and L.D. Johnston. 1996. "Routine Activities and Individual Deviant Behaviour." *American Sociological Review* 61: 635–55.

Ouimet, M. 2002. "Explaining the American and Canadian Crime 'Drop' in the 1990s." *Canadian Journal of Criminology.* 44(1): 33–50.

Packer, H.L. 1969. *The Limits of the Criminal Sanction.* Stanford: Stanford University Press.

Paetsch, J.J., and L. D. Bertrand. 1999. "Victimization and Delinquency among Canadian Youth." *Adolescence* 34(134): 351–67.

Pagelow, M.D. 1989. "The Incidence and Prevalence of Criminal Abuse of Other Family Members." In L. Ohlin and M. Tonry (eds.), *Family Violence*. Chicago: University of Chicago Press.

Palenski, J.E. 1984. "The Use of Mediation by Police." *Mediation Quarterly* 5: 31–8.

Papadopoulos, C. 1997. *A Comparison of Crime in the U.S. and Canada*. Unpublished MA thesis. Edmonton: University of Alberta.

Parks, G. 2000. "The High/Scope Perry Preschool Project." *OJJDP Juvenile Justice Bulletin*. Washington, DC: Office of Justice Programs, U.S. Department of Justice.

Parnaby, P., and V.F. Sacco, 2004. "Fame and Strain: The Contributions of Mertonian Deviance Theory to an Understanding of the Relationship between Celebrity and Deviant Behavior." *Deviant Behavior* 25: 1–26.

Parsons, T. 1951. *The Social System*. Glencoe: Free Press.

Passas, N., and R. Agnew. 1997. *The Future of Anomie Theory*. Boston: Northeastern University Press.

Paternoster, R., and R. Brame. 1997. "Multiple Routes to Delinquency? A Test of Developmental and General Theories of Crime." *Criminology* 35(1): 49–84.

Paternoster, R., and P. Mazerolle. 1994. "General Strain Theory and Delinquency: A Replication and Extension." *Journal of Research in Crime and Delinquency* 31(3): 235–63.

Patterson, G.R., and T.J. Dishion. 1985. "Contributions of Families and Peers to Delinquency." *Criminology* 23: 63–79.

Paulsen, D.J. 2003. "Murder in Black and White: The Newspaper Coverage of Homicide in Houston." *Homicide Studies* 7(3): 289–317.

Pearce, F., and L. Snider. 1995. *Corporate Crime: Contemporary Debates*. Toronto: University of Toronto Press.

Pease, K., and G. Laycock. 1996. *Revictimization: Reducing the Heat on Hot Victims*. Washington: National Institute of Justice.

Pepler, D.J., W.M. Craig, and J. Connolly. 1997. *Bullying and Victimization: The Problem and Solutions for School-Aged Children*. Ottawa: National Crime Prevention Council.

Perrone, D., C.J. Sullivan, T.C. Pratt, and S. Margaryan. 2004. "Parental Efficacy, Self-Control, and Delinquency: A Test of a General Theory of Crime on a Nationally Representative Sample of Youth." *International Journal of Offender Therapy and Comparative Criminology* 48(3): 298–312.

Peters, T., T.C. LaGrange, and R.A. Silverman. 2003. "Investigating the Interdependence of Strain and Self-Control." *Canadian Journal of Criminology and Criminal Justice* 45(4): 431–64.

Pfohl, S. 1977. "The Discovery of Child Abuse." *Social Problems* 24(3): 315–21.

Pfuhl, E.H. 1986. *The Deviance Process.* 2nd ed. Belmont: Wadsworth.

Phelps, T.G. 1983. "The Criminal as Hero in American Fiction." *Wisconsin Law Review* 6: 1427–54.

Pillemer, K.A., and D. Finkelhor. 1988. "The Prevalence of Elder Abuse: A Random Sample Survey." *The Gerontologist* 28(1): 51–57.

Pipes, D. 1997. *Conspiracy: How the Paranoid Style Flourishes and Where it Comes From.* New York: Free Press.

Piquero, A.R., and M. Hickman. 2003. "Extending Tittle's Control Balance Theory to Account for Victimization." *Criminal Justice and Behavior* 30(3): 282–301.

Piquero, A.R., R. MacIntosh, and M. Hickman. 2000. "Does Self-Control Affect Survey Response? Applying Exploratory Confirmatory, and Item Response Theory Analysis to Grasmick et al.'s Self-Control Scale." *Criminology* 38(3): 897–929.

Piquero A., and R. Paternoster. 1998. "An Application of Stafford and Warr's Reconceptualization of Deterrence to Drinking and Driving." *Journal of Research in Crime and Delinquency* 35(1): 3–39.

Piquero, N.L., and M.D. Sealock. 2004. "Gender and General Strain Theory: A Preliminary Test of Broidy and Agnew's Gender/GST Hypotheses." *Justice Quarterly* 21(1): 125–58.

Piquero, A., and R. Tibbetts. 2002. *Rational Choice and Criminal Behavior.* New York: Routledge.

Pizam, A., and Y. Mansfeld. 1996. *Tourism, Crime and International Security Issues.* New York: Wiley.

Pogarsky, G., and A.R. Piquero. 2003. "Can Punishment Encourage Offending? Investigating the 'Resetting' Effect" *Journal of Research in Crime and Delinquency* 40(1): 95–120.

Pogarsky, G., A.R. Piquero, and R. Paternoster. 2004. "Modeling Change in Perceptions about Sanction Threats: The Neglected Linkage in Deterrence Theory." *Journal of Quantitative Criminology* 20(4): 343–69.

Porter, P. 2005. "Kingston Police Race Study Attacked; Officers' Group, Professor Dispute Claim of Race Bias; Police Chief Says the Criticism Was Expected." *Toronto Star,* June 8, 2005: A14.

Potter, R.H., and L.E. Saltzman. 2000. "Violence Prevention and Corrections-related Activities of the Centers for Disease Control and Prevention." *The Criminologist* 25(2): 1, 4–6.

Pound, R. 1943. "A Survey of Social Interests." *Harvard Law Review* 53: 1–39.

Pratt, T.C., and F.T. Cullen. 2000. "The Empirical Status of Gottfredson and Hirschi's General Theory of Crime: A Meta-Analysis." *Criminology* 38(3): 931–64.

Presser, L. 2003. "Remorse and Neutralization among Violent Male Offenders." *Justice Quarterly*. 20(4): 801–25.

Prinz, R. 2000. "Research-Based Prevention of School Violence and Youth Antisocial Behavior: A Developmental and Education Perspective." In *Preventing School Violence: Plenary Papers of the 1999 Conference on Criminal Justice Research and Evaluation—Enhancing Policy and Practice Through Research*. Vol. 2. Washington, DC: U.S. Department of Justice.

Public Safety and Emergency Preparedness Canada. *National Crime Prevention Strategy*. http://www.psepc-sppcc.gc.ca/prg/cp/ncps-en.asp#1

Putnam, R.D. 2000. *Bowling Alone: The Collapse and Revival of American Community*. New York: Simon and Schuster.

Quinn, M.J., and S.K. Tomita. 1986. *Elder Abuse and Neglect: Causes, Diagnosis and Intervention Strategies*. New York: Springer-Verlag.

Rader, N.E. 2004. "The Threat of Victimization: A Theoretical Reconceptualization of Fear of Crime." *Sociological Spectrum* 24: 689–704.

Radford, B. 2003. *Media Mythmakers: How Journalists, Activists and Advertisers Mislead Us*. Amherst, NY: Prometheus Books.

Ramos, Reyes. 1998. "Anatomy of a Drive-By: What Can We Learn from an Unexpected Death?" *The Sociological Quarterly* 39(2): 271–88.

Randall, D.M., L. Lee-Sammons, and P.H. Hagner. 1988. "Common versus Elite Crime Coverage in Network News." *Social Science Quarterly* 69(4): 910–29.

Rankin, J.H., and L.E. Wells. 1990. "The Effect of Parental Attachments and Direct Controls on Delinquency." *Journal of Research in Crime and Delinquency* 27(2): 140–65.

Reasons, C.E., L. Ross, and C. Paterson. 1981. *Assault on the Worker: Occupational Health and Safety in Canada*. Toronto: Butterworths.

Reckless, W. 1967. *The Crime Problem*. 4th ed. New York: Meredith.

Redmon, D. 2003. "Examining Low Self-control Theory at Mardi Gras: Critiquing the General Theory of Crime Within the Framework of Normative Deviance." *Deviant Behavior* 24(4): 373–392.

Reiman, J. 2003. *The Rich Get Richer and the Poor Get Prison*. 7th ed. Boston: Allyn and Bacon.

Reinarman, C., and H.G. Levine. 1989. "The Crack Attack: Politics and Media in America's Latest

Drug Scare." In J. Best (ed.), *Images of Issues.* New York: Aldine de Gruyter.

Reiss, Jr., A.J. 1951. "Delinquency as the Failure of Personal and Social Control." *American Sociological Review* 16 (April): 196–207.

———— 1984. "Consequences of Compliance and Deterrence Models of Law Enforcement for the Exercise of Police Discretion." *Law and Contemporary Problems* 47(4): 83–122.

———— 1986. "Official and Survey Crime Statistics." In E.A. Fattah (ed.), *From Crime Policy to Victim Policy—Reorienting the Justice System.* London: Macmillan.

Reppetto, T. 1974. *Residential Crime.* Cambridge: Ballinger.

Resick, P.A. 1987. "Psychological Effects of Victimization: Implications for the Criminal Justice System." *Crime and Delinquency* 33: 468–78.

Reuter, P. 1984a. "The (Continued) Vitality of Mythical Numbers." *Public Interest* 75: 135–47.

———— 1984b. "Social Control in Illegal Markets." In D. Black (ed.), *Toward a General Theory of Social Control, Volume 2: Selected Problems.* Orlando: Academic Press.

———— 1995. "The Decline of the American Mafia." *The Public Interest* 120: 88–89.

Rice, T.W., and C.R. Goldman. 1994. "Another Look at the Subculture of Violence Thesis: Who Murders Whom under What Circumstances?" *Sociological Spectrum* 14: 371–84.

Richie, B.E. 2000. "Exploring the Link Between Violence Against Women and Women's Involvement in Illegal Activity." *Research on Women and Girls in the Justice System.* Vol. 3. Washington: Office of Justice Programs, National Institute of Justice.

Riger, S., S. Raja, and J. Camacho. 2002. "The Radiating Impact of Intimate Partner Violence." *Journal of Interpersonal Violence* 17(2): 184–205.

Riley, D. 1987. "Time and Crime: The Link between Teenager Lifestyle and Delinquency." *Journal of Quantitative Criminology* 3(4): 339–54.

Rinfret-Raynor, M., A. Riou, and S. Cantin. 2004. "A Survey on Violence Against Female Partners in Quebec, Canada." *Violence Against Women* 10(7): 709–28.

Roberts, D. 1999a. "Insanity Rulings Blasted after Killings in Winnipeg." *Globe and Mail,* January 5, 1999: A1, A7.

———— 1999b. "Man Gets Two Life Sentences in Killings." *Globe and Mail,* December 4, 1999: A2.

Roberts, J.V. 1994. "Crime and Race Statistics: Toward a Canadian Solution." *Canadian Journal of Criminology* 36(2): 175.

Roberts, J.V., and A.N. Doob. 1997. "Race, Ethnicity and Criminal Justice in Canada." In M. Tonry (ed.), *Ethnicity, Crime and*

Immigration: Comparative and Cross-National Perspectives, Vol. 21, Crime and Justice. Chicago: University of Chicago Press.

Roberts, J.V., and R. Melchers. 2003. "The Incarceration of Aboriginal Offenders: Trends From 1978 to 2001." *Canadian Journal of Criminology and Criminal Justice* 45(2): 211–42.

Roberts, K. 1983. *Youth and Leisure.* London: George Allen & Unwin.

Robinson, M.B., and B.H. Zaitzow. 1999. "Criminologists: Are We What We Study? A National Self-Report Study of Crime Experts." *The Criminologist* 24(2): 1, 4, 17–19.

Rome, D. 2004. *Black Demons: The Media's Depiction of the African American Male Criminal Stereotype.* Westport, CT: Praeger.

Roncek, D.W., and P.A. Maier. 1991. "Bars, Blocks and Crimes Revisited: Linking the Theory of Routine Activities to the Empiricism of 'Hot Spots.'" *Criminology* 29(4): 725–53.

Roncek, D.W., and M.A. Pravatiner. 1989. "Additional Evidence That Taverns Enhance Nearby Crime." *Sociology and Social Research* 73(4): 185–8.

Rosenbaum, D.P. 1987. "The Theory and Research behind Neighborhood Watch: Is It a Sound Fear and Crime Reduction Strategy?" *Crime and Delinquency* 33(1): 103–34.

———— 1988. "Community Crime Prevention: A Review and Synthesis of the Literature." *Justice Quarterly* 5(3): 323–95.

Rosnow, R.L. 1988. "Rumour as Communication: A Contextual Approach." *Journal of Communication* 38(1): 12–28.

Rosnow, R.L., and G.A. Fine. 1976. *Rumor and Gossip.* New York: Elsevier.

Ross, H.L. 1982. *Deterring the Drinking Driver.* Lexington, MA: Lexington Books.

Ross, R., and G.L. Staines. 1972. "The Politics of Analyzing Social Problems." *Social Problems* 20(1): 18–40.

Rossmo, D. K. 2000. *Geographic Profiling.* Boca Raton, FL: CRC Press.

Roth, D., and S.L. Muzzatti. 2004. "Enemies Everywhere: Terrorism, Moral Panic and US Civil Society." *Critical Criminology* 12(3): 327–50.

Rountree, P.W. 2000. "Weapons at School: Are the Predictors Generalizable Across Context?" *Sociological Spectrum* 20: 291–324.

Rowe, D.C. 2001. *Biology and Crime.* Los Angeles: Roxbury Publishing Company.

Ruback, R.B., and M.P. Thompson. 2001. *Social and Psychological Consequences of Violent Victimization.* Thousand Oaks, CA: Sage Publications.

Rubington, C., and M.S. Weinberg. 1987. *Deviance: The Interactionist Perspective.* New York: Macmillan.

Rush, G. 1994. *The Dictionary of Criminal Justice.* 4th ed. Guilford: Dushkin.

Sacco, V.F. 1990. "Gender, Fear and Victimization: A Preliminary Application of Power–Control Theory." *Sociological Spectrum* 10: 485–506.

——— 1995. "Media Constructions of Crime." *The Annals of the American Academy of Political and Social Science* 539: 141–54.

——— 1998. "Evaluating Satisfaction." In J-P. Brodeur (ed.), *How to Recognize Good Policing: Problems and Issues,* pp. 123- 37. Thousand Oaks, CA: Sage.

——— 2000. "News that Counts: Newspaper Images of Crime and Victimization Statistics." *Criminologie* 33(1): 203–23.

——— 2005. *When Crime Waves.* Thousand Oaks, CA: Sage Publications.

Sacco, V.F., and B.J. Fair. 1988. "Images of Legal Control: Crime News and the Process of Organizational Legitimation." *Canadian Journal of Communication* 13: 113–22.

Sacco, V.F., and H. Johnson. 1990. *Patterns of Criminal Victimization in Canada.* Ottawa: Minister of Supply and Services.

Sacco, V.F., H. Johnson, and R. Arnold. 1993. "Urban–Rural Residence and Criminal Victimization." *Canadian Journal of Sociology* 18(4): 431–51.

Sacco, V.F., and M.R. Nakhaie. 2001. "Coping With Crime: An Examination of Elderly and Nonelderly Adaptations." *International Journal of Law and Psychiatry* 24: 305–23.

Sacco, V.F., and R.A. Silverman. 1982. "Crime Prevention through Mass Media: Prospects and Problems." *Journal of Criminal Justice* 10: 257–69.

Sacco, V.F., and E. Zureik. 1990. "Correlates of Computer Misuses: Data from a Self-Reporting Sample." *Behaviour and Information Technology* 9(5): 353- 69.

Sagarin, E. 1975. *Deviants and Deviance.* New York: Praeger.

Sugrestano, L.M., C.L. Heavey, and A. Christensen. 1999. "Perceived Power and Physical Violence in Marital Conflict." *Journal of Social Issues* 55(1): 65–79.

Sailer, S. 2006. "Analysis: IQ defenders feel vindicated." (June 24). United Press International.

Saleno, A.W. 1994. "Boot Camps: A Critique and Proposed Alternative." *Journal of Offender Rehabilitation* 20: 147–58.

Sales, E., M. Baum, and B. Shore. 1984. "Victim Readjustment Following Assault." *Journal of Social Issues* 40(1): 117–36.

Salinger, L.R., P. Jesilow, H.N. Pontell, and G. Geis. 1993. "Assaults against Airline Flight Attendants: A Victimization Study." In H.N. Pontell (ed.), *Social Deviance.* Englewood Cliffs: Prentice-Hall.

Sampson, R.J. 1985. "Race and Criminal Violence: A Demographically Disaggregated Analysis of Urban Homicide." *Crime and Delinquency* 31(1): 47–82.

——— 2000. "Whither the Sociological Study of Crime?" *Annual Review of Sociology* 26: 711–14.

Sampson, R.J., and W.B. Groves. 1989. "Community Structure and Crime: Testing Social Disorganization Theory." *American Journal of Sociology* 94: 774–802.

Sampson, R.J., and J.L. Lauritsen. 1990. "Deviant Lifestyles, Proximity Crime, and the Offender-Victim Link in Personal Violence." *Journal of Research in Crime and Delinquency* 27(2): 110–39.

Sampson, R.J., and S.W. Raudenbush. 1999. "Systematic Social Observations of Public Spaces: A New Look at Disorder in Urban Neighborhoods." *American Journal of Sociology* 105(3): 603–651.

Sampson, R.J., S. Raudenbush, and F.J. Earls. 1997. "Neighborhoods and Violent Crime: A Multilevel Study of Collective Efficacy." *Science* 277: 918–24.

Sanders, T. 2005. "Rise of the Rent-a-Cop: Private Security in Canada, 1991–2001." *Canadian Journal of Criminology and Criminal Justice* 47(1): 175–91.

Sasson, T. 1995. *Crime Talks.* New York: Aldine de Gruyter.

Sauvé, J. 2005. "Crime Statistics in Canada 2004." *Juristat* 25(5).

Savelsberg, J.J. 1999. "Human Nature and Social Control in Complex Society: A Critique of Charles Tittle's Control Balance." *Theoretical Criminology* 3(3): 331–38.

Savelsberg, J.J., R. King, and L. Cleveland. 2002. "Politicized Scholarship? Science in Crime and the State." *Social Problems* 49(3): 327–48.

Savitz, L.D. 1978. "Official Police Statistics and Their Limitations." In L.D. Savitz and N. Johnston (eds.), *Crime in Society.* New York: John Wiley.

Scheingold, S.A. 1984. *The Politics of Law and Order: Street Crime and Public Policy.* New York: Longman.

Schelling, T.C. 1967. "Economic Analysis of Organized Crime." In *President's Commission on Law Enforcement and Administration of Justice Task Force Report: Organized Crime, Annotations and Consultant's Papers,* pp. 114–26. Washington: U.S. Government Printing Office.

Scheppele, K.L., and P.B. Bart. 1983. "Through Women's Eyes: Defining Danger in the Wake of Sexual Assault." *Journal of Social Issues* 39: 63–81.

Schissel, B. 1992. "The Influence of Economic Factors and Social Control Policy on Crime Rate Changes in Canada, 1962–1988." *Canadian Journal of Sociology* 17(4): 405–28.

Schlesinger, P., R.E. Dobash, R.P. Dobash, and C.K. Weaver. 1992. *Women Viewing Violence.* London: BFI.

Schmid, D. 2005. *Natural Born Celebrities: Serial Killers in American Culture.* Chicago: University of Chicago Press.

Schneider, J.L. 2005. "Stolen-goods Markets: Methods of Disposal." *British Journal of Criminology* 45(2): 129–40.

Schneider, M.C., T. Rowell, and V. Bezdikian. 2003. "The Impact of Citizen Perceptions of Community Policing on Fear of Crime: Findings from Twelve Cities." *Police Quarterly* 6(4): 363–86.

Schneider, S. 2004 "Money Laundering in Canada: A qualitative Analysis of Royal Canadian Mounted Police Cases." *Journal of Financial Crime* 11(3): 282–91

Schneider, V.W., and B. Wiersema. 1990. "Limits and Use of the Uniform Crime Reports." In D.L. MacKenzie, P.J. Baunach, and R.R. Roberg (eds.), *Measuring Crime: Large-Scale, Long-Range Efforts.* Albany: State University of New York Press.

Schreck, C.J. 1999. Criminal victimization and low self-control: An extension and test of a general theory of crime." *Justice Quarterly* 16(3): 633–54.

Schreck, C.J., J.M. Miller, and C. Gibson. 2003. "Trouble in the Schoolyard: A Study of Risk Factors of Victimization at School." *Crime and Delinquency* 49(3): 460–84.

Schulenberg, J. 2003. "The Social Context of Police Discretion with Young Offenders." *Canadian Journal of Criminology and Criminal Justice* 45(2): 127–58.

Schur, E.M. 1965. *Crimes without Victims.* Englewood Cliffs: Prentice-Hall.

Schwartz, M.D., W.S. DeKeseredy, D. Tait, and S. Alvi. 2001. "Male Peer Support and a Feminist Routine Activities Theory: Understanding Sexual Assault on the College Campus." *Justice Quarterly* 18(3): 623–49.

Scott, M.S. 2006. "Assaults in and Around Bars." 2nd ed. Center for Problem Oriented Policing. http://www.popcenter.org/Proble ms/problem-assaults.htm

Scott, M.S., and H. Goldstein, 2005. *Shifting and Sharing Responsibility for Public Safety Problems.* Washington, DC: U.S. Department of Justice, Office of Community Oriented Policing Services.

Scott, M., and S. Lyman. 1968. "Accounts." *American Sociological Review* 33: 42–62.

Scully, D., and J. Marolla. 1984. "Convicted Rapists' Vocabulary of

Motive: Excuses and Justifications." *Social Problems* 31(5): 530–44.

Sellin, T. 1938. "Culture Conflict and Crime." A Report of the Subcommittee on Delinquency of the Committee on Personality and Culture. *Social Science Research Council Bulletin* 41.

Shaffer, E.B. 1980. *Community Policing.* London: Croon Helm.

Shamsie, J., S. Nicholl, and K.C. Madsen. 1999. *Antisocial and Violent Youth.* Toronto: Lugus.

Shaw, C.R., and H.D. McKay. 1942. *Juvenile Delinquency in Urban Areas.* Chicago: University of Chicago Press.

Sheldon, W.H. 1949. *Varieties of Delinquent Youth: An Introduction to Constitutional Psychiatry.* New York: Harper and Brothers.

Sheley, J.F. 1991. "Conflict in Criminal Law." In J.F. Sheley (ed.), *Criminology: A Contemporary Handbook.* Belmont: Wadsworth.

Sheley, J.F., and J.D. Wright. 1998. "High School Youths, Weapons, and Violence: A National Survey." National Institute of Justice Research in Brief. Washington: Office of Justice Programs, National Institute of Justice.

Sherley, A.J. 2005. "Contextualizing the Sexual Assault Event: Images From Police Files." *Deviant Behavior* 26: 87–108.

Sherman, L. 1992. *Policing Domestic Violence: Experiments and Dilemmas.* New York: The Free Press.

Sherman, L., and R. Berk. 1984. "The Specific Deterrent Effects of Arrest for Domestic Assault." *American Sociological Review* 49: 261–72.

Sherman, L., P.R. Gartin, and M.E. Buerger. 1989. "Routine Activities and the Criminology of Place." *Criminology* 27(1): 27–55.

Sherman, L., D.C. Gottfredson, D.L. MacKenzie, J. Eck, P. Reuter, and S.D. Bushway. 1998. *Preventing Crime: What Works, What Doesn't, What's Promising.* National Institute of Justice Research in Brief. Washington, DC: Office of Justice Programs, U.S. Department of Justice. http://www.ncjrs.org/works/

Sherrill, R. 1997. "A Year in Corporate Crime." *The Nation,* April 7: 11–12, 14, 16–20.

Shibutani, T. 1966. *Improvised News: A Sociological Study of Rumor.* Indianapolis: Bobbs-Merrill.

Shotland, R.L. 1976. "Spontaneous Vigilantism: A Bystander Response to Criminal Behavior." In H.J. Rosenbaum and P.C. Sederberg (eds.), *Vigilante Politics.* Philadelphia: University of Pennsylvania Press.

Shotland, R.L., and L.I. Goodstein. 1984. "The Role of Bystanders in Crime Control." *Journal of Social Issues* 40(1): 9–26.

Shotland, R.L., and M.K. Straw. 1976. "Bystander Response to an Assault: When a Man Attacks a Woman." *Journal of Personality and Social Psychology* 34: 990–9.

Shover, N. 1973. "The Social Organization of Burglary." *Social Problems* 201 (Spring): 499–513.

——— 1983. "The Later Stages of Ordinary Property Offender Careers." *Social Problems* 30: 208–18.

Silver, W., K. Mihorean, and A. Taylor-Butts. 2004 "Hate Crime in Canada." *Juristat* 24(4).

Silverman, R.A., and L.W. Kennedy. 1993. *Deadly Deeds: Murder in Canada.* Scarborough: Nelson Canada.

Silverman, R.A., and M.O. Nielsen. 1992. *Aboriginal Peoples and Canadian Criminal Justice.* Toronto: Butterworths.

Silverman, R.A., J.J. Teevan, and V.F. Sacco (eds.). 2000. *Crime in Canadian Society.* 6th ed. Toronto: Harcourt Brace.

Simon, D.R. 1996. *Elite Deviance.* 5th ed. Boston: Allyn & Bacon.

Simon, D.R., and D.S. Eitzen. 1993. *Elite Deviance.* 4th ed. Boston: Allyn & Bacon.

Simourd, L., and D.A. Andrews. 2000. "Correlates of Delinquency: A Look at Gender Differences." In R.A. Silverman, J.J. Teevan, and V.F. Sacco (eds.), *Crime in Canadian Society*, 6th ed. Toronto: Harcourt Brace.

Simpson, S.S. 1989. "Feminist Theory, Crime and Justice." *Criminology* 27(4): 605–31.

Simpson, S.S., and C.S. Koper. 1992. "Deterring Corporate Crime." *Criminology* 30(3): 347–75.

Simpson, S.S., and N.L. Piquero. 2002. "Low Self Control, Organizational Theory and Corporate Crime." *Law and Society Review.* 36(2): 509–47.

Singer, S.I., and M. Levine. 1988. "Power–Control Theory, Gender and Delinquency: A Partial Replication with Additional Evidence on the Effect of Peers." *Criminology* 26: 627–47.

Skaret, D., and C. Wilgosh. 1989. "Learning Disabilities and Juvenile Delinquency: A Causal Relationship." *International Journal for the Advancement of Counselling* 12: 113–23.

Skipper, J.K. 1985. "Nicknames of Notorious American Twentieth Century Deviants: The Decline of the Folk Hero Syndrome." *Deviant Behavior* 6: 99–114.

Skogan, W.G. 1976. "Citizen Reporting of Crime: Some National Panel Data." *Criminology* 13(4): 535–49.

——— 1977. "Dimensions of the Dark Figure of Unreported Crime." *Crime and Delinquency* 23: 41–50.

——— 1981. "On Attitudes and Behavior." In D.A. Lewis (ed.), *Reactions to Crime.* Beverly Hills: Sage.

——— 1986. "Methodological Issues in the Study of Victimization." In E.A. Fattah (ed.), *From Crime Policy to Victim Policy—Reorienting the Justice System.* London: Macmillan.

———— 1987. "The Impact of Victimization on Fear." *Crime and Delinquency* 33: 135–54.

———— 1990a. "The National Crime Survey Redesign." *Public Opinion Quarterly* 54: 256–72.

———— 1990b. *Disorder and Decline.* New York: The Free Press.

———— 1993. "The Various Meanings of Fear." In W. Bilsky, C. Pfeiffer, and P. Wetzels (eds.), *Fear of Crime and Criminal Victimization.* Stuttgart: Ferdinand Enke Verlag.

Skogan, W.G., and M.G. Maxfield. 1981. *Coping with Crime: Individual and Neighborhood Reactions.* Beverly Hills: Sage.

Skogan, W.G., and M.A. Wycoff. 1987. "Some Unexpected Effects of a Police Service for Victims." *Crime and Delinquency* 33: 490–501.

Skolnick, J. 1966. *Justice without Trial.* New York: John Wiley.

Smith, D. 1975. *The Mafia Mystique.* New York: Basic Books.

Smith, D.A. 1987. "Police Response to Interpersonal Violence: Defining the Parameters of Legal Control." *Social Forces* 65(3): 767–82.

Smith, D.A., and G.R. Jarjoura. 1989. "Household Characteristics, Neighborhood Composition and Victimization Risk." *Social Forces* 68(2): 621–40.

Smith, R.S., S.G. Frazee, and E.L. Davison. 2000. "Furthering the Integration of Routine Activity and Social Disorganization Theories: Small Units of Analysis and the Study of Street Robbery as a Diffusion Process." *Criminology* 38(2): 489–524.

Snider, L. 1992. "Commercial Crime." In V.F. Sacco (ed.), *Deviance: Conformity and Control in Canadian Society,* 2nd ed. Scarborough: Prentice-Hall.

———— 1993. *Bad Business: Corporate Crime in Canada.* Scarborough: Nelson Canada.

Solicitor General of Canada. 1983. *Canadian Urban Victimization Survey Bulletin 1: Victims of Crime.* Ottawa: Programs Branch/Research and Statistics Group.

———— 1998. *The Organized Crime Impact Study.* Ottawa: Solicitor General of Canada.

———— 2005. *Basic Facts about the Correctional Service of Canada.* Ottawa: Public Works and Government Services Canada.

Sorenson, A.M., and D. Brownfield. 1995. "Adolescent Drug Use and a General Theory of Crime: An Analysis of Theoretical Integration." *Canadian Journal of Criminology* 37(1): 19–37.

Spahr, L.L., and L.J. Alison. 2004. "US Savings and Loan Fraud: Implications for General and Criminal Culture Theories of Crime." *Crime, Law and Social Change* 41: 95–106.

Sparks, R. 1992. *Television and the Drama of Crime.* Buckingham: Open University Press.

Spector, M., and J.I. Kitsuse. 1977. *Constructing Social Problems.* Menlo Park: Cummings.

Sprott, J.B., and C. Cesaroni. 2002. "Similarities in trends in homicide in the United States and Canada: Guns, crack or simple demographics?" *Homicide Studies.* 6(4), 348–59.

Sprott, J.B., and A.N. Doob. 2000. "Bad, Sad, and Rejected: The Lives of Aggressive Children." *Canadian Journal of Criminology* 42(2): 123–34.

———— 2003. "It's All in the Denominator: Trends in the Processing of Girls in Canada's Youth Courts." *Canadian Journal of Criminology and Criminal Justice* 45(1): 73.

St. Cyr, J.L. 2003. "The Folk Devil Reacts: Gangs and Moral Panic." *Criminal Justice Review* 28(1): 26–46.

St. John, C., and T. Heald-Moore. 1996. "Racial Prejudice and Fear of Criminal Victimization by Strangers in Public Settings." *Sociological Inquiry* 66(3): 267–84.

Stafford, M.C., and O.R. Galle. 1984. "Victimization Rates, Exposure to Risk, and Fear of Crime." *Criminology* 22(2): 173–85.

Stafford, M.C., and J.P. Gibbs. 1980. "Crime Rates in an Ecological Context: Extension of a Proposition." *Social Science Quarterly* 61(3–4): 653–65.

Stafford, M.C., and M. Warr. 1993. "A Reconceptualization of General and Specific Deterrence." *Journal of Research in Crime and Delinquency* 30(2): 123–35.

Standing Committee on Justice and the Solicitor General. 1993. *Crime Prevention in Canada: Toward a National Strategy.* Ottawa: Queen's Printer.

Stanko, E.A. 1995. "Women, Crime, and Fear." *Annals of the American Academy of Political and Social Science* 539: 46–58.

Statistics Canada, Canada e-book. 2005. http://142.206.72.67/r006_e.htm

Statistics Canada. 2006. "Television Viewing, by Age and Sex, by Province." http://www40.statcan.ca/l01/cst01/arts23.htm

Steffensmeier, D., and E. Allan. 1995. "Criminal Behaviour: Gender and Crime." In J.F. Sheley (ed.), *Criminology: A Contemporary Handbook,* 2nd ed. Belmont: Wadsworth.

Steffensmeier, D.J., and R.H. Steffensmeier. 1977. "Who Reports Shoplifters?: Research Continuities and Further Developments." *International Journal of Criminology and Penology* 3: 79–95.

Steinmetz, S. 1977–78. "The Battered Husband Syndrome." *Victimology: An International Journal* 2: 499–509.

Stenning, P.C. 2003. "Long Gun Registration: A Poorly Aimed Longshot." *Canadian Journal of Criminology and Criminal Justice* 45(4): 479–89.

Sternheimer, K. 2003. *It's Not the Media: The Truth about Pop Culture's Influence on Children.* Boulder Colo: Westview Press.

Stevenson, K., J. Tufts, D. Hendrick, and M. Kowalski. 1998. *A Profile of Youth in Canada.* Ottawa: Minister of Industry.

Stewart, E.A., K.W. Elifson, and C.E. Sterk. 2004. "Integrating the General Theory of Crime into an Explanation of Violent Victimization among Female Offenders." *Justice Quarterly* 21(1): 159–81.

Stone, S. 1993. "Getting the Message Out: Feminists, the Press and Violence against Women." *Canadian Review of Sociology and Anthropology* 30(3): 377–400.

Strike, C. 1995. "Women Assaulted by Strangers." *Canadian Social Trends* 36: 2–6.

Straus, M.A. 1991. "Discipline and Deviance: Physical Punishment of Children and Violence and Other Forms of Crime in Adulthood." *Social Problems* 38(2): 133–52.

Stylianou, S. 2002. "The Relationship between Elements and Manifestations of Low Self-Control in a General Theory of Crime: Two Comments." *Deviant Behavior* 23(6): 531–57.

Sugarman, D.B., and G.T. Hotaling. 1989. "Dating Violence: Prevalence, Context and Risk Markers." In M.A. Pirog-Good and J.E. Stets (eds.), *Violence in Dating Relationships.* New York: Praeger.

Sumser, J. 1996. *Morality and Social Order in Television Crime Drama.* Jefferson: McFarland and Co.

Sun, I.Y., R. Triplett, and R.R. Gainey. 2004. "Neighborhood Characteristics and Crime: A Test of Sampson and Groves' Model of Social Disorganization." *Western Criminology Review* 5(1): 1–16.

Surette, R. 1992. *Media, Crime, and Criminal Justice: Images and Realities.* Pacific Grove: Brooks/Cole.

Sutherland, E.H. 1940. "White-Collar Criminality." *American Sociological Review* 5: 1–12.

————— 1947. *Principles of Criminology.* 4th ed. Chicago: Lippincott.

————— 1961. *White Collar Crime.* New York: Holt, Rinehart & Winston.

Tanner, J. 2001. *Teenage Troubles.* 2nd ed. Scarborough: Nelson Canada.

Tanner, J., and S. Wortley. 2002. *The Toronto Youth Crime and Victimization Survey: Overview Report.* Toronto: University of Toronto, Centre of Criminology.

Tate, E.D. 1998. "The Ontario Royal Commission on Violence in the Communications Industry: Twenty Years Later." *British Journal of Communication Studies* 13(1): 148–63.

Taylor, R.B. 2001. *Breaking Away from Broken Windows.* Boulder CO: Westview.

Taylor, R.B., and S. Gottfredson. 1986. "Environmental Design and Prevention: An Examination of Community Dynamics." In A.J. Reiss, Jr., and M. Tonry (eds.), *Communities and Crime*. Chicago: University of Chicago Press.

Taylor, R.B., and A.V. Harrell. 1996. *Physical Environment and Crime*. Washington: U.S. Department of Justice.

Taylor, S.E., J.V. Wood, and R.R. Lichtman. 1983. "It Could Be Worse: Selective Evaluation as a Response to Victimization." *Journal of Social Issues* 39: 19–40.

Taylor-Butts, A. 2004. "Private Security and Public Policing in Canada, 2001." *Juristat* 24(7).

——— 2005. "Canada's Shelters for Abused Women, 2003/04." *Juristat* 25(3).

Teevan, J.J., and H.B. Dryburgh. 2000. "First Person Accounts and Sociological Explanations of Delinquency." *Canadian Review of Sociology and Anthropology* 37(1): 77–93.

Thomas, J. 2005. "Youth Court Statistics, 2003/04." *Juristat* 25(4).

Thomas, M. 2004. "Adult Criminal Court Statistics, 2003/04." *Juristat* 24(12).

Thompson, M.P., L.E. Saltzman, and H. Johnson. 2003. "A Comparison of Risk Factors for Intimate Partner Violence-related Injury Across Two National Surveys on Violence Against Women." *Violence Against Women* 9(4): 438–57.

Thornberry, T.P. 1987. "Toward an Interactional Theory of Delinquency." *Criminology* 25(4): 863–92.

Thornberry, T.P., A.J. Lizotte, M.D. Krohn, M. Farnworth, and S.J. Jang. 1991. "Testing Interactional Theory: An Examination of Reciprocal Causal Relationships Among Family, School, and Delinquency." *Journal of Criminal Law and Criminology* 82(1): 3–33.

Tibbetts, S.G., and C.L Gibson. 2002. "Individual Propensities and Rational Decision-Making: Recent Findings and Promising Approaches". In A.R. Piquero and S.G. Tibbetts (eds.), *Rational Choice and Criminal Behavior: Recent Research and Future Challenges*. New York: Routledge Press.

Tibbetts, S.G., and D.C. Herz. 1996. "Gender Differences in Factors of Social Control and Rational Choice." *Deviant Behavior: An Interdisciplinary Journal* 17: 183–208.

Tierney, K. 1982. "The Battered Women Movement and the Creation of the Wife Beating Problem." *Social Problems* 29: 207–20.

Timmer, D.A., and W.H. Norman. 1984. "The Ideology of Victim Precipitation." *Criminal Justice Review* 9: 63–68.

Tittle, C.R. 1995. *Control Balance: Toward a General Theory of Deviance*. Boulder: Westview Press.

—— 2004. "Refining Control Balance Theory." *Theoretical Criminology* 8(4): 395–428.

Tittle, C.R., and H.G. Grasmick. 1998. "Criminal Behavior and Age: A Test of Three Provocative Hypotheses." *Journal of Criminal Law and Criminology* 88: 309–42.

Tjaden, P., and N. Thoennes. 1998. "Prevalence, Incidence, and Consequences of Violence Against Women: Findings from the National Violence Against Women Survey." *National Institute of Justice Centers for Disease Control and Prevention.* Washington: U.S. Department of Justice.

Toby, J. 1995. "The Schools." In J.Q. Wilson and J. Peterson (eds.), *Crime: Twenty-eight Leading Experts Look at the Most Pressing Problem of our Time.* San Francisco: Institute for Contemporary Studies Press.

Tracy, P.E., and J.A. Fox. 1989. "A Field Experiment on Insurance Fraud in Auto Body Repair." *Criminology* 27: 509–603.

Traub, S.H., and C.B. Little (eds.). 1980. *Theories of Deviance.* 2nd ed. Itasca: F.E. Peacock.

Tremblay, M., and P. Tremblay. 1998. "Social Structure, Integration Opportunities, and the Direction of Violent Offenses." *Journal of Research in Crime and Delinquency* 35(3): 295–315.

Tremblay, S. 2000. "Crime Statistics in Canada, 1999." *Juristat* 20(5).

Tufts, J. 2000. "Public Attitudes Towards the Criminal Justice System." *Juristat* 20(12).

Tunnell, K.D. 1992. *Choosing Crime: The Criminal Calculus of Property Offenders.* Chicago: Nelson-Hall.

—— 1998. "Reflections on Crime, Criminals, and Control in Newsmagazine Television Programs." In F. Bailey and D. Hale (eds.), *Popular Culture, Crime and Justice.* Belmont: West/Wadsworth.

Turk, A. 1976. "Law as a Weapon in Social Conflict." *Social Problems* 23: 276–92.

Turner, M.G., and A.R. Piquero. 2002. "The Stability of Self-control." *Journal of Criminal Justice* 30(6): 457–71.

Turner, P.A. 1993. *I Heard It Through the Grapevine.* Berkeley: University of California Press.

Tyler, K.A., and K.A. Johnson, 2004. "Victims and Offenders: Accounts of Paybacks, Invulnerability and Financial Gain among Homeless Youth." *Deviant Behavior* 25(5): 427–49.

Tyler, T. 1990. *Why People Obey the Law.* Chicago: University of Chicago Press.

Uggen, C. 2000. "Class, Gender, and Arrest: An Intergenerational Analysis of Workplace Power and Control." *Criminology* 38(3): 835–62.

Unnever, J.D., M. Colvin, and F.T. Cullen. 2004. "Crime and Coercion: A Test of Core

Theoretical Propositions." *Journal of Research in Crime and Delinquency* 41(3): 244–68.

Upson, A. 2004. *Violence at Work: Findings from the 2002/2003 British Crime Survey.* London: British Home Office.

U.S. Department of Justice. 1988. *Report to the Nation on Crime and Justice.* 2nd ed. Washington: Bureau of Justice Statistics.

Useem, B.1998. "Breakdown Theories of Collective Action." *Annual Review of Sociology* 24: 215–238.

Van Brunschot, E. 2000. "Assault Stories." In R.A. Silverman, J.T. Teevan, and V.F. Sacco (eds.), *Crime in Canadian Society,* 6th ed. Toronto: Harcourt Brace.

Van Brunschot, E.G. 2003. "Community Policing and Johns Schools." *Canadian Review of Sociology and Anthropology.* 40(2): 215–32.

Van Brunschot, E.G., and A. Brannigan. 2002. "Childhood Maltreatment and Subsequent Conduct Disorders: The Case of Female Street Prostitution." *International Journal of Law and Psychiatry* 25(3): 219–34.

Van den Haag, E. 1975. *Punishing Criminals: Concerning a Very Old and Painful Question.* New York: Basic Books.

van Dijk, J.J.M., and J. de Waard. 1991. "A Two-Dimensional Typology of Crime Prevention Projects with a Bibliography." *Criminal Justice Abstracts* (September).

van Wormer, K.S., and C. Bartollos. 2000. *Women and the Criminal Justice System.* Boston: Allyn & Bacon.

Vancouver Sun, July 15, 2005.

Venkatesh, S.A. 1997. "The Social Organization of Street Gang Activity in an Urban Ghetto." *American Journal of Sociology* 103(1): 82–111.

Veysey, B.M., and S.T. Messner. 1999. "Further Testing of Social Disorganization Theory: An Elaboration of Sampson and Groves's 'Community Structure and Crime.'" *Journal of Research in Crime and Delinquency* 36(2): 156–74.

Vogel, R.E., and M.J. Himlein. 1995. "Dating and Sexual Victimization: An Analysis of Risk Factors among Precollege Women." *Journal of Criminal Justice* 23(2): 153–62.

Vold, G.B., T.J. Bernard, and J.B. Snipes. 1998. *Theoretical Criminology.* 4th ed. New York: Oxford University Press.

Voumvakis, S.E., and R.V. Ericson. 1984. *News Accounts of Attacks on Women: A Comparison of Three Toronto Newspapers.* Toronto: Centre of Criminology, University of Toronto.

Vowell, P.R., and D.C. May. 2000. "Another Look at Classic Strain Theory." *Sociological Inquiry* 70(1): 42–60.

Wachs, E. 1988. *Crime-Victim Stories: New York City's Urban Folklore.*

Bloomington and Indianapolis: Indiana University Press.

Wagner, D. 1997. *The New Temperance: The American Obsession with Sin and Vice.* Boulder: Westview Press.

Walby, K. 2005. "Open-Street Camera Surveillance and Governance in Canada." *Canadian Journal of Criminology and Criminal Justice* 47(4): 685–708.

Walby, S., and A. Myhill. No Date. *Reducing Domestic Violence . . . What Works?* London: Home Office Research.

Walker, S.G., and C.R. Walker. 1993. "The Victoria Community Police Stations: An Exercise in Innovation." In J. Chacko and S.E. Nancoo (eds.), *Community Policing in Canada*, pp. 47–89. Toronto: Canadian Scholars' Press.

Walklate, S. 1989. *Victimology: The Victim and the Criminal Justice System.* London: Unwin Hyman.

Wallace, M. 2004. "Crime Statistics in Canada, 2003." *Juristat* 24(6).

Waller, I. 1982. "Victimization Studies as Guides to Action: Some Cautions and Suggestions." In H.J. Schneider (ed.), *The Victim in International Perspective.* New York: Aldine de Gruyter.

——— 1989. *Current Trends in European Crime Prevention: Implications for Canada.* Ottawa: Department of Justice Canada.

Waller, I., and N. Okihiro. 1978. *Burglary: The Victim and the*

Public. Toronto: University of Toronto Press.

Waller, I., and R. Weiler. 1984. *Crime Prevention through Social Development.* Ottawa: Canadian Council on Social Development.

Walsh, L., and A. Ellis. 1999. "Criminologists' Opinions about Causes and. Theories of Crime." *The Criminologist,* 24(4): 1–6.

Walters, G.D., and T.W. White. 1989. "Heredity and Crime: Bad Genes or Bad Research." *Criminology* 27(3): 455–8.

Walters, R. 2003a. *Deviant Knowledge: Criminology, Politics and Policy.* Cullompton: Willan Publishing.

——— 2003b. "New Modes of Governance and the Commodification of Criminological Knowledge." *Social and Legal Studies* 12(1): 5–26.

Warchol, G. 1998. *Bureau of Justice Statistics Special Report, National Crime Survey, Workplace Violence.* Washington: U.S. Department of Justice.

Warr, M. 1985. "Fear of Rape among Urban Women." *Social Problems* 32: 238–50.

——— 1988. "Rape, Burglary, and Opportunity." *Journal of Quantitative Criminology* 4(3): 275–88.

——— 1990. "Dangerous Situations: Social Control and Fear of Victimization." *Social Forces* 68(3): 891–907.

——— 1991. "America's Perceptions of Crime and Punishment." In J.F. Sheley (ed.), *Criminology: A Contemporary Handbook.* Belmont: Wadsworth.

——— 1998. "Life Course Transitions and Desistance from Crime." *Criminology* 36(2): 183–216.

——— 2002. *Companions in Crime: The Social Aspects of Criminal Conduct.* New York: Cambridge University Press.

Warr, M., and M.C. Stafford. 1983. "Fear of Victimization: A Look at Proximate Causes." *Social Forces* 61: 1033–43.

Weaver, G.S., J.E.C. Wittekind, J. Corzin, L. Huff-Corzine, T.A. Petee, and J.P. Jarvis. 2004. "Violent Encounters: A Criminal Event Analysis of Lethal and Nonlethal Outcomes." *Journal of Contemporary Criminal Justice* 20(4): 348–68.

Weed, F. 1995. *Certainty of Justice: Reforms in the Crime Victim Movement.* New York: Aldine de Gruyter.

Weeks, E.L., J.M. Boles, A.P. Garbin, and J. Blount. 1986. "The Transformation of Sexual Harassment from a Private Trouble to a Public Issue." *Sociological Inquiry* 56: 432–55.

Weerman, F.M. 2003. "Co-offending as Social Exchange: Explaining Characteristics of Co-Offending." *British Journal of Criminology* 43(2): 398–416.

Weis, J.G. 1989. "Family Violence Research Methodology and Design." In L. Ohlin and M. Tonry (eds.), *Family Violence, Crime and Justice—A Review of Research,* Vol. 11. Chicago: University of Chicago Press.

Welch, D. 2000. "News into the Next Century: Introduction." *Historical Journal of Film, Radio and Television* 20(1): 5–13.

Wellford, C. 1975. "Labelling Theory and Criminology: An Assessment." *Social Problems* 22: 332–45.

Wellford, C.F. 1997. "Victimization Rates for Domestic Travelers." *Journal of Criminal Justice* 3: 205–10.

Wells, L.E., and J.H. Rankin. 1986. "The Broken Homes Model of Delinquency: Analytical Issues." *Journal of Research in Crime and Delinquency* 23(1): 68–93

——— 1991. "Families and Delinquency: A Meta-Analysis of the Impact of Broken Homes." *Social Problems* 38(1): 71–93.

Welsh, B.C., and D.P. Farrington. 2003. "Effects of Closed-Circuit Television on Crime." *The Annals of the American Academy of Political and Social Science* 587 (May): 110–35.

——— 2005. "Evidence Based Crime Prevention: Conclusions and Directions for a Safer Society." *Canadian Journal of Criminology and Criminal Justice* 47(2): 337–54.

Whitaker, C.J., and L.D. Bastian. 1991. *Teenage Victims.* A National Crime Survey Report. Washington: U.S. Department of Justice.

White, R., and F. Hanes. 2000. *Crime and Criminology.* 2nd ed. Oxford: Oxford University Press.

Widom, C.S. 1995. "Victimization of Childhood Sexual Abuse—Later Criminal Consequences." Washington: U.S. Department of Justice.

Wilcox, P., K.C. Hand, and S.A. Hunt. 2003. *Criminal Circumstance: A Dynamic Multi-Contextual Criminal Opportunity Theory.* New York: Aldine de Gruyter.

Will, J.A., and J.H. McGrath. 1995. "Crime, Neighborhood Perceptions, and the Underclass: The Relationship between Fear of Crime and Class Position." *Journal of Criminal Justice* 23(2): 163–76.

Williams, F.P., M.D. McShane, and R.L. Akers. 2000. "Worry About Victimization: An Alternative and Reliable Measure for Fear of Crime." *Western Criminology Review* 2(2). http://wcr.sonoma.edu/v2n2/williams.html

Williams, K.R., and R.L. Flewelling. 1988. "The Social Production of Criminal Homicide: A Comparative Study of Disaggregated Rates in American Cities." *American Sociological Review* 53: 421–31.

Williams, K.R., and R. Hawkins. 1986. "Perceptual Research on General Deterrence: A Critical Review." *Law and Society Review* 20: 545–72.

Williams, L.M. 2003. "Understanding Child Abuse and Violence Against Women: A Life Course Perspective." *Journal of Interpersonal Violence* 18(4): 441–51.

Wilson, J. 1980. "Sociology of Leisure." *Annual Review of Sociology* 6: 21–40.

Wilson, J.Q. 1983. *Thinking About Crime.* New York: Vintage.

Wilson, J.Q., and R.J. Herrnstein. 1985. *Crime and Human Nature.* New York: Simon & Schuster.

Wilson, J.Q., and G.L. Kelling. 1982. "Broken Windows." *Atlantic Monthly* (March): 29–38.

Wilson, W.J. 1987. *The Truly Disadvantaged: The Inner City, the Underclass, and Public Policy.* Chicago: University of Chicago Press.

Windsor Police Department Scam Alert. http://www.police.windsor.on.ca/Senior%20Moment/scam_alert.htm

Wirth, L. 1938. "Urbanism as a Way of Life." *American Journal of Sociology* 44: 3–24.

Wittebrood, K., and P. Nieuwbeerta. 2000. "Criminal Victimization During One's Life Course: The Effects of Previous Victimization and Patterns of Routine Activities." *Journal of Research in Crime and Delinquency* 37(1): 91–122.

Wolf, L. 1991. "Drug Crimes."
Canadian Social Trends 20: 27–29.

Wolfgang, M. 1958. *Patterns in Criminal Homicide.* Philadelphia: University of Pennsylvania Press.

Wolfgang, M., and F. Ferracuti. 1967. *The Subculture of Violence: Towards an Integrated Theory in Criminology.* Beverly Hills: Sage.

Wong, S.K. 1999. "Acculturation, Peer Relations and Delinquent Behavior of Chinese-Canadian Youth." *Adolescence* 34(133): 107–19.

Wood, C. 2000. "Why Do Men Do It?" *Maclean's*, August 7: 34–7.

Wood, D.S., and C.T. Griffiths. 2000. "Patterns of Aboriginal Crime." In R.A. Silverman, J.T. Teevan, and V.F. Sacco (eds.), *Crime in Canadian Society,* 6th ed. Toronto: Harcourt Brace.

Woodiwiss, M. 2001. *Organized Crime and American Power.* Toronto: University of Toronto Press.

Wortley, S. 2005. *Profiling a Problem in Canadian Police Leadership: The Kingston Police Data Collection Project.* Institute of Public Administration of Canada; City of Kingston Police. http://www.police.kingston.on.ca

Wortley, S., and J. Tanner. 2005. "Inflammatory Rhetoric? Baseless Accusations? A Response to Gabor's Critique of Racial Profiling Research in Canada."
Canadian Journal of Criminology and Criminal Justice 47(3): 581–609.

Wright, J.P., and F.T. Cullen. 2004. "Employment, Peers and Life-Course Transitions." *Justice Quarterly* 21(4): 183–205.

Wright, J.D., and P. Rossi. 1986. *Armed and Considered Dangerous: A Survey of Felons and Their Firearms.* Hawthorne: Aldine de Gruyter.

Wright, R., and T. Bennett. 1990. "Exploring the Offender's Perspective: Observing and Interviewing Criminals." In K.L. Kempf (ed.), *Measurement Issues in Criminology.* New York: Springer-Verlag.

Wright R., and S.H. Decker. 1994. *Burglars on the Job: Streetlife and Residential Break-Ins.* Boston: Northeastern University Press.

Wright, R., R.H. Logie, and S.H. Decker. 1995. "Criminal Expertise and Offender Decision Making: An Experimental Study of the Target Selection Process in Residential Burglary." *Journal of Research in Crime and Delinquency* 32(1): 39–53.

Wright, R.A., and J.M. Miller. 1998. "Taboo Until Today: The Coverage of Biological Arguments in Criminology Textbooks, 1961 to 1970 and 1987 to 1996." *Journal of Criminal Justice* 26(1): 1–19.

Yin, P. 1980. "Fear of Crime among the Elderly: Some Issues and Suggestions." *Social Problems* 27: 492–504.

——— 1982. "Fear of Crime as a Problem for the Elderly." *Social Problems* 30: 240–5.

Zawitz, M.W., P.A. Klaus, R. Bachman, L.D. Bastian, M.M. DeBerry, Jr., M.R. Rand, and B.M. Tayler. 1993. *Highlights from 20 Years of Surveying Crime Victims.*

Washington: Bureau of Justice Statistics.

Ziegenhagen, E.A., and D. Brosnan. 1985. "Victims' Responses to Robbery and Crime Control Policy." *Criminology* 23: 675–95.

CREDITS

Cover: Jeff Spielman/Getty Images; page 14: Courtesy www.snopes.com;
page 36: Courtesy Windsor Police Department; page 39: Statistics Canada, 2005,
Exploring Crime Patterns in Canada, Catalogue no. 85-561-XIE2005005. Used
by permission of Statistics Canada; page 42: Public Works and Government
Services Canada; page 43: M. Wallace (2004), "Crime Statistics in Canada 2003,"
Statistics Canada, Juristat, Catalogue No. 85-002, Volume 24, Number 6: 25. Used
by permission of Statistics Canada; page 48: M. Gannon and K. Mihorean. 2005.
Criminal victimization in Canada: 2004. 85-002-XPE. Juristat. 25 (7):23; page 49:
M. Gannon and K. Mihorean. 2005. Criminal Victimization in Canada: 2004.
85-002-XPE. Juristat. 25 (7): 26. Used by permission of Statistics Canada;
page 58: Adapted from the Statistics Canada publication "Juristat", *Crime
Statistics in Canada,* 2004, Catalogue 85-002, Volume 25, Number 5, page 18,
released July 21, 2005; page 62: Adapted from the Statistics Canada publication
"Juristat", *Crime Statistics in Canada,* 2004, Catalogue 85-002, Volume 25,
Number 5, page 4, released July 21, 2005; page 81: International Crime
Victimization Survey, 2000, Statistics Canada 85-565-XIE Juristat Catalogue #
85-002-XPE Vol. 22 no. 4; page 84: Canadian General Social Survey, 2005,
Statistics Canada, Family, Household and Social Statistics Division. Used by
permission of Statistics Canada; page 122: Bartol, Curt R. *Criminal Behaviour:
Psychosocial Approach,* 3rd, © 1991. Electronically reproduced by permission
of Pearson Education, Inc., Upper Saddle River, New Jersey; page 140: Elaine
Cressey, executor, Donald R. Cressey Estate for a passage from Edwin H.
Sutherland, Principles of Criminology 4th edition (Chicago: J.B. Lippincott,
1947); page 154: Obeidallah, D., & F.J. Earls. 1999. Adolescent Girls: The Role of
Depression in the Development of Delinquency. Washington: Office of Justice
Programs, U.S. Department of Justice: 3; page 175: D. Janhevich, M. Gannon
and N. Morisset (2003). "Impaired Driving and Other Traffic Offences-2002."
Juristat. 23 (9): page 3. Used by permission of Statistics Canada; page 183:
Gannon, M., and K. Mihorean. 2005. "Criminal Victimization in Canada 2004."
Juristat 25(7): 23. Used with permission of Statistics Canada; page 184:
Fitzgerald, Robin, Michael Wisener, and Josée Savoie. 2004. Neighbourhood
Characteristics and the Distribution of Crime in Winnipeg. Ottawa: Canadian
Centre for Justice Statistics, Statistics Canada. page 30; page 186: C. Kershaw,
S. Nichols, D. Povey, A. Walker and A. Mayhill. 2005. Crime in England and Wales
2004/2005. London: The Home Office; page 192: Courtesy U.S. Department of
Justice; page 198: Luckenbill, D.F. 1977. "Criminal Homicide as a Situated
Transaction." Social Problems 25 (2): 176–86. Used by permission; page 208:
M. Gannon and K. Mihorean. 2005. Criminal Victimization in Canada, 2004.
Ottawa: Centre for Justice Statistics, Statistics Canada: pg. 12. Used by

permission of Statistics Canada; page 214: S. De Leseleuc & R. Kong. 2004. Victim Services in Canada: National, Provincial and Territorial Fact Sheets. Ottawa: Canadian Centre for Justice Statistics, Statistics Canada, Catalogue 85-003. Used by permission of Statistics Canada; page 215: Source: R. Kong. Criminal Justice Indicators, 2005. Ottawa: Centre for Justice Statistics, Statistics Canada: pg. 51. Used by permission of Statistics Canada; page 216: M. Gannon. 2005. "General Social Survey on Victimization, Cycle 18: An Overview of Findings." Statistics Canada Catalogue 85-565-XIE. Ottawa. Used by permission of Statistics Canada; page 239: K. Mihorean. 2005. "Trends in Self-Reported Spousal Abuse." In K. AuCoin (ed.) Family Violence in Canada: A Statistical Profile. Ottawa: Canadian Centre for Justice Statistics, Statistics Canada: pg. 15. Used by permission of Statistics Canada; page 241: S. Walby and A. Myhill, No Date. Reducing Domestic Violence . . . What Works? London: Home Office Research. Used by permission; page 248: M. Gannon and K. Mihorean. 2005. "Criminal Victimization in Canada, 2004," Juristat 25 (7): p. 26. Used by permission of Statistics Canada; page 252: O. Fedorowycz. 2004. "Breaking and Entering in Canada-2002." Juristat 24 (5): p. 3. Used by permission of Statistics Canada; page 262: Source: Statistics Canada. http://www40.statcan.ca/l01/arts23.htm. Used by permission of Statistics Canada; page 274: T. Burgmann, The Queen's Journal. Volume 133, Issue 9. September 27, 2005; page 276: Courtesy Center for Problem Oriented Policing; page 277: Courtesy Center for Disease Control and Prevention; page 290: Duhart, D.T. 2001. Violence in the Workplace: 1993-99. Washington, D.C.: U.S. Department of Justice; page 295: Upson, A. 2004. Violence at Work: Findings from the 2002/2003 British Crime Survey. London: British Home Office; page 302: Conrad Winn and Tamara Gottlieb, Compas Inc. 2005. Crime, Punishment, Compensation and CEOs; page 304: Coleman, J.W. 1987. "Toward an Integrated Theory of White-Collar Crime." American Journal of Sociology 93 (2): 406–39. Univeristy of Chicago Press; page 307: Snider, L. 1992. "Commercial Crime." In V.F. Sacco (ed.), Deviance: Conformity and Control in Canadian Society 2nd ed. Scarborough: Prentice-Hall. Reprinted with permission by Pearson Education Canada Inc.; page 310: R. Kong (ed). 2005. Criminal Justice Indicators. Ottawa: Centre for Justice Statistics. Used by permission of Statistics Canada; page 312: Criminal Intelligence Service of Canada, 2004; page 332: A. Doob and C. Cesaroni. 2004. Responding to Youth Crime in Canada. Toronto: University of Toronto Press. A.W. Saleno (1994), " Boot Camps: A Critique and Proposed Alternative," Journal of Offender Rehabilitation 20: 147–58. J. Shamsie, S. Nicholl, and K.C. Madsen (1999), Antisocial and Violent Youth. Toronto: Lugus; page 337: J. Lasley (1998), "'Designing Out' Gang Homicides and Street Assaults," National Institute of Justice: Research in Brief, Washington, D.C. : U.S. Department of Justice. Used by permission; page 340: R. Prinz (2000), "Research-Based Prevention of School Violence and Youth Antisocial Behavior:

A Developmental and Education Perspective," in Preventing School Violence: Plenary Papers of the 1999 Conference on Criminal Justice Research and Evaluation—Enhancing Policy and Practice Through Research, Vol. 2. Washington, D.C. : U.S. Department of Justice. Used by permission; page 344: Eck, J.D. 2001. "Problem-Oriented Policing and Crime Event Concentration." In R.F. Meier, L.W. Kennedy, and V.F. Sacco (eds.), The Process and Structure of Crime. Vol. 9, Advances in Criminological Theory. Piscataway: Transaction Press; page 347: Goldstein, H. 1990. Problem-Oriented Policing. New York, McGraw-Hill, Inc.

NAME INDEX

SUBJECT INDEX

on race/ethnicity, 47, 94–99, 106
reports (*See* Crime reports)
specification problem and, 205
Resetting account, 161
Retreatism, 130
Retreatist patterns, 133
Riots, 274
Risk factors
in break-and-enter incidents,
253–255
of courtship violence, 277
fear of crime and, 217–218, 230
for gender and delinquency, 44
in opportunity theories, 190–193
Risky lifestyles, 269, 284
Ritualism, 130
Robberies. *See* Thefts
Routine activities theory, 184–188, 201,
224, 247, 269–270, 327
Routine conflict theory, 188–189
Rumours and legends, 12–14
Rural/urban distinctions.
See Community settings

S

Safe houses/shelters, 245, 258
Safe street laws, 27
"Scared straight" approaches, 330
School failure hypothesis, 126–127
School violence, 72, 292–295, 296–297
Scripts, 189
Secondary deviance, 160
Selection account, 160–161
Self-control, 155–157, 161, 189,
305–306
Self-defence, 20
Self-fulfilling prophecy, 160
Self-identity, 160
Self-report studies, 84–87, 88–89
Serial killers
moral panics about, 228
myths about, 15
public interest in, 10, 12, 136
situated transactions and, 199

Severity of punishment, 168–169, 173
Sex crimes, 175, 264
Sexist beliefs, 45
Sexual assaults
conduct norms and, 30
in crime news, 7
"date rape" (*See* Date rape)
physical settings of, 270
as predatory/moralistic crime, 31
rape (*See* Rape)
reporting of, 51–52, 75, 93
social domains of, 61, 275–279
temporal settings of, 183
Sexual behaviours, 53
Sexual harassment, 93, 289
Shoplifting, 30–31
Simplification of reality, 10
Situated transactions, 197–199, 202, 327
Situational crime prevention, 335
Situational deterrence, 171–173
Situational prevention, 337–339
Smartness, 141
Social agendas, 16
Social barometers, 101
Social bonds, 153–155, 159, 161,
177, 246
Social capital, 167
Social classes, 26, 131, 141, 147, 315
Social conditions
American dream and, 130, 137–138
anomie theory, 131
celebrity, 136
crime news reporting on, 6
as criminal motivation theory,
129–138, 147, 200
frustrated ambitions theory,
129–131, 147, 326
legitimate/illegitimate means in,
132, 147
status deprivation theory, 131–132
status quo representations of, 11
strain theory, 132–138, 162,
176, 242
welfare-state fallacy and, 16